THE LEARNING SOCIETY IN A POSTMODERN WORLD

THE LEARNING SOCIETY IN A POSTMODERN WORLD

Studies in the Postmodern Theory of Education

Joe L. Kincheloe and Shirley R. Steinberg
General Editors

Vol. 260

PETER LANG
New York • Washington, D.C./Baltimore • Bern
Frankfurt am Main • Berlin • Brussels • Vienna • Oxford

KENNETH WAIN

THE LEARNING SOCIETY IN A POSTMODERN WORLD

• *The Education Crisis* •

PETER LANG
New York • Washington, D.C./Baltimore • Bern
Frankfurt am Main • Berlin • Brussels • Vienna • Oxford

Library of Congress Cataloging-in-Publication Data

Wain, Kenneth.
The learning society in a postmodern world:
the education crisis / Kenneth Wain.
p. cm. — (Counterpoints; v. 260)
Includes bibliographical references and index.
1. Continuing education—Philosophy. 2. Adult learning.
3. Postmodernism and education. I. Title.
II. Counterpoints (New York, N.Y.); v. 260.
LC5219.W35   374'.001—dc21   2003009948
ISBN 0-8204-6836-3
ISSN 1058-1634

Bibliographic information published by **Die Deutsche Bibliothek**.
Die Deutsche Bibliothek lists this publication in the "Deutsche
Nationalbibliografie"; detailed bibliographic data is available
on the Internet at http://dnb.ddb.de/.

Cover art by Raphael Vella
Cover design by Sophie Boorsch Appel

The paper in this book meets the guidelines for permanence and durability
of the Committee on Production Guidelines for Book Longevity
of the Council of Library Resources.

© 2004 Peter Lang Publishing, Inc., New York
275 Seventh Avenue, 28th Floor, New York, NY 10001
www.peterlangusa.com

Printed in the United States of America

Table of Contents

Introduction   ix

Chapter 1
The Lifelong Education Movement: The Learning Society as Utopia

The Challenge of Lifelong Education   1
Education and the Problem of Change   3
The Learning Society   9
Amor Fati: The Individual   11
Scientific Humanism: The Culture   16
The Two Strands   19
Defining Education   21
The Challenge to Schooling   24
Illich's Postmodern Learning Society   28
Living Together Educates: Education Lifewide   33
The Maximalist View   37
The Education Research Project   41

Chapter 2
Death of the Movement: The Learning Society as Postmodern Myth

Problems with Utopia   45
The Postmodern World   50
The Information Society and Postmodern Culture   57
The Return of the Learning Society   62
The Employers' Agenda   67
Learning Organizations   72
Having or Being?   75
Adult Education as a Welfare Right   81
Counter-Discourse, Utopia?   87

CHAPTER 3
MacIntyre's Educated Public

The Crisis of Modernity   91
Escatological Utopianism   97
MacIntyre's Challenge   100
The Educated Public   105
Death of the Liberal University   110
MacIntyre's Politics   115
Dependent Rational Animals   120
Similarities with MacIntyre   124
MacIntyre's Learning Communities   128

CHAPTER 4
Habermas: The Rational Society

Habermas and Education   135
The Rational Society   139
The Culture Industry   144
The Bourgeois Public   146
Critical Reactions   153
The Publics Compared   158
Utopia   163
Habermas and the Welfare State   167
Emancipation, Democracy, and Justice   170
Habermas's Learning Society   177

CHAPTER 5
The Learning Society and the Third Way

The Learning Democracy   183
The Welfare State Reconsidered   188
Adult Welfare Rights Revisited   195
A Japanese "Postmodern" Model?   198
The New Left   202
New Labour's Learning Society   210
The Civic Learning Culture   215
The Present   220

CHAPTER 6
The Politics of Hope

Postmodernism: The Objections 229
Poststructuralism 238
Philosophy and Strong Poetry 246
Deconstructive Politics 250
Derrida and the Learning Society 255
Rorty's Liberal Utopia 258
Philosophy and Achieving the Left 264
Rorty and Education 269

CHAPTER 7
The Politics of Suspicion

Dystopian Writing 277
The Panopticon Society 281
The Obscene Society 287
Radical Individualism 297
Self-Care and Self-Creation 301
Foucaultian Politics and the Specific Intellectual 306
Foucault, the Learning Society, and Education 313

NOTES 321

BIBLIOGRAPHY 339

INDEX 351

Introduction

This book depends on some key theses, which it assumes and discusses, and around which it is structured. First, that today's world is in a postmodern condition. Second, that lifelong learning and the learning society are key priority areas of policy interest in today's postmodern world, to a large extent displacing the modern world's focus on mass schooling. Third, that a feature of the postmodern condition is the death of education as we have understood it since the time of the Greeks, namely as a way of being an individual, as distinct from mere enculturation. Fourth, that what is called *postmodernism* threatens the existence of educational theory and, more specifically, of philosophy of education.

My narrative about how lifelong learning and the learning society became priority areas in the postmodern world occupies mainly Chapters 1, 2, and 5 of the book. It starts in the mid-1960s and early 1970s when the notion of *lifelong education* burst on the scene in the ambits of UNESCO, promoted by what could loosely be described as a movement made up of educators and educationalists of different kinds, but mainly from adult education, with a well-defined leftist political agenda. They supported the creation of a learning society with participatory democratic credentials and a scientific humanistic culture. This movement, during the two decades or so of its existence, had two strands. The first dominated up to and beyond the early 1970s when the Faure Report *Learning to be* (1972) anticipated the advent of a learning society of the future supporting individual and collective lifelong education. With the receding of these utopian aspirations in the late 1970s and beginning of the 1980s, however, a second pragmatic strand grew more dominant within the movement. It stopped theorizing the learning society in abstract "philosophical" terms and focused on strategy instead, on the prospects for lifelong education policies in different countries.

Chapters 1 and 2 describe the educational aspirations of both strands of the movement, which petered out in the late 1980s for a number of reasons. After a break of two chapters, Chapter 5 takes up the narrative again beginning from the early 1990s to provide the background to the contemporary debate on lifelong learning and the learning society. The background provided in the first two chapters, however, is nearly always neglected when the two subjects are discussed today. It enables one to appreciate how the movement's discourse elaborating them—or, more accurately, its vocabulary—reappropriated in the beginning of the 1990s, is distorted today from its original agenda set by the movement, hijacked by an agenda that is economic and vocationalist instead of humanist and educationist, subscribing to a different set of criteria and values (those of performativity rather than human growth), and set by very different protagonists, employers and national governments, with very different interests from those of the movement. Chapter 2, in particular, takes up this part of the narrative, which is completed in Chapter 5 where the reader is brought up to date on the most recent developments in the debate on lifelong learning, which, in Europe, has been appropriated by the European Union with its powerful Commission. Meanwhile, Chapters 1 and 2 also contain some description of the postmodern world, or the postmodern condition of the world, dwelling mainly on the existential demands made on individuals in postmodern societies that are described as "risk" societies, besides having the character of information societies in which the media are key protagonists.

A key feature of the change in discourse from the movement's to the contemporary is the substitution of the expression lifelong *education* with lifelong *learning*. This is not, in my view, an innocuous change, an innocent switch reflecting a mere change in fashion or something like that, but suggests a trend toward abandoning our normative understanding of education for the normatively neutral "learning." It corresponds with the postmodern turn toward a nonideological world (with the collapse of any viable alternative to capitalism and liberal democracy) and with the consequent dominance of the criterion of performativity in all its affairs, including those that fall under the name of "education." This turn of events, reflected in the decline of nonvocational adult learning everywhere in the 1990s, becomes a central preoccupation of this book, which also interprets this crisis of education as an aspect of the crisis of modernity itself. The project of modernity, child of the Enlightenment, has come under different challenges over these last decades, and I identify three very different ones as particularly relevant to my purposes—Alasdair MacIntyre's, Jurgen Habermas's, and postmodernism's. MacIntyre is an enemy of modernity, Habermas a sympathetic critic who believes in revision, postmodernism is ambiguous—the "post" in the term subject to different interpretations. Chapter 6 deals with important distinctions between postmodernism as an *ism* (to be distinguished from the postmodern condition) and *poststructuralism*, the term I prefer to use instead for what the writers I am interested in (those usually labeled postmodernists, namely Derrida, Lyotard, Foucault, Baudrillard, Rorty, and so on) produce.

For MacIntyre the crisis in modern education is reflected in its inability to resolve the tension between two tasks that teachers and educational institutions from schools to universities are required to perform in our societies: that of enculturation and individuation, of preparing individuals to perform their social roles while making them independent thinkers. Rorty refers to it as the tension between the joint demands of truth and freedom. Or, put differently, from the individual's rather than society's point of view, between reassurance and freedom. This is a tension that has grown considerably in a postmodern world where risk is a crucial protagonist. MacIntyre argues that the way to resolve it is to restore the notion of an educated public to the postmodern world and to reform the university system for this purpose. His account of an educated public, his views about the university, and the more general project for a learning community developed in his work since *After Virtue* (1981), are the subject of Chapter 3. Chapter 4 is devoted to the Frankfurt School theorists and to Habermas in particular. What is particularly interesting and relevant to the subject of this work in the former is their utopian dream of a rational society, which they hold out against the instrumental rationality of the developing capitalist liberal democracies of the Western world that they describe in their sociologies, influenced also by the work of Max Weber. Adorno and Horkheimer were, of course, as critical of modernity as MacIntyre and even more pessimistic of the possibility of such a society emerging under modern conditions than he was, regarding them as overwhelmingly oppressive and manipulative.

Habermas did not share their pessimism, though he shared much of their social analysis of contemporary Western societies as well as their interest in the rational society. The latter he found modeled, more or less, in the critical liberal bourgeois public that formed in the salons of Europe in the eighteenth century, the same century as the Scottish public, which MacIntyre, on his part, adopted as his model educated public. Inevitably Chapter 4 contains a comparison between these two publics, Habermas's and MacIntyre's, which, as may easily be supposed, are very different from one another. Chapter 4, however, also includes a critique of the development of the relevant aspects on Habermas's thinking following the publication of *The Structural Transformation of the Public Sphere* (1989a), in which he described the rise and fall of the bourgeois public—namely, his work on communicative action and the communicative community, their link with the politics of emancipation, and the workings and role of the public and general possibility of various different publics in modern-day liberal democracies. What is especially interesting is the suggestion found in his work of the need for two kinds of publics: one general and more measured, a critical public formed at the interface between systems and lifeworld; the other, or others, emerging spontaneously from the lifeworld in response to crises experienced in the interaction between systems and lifeworld or around specific issues. Chapter 5 picks up from Chapter 4 with a discussion of the work of Stewart Ranson, who theorizes a learning democracy based largely on Habermas's work, before it turns to developments in Britain in the last years of the twentieth century as a Labour Party came to power in that country expressly committed to policies of lifelong learning and to creating a learning society with social democrat political credentials.

At this stage, I need to say something about the personal background to the writing of this book, which was intended to follow up on *Philosophy of Lifelong Education* (*PLE*), which I published in 1987. That work ended with a chapter on the lifelong education movement's description of the learning society. My project when I finished that book was to write another one elaborating an *education research project* for a learning society with a *maximalist* operational approach in line with that supported by the movement (the term is explained in Chapter 1) and a social democrat political outlook. So my intentions at the time were politically quite similar to Ranson's. The notion of an education research project was elaborated in the 1987 book and is redescribed with some critical comments in Chapter 2 of this book. In Chapter 3 I show how it could perfectly well accommodate theoretical approaches to the learning society like MacIntyre's, since what I do there is re-present MacIntyre's writings as such a project. The way *PLE* proposed dealing with educational theory was to rationalize competing discourse on education, the liberal, the Marxist, the social democrat, and so on, as research projects with a well-defined role for philosophy in them. Had I continued with my original idea this book would have been finished some years ago. It would have been interesting to compare it with Ranson's work today and, more especially, with the education project of the new social democrat politics of the "Third Way" that came to define the political outlook of the British Labour Party and many other left parties in the Western world in the 1990s. At a certain stage of writing, however, when I was working on MacIntyre and Habermas, I found myself looking at what was being said about postmodernism at the time, especially at what the postmodernists were saying. This was really already in the cards when I wrote *PLE* and used Rorty's hermeneutical account of philosophy in *Philosophy and the Mirror of Nature (PMN)* (1980). But when I started reading up on Rorty after *PLE* I found that he had abandoned his approach in *PMN* and that his postmodernism was more pronounced. From there it was a short trip to Lyotard, then to Foucault, Derrida, and Baudrillard. Immediately I found my writing project challenged in several ways.

What was most evidently challenged was the methodology of an education research project. The model contemplates a "hard" ideological core that determines the normative dimension of the project and gives it its political identity; in my case, as I have been saying, being a social democrat, I intended a social democrat education project. The fashionable way to describe the contents of the core today would be as a "master narrative," and the master narratives of the modern world are greeted with skepticism in the postmodern. More seriously, poststructuralists like Foucault, whose narratives immediately captivated me, encourage us to live without master narratives *of any kind*, to "cut off the king's head," as he put it, rather than replace some old king with the new, as a sign of our postmodern ("countermodern," Foucault [1984a]) maturity. Poststructuralists in general are also skeptical of theory in general, of theoretical or constructive approaches, and my project was to construct a theory of a learning society as a strategic tool for action. Rorty has described the poststructuralist outlook as "reactive" as opposed to the constructive, and their politics as particularistic and "tactical" rather than holistic (*maximalist* in my case) and strategic. And this suggests a wholly different way of approaching the learning society than what I had contemplated—as an existing reality rather than a promise for the future. Foucault and Baudrillard are particularly interesting poststructuralists in this sense because they describe the postmodern learning society vividly in their work, the former as a policed, the latter as obscene, society. Both render the case for an educated public impossible and undesirable. Their dystopian accounts are the subject of Chapter 7. Rorty describes Foucault's politics as the politics of despair. Chapter 6, on the other hand, describes his politics of hope and that of Derrida. Both describe themselves as belonging politically to the left with the crucial difference that where Rorty gets his politics (or so he says) from Dewey, Derrida gets his from Marx.

Of the two, Rorty is more interesting for me since his self-declared business is to articulate the evolving vocabulary of a new liberal-social democrat utopia as he sees it emerging within the left's political discourse in the postmodern world.

Does it in any way resemble the political project for a new social democracy promised by the Third Way social democrats, whose vision of a learning society is also described in Chapter 5? The question is a complex one, but interestingly the new social democrats also find it more comfortable to live without a hard ideological core for their project and prefer to describe their politics within a center that is fluid, not a synthesis of some sort of left and right, but a creative way of recasting the left, which is also what the poststructuralists of the left are after. While Rorty describes himself as an orthodox social democrat reformist, Foucault and Baudrillard are uninterested in situating themselves politically either way. The latter pronounces himself uninterested in politics altogether, the former as interested in politics in a different way. Baudrillard is a thoroughgoing nihilist with a narcissistic outlook who seeks an ecstatic identification with "the object." Foucault can be described as a "weak anarchist," as Todd May calls him, both in his political outlook, which is suspicious of power relations, and in his tactical approach, which engages in politics at the microlevel and aims to subvert relations of dominance and manipulation where these exist. More generally Foucault is concerned with the workings of power in the construction of modern societies, analyzing them in his genealogies. Foucault's is a politics of combat and suspicion rather than despair. It is suspicious particularly of projects intended to establish the ideal conditions for a politics of consensus, like those of Habermas and Gadamer. It focuses its suspicion on postmodern learning societies, suggesting that the kind of work we should do on them is not theoretical or utopian but genealogical; mapping out the economics of power within them, with the ultimate object of unmasking their repressive features and freeing individuals to create their own self-individuating projects.

Indeed, the *ethos* Foucault encourages, unlike Derrida, is individualist, and the same is true of Rorty and Baudrillard, though their individualism is different from his. Rorty and Foucault both encourage an ethics of self-creation, though where Rorty's notion of self-creation is essentially Sartre's, Foucault's is Nietzsche's. Baudrillard's, on the other hand, is an ethics not of self-creation but of self-destruction. This is what renders it nihilistic where Foucault's is not. Both Rorty and Foucault propose individual self-creation rather than the reconstitution of educated publics as their response to the question of education in our postmodern world, though even here, the way they deal with the tension between enculturation and individuation raised by that question is very different. Rather than propose their synthesis in a public, Rorty advocates their separation into distinct activities and practices, distinct stages of life, different institutions—the first, enculturation, being the proper task of schooling, the second, individuation, of the nonvocational university. Foucault does not deal directly with the idea of identifying schooling with enculturation, so one does not know how attractive he would have found it. Foucault was very concerned with how enculturation works in our societies, with how we are made *subjects*, as he puts it, by different economies of disciplinary power. Thus, in the Nietzschean manner (and unlike Rorty), he identifies self-refusal, the refusal of aspects of one's subjectification, as indispensable for self-creation, which lies beyond the indispensable commitment to self-care. Identifying lifelong education with the individual's ongoing self-creation is, however, undoubtedly taking it out of the remit of schooling. A culture of self-care in the sense of individual self-dependence, economic and vocational, lies at the heart of the Third Way's social philosophy. It is also identified as the key object of lifelong learning in the current discourse of the European Union. Foucault, however, understands care for self differently, tying it to a project of being rather than having, to draw on Fromm's famous distinction, and drawing on an understanding of the expression that goes back to antiquity. Self-creation is also very different for Foucault than it is for Rorty, since the latter envisages it as an entirely private matter, its irony unsuitable for public life, while the former wants to carry it into the public sphere and does not countenance Rorty's radical distinction between public and private self.

Rorty believes that philosophy, though it could contribute to one's private self-creation, has nothing to say to the citizen, since it has nothing to say to politics. He also says that it has nothing to say to education as a public enterprise, thus denying the need for a philosophy of education. This view has created other difficulties for me in writing this book, as not only was my notion of an education research project challenged but also my own self-perception as a philosopher of education (a label, to be honest, that I have always felt uncomfortable with). In the hermeneutic "postphilosophical culture" he describes in *Consequences of Pragmatism* (1982:xxix), Rorty replaces philosophers with all-purpose intellectuals with "no special 'problems' to solve, nor any special 'method' to apply," who "abided by no particular disciplinary standards," and "had no collective self-image as a 'profession.'" Perceiving oneself as an intellectual also implies a willingness to play some sort of public role in one's society. But his proposal comes at a time when the intellectual's role in a postmodern world, cast as the universal intellectual at home in the modern world, is threatened by the figure of the *imagologue*, as Kundera calls her. Views like Kundera's that the intellectual is dead are shared by many, and are responded to in different ways by Habermas, Foucault, MacIntyre, and others in the book. Again I feel myself drawn to Foucault's description of the specific intellectual and the role he assigns to her in public life. But Kundera raises a more general question than that of the intellectual's future or, better still, frames the question within the more general one about the role of the media (which turns out to be crucial in several ways) in shaping the postmodern learning society. Much space is given to this concern in the book, mainly via the work of Adorno and Horkheimer, Baudrillard, and Gianni Vattimo.

Finally, with respect to the future of the education research project, as I wrote earlier it is not a notion or tool that will interest the poststructuralist. Do I now, therefore, think it useless? One of the many things that have interested me in Rorty's work is his suggestion that often it is not a question of choosing between one thing and another, of deciding what to keep and what to abandon, whether to be a constructive philosopher or a reactive intellectual, whether to be theoretical or subversive, but of realizing that the alternatives can and need to be put to different purposes. Rorty contends that both creative and reactive discourses are required, and that reactive discourse is perforce reactive to *something*, something that is itself constructive. Constructive discourse, theory, will always be needed by those who are concerned with making policies and setting up programs or projects in the name of public education. For these, I believe, the education research project could still be a useful tool, and philosophers could still indulge in their traditional work of justification and critique. For those, on the other hand, who have to submit to policies, programs, and projects that are made for them by others, or who, as specific intellectuals, work with those who submit, the story is different.

CHAPTER ONE

The Lifelong Education Movement: The Learning Society as Utopia

The Challenge of Lifelong Education

I first came across the idea of a learning society in the late 1970s when I took an interest in the phenomenon of lifelong education as an emerging concept, started teaching a course on the subject in the teacher education program at the University of Malta, and decided to make it the subject of my Ph.D. research.[1] The literature I read at the time in connection with my research, and which saw its heyday during the 1960s and 1970s, had as its point of departure the claim that education in the second half of the twentieth century is in a state of deep crisis, a claim that both struck and convinced me. It identified this crisis as the failure of our contemporary education systems and practices to adapt to the demands of a fast-changing world, argued that in such a world they are facing the threat of obsolescence, and claimed that the sensible response to this threat is to promote lifelong learning for all. In the early 1960s UNESCO formally announced lifelong education as the "master concept" for the planning and programming of education for the second half of the twentieth century.[2] Gradually, my attention began to focus on a group of writers on the subject who were operating within, or were sponsored by, UNESCO and were interested not merely in lifelong learning but in the more radical reconceptualization of the whole of education as a lifelong process. They thus distinguished it from other terms also circulating at the time that confused lifelong learning with adult or even professional education. With the passing of time this body of writers had acquired enough consistency and unity of thought and purpose to qualify as a movement, though only in the loosest sense, since they never actually banded themselves as a movement.

The movement emphasized the universality and ancient lineage of the idea of lifelong education. Its presence in a diversity of cultures, they argued, has acted as a civilizing force, and thus as a value inherent to human life and experience. Besides the liberal and humanist tradition of the West, where it was captured in the thoughts of writers like Comenius, Matthew Arnold, and John Dewey, it appeared in Islam, where the Koran exhorts the faithful to learn from the cradle to the grave, and in ancient Chinese, Indian, and Greek traditions as well. This universality of the notion more or less justified UNESCO's concern with it as a global organization.[3] Bogdan Suchodolski (1979:38), one of the movement's foremost pioneers, attributed to Comenius the writing of the first treatise on lifelong education. But the movement in general identified its own modern, socially conscious, egalitarian "doctrine of lifelong education" more immediately with the memorandum connected with the report of the Adult Education Committee of the United Kingdom, published in 1919, which had concluded that in the new postwar world, "Adult education is not a luxury for a limited, exclusive group of specially selected individuals, but an integral part of social life," and should, therefore, "be made available for all as well as be made permanent" (Dave 1976:58). Quoting from the same memorandum, F.W. Jessup (1969:18) noted that besides linking lifelong learning with the ideal of national economic recovery, the report had an explicit political agenda: cultivating "a new spirit of assertion among the rank-and-file" through the exercise of their democratic responsibilities, and responding to "the need for a far wider body of intelligent public opinion." These were concerns that were also taken up and articulated by the writers of the movement in the 1960s and 1970s. But Suchodolski (1976:58) identified A.B. Yeaxlee's *Lifelong Education* (1929) as the first to address these issues seriously and try to work out what they could mean in terms of practical policies. Yeaxlee was already speaking about the growing demand for "education as a lifelong process" in Britain in 1920 (Field 2001:5). In France the concept of lifelong education began to take shape in the 1930s "in the hands of the philosopher Bachelard," but was not adopted in educational circles until after World War II (Furter 1977:13).[4]

The importance of the fast-decreasing time span of change and its impact on education that so struck the writers of the movement had already been identified and highlighted in the 1930s by A.N. Whitehead (Dave 1976:15). By the 1960s, when the notion of lifelong education burst on the scene, this phenomenon of fast-accelerating change had taken new and different forms and global proportions, creating urgent challenges and infiltrating the world of politics and culture, as well as the social and economic world, where it had its most immediate impact. What was particularly remarkable about it were its speed and permeability, its rate and penetration into the everyday lives of ordinary people. In such a situation, as Paul Lengrand (1975:16) pointed out, "the notion that man can accomplish his life-span with a given set of intellectual and technical luggage is fast disappearing," and we are faced with the necessity of lifelong learning. Lengrand conceded that change has always been a challenge for humanity but argued that the difference today was that it had modified the very terms of individual and community fate, rendering the actions of the world both more complex and more involved, and jeopardizing the traditional patterns of explanation for coming to terms with them. In short, it threatened people with *anomie*, with becoming strangers in the world they inhabit. The challenges he identified were those created by a growing demand for democratic citizenship in the political field; by the explosion of information technology, which has given our civilization a planetary character but which also requires a more discriminating selection because of the quality of its products; by the growth of leisure time and its use; by the "crisis" in patterns of life and in relationships as well as in ideologies; and by the changing perception of the human body, including the place that sexuality has come to play in our culture. This is no different from the way social theorists describe today's challenges. Against them, Lengrand described educational systems as characterized by only very fractional links with life, by nearly complete isolation from concrete realities, by a rift between enjoyment and "education," and by a nearly total absence of a political culture of dialogue and participation.

Education and the Problem of Change

The importance of the impact of the fast-changing world on everyday life has grown, if anything, in the estimation of social theorists. In 1992, Barry Smart (1992:1) was arguing like Lengrand that change "constitutes an increasingly prominent aspect of modern life," that it "might be regarded as the defining feature" of modern times in that it "radically alters the nature of day-to-day social life and affects the most personal aspects of experience," and that it has become an increasingly dramatic reality for ordinary people and societies. In *Modernity and Self-Identity*, Anthony

Giddens (1991:2) described the net effect of change on people's lives in postmodern information societies, especially through the mass media, as one of disorientation. "Modern social life," Giddens (1991:4) said, "is characterized by profound processes of the reorganization of time and space, coupled to the expansion of disembedding mechanisms, mechanisms which prize social relations free from the hold of specific locales, recombining them across wide time-space distances." As a result, traditional habits and local customs are undermined, creating unaccustomed tensions between the poles of extensionality and intensionality that constitute everyday experience. In sum, the late modern world, he tells us, is in many ways a paradoxical world that, while "having a unitary framework of experience, creates new forms of fragmentation and dispersal" (1991:5). He goes on to describe its culture as "a risk culture," in the sense that "the concept of risk becomes fundamental to the way both lay actors and technical specialists organize the social world," which cannot, in some of its aspects, avoid appearing "apocalyptic" (1991:3). Not, he swiftly adds, "because it is inevitably heading towards calamity as some prophets of doom forecast," but because the risks it introduces are such as no previous generation has had to face (1991:4).

In this situation of change and constant risk, Giddens continues, self-identity requires of the individual a reflexively organized endeavor as the self increasingly becomes the only point of reference available to it and as it needs constantly to be remade in the light of the fast-changing world. Giddens (1991:5) disagrees that the decline of traditional reference points means that all kinds of standardizing influences have disappeared from today's world. The truth is, he holds, that "because of the 'openness' of social life today, the pluralization of contexts of action and the diversity of 'authorities' people within the same society are prepared to refer to, lifestyle choice is increasingly important in the constitution of self-identity and daily activity." In this context the notions of a lifestyle and a plan of life acquire a particular significance. He introduces a political caveat here that is important in the light of his later political writing, namely that the ideal of "life planning" is meaningless for the many whose circumstances deprive them of the means to plan, namely the poor and socially marginalized. "Modernity," Giddens (1991:6, italics in original) reminds us grimly, is not only about disorientation, it also "produces *difference, exclusion,* and *marginalization.*" In short, it produces social injustice. "It would be a major error," he warns, "to suppose that the phenomena analyzed in the book are confined in their impact to those in more privileged material circumstances" (1991:6). Cutting across traditional class barriers and across traditional gender and other distinctions, the risk society concerns everyone. The object of this caveat is obviously to highlight the point that the problem of change is also, if not primarily, a problem of *justice*.

Ulrich Beck (1994) similarly refers to contemporary societies as "risk societies," and to the kinds of risks they involve as unique to the process of modernization.[5] Scott Lash and Brian Wynne (Beck 1994:3), in their introduction to the English version of his book, summarize Beck's view as holding that "risk has become an intellectual and political web across which thread many strands of discourse relating to the slow crisis of modernity and industrial society." Referring to the age as one of "reflexive modernity," Beck (1994:21) argues, like Giddens, that "as opposed to older dangers," the risks "are consequences that relate to the threatening force of modernization and to its globalization of doubt." Like Beck, Giddens (1991:3) says that doubt "forms a general existential dimension of the contemporary social world." Stewart Ranson (1994:39) notes, quoting Hobsbawm (1981), a search for increasingly private and personal satisfactions in these circumstances as "a rational response for the many who feel they have little sense of control over their destinies in the face of a public world that is in their perception growing more intractable." Today, he continues, social identities are more typically formed in the private domain than at work. John Quicke (1997:141), drawing on Lash, identifies the "gradual 'freeing of agency from structure'" referred to by Giddens as a key mark of "reflexive modernity" (the term he also uses), and an outstanding cause of this strong trend toward individualism that Ranson refers to. It has, he says, impacted various social structures like the nuclear family, the nation, and the state, and has led to the growing atomization of society. Back in the 1970s the lifelong education writers had warned of these trends, that we could see a society coming into being whose members would see themselves as private consumers of information and adult vocational services that respond to the demands of the economy and to their working prospects, and little else. A society devoid of any substantial moral or political vision, whose members lack any perception of themselves as lifelong learners in any more than the minimal sense in which this requirement is forced on them by their practical, vocational, or professional needs, or to respond to fashion, because it is the "in" thing, or because learning is presented to them as a form of leisure entertainment. In other words, a society where learning is valued only for economic survival or because it satisfies the hedonistic self-satisfaction of consumers, mainly of the offerings of the media but also of a broader learning market. Suchodolski (1976:69), in particular, warned of our advance toward a late capitalist world that focuses attention almost entirely on material values, and "lays the foundations of rivalry and aggression and encourages exaggerated consumption," rather than education. A world that "makes man a slave of ambition and status symbols." There was a lot of prescience in these warnings, as will be seen in the next chapter.

Meanwhile, against the pragmatic argument for lifelong education, Charles Bailey (1988:122) has argued that acknowledging the existence of change does not commit us to educate *for* change. We need some deeper reason for that. For change, he points out quite rightly, is not an unqualified good. One may want to resist it in the form it takes, if it harms persons, for instance. The argument paraphrases the one made against Dewey's famous definition of education as growth, which, Dewey's critics have argued, is not necessarily good or desirable. There are instances when it is positively harmful or evil. And the same can be said of change. Both terms, growth and change, are normatively neutral or indeterminate terms and need to be given substance before one can assess their desirability or otherwise. One needs to say what kind of change or growth there is, and where and what it leads to. In Dewey's case the argument of his critics was that normative aims are required to direct education. Bailey (1988:122), on his part, was worried that the "developments and changes of a technological nature," cited to support the argument for lifelong education, "are often no more than the impositions of the actions of some people upon others, with the presupposed values and their vested interests being unavailable for discussion." He did not elaborate on who these "some people" are, but his words seem prophetic, as we shall see, in the light of what is happening today in lifelong learning. His more general point, and it seems a perfectly valid one as far as it goes, is that pragmatic arguments are never enough by themselves; one has to see how the practices they endorse are justified. In this sense, he argued, satisfying the criterion of relevance to historical, social, and technological circumstances—even if it is conceded that the notion of relevance is unproblematic—is insufficient reason to subscribe to the concept of lifelong *education*. In short, what Bailey is saying, like Dewey's critics, is that "education" is a normative concept; it must refer back to a set of values and cannot be justified on purely pragmatic grounds. Dewey's persistence in eschewing the need for any other criterion for growth, except that it is open-ended and leads to more growth, seems to violate this understanding of the concept.

In fact, however, despite his resistance to further definition, Dewey's theory of growth was far from vacuous or permissive. As he tells us himself, the whole object of his reflections on education was "to detect and state the ideas implied in a democratic society and to apply these ideas to the problems of the enterprise of education" (1966a:iii). So there is a clear normative point of reference for his conception of growth; namely, the promotion of democratic life. But the problem is that he was equally vacuous about democracy, having simply described it as a form of life characterized by criteria of unrestricted communication. His critics wanted more from him, but do we need something more substantive than that? That is one of the questions that will dog the writing of this book. Dewey, on his part, assumed that the most generic criteria will do, that one does not need anything more refined or definite; any models or any theoretically supported theories of justice or of the good society, or the good life, or of human progress to strive for or to measure practices or policies by. Meanwhile, on the matter of change and its value Dewey would have conceded that it is not an unconditional good but argued that a politically positive attitude toward change is required *a priori* in a democracy. In Dewey's view a democratic society must perforce value change in principle, since its progress depends on its members' willingness to experiment socially and politically. But this does not mean giving absolute value to change any more than a liberal society gives absolute value to liberty. Liberals value liberty, as Dewey values change and postmodernists difference, *in principle*, not as an unconditional good but as an *a priori* good, with the onus of proof falling on those who would restrict or suspend it in some way. The way the democrat values change can be contrasted with the way the Platonist values permanence. Karl Popper (1965) has argued, like Dewey, that the principled resistance to change produces "closed" totalitarian societies that censor ideas and control the flow of information. Open democratic environments are, to the contrary, as Dewey held them to be, necessarily fluid and dynamic, constituted experimentally and reformed piecemeal, rather than according to a blueprint. This is why they are resistant to utopian modeling.

Meanwhile, one needs to note that Dewey understands growth, in educational terms, as a process that is ongoing and cumulative or "reconstructive": a process that is obedient to some principle or directive force in contrast with that kind of change that is degenerative or chaotic, or generally unintelligent and blind. In the very first pages of *Democracy and*

Education (1966a, henceforth *DE*), he establishes the basic Darwinian point that learning is, for all living beings, humans included, most fundamentally a matter of survival; that survival is the first and most basic motive for all organisms to learn, including the human. Bailey (1988:122) concedes that "there may be certain aspects of our physical environment that we can do no other than adapt to." But when he adds, "even here human beings have proved to be remarkably ingenious in the manner of their adaptation to, say, gravity," he shows that he has failed to grasp what the lifelong education writers understood by a pragmatic adaptation to change. Dewey points out in those same pages in *DE*, that adaptation to one's environment, changing or otherwise, need not be, and ideally is not, passive. It can be, and he wanted it to be, "ingenious" or creative. And so did the lifelong education writers. Like Dewey, they held that it is only the kind of living that is critical and creative, interactive rather than passive, having the power to *change* the environment, not just to adjust to it, that deserves to be called "human." The power of agency that takes human potential far beyond passive adaptation into the realm of creativity and risk is for Dewey, as it was for Marx and for Nietzsche, and for the lifelong education writers (as we shall see), the higher, optimal objective of the human enterprise that we may call education.

Finally, the environment Dewey had in mind was mainly, though not only, social. Survival in our social environment is the task we are prepared for by our upbringing, or enculturation, and it is an inescapable experience for all social animals. It implies the need to learn to cope with the conditions of living in one's contemporary world without going down in it, without being alienated or submerged into an underclass. By describing lifelong learning as necessary in today's world, the movement's writers were reacting to this need for social survival in the kind of world described by the social theorists. Their point was that even if one always has the choice of opting out of lifelong learning, it would always be at a terrible price. A more general Deweyan reply to Bailey would be that foregoing pragmatic considerations, ignoring the actual sociocultural, political, and economic context one lives in, however possible this may be in theory and even perhaps in practice, cannot be a coherent choice for anyone. For, whether one likes it or not, that context sets the agenda for one's life. And even if one needs to struggle against it, or some particular aspect of it, one can do so only from within that context itself, not from some theoretical point outside it. And this is more dramatically true with the contemporary sociocultural and political context that, as Giddens and Beck and other social theorists argue, is intrusive into our lives and influential in a way that it has never been at any time before, thanks mainly to the pervasiveness of the mass media and the implements of the information society generally. In today's information society the number of secluded woods available for an Emile to roam in, or peaks for a Platonic hero to ascend to, away from the harsh material realities of the cave, are in very short supply indeed. And, in any case, Aristotle's warning that only gods and animals can make any sense of life outside the cave continues to ring true to us through the ages. Plato himself considered socialization into the inferior reality of the cave as the indispensable first stage of one's education into being a philosopher, if for no other reason than because it will eventually be the philosopher's moral duty anyway to return to that cave to enlighten its occupants once he has obtained his own intellectual freedom and enlightenment outside it.

The Learning Society

In a succinct statement, R. H. Dave (1976:34, italics in original) outlined the philosophy of lifelong education and the politics of the movement as follows: "*Lifelong education is a process of accomplishing personal, social and professional development throughout the life-span of individuals in order to enhance the quality of life of both individuals and their collectives. It is a comprehensive and unifying idea, which includes formal, non-formal and informal learning for acquiring and enhancing enlightenment so as to attain the fullest possible development in different stages and domains of life. It is connected with both individual growth and social progress. That is why ideas such as 'learning to be' and 'a learning society' or 'an educative society' are associated with this concept.*"

This statement, unpacked, makes two claims on behalf of the movement's project of lifelong education: (1) that it is holistic and comprehensive; that it has to do with the overall development of individuals throughout their life spans and in all life's domains, aiming to enhance the quality of their lives and that of their collectives, and is, therefore, related to the twin educational aims of modernity—individual growth ("learning to be") and collective enlightenment; and (2) that it is based on a comprehensive and unifying idea of education, which includes learning of all kinds—formal, non-formal and informal—and is, therefore, tied to the idea of a "learning" or "educative" (which are not the same thing) society. These two claims made up the normative and "technical" (a distinction I shall explain later) aspects of the project, distinguishing it from the projects falling under the competing expressions similarly incorporating the idea of lifelong learning that were around at the time: "recurrent education" (Organisation for Economic Cooperation and Development, or OECD), "continuing education," and "permanent education" (Council of Europe), to name the most prominent. More than just a platform to argue the "pressures" for the acceptance of lifelong learning, as one writer, Huey B. Long (1974) put it, the movement's concern was with the "deeper sense of the term" lifelong education, in which it "represents an entire philosophical system centered upon man and his creative development," and grounded in "modern psychology" and anthropology (Suchodolski 1976:77). A humanistic philosophical system in which "man in all his aspects, in the diversity of his situations and in the breadth of his responsibilities, in short, man as he really is," becomes the "true subject of education" (Lengrand 1975:95).

Lengrand (1975:95) makes Giddens's and Beck's point that today's "man", is "the victim of abstraction," that everything in today's world "conspires to divide him and break his unity," that "he" is "lost amidst a multitude of incoherent and contradictory situations, trends and definitions." He further argues that contemporary schooling not only fails to respond to this state of affairs, it contributes to the situation by "arbitrarily isolating" the intellectual aspect of the human personality in its cognitive form for the "needs of instruction," causing the self to "either shrink to an embryonic state or develop in a disordered fashion" thereby "threaten[ing] the balance of the personality."[6] Lengrand (1975:36) describes the "fundamental crisis" facing the fast-changing contemporary world as obvious in the sphere of morals and interpersonal relations but also "in the realm of thought." He writes of it as "an alien, unfriendly world" in which people "do not recognise themselves," echoing the then topical and influential UNESCO-commissioned *Learning to be*, published in 1972 by a group of experts chaired by Edgar Faure, and presented as a "report" about "the world of education today and tomorrow," but reading more like a manifesto and afterwards regarded as a canonical text within the lifelong education literature. Like Lengrand, and sounding like Dewey, the report (1972:158) emphasized "the permanent immaturity and incompleteness" of the human being, "a batch of potentialities that can either evolve or miscarry," that "never ceases to 'enter life,' to be born in human form"; that one is permanently in a state of becoming, a fact that makes lifelong education "natural" for human beings. So that, in promoting it one does no more than return education to its "true nature," its "full significance ... which is not the acquisition of a hoard of knowledge but the development of the individual attaining increasing self-realization as a result of successive experiences" (1972:50).

Faure (1972:69) emphasized that this view of education needs to be upheld against the conventional view that regards it as a matter of "preparing for stereotyped functions, stable situations, for one moment in existence, for a particular trade or a given job," as the inculcation of "conventional knowledge in time-honored categories" related to the prevailing "idea of acquiring, at an early age, a set of intellectual and technical equipment valid for a lifetime." This, he says, is a "fundamental axiom" that "is crumbling" in today's world that demands something different: "Learning to live, learning to learn, so as to be able to absorb new knowledge all through life; learning to think freely and critically; learning to love the world and make it more human; learning to develop in and through creative work" (1972:145). Today's world, the report continued, demands that education be viewed as a process that "transcends the limits of institutions, programs and methods imposed on it down the centuries" (1972:145). It demands an "indispensable remolding" away from education's traditional focus on schooling, since in any case, society today "cannot exercise broad, efficient action on all its components—in any domain—through one single institution, however extensive it may be" (1972:161). In short, the report concluded, the world today demands "that all its elements [the elements of education]—theory and practice, structures and methods, management and organization—be completely rethought from one and the same point of view," i.e., that of the learning society (1972:233).

Amor Fati: **The Individual**

In response to the threat of disorientation to the individual, the lifelong education writers militated for a holistic education that respects the unity and complexity of the person, that caters to "every aspect and dimension of the individual as a physical, intellectual, emotional, sexual, social and spiritual being" and corresponds with the activity of multiplying the dimensions of human existence rather than shrinking them to one kind, the intellectual (Lengrand 1975:96). Thus Suchodolski (1976:74), appropriating Herbert Marcuse's 1964 famous expression, complains about the "one-dimensional man" who needs hardly any education at all since the guiding principles of "his" life are governed solely by criteria of efficiency, and "his" prospects for the future are limited by utility and power. Lengrand (1975:36) contrasts the "attitude of resignation and surrender" of those reduced to being helpless spectators with the disposition to live with disorientation and risk that is alone "compatible with a full and wholehearted acceptance of the condition of man." This is a condition that requires "radical transformations and changes in minds and attitudes with regard to life" itself, starting with a changed attitude toward time, which should be regarded not as the enemy to be constantly defeated but as "something positive, bringing human experience discoveries and progress" (1975:100). It corresponds with what Nietzsche called *amor fati*: an attitude that "implies acceptance of risk and taste for adventure of all kinds" and signifies an acceptance of one's lot that comes with self-confidence, with confidence in one's own powers, not with resignation (1975:100).

In the face of disorientation, Lengrand (1975:100) argues, education seeks not the false security of permanence but "the discovery of true security by becoming part of the movement" of change, or flux itself, accepting and welcoming it in the form of risk-taking "as experience of life in action." We need, he says, echoing the Faure report (1972)—which similarly affirms the value of creativity in the face of rapid change—to accept risk and to respond to it creatively and fearlessly. Suchodolski (1976:74) too contrasts the experience of "one-dimensional man" with a way of being that is a field of creativity and of contacts that enrich the mind. The Faure report (1972:148) speaks of the same tension that Lengrand does, between a yearning for security and a willingness to risk, as fundamental to the human outlook. It speaks of "man's nature" being "torn between two longings: for security and for adventure." The first forces "him" to seek out shelter and reassurance while the second inclines "him" in the contrary direction toward exposure and risk. The existence of disorientation and risk is not, the report insists, something necessarily negative or calamitous, nor is the willingness to accept or take risks an unnatural one for human beings to adopt.

Quite the contrary, risk-taking is natural. We are inclined to accept it as a part of life and even to have a taste for it in all its forms, "the risk of being wrong or led astray as much as the risk involved in discovering, in being discovered and in facing life's great experiences." There is in life, it says, always a price to be paid for everything. Security, to be sure, demands a low price, "the modest one of discipline." Risk demands a much greater one, that of creativity. Nevertheless, creativity, the readiness to risk, it insists, is the only true condition of "man." The creature of the spirit of curiosity and adventure it alone is compatible with living a truly human existence.

Lengrand (1975:100) asks whether this conclusion does not conflict with the common assumption that it is "the aim of education to make men happy." Yes, he answers, if happiness is confused with a life of untroubled adaptation, for risk-taking is necessarily stressful and troubled. But this happiness has nothing to do with education. Education has nothing to do either with happiness that is "made to depend on the possession or lack of an object" material or "moral," "such as the possession of someone loved or public esteem." It has nothing to do, he insists, with *having* anything at all.[7] It does, however, have to do with happiness "given its true meaning as a mode of being and a way of living one's life" linked with the exercise and feeling of power (1975:101): "True power, not the deceptive, alienating and dangerous power of controlling other people but the power which really deserves the name, that of self-control" (1975:101). This power, Lengrand (1975:101) points out, is within everybody's reach: "Everyone is capable of making this effort to control himself on the countless occasions when lucidity must triumph over illusion, knowledge over ignorance, hope over despair and discouragement, confidence in others over mistrust and suspicion, love and understanding over hatred and misanthropy, and availability and transparency over refusal and opacity." It also demands the Socratic readiness to state one's own feelings in opposition to the herd, to counter ready-made conceptions with a personal and original view of the world, to be authentic in the positive sense of being self-created, and to prefer judgments that have been formed on the basis of knowledge and reflection to vague, fluctuating opinions. Power of this positive kind, Lengrand contends, can be acquired only through work. And work means study, discipline, and the discovery and use of gifts and abilities that enable us to understand and communicate with others to find answers to the questions constantly presented by life, the world, and the vicissitudes of the heart and mind, even when we keep them on the confines of consciousness. No one, Lengrand (1975:103) argues, can hope to find happiness in life without resigning oneself to being constantly challenged, without being prepared to meet with shocks and changes, with separations and disappearances, and finally, with the unavoidable need to die. While the patterns of family and school education have hitherto led to an untrue, frail, and fixed image of happiness resting on an illusion of security, he contends, real education—an education that is truly at the service of individuals—must teach them resolutely to accept risk, alteration, and insecurity and to ally themselves with time, the destroyer of all things.

There is much of Michel Foucault in all this, as we shall see in the final chapter, because there is much of Nietzsche. Lengrand (1975:14) follows up these reflections on life, education, and happiness with closely related reflections about culture. As with education, he rejects the common view of culture as some*thing* lying there waiting to be occupied or "possessed"; "a self-contained domain" or "territory," "the sum total of knowledge accumulated over the centuries and the sum total of experiences and achievements in the various sectors of science, art and literature." This "geographical" conception of culture, he says, is intrinsically nonegalitarian in that it distinguishes the "possessors" of culture from the rest, the dispossessed. It "creates the cultural rich and the cultural poor, the privileged and the victims, the initiates and the uninitiated." We need, he says, to stop thinking in terms of a "ready made, cut-and-dried culture" that we have inherited and to locate it "in its rightful place" where it is "integrated into a living, fighting being and into a series of experiences of life, each individual and unique" (1975:14). Acknowledging the positive motives and efforts of those who have tried "to reduce inequality and open wide the doors and broaden the paths of access to culture" in the past as undoubtedly well-meaning, they were, he says, always doomed to fail because their thinking was fundamentally flawed, precisely because it was based on this geographical notion of culture that we should reject outright (1975:13). The way we should answer the problem of inequality, for Lengrand, is not primarily by seeking to solve the problem of access (though this problem needs to be addressed too), but by solving that of motivation.

The Faure report (1972:xxviii) shares this view. It also identifies motivation as "the key to every modern educational policy," distinguishing two kinds: the materialistic, related to ambition and to the search for employment, to having; and that inspired by the human instinct to know and learn, the *libido sciendi* related to being. Predictably, it rejects the first and favors the second, relating it with "modern democratic education," which, it says, "requires a revival of man's natural drive towards knowledge" (1972:xxix). Suchodolski (1976:72) says the same thing. He describes the policy of generating and sustaining the motivation to learn as the major challenge for a democratic learning society, tying it in with participation and a sense of personal responsibility for one's learning. Many writers of the movement identify self-direction, motivation, and equality of opportunity as the politically desirable features of the learning society. Lengrand, as we saw, ties it more with the individual's willingness to fight and the thirst for adventure. Besides motivation, he emphasizes the importance of learning to learn, a "much-worn formula" constantly abused, he says, but meaning exactly what it says, denoting the ability to understand, assimilate, and analyze, put order into the knowledge acquired, handle with ease the relationship between the abstract and the concrete, the general and the particular, relate knowledge to action, and coordinate training with information (Lengrand 1975:54–55). Motivation and learning to learn are the main components of self-directed learning, which the lifelong learning writers considered as indispensable for lifelong learning.[8] A. J. Cropley (1979:3), in fact, includes it in the technical understanding of lifelong education appearing in the literature, described as education that:

1. lasts the whole life of the individual;
2. leads to the systematic acquisition, renewal, upgrading, and completion of knowledge, skills, and attitudes made necessary by the constantly changing conditions in which people now live;
3. has as its ultimate goal the promotion of the self-fulfillment of each individual;
4. depends for its successful implementation on people's increasing ability and motivation to engage in self-directed learning activities;
5. acknowledges the contribution of all available educational influences, including formal, non-formal, and informal.

Rodney Skager (1978) defined the concept of self-direction as including: (1) motivation toward self-improvement, (2) recognition of the importance and value of continuing to learn as a means of satisfying this motive, (3) possession of the skills necessary to engage in learning through a variety of modes and in different settings, and (4) living in a communal and societal setting that provides opportunity for variegated patterns of learning throughout one's lifetime (the support of a learning society). Skager (1978) went on to identify three personal qualities required of the self-directed learner: "self-awareness," "self-confidence," and "self-acceptance." He also referred to Dave's (1973) five skills of self-directed learning, namely: (1) the ability to use strategies to work independently and cooperatively in groups, (2) competence in the basic learning skills, such as purposeful reading, observing, listening, comprehension, and communication, (3) developed intellectual skills such as reasoning, critical thinking, organizing, and application, (4) the ability to use various learning media including textbooks, periodicals, and programmed aids, and (5) the ability to organize one's own learning experiences through the identification of needs, planning and carrying out learning activities, and evaluating one's accomplishments. Lengrand himself refers self-directed learning to the broader requirement of self-education, with education, described as above, as something that belongs to a particular way of being, in contrast with the economic, vocational, or other purposes to which it may be, and has been, put.

Scientific Humanism: The Culture

The Faure report sought to assimilate the pedagogical resources of progressive education, focusing on the learner's holistic "growth" and, like Dewey, linking education closely with "life," thereby highlighting the educative importance of experiential learning, both inside and outside the school, and emphasizing the open-ended and dynamic quality of lifelong education as a process of constant "becoming." The first wave of the movement influenced by Faure (there was, as I shall point out, a second wave) was utopian, referring to "the need of contemporary man to control, adapt and create the relevant technological and social organization for a new quality of life and for a meaningful quest of more effective and appropriate values of the spirit" (Kirpal 1976:98). Identifying a sense of "a growing crisis of contemporary civilization," it called for a revival of the humanistic aspirations of modernity that would steer "man" away from the dominant materialistic values of consumerism (Suchodolski 1976). This sense of a modernity in crisis, which permeates Suchodolski's work in particular (but also to a lesser extent Lengrand), departs from a deep philosophically and politically familiar discontent with the "inhuman" state of modern capitalist civilization, particularly with its market-driven consumerism, which these writers blamed for producing conditions of alienation and anomie that are reflected in and reproduced by its education systems. It is easy to detect within their writing the same preoccupations of Marxist and existentialist critics of the times that educational systems replicate the injustices and forms of alienation of the capitalist social order and productive system. In sum, the call to radical rethinking in the name of lifelong education was a political one as much as anything else, and its tone was decidedly leftist and humanistic.

And the same is true of Ettore Gelpi, the leading exponent of the second, post-Faure, wave of writers of the movement, who was an early supporter and collaborator with the left-wing Italian Radical Party. Suchodolski, himself a more orthodox Polish Marxist scholar, believed that socialist countries are more qualified as humane learning societies than the capitalist countries of the West. All three (who were, in my view, the most ideological members of the movement) came from an adult education background, and all tended to agree with the authors of the Faure report that the learning society (or "education-centered society," as Suchodolski preferred to call it) is an ideal to be achieved in struggle. All expressed *"strong support"* for democracy *"as the only way for man to avoid becoming enslaved to machines, and the only condition compatible with the dignity which the intellectual achievements of the human race require,"* but argued that *"the concept of democracy itself must be developed, for it can no longer be limited to a minimum of juridical guarantees protecting citizens from the arbitrary power in a subsistence society"* (Faure 1972:xxvi, italics in original). While Suchodolski (1976:59), as we saw, attacked our contemporary societies as "one-dimensional," the Faure report (1972:26) heavily criticized "blocked societies whose sole purpose is their own perpetuation," as antithetical to the progress of both democracy and education. Democratic education, it said, should aim at "raising the people's cultural level and enhancing their consciousness." It must be "concern[ed] to create the conditions for greater mass participation in democratic processes," which should be valued as learning processes. Today's citizens, it continued, want more than protection from the arbitrary exercise of power, they want to exercise power themselves (1972:xxiv). So education in democratic societies cannot be restricted to "training the leaders of tomorrow's society," or treated as the "privilege of an elite or the concomitant of a particular age" (1972:160). Or, worse still, "as if it were a gift or a social service handed out to [citizens] by [their] guardians, the powers-that-be" (1972:161). In this same vein, Suchodolski (1976:81) also criticizes the welfare state, arguing that though it has freed people from need and fear and raised the level of material living standards, it leaves its members in a "spiritual desert" and perpetuates the pernicious myth that welfare is the only basic requirement for human happiness. The slogan

"Welfare—what more does man need?" soon leads, he says, to a degree of satisfaction with one's condition beyond which lies boredom and satiated indifference toward activities that require effort or some degree of sacrifice.

This commitment to democracy and to democratic processes is common to all the writers of the movement. "All educational programs and methods," Lengrand (1975:130) states, "at all levels—should be actuated by this concern to awaken political consciousness and develop the virtues of democratic man." These virtues are qualified in a footnote on the same page as "the civic virtues which formed the basis of the individual citizen's morality in the *polis* of antiquity," which with time "have gradually depreciated and given way to the virtues prescribed by a theological and moralistic conception of existence." The idea of individual empowerment that Lengrand also promotes is endorsed by Faure (1972:161, italics in original), which proclaims that education should be "no longer focused *on* the learner, nor anyone, nor anything. It must necessarily proceed *from* the learner." In short, the writers of the movement come out strongly in favor of a participatory democracy in which the individual citizen is the active, combative protagonist of the learning society. "*An individual,*" Faure (1972:151, italics in original) states, "*comes to a full realization of his own social dimensions through an apprenticeship of active participation in the functioning of social structures and, where necessary, through a personal commitment in the struggle to reform them.*" The culture of their learning society is "scientific humanism," where science is at the service of "man," not of capital, the state, or the military (1972:146). Suchodolski (1976:88) amplifies that "we are using humanism in the modern sense," connected "with the classical European tradition, but its essence consists in the conception of the world created by man for man." It involves the perception that "what is needed is a new kind of belief, a spirit common to all mankind, beyond all regional differences" (1976:90); a truly global humanism, a more universal vision that "seeks to substitute love for power, stresses the brotherhood of man and his common humanity, and probes toward a new relationship of man with the cosmos" (Kirpal 1976:106). Kirpal finds it implicit in Julian Huxley's idea of evolutionary humanism (1976:107).[9]

For Faure (1972:146), scientific humanism "rejects any preconceived, subjective or abstract idea of man" and concerns itself with "man as he is," a "concrete being, set in a historical context, in a set period," who "depends on objective knowledge," especially on the contributions of science, for "his" progress. More than that, it concerns the "complete man," one who goes out and "questions the world in ways combining the scientific and the poetical frames of mind" (1972:155). This "complete man" ("total man" is the expression Lengrand uses) is a pedagogic ideal, Faure (1972:156) says, which has appeared and reappeared at various times throughout human history and in different countries. It has been "one of the fundamental themes for humanist thought in all times." Such a "man" is "universal," in the sense of being "in large measure ... the same, at all times and in every place," and particular in the sense of being an individual with a history that cannot be confused with that of any other individual's (1972:156).

The Two Strands

In the previous section I referred to two phases in the history of the lifelong education movement. The first phase, *utopian*, which coincided with and followed the Faure report in 1972, *theorized* or philosophized lifelong education and the learning society; the second phase, *pragmatist*,—which started in the late 1970s and continued until the movement's decline in the late 1980s—reacting to the criticism of the report's utopian approach, was more interested in concrete practices of lifelong education. Its approach was historical and comparative, and it focused on present realities rather than the future possibilities of lifelong education (Ireland 1978). It was also particularly sensitive to the criticism that there could be different accounts of lifelong education and the learning society, emancipatory *and* repressive.[10] Acknowledging that there was nothing intrinsically positive about either notion from a political viewpoint, they were also more sensitive than their predecessors to the ambiguity of the notion of lifelong education itself; to the fact that the meaning of "lifelong" is variable, that learning does not automatically mean education, and that there are different views about the kind of "life" that is desirable and the kind of experiences that are educative and should be promoted. There was also the question of distinguishing *lifelong* education from the other contemporaneous terms that I mentioned earlier: *continuing* education, *recurrent* education, and *education permanente*. All similarly related to the idea of lifelong learning, but denoted very different understandings of it.

The first, *continuing* education, commonly used in the United States, suggested a lifelong learning continuum in which adult education "tops up," or adds to, the earlier experience of schooling, and professional development courses with that name and departments of "adult and continuing education" were common at the time even outside the United States.[11] *Recurrent* education, on the other hand, was the term used in the OECD where the idea of lifelong learning "was couched more in terms of human capital thinking, albeit laced with a few dashes of social democracy. OECD's ideal socioeconomic model at this time would probably have been a pragmatic one, blending the dynamism and openness of the USA with the security and civic virtues of Sweden" (Field 2001:6).[12] *Education permanente* was an expression used by the Council of Europe. The notion of recurrent education itself suggests a stop-start, rather than the adding-to, process associated with continuing education, with schooling coming first followed by alternating periods of "education" and non-education throughout one's life. Both notions held a much narrower understanding of lifelong learning than that of the movement's writers. The first visualized it as a two-phased process in which adult education initiatives and policies build on formal schooling, while the second regarded it as continuous and multiphased. Both were really about reforming adult education and professional development and by and large assumed schooling to be another matter. Neither represented itself, like lifelong education, as a *philosophy* of education. They both constituted, as Angela Cross-Durant (1984:115) put it, a mere "tinkering with an existing engine," while the lifelong education writers' undertaking to *reconceptualize* education as a lifelong process was a "shift of paradigm" in the way we think about education, which included a reconsideration of the role and function of schooling itself in a learning society. It challenged the politics of mass schooling, questioning the centrality and priority the school has typically enjoyed in modern societies and in our customary thinking about education. In this sense it was nearly (but not quite) as radical as the deschooling movement, which was contemporaneous with it but enjoyed much greater publicity at the time among philosophers of education and education theorists mainly for this reason: because it sounded more outrageous, but also because of the prevalent tendency to identify lifelong education with adult education, an area to which philosophers in particular gave (and still give) only the scantiest attention.

For the writers of the movement, reconceptualizing education as a lifelong process commits us to three things in our *technical* or *operational* definition of education. First, it involves *all ages and stages of life* rather than just the hitherto privileged stages of childhood and youth. Secondly, it includes *all kinds, sources of, and avenues to learning*, including informal, and not just the hitherto privileged ones that are formal and teacher-directed and typically set in schools and other formal learning institutions or settings. And thirdly, as a consequence of the second item, it acknowledges as "educationally relevant" *all sites where people learn* other than the formal ones that have *not* traditionally been so classified in the past, such as the home, the factory or workplace, the church, the market, and so on. Henri Janne, quoted by Dave (1976:129, italics in original), captures their thinking: "If education is to constitute an aspect of every phase of life, it must necessarily enter into *all* human activities *wherever they take place.* To summarize," Janne says, "education, as another writer put it, will no longer be confined in time and place to youth and school: it will be 'diffused.'" In other words, it will be *lifewide* besides being lifelong, and the business not of the school but of the learning society. This thinking requires us to reconstitute the school as a component of the learning society and divests it of its exclusivity over education.

Defining Education

At this point, before I say any more about lifelong education and mass schooling, I must explain this distinction I have been making between *technical* (or *operational*) and *normative* definitions of education. As I have pointed out elsewhere (Wain 1993), the distinction is not mine. Dewey (1966a:76—77, 80) refers to a technical definition of education in *DE* where he makes it clear that his definition of education as "growth," understood as "that reconstruction or reorganization of experience which adds to the meaning of experience, and which increases ability to direct the course of subsequent experience," is, as I said earlier, a technical one. And he distinguishes it from other technical definitions where education is seen "as preparation for a remote future, as unfolding, as external formation, and as recapitulation of the past" (1966:80). Dewey unpacked his own technical definition of education as growth in his extensive discussions of what this reconstruction or reorganization of experience means. Once it is understood that growth was only his technical definition of education, not his definition of education *in toto*, one starts to better understand how he uses it in his work. His apparent reluctance to engage a normative definition of education, which gives the impression that he deemed a technical definition enough, is a different matter. I argued earlier that this is not so, that Dewey envisaged growth as educative only within democratic forms of life, permitting a creative individuality to grow in communication with others. This is however, as far, as he was ready to go by way of normative definition. The lifelong education writers of the first strand were not so prudent; they wanted to theorize a utopian democratic learning society. Moreover, they worried that lifelong education was still undefined in any conclusive way and was being used to suit all sorts of different needs and purposes (Cropley 1979).[13] I disagree, however, with David Aspin and Judith Chapman's (2001:7) view that their approach to its definition was "essentialist." At least I found no evidence of essentialism in the literature to confirm this charge. Their concern seems to have been rather that confused statements about lifelong education would convey the impression of a lack of seriousness in the debate on the subject and in the proposals that were being made in its name.

To return to the distinction between the normative and technical or operational definitions of education, the latter, in my understanding, identifies what manifestations, processes, and practices of learning, which periods of life, and which sites, one decides to include in one's general definition of education. If we look to traditional education, we find that it identifies education technically or operationally with childhood and youth, with schooling, and with formal and teacher-directed (or at least intended or planned) learning—the very opposite of the thinking of Dewey and the lifelong education writers. At this stage I shall continue to use the term "operational" instead of "technical." The distinction between operational and normative definitions of education helps us clarify another confusion that has been going about since the early days: between the terms lifelong *education* and lifelong *learning*. In the past the two expressions were often used interchangeably, insensitive to any need to distinguish between them, with the former, perhaps, more widely used than the latter. But things have been reversed today, and the term lifelong education has gone practically into disuse, replaced by lifelong learning. Some see this as a good thing and contend that the trend should continue. Aspin and Chapman (2001:10) describe how the change of fortune came about. It began, they say, when authors and participants in "the discussion of several international bodies noted that the emphasis on the idea of 'lifelong education' placed great weight—perhaps too great—on teaching and learning transactions within the norms and conventional boundaries of an institutional environment and within education seen in institutional terms." This emphasis, these authors and participants argued, rendered it restrictive in terms of the environments in which learning takes place, and in terms of the desirability of individual initiatives and learning styles (2001:10).

Comparing it with the definition of education promoted by liberal philosophers like Richard Peters (which, they say, was similarly restrictive in the way it confined education to certain types of "worthwhile knowledge"), Aspin and Chapman (2001:11) argue that lifelong education was unduly restrictive on policy-making, since how it was understood had a substantial impact "among those planning, funding, and putting on the programs of educational institutions in those days." In the same way, however, the decision to abandon it completely for learning, to *substitute* learning for education cannot be just a matter of sorting out confusion between the two terms. It has important policy implications also. For this reason one needs to probe it further, much further to see what lies behind it, not the least because the change from lifelong education to lifelong learning coincides with a broader trend to regard the normative definition of education as either unimportant or given and to measure learning in terms of criteria of performativity instead. It could well suggest that in today's "postideological" world we can take our normative commitments for granted and uncontested, at least in the West. In which case, we may feel that the word education has become redundant, an invitation to useless debate and confusion and, therefore, to be safely dropped from our vocabulary. Or maybe education has fallen victim to our postmodern penchant to distrust the master narratives of modernity, in which case the switch from lifelong education to lifelong learning could be explained very simply as coinciding with this fact.[14] In any case, I myself am not so complacent about this trend; to the contrary, I am exceedingly suspicious of it.

My reaction to Aspin and Chapman's restrictive account of "lifelong education" is that I fail to recognize it. It has nothing to do with the way it is represented in the lifelong education literature I have been describing, and this will become even more evident as the chapter proceeds. The movement's operational definition of lifelong education was as permissive as they come, and this is the more usual objection to it by its critics. Another tendency the writers of the movement were criticized for in the 1970s and 1980s was that of assimilating education as a whole to lifelong education, somewhat in the way that liberal philosophers of education of the same period tended to assimilate the whole of education with liberal education.[15] There is, of course, a difference between the two; there is no inbuilt normative component to the concept of lifelong education as there is to liberal education, where it stands for a political and ethical outlook of a specified kind. Lifelong education is a contestable concept capable, as the writers of the movement themselves said many times, of different resolutions depending on how one defines education normatively and "lifelong" operationally. One could, for instance, speak of a liberal philosophy of lifelong education, or a socialist. The writers of the movement felt they needed to specify their own philosophy of lifelong education in order to distinguish it from others that could be repressive and operationally more restrictive. The Faure-inspired theorists gave the impression that theirs was the model for lifelong education and the learning society but not the pragmatists who followed. Both sets of writers assumed the argument for lifelong learning self-evident, that however education is defined normatively it must be identified operationally with lifelong learning. Bailey argued correctly that this was not so, that the fact of a fast-changing world need not imply adopting lifelong education as an operational response to it. The decision to adopt it is not a necessary one, just like the decision to think in the *lifewide* terms of a learning society instead of schooling. One could have a philosophy of lifelong education that continues to prioritize schooling and that is individualistic and has no need for the notion of a learning society.

The Challenge to Schooling

Writers like Lengrand and Gelpi, possibly because of their backgrounds in the field, viewed adult education as the instrument to reform education and society. They had little if any faith in the ability of schools and professional teachers to carry out the job. They differed in this respect from Dewey who, to the contrary, saw schools as the instruments of change and social reconstruction.[16] In valuing adult education in this way and advocating the learning society as their operational focus instead of schools, they undoubtedly devalued the role of schooling in today's world, which was not the case with the proponents of continuing, and recurrent, education, though it seems to me that a decision for lifelong learning, in itself, implies that schooling must include some preparation for it, for the continuation of learning in adult life. From the point of view of the movement's writers this consideration, in itself, meant many things. Primarily, as I said earlier, it meant giving young people the tools to be self-directed learners and the motivation to continue with their education throughout their lives. But the writers' revaluation of schooling, as I also said in the previous sections, stemmed from their unhappiness with many of its contemporary aspects that had nothing to do with the strategic demands of lifelong education but with its normative understanding of education also—apart, of course, from their unhappiness with the modern tendency to think of education in terms of schools and professional teachers. Gelpi (1984a) expressed concern on this matter more forcefully and repeatedly than most:

> [L]ifelong education is confused with the practices of teachers, but my own experience is that, frequently, it is non-teachers who are producing the most interesting things. I am not, of course, against schools, on the contrary I think they perform a very relevant role in lifelong education. But teachers are not the sole educators; people in the productive line, scientists, artists, medical doctors, play a fundamental role in education as well. Unfortunately, more often than not, they are not considered part of the educational system, though they may be producing innovative (educational) theories and valid programs. (18)

One could add others to this list of non-professional educators (non-teachers, Gelpi calls them)—parents, therapists, priests and pastors, social workers, communication experts, union leaders, and so on. Indeed, for the lifelong education writers, it should include anyone with a progressive and experimental outlook who, at any stage in life, undertakes the role of "educator"; who has anything to teach anywhere to anyone; and who produces "valid programs" for the purpose. Which is why some considered not just learning to learn but learning to teach as a primary responsibility for schools in a learning society.

Gelpi's strong disclaimer, on the other hand, that he is not "against schools" as such and sees a role for them in lifelong education, was also echoed and insisted on by his fellow lifelong education writers. It reflects their sensitivity to the possibility that they could be identified with the deschoolers, who, as I said earlier, were on the scene at about the same time. Notwithstanding the criticisms of contemporary schooling and the questions about its future they shared with the deschoolers, the writers of the movement were not interested in the project of deschooling society. They still thought of schools, as Gelpi says, as "very relevant" institutions. Indeed, the Faure report's (1972:xxxii) view about deschooling theories was that if they "were put into practice on any scale their effects would certainly be of a reactionary nature, like the economic ideas of the partisans of 'zero growth' to which they are often linked." It affirmed that "schools, that is to say establishments devised to dispense education systematically to the rising generations, are now and will remain in the future, [however], the decisive factor in training men to contribute to the development of society, to play an active part in life, men properly prepared for work" (1972:xxxii). What both the lifelong education writers and the deschoolers questioned was the justice and economic wisdom of perpetuating the priority enjoyed by schools and other sites of formal education in the distribution and allocation of late modern society's human and economic resources. Schools had grown irrelevant to contemporary times, they argued, because they are characterized by "fractional links with life, isolation from concrete realities, a rift between enjoyment and education, and an absence of all dialogue and participation" (Lengrand 1975:39). Dewey had similarly worried about the remoteness from "life" of modern school regimes. The Faure report (1972:xxx) emphasized that schools "must not be separated from life; [that] the child's personality must not be split between two worlds, each out of contact with the other—one in which he learns like a disembodied creature, and the other in which he fulfils himself through some anti-educational activity." And Dewey made precisely the same pleas for the relevance of what is learned at school to the child's life, most pointedly in *The Child and the Curriculum* (1966b) but in other places also.[17]

Similar dissatisfactions have been expressed more recently by writers who have referred to the single-classroom, single-lesson, single-teacher format typical of today's schools as more suited to the late nineteenth- and early twentieth-century preoccupations with mass education and basic skills and with rigid educational selection for future work roles that are expected to stay fixed over time, than to the complex needs of the postindustrial order. The lifelong education writers made the more general point (with which I agree) that, as a matter of sheer logic, the restructuring of contemporary societies in their transition from industrial to postindustrial, modern to postmodern, liberal to postliberal, demands the restructuring of education to respond to it. Alasdair MacIntyre (1987), as we shall see in Chapter 3, makes a very different complaint against mass schooling: that it has failed to resolve the fundamental challenge entrusted to it by the project of modernity of resolving the tension between the concurrent claims of preparing children for their role in society and making them enlightened individuals. He does not blame the schools themselves for this failure, however, but the project of modernity itself, which, he says, gave them an impossible agenda to fulfill. He believes that the solution for education is to be sought elsewhere than in a simple reform of the schooling system. Other writers have pointed to this same tension, which was there from the start when mass schooling was introduced to accommodate the contrasting cries for more social control, for "gentling the masses," and economic efficiency that came from conservatives, and for enlightenment, political participation, and economic opportunity that came from liberal reformists.

The Marxian thesis is that the former won, and that modern schools are instruments of capitalist power. Foucault agrees. John Knight (1995:23–24), echoing him, says that with the growth of the modern state, mass schooling became an "attempt to produce personalities and subjected and docile bodies suited to the need of work and the practices of power; the infinite reproduction of schooled workers." Helmut Peukert (1992) has argued that the suspicion about modernity is itself primarily a suspicion about its program of mass education for enlightenment. And Knight (1995:23) has argued that that suspicion has been confirmed by the "failure" of that program stemming from its own internal contradictions. "Despite the rhetorics of classical humanism, liberal humanism, child-centered education, personal growth and progressivism, which have been deployed variously in education's justification," he claims, "mass schooling has been characterized by practices which are substantially otherwise" than humane. Knight, thus, does not even share the lifelong education writers' view that we should take progressivism more seriously, laying the blame for the plight of mass modern schooling squarely, like Foucault, on the same "rhetorics of classical humanism" that progressivism shares. The criticism mostly made today against mass schooling is that its agenda is set by performativist rather than humane criteria, though its agenda is an offshoot of humanism. The "complex needs of the postindustrial order" were not mainly what concerned the lifelong education writers in their criticism of schooling. They were concerned rather with the needs, with the quality of life, of individuals who live in the contemporary world and are subjected to its demands and challenges; individuals and societies at risk.

To conclude, the main pragmatic factor that gave rise to mass schooling was undoubtedly the perception that an adequate preparation for life in modern industrialized societies was beyond the power and means of most families to provide for in the home. That family and neighborhood were no longer effective agencies for socializing the young; for initiating them into a modern literate, technological world; and, in general, preparing them adequately for the workplace, which had also moved decisively out of the home and into the more anonymous reality of factories and bureaucracies. Ian Hunter (1994:xviii), playing down the contribution of both reformers and conservatives to mass schooling, says that "the school emerges not as the expression of some pre-given economic interests, intellectual capacities, or moral principles, but as an improvised 'technology for living.'" Without a specialized agency such as the school, it was realized in early modern times, individuals would be lost and would turn politically dangerous, and the economic and social progress of their societies completely prejudiced. The same assumption about lifelong learning and the learning society underlines the rhetoric on its behalf today. They have similarly emerged as an improvised "technology for living" in a postmodern, postindustrial world, for which schooling is no longer enough. The question, of course, is to what extent that rhetoric is continuous with that of the lifelong education movement, which will be the subject of the next chapter.

Illich's Postmodern Learning Society

Ivan Illich was hostile toward the lifelong education movement, mistakenly identifying it with a lifelong *schooling* movement, but his rejection of schooling as an institution led him to theorize what was, in effect, a learning society. His book *Deschooling Society* (1978), first published in 1971, and the deschooling literature in general, became something of a *cause célèbre* in the 1970s. Today, it is mentioned only very occasionally in education seminars or classes as a curiosity of radical educational theorizing, or as an example of the eccentricities of the 1970s. Not only has society not been deschooled, the contrary has happened, as James G. Ladwig (1995:219–220) remarks: "There is a growing body of literature in the sociology of education which examines the global expansion of industrialized forms of schooling and which is working with a general notion of schooling as a world culture in itself (Benavot et al., 1991; Boli and Ramirez, 1986; Ramirez and Meyer, 1985; Meyer 1980; Ramirez and Soysal, 1992)," consolidating the trend toward increasingly schooled societies.[18] The substance of Illich's project was very similar to that of the lifelong education writers in that, though he didn't put it this way himself, he wanted to replace the modern focus on mass schooling with a postmodern focus on a learning society (1978:29). His characterization of the deschooled society as a society without any formal education institutions left him with no option, in fact, but to theorize an alternative as a society mobilized for non-formal learning.

The broader political target of Illich's (1978:9) attack was the "institutionalization of values" in the modern welfare state, which, in his view, leads "inevitably to physical pollution, social polarization and psychological impotence ... three dimensions in a process of global degradation and modernized misery," and to which he believed the schooling system contributed. Redressing these effects is not, he held, a matter of social reform or more schooling, or better schooling, or of creating new kinds of schools, but a paradigm shift in our thinking about education that abolishes schooling and creates "institutions which serve personal, creative and autonomous interaction and the emergence of values which cannot be substantially controlled by technocrats" (1978:9–10). "The current search for new educational funnels," he said, "must be reversed into the search for their institutional inverse; educational webs which heighten the opportunity for each one to transform each moment of his living into one of learning, sharing and caring" (1978:8). These "webs" would form the structure of his learning society and the conduit for life long learning. And he believed that serious research into the strategic possibilities of the new communications technologies could show us how to create them. In short, Illich was not the destructive anarchist or iconoclast he was often represented to be; he was not against institutions as such but against institutional structures controlled by technocrats, who discipline life, conditioning it and our expectations. Apart from objecting to the schooling culture and its compulsory nature and advocating a learning society without schools, Illich also objected, like the lifelong education writers, to identifying education with childhood and youth and to the model of education as a linear process concentrated in and sustained through a fixed determined period of the individual's life. In short, he shared the Faure report's (1972:186, italics in original) belief that *"each person should be able to choose his path more freely, in a more flexible framework, without being compelled to give up educational services for life if he leaves the system."* "Ultimately," Illich (1978:21) says, "there should be no obstacle for anyone at any time of his life to be able to choose instruction among hundreds of definable skills at public expense." What he suggests is not, however, as with the lifelong education writers, some indefinite right to continuing learning, but the introduction of an "edu-credit card" issued to each citizen at birth and cashable at any time during her life according to her own needs or wishes.

Illich was even more skeptical toward professional teachers than Gelpi, to the extent that he proposed deprofessionalizing teaching and opening the teacher market to anyone with skills or knowledge to provide or to exchange with willing partners. "The right to teach any skill," he contended, "should come under the protection of freedom of speech" (1978:92). Evidently, without schools and professional teachers one needs to create alternative ways of matching educator with learner, and Illich proposed that these be modeled on the way one sets out to find partners for a game, namely by advertisement or invitation. He also suggested creating a "bank" for skill exchange (1978:92), together with a peer-matching network run by professional "educational guides" who would assist the immature or inept to choose from the advertised services open to all who wish to share them. In this case there are also similarities with the lifelong education writers, who, besides motivation—which, as we saw, they identified as the key to lifelong education—emphasized the need for efficient guidance services in the learning society. Illich (1978) provides a graphic account of how his learning society would work:

> Each man, at any given moment and at a minimum price, could identify himself to a computer with his address and telephone number, indicating the book, article, film or recording on which he seeks a partner for discussion. Within days he could receive by mail the list of others who recently had taken the same initiative. The list would enable him by telephone to arrange for a meeting with persons who initially would be known exclusively by the fact that they requested a dialogue about the same subject. (26)

Today's communications technology, of course, makes these kinds of transactions simpler, quicker, and more efficient. Illich (1978:45, italics in original) resisted the idea that the individual's self-identification in this enterprise be based "also on an *idea* or an issue," or that it should include additional information about oneself (such as one's age, background, worldview, competence, experience, etc.) beyond one's immediate interest, or other "incidental assistance that will facilitate their meetings—with space schedules, screening and protection." This information, he contended, would spoil the spontaneity of the meetings and constitute steps toward the technocratic institutionalization of the webs. In short, we would be back where we started with schooling and other formal education agencies and networks.

Apart from the spontaneity and transitory nature of the learning meetings, the other thing he emphasized, again like the lifelong education writers, was individual choice and self-direction. Like the writers of the lifelong education movement, he operated with the general principle that one's responsibility for one's own life, as for one's learning, should be one's own, that the "transfer of responsibility from self to institution guarantees social regression, especially once it has been accepted as an obligation" (1978:45). His emphasis on the transitory and impermanent nature of learning encounters—on impermanence generally—resonates, as we shall see in later chapters, with poststructuralist politics in general. With Jean-François Lyotard, in particular, he shares a criticism of the modern university, which, he says, "forfeited its chance to provide a simple setting for encounters which are both autonomous and anarchic, focused yet unplanned and ebullient," the sort he envisaged for his learning society, "and has chosen instead to manage the process by which so-called research and instruction are produced" (1978:41). If the schooling system is "the repository of society's myth, the institutionalization of that myth's contradictions, and the locus of the ritual, which reproduces and veils the disparities between myth and reality," the university complements this process (1978:43). It perpetuates the social myth that legitimizes modern schooling: that human learning needs manipulating by others, that it is measurable, that it can be packaged and valued, that it is driven by self-perpetuating progress, and that it is a good capable of unending consumption. Backed by a suitable ritual, this myth became a world religion in modern times with the promise of a coming kingdom that would universalize the expectations for humanity raised by the project of modernity. Illich proposed to fight it with his countermyth of a deschooled learning society, the first wave of lifelong education writers with their myth of a learning society though not constructed, like his, on the death of schooling.

Illich (1978:57) on his part, while he believed that the opportunities offered by new communication technologies could help his deschooled utopia to materialize, warned with prescience that "the future depends more upon our choice of institutions which support a life of action than on our developing new ideologies and technologies." For this reason he promoted *convivial* institutions for his deschooled learning society, which "exist to be used rather than to produce something," as opposed to the current *manipulative* ones. The regulations of convivial institutions "have mainly the purpose of avoiding abuses which would frustrate their general accessibility," rather than any strict or efficient management (1978:59). Such institutions are telephone linkups, subway lines, mail routes, public markets, and exchanges—services that "do not require hard or soft sells to induce their clients to use them" (1978:59). He would have included e-mail, Internet, and other computer-created services today. He went on to identify just four indispensable resources for learning: things, models, peers, and elders. Developing these resources outside the parameters of a schooling model would be the basis of his learning society, which, though it excluded professional teachers, required professional educators of a different type. Two types, to be exact: (1) individuals "with practical wisdom who would be willing to sustain the newcomer in his educational adventure" and (2) web "masters" or leaders who would operate the different networks; guide parents, students, and other "natural" educators in their use; and "act as *primus inter pares* in undertaking difficult intellectual exploratory journeys." The first kind would be professional educational administrators and pedagogical counselors who would, as Illich (1978:99) puts it, build and maintain the roads providing access to the resources and help students along their chosen roads economically and efficiently. The second, the initiator or leader, the "master," Illich (1978:102) confesses to be harder to define. Even more difficult to define would be the relationship between master and learner, for which, however, he turns to Aristotle's description of a "moral type of friendship, which is not on fixed terms: it makes a gift, or does whatever it does, as to a friend."

Illich (1978:103) concedes that relying for intellectual leadership on this kind of motive, the free desire of people to provide it as a gift, is highly difficult to visualize in our present society. So, "we must first construct a society in which personal acts themselves re-acquire a value higher than that of making things and manipulating people." We should not just wait around for such a society to come into being by itself; masters assembling "congenial disciples" could set it going. This suggestion, as we shall see in Chapter 3, finds its echo in MacIntyre, but it also finds an echo in lifelong education writers like Gelpi, who similarly pins his hopes for educational change on radical enlightened educators, even if he would not characterize them as masters. Illich (1978:106) also shares with MacIntyre and other philosophers a basic negative assessment of modern society, likening it (using metaphors reminiscent of Weber) to "the ultimate machine which I once saw in a New York toyshop. It was a metal casket which, when you touched a switch, snapped open to reveal a mechanical hand. Chromed fingers reached out for the lid, pulled it down and locked it from the inside. It was a box; you expected to be able to take something out of it; yet all it contained was a mechanism for closing the cover. This contraption is the opposite of Pandora's box" with which "modern man" began only, he laments, to end up with "the self-sealing casket." His vision of the modern learning society!

Living Together Educates: Education Lifewide

The lifelong education writers knew Illich's work and the deschooling philosophy well, and it evidently influenced them in some ways. Dewey, however, is the obvious philosophical point of reference for anyone interested in the project of reconceptualizing education as a lifelong project. Angela Cross-Durant describes lifelong education as "the expedient term which most clearly reflects John Dewey's vision of education" (1984:115), and George Parkyn (1973:115) makes the same point.[19] It is, in fact, easy to find statements in *DE* that identify Dewey as a forerunner to the lifelong education movement. His operational definition of education as growth conceived as an ongoing reconstruction of experience, and his refusal to identify it with schooling and formal learning, clearly anticipates the movement, including the latter's incorporation of the notion of the learning society. At one point early in *DE* the value of the social dimension of learning as life led Dewey (1966a:6) to conclude that "the very process of living together educates," in that it "enlarges and enlightens experience," and as communication it "stimulates and enriches imagination; it creates responsibility for accuracy and vividness of statement and thought." And "living together educates" could be an effective slogan for a learning society, capturing Dewey's, Illich's, and the lifelong education movement's emphasis on learning together in such a society. But Dewey never actually theorized the learning society (an expression that, to my knowledge, he never used) any more than he adequately theorized the closely related idea of a public, which is what he thought communication in healthy democracies requires. Though he gestured strongly toward both, in the final analysis he was more interested in the democratic and socially reconstructive potential of teachers and schools than that of the wider society as a learning society.

"Living together educates" suggests that, like the writers of the movement, we should understand education operationally to include not just *formal* and *non-formal* learning, which imply some element of purpose or intention on the part of teachers and/or learners, but also *informal* learning, which is unconscious and comes to us from experience, from the way we live with things and with other human beings. The term *informal* learning has been used in many different ways, but I shall use it as an umbrella term for unconscious experiential learning of all kinds on the learner's part. By *non-formal* learning, on the other hand, I shall mean those learning activities and processes, whether solitary or collective, that are intended as such but do not involve someone in the role of teacher. In *DE*, Dewey (1966a:9) held "the method of keeping a proper balance between the informal and the formal, the incidental and the intentional, modes of education," as "one of the weightiest problems with which the philosophy of education has to cope."[20] A view not commonly shared afterwards by philosophers of education, who for the most part have tended to restrict their interest and operational definition of education to formal learning activities and processes in schooling contexts. Dewey (1966a:19) elaborates the distinction in his discussion on the constitution of learning environments, distinguishing the "chance" that we *permit* or use, from "structured" environments that we *design* for some given purpose. Schools are of the latter kind, designed to influence "the mental and moral disposition of their members."

Far from dismissing the chance or informal learning environment as irrelevant, he strongly emphasized its importance as "an educative or formative influence unconsciously and apart from any set purpose," which "furnishes the basic nature of even the most insistently schooled youth ... the main texture of disposition." Indeed, he points out, the "unconscious influence of the environment" is so subtle and pervasive that it affects every fiber of character and mind" (1966a:17). And it is mainly "in the ordinary intercourse of life" that people learn such fundamental things as their native language, manners, good taste, and aesthetic appreciation (1966a:17). This priority he gave to raw over schooled experience, to life over schooling, took him so far as to declare strongly that "we never educate directly, but indirectly by means of the environment" (1966a:19), confirming my point earlier that the normative element in Dewey's definition of education is his description of a democratic environment where people grow individually and together in and through communication.

Not everyone, however, shares this priority he gave to informal learning. Even though the notion of the "hidden curriculum" has familiarized us with this idea and has been with us now for a good many years, the inclusion of informal learning in our technical definition of education has been challenged by many. Critics of the lifelong education literature like Richard Bagnall (1990) and Kenneth Lawson (1982) have argued against it on the grounds that it identifies education with life, thus robbing education of any distinctive meaning. Bagnall (1990:2) put his objection in a nutshell: with the inclusion of informal learning, he argued, "traditional conceptions, such as that of education as an essentially intentional activity directed in desirable ways towards desirable learning ends, or as the learning outcomes of such an activity (Bagnall 1987), are denied." It begs the question why we should worry about denying "traditional conceptions" of education if we have good reasons for it; if they appear outdated to us or wrong, or if retaining them has become problematic, as the lifelong education writers argued. Today there is universal accord, or close to it, that education is an essentially contestable concept. This "essential contestability" of education, however, is not restricted to its normative definition; it applies to the operational definition also. Bagnall's (1990:2) other point is about meaning: that the word education must have some more distinct referent than to life itself, otherwise there would be no point in using it; it would be redundant since nothing could be claimed specifically in its name.[21] He believes that this also has illiberal consequences, since it precludes "the practical possibility of individual and collective rights to educational engagement and hence also to such engagement as a means both to individual liberation and to democratic involvement in public affairs." This is because if education has no particular meaning, it cannot be claimed as a right, for it would be unclear what one is claiming in its name. A clear-cut distinction between education and life, he concludes, is required, otherwise education "is precisely that which happens to each one of us in our life-spans; it is both desirable and actual; we could not ask for more, because there is no more" (1990:2).

This criticism seems compelling, but only if the crucial distinction between operational and normative definitions of education is neglected, so that Dewey's (who Bagnall ultimately blames for first mixing education with life) operational definition of education as growth to include informal learning is taken as his *general* definition of education. As I have argued, Dewey does tell us what *kind* of "living together" he regarded as educative. And the same is true of the lifelong education writers, as we saw earlier, who were similarly clear about the sociopolitical and cultural aims of their learning society. Where Dewey is concerned, the starkness of statements like "living together educates" and "we never educate directly" seem like deliberate provocations; his way of shaking us out of our complacent identification of education with instruction. In this sense, contrary to what some of his critics contend, it is not trivial to make the point, as Dewey does, that learning is continuous with life, that one necessarily learns in the process of living, that that learning is as valuable for life itself (if not more so) as schooled learning, and that it should not, therefore, as Bagnall feels, be excluded from our understanding of education. He would possibly reply, as have other liberal philosophers of education, that wanting to so exclude it does not mean that he wants it devalued or its importance in life reduced. But this is the inevitable outcome, as was pointed out in my earlier discussion of Aspin and Chapman; excluding informal learning from our discourse about education *is* devaluing it, obscuring its worth, and discouraging policy-makers to take any notice of it. Bagnall's objection to informal learning, in fact, corresponds with the liberal prejudice for identifying "worthwhile" or non-trivial knowledge with academic knowledge, which is not, of course, typically acquired informally.

Dewey, for his part, was not simply trying to warn us that we are neglecting something crucial to our understanding of how people learn when we ignore the value of informal learning; he was evidently also after reversing the liberal prejudice in favor of academic knowledge. His emphasis on the prior value of informal learning to other kinds does not merely seek to make a pedagogical point; it is also, primarily, a fundamental political statement about education itself. In saying that what has educative value is what is learned informally through the environment, he was expressing his well-known distaste for the idea that education is about *forming* people according to the preset ideas or predefined aims of other people. One notes, in this respect, the force Dewey gives to his statement: We never, he says, educate except through the environment. Which means that we never educate formally through direct teaching or instruction. He seems in this way actually to *identify* education with informal learning, and this, of course, fits with his operational definition of education as growth, since growing is not something people, teachers, and others, can do for us but something we necessarily do ourselves. The role of others in the process is simply to assist us with the best conditions to grow. The horticultural metaphor quickly comes to mind here, in which the educator is one who provides the best soil and manure for healthy growth and waters it judiciously. But viewed in this way, the true contribution of education theorists, for Dewey, lies not in reasoning or arguing out some particular set of educational aims for schools and teachers to adopt, or justifying some particular philosophy of the curriculum with epistemological, psychological, and sociopolitical arguments, but in describing environments for learning that are truly educative; that is, that are democratic (in his sense of the word), and facilitate creative individual and collective growth, whether these are the more deliberately engineered institutional environments of schools and classrooms or the other, more spontaneous, sites of the learning society.

The Maximalist View

Bagnall (1990:2), quoting me, refers to the view of lifelong education that "encompasses those sectors of education commonly described as formal, non-formal and informal (Wain 1987, 37)" as *maximalist*.[22] He distinguishes three different accounts of lifelong education, each having its own policy implications, namely: (a) as the preparation of individuals for the management of their adult lives; (b) as the distribution of education *throughout* the life span of the individual; and (c) as the identification of education with the whole of life (1990:1). The first two clearly correspond with the notions of "continuing" and "recurrent" education, while the third he wrongly, as I argued in the previous section, attributes to the maximalist position of the lifelong education writers, which, in fact, refers *only* to the operational definition of education. Another argument he fetches against the maximalist position is that it is oppressive because it embraces a program "to institutionalize all learning." He cites Illich and Verne's fear that it threatens the "enschooling" of society as a whole (1990:3). Illich and Verne (1976) raise the specter of a "global classroom"—of a learning society where the ethos and practices of schooling are extended into the whole social fabric by a repressive paternalistic state that treats its adult citizens as "immature children." Bagnall (1990:14) reminds us of their warning that "the ultimate success of the schooling instrument is the extension of its monopoly, first to all youths, then to every age, and, finally, to all areas." He continues, "While the nature of this institutionalization is not explicated, it clearly involves at least the general acceptance of this view of Lifelong Education as the only correct view of education." At any rate, he goes on, "the vagueness of the program on this point leaves open the opportunity for it to be interpreted as calling for public programs to monitor and control (to 'institutionalize' in the ordinary language sense) those categories of events which fall within the definition of education" (1990:3).

Bagnall puts "Lifelong Education" in capitals, but there is nowhere in the literature of the movement even the slightest suggestion that it intended its philosophy as *the* correct or true version of lifelong education as the capitals suggest. Not among the utopians, nor among the pragmatists. The latter, in fact, insisted that there is *no* universal blueprint for lifelong education, just as there is no universal blueprint for a learning society. Nowhere, either, does the literature suggest that the learning society the movement contemplated was a "schooled society." In this respect, what the

Faure report (1972:220, italics in original) says about education is relevant: *"It should be made a principle to center educational activity on the learner, to allow him greater and greater freedom, as he matures, to decide for himself what he wants to learn, and how and where he wants to learn it and take his training."* I described, three sections above, the way the lifelong education writers regarded schooling as a necessary aspect of the learning society, not as its model. In this respect, Cropley (1979:105) described the maximalist view as one that "sees lifelong education as involving a fundamental transformation of society, so that the whole society becomes a learning resource for each individual, and is aware of its responsibility," and I share this same understanding of the term. In *Philosophy of Lifelong Education* (1987, henceforth *PLE*), I similarly described the learning society as a society "mobilized for learning." And it must be admitted that speaking of mobilization does indicate the possibility of some institutionalization of lifelong education. But institutionalization is not something bad. The institutionalization of learning in schools, colleges, universities, and so on, is a feature of all modern societies. This is the institutionalization Illich objected to and wanted to replace with his learning webs, but even his learning webs, as we saw, require institutional support. Institutionalization is bad only if one philosophy is imposed on a society in totalitarian fashion.

The ironic thing in this respect is that, if my memory serves me, I came across the "mobilization" metaphor in Illich as a description of his deschooled society before I used it. But this just shows that "mobilization" can have different purposes, serve different causes, and involve different forms of institutionalization. Recently the institutionalization of lifelong learning has been recommended by the European Union, as we shall see, but it was already decided on in Japan in 1990. In the language game of war, where it is originally at home, a society's resources, human and material, are mobilized when it defines its priorities in terms of the "war effort." By analogy, a society mobilized for learning does the same for learning, valorizing it to the same degree that actions and policies related to the "war effort" are valorized in a society mobilized for war, giving them priority. In this respect, what is mobilized in a learning society, apart from its resources, is the minds and efforts of its members in favor of a civic culture of learning. As MacIntyre (1987) put it in the case of the notion of an educated public, it requires members who *recognize themselves* as members of a learning society. "Mobilizing minds and motives" may sound sinister because of its association in our minds with the indoctrination of mass societies under totalitarian regimes more than familiar to the modern age. The Faure report is reassuring in this respect with regard to its utopian intentions, repeatedly emphasizing its own democratic and humane credentials. But it must be confessed that the lifelong education literature's reference to the two key strategies of mobilization as *integration*, "vertical" (occurring along the learner's life span and referring to the learning experiences of the individual) and "horizontal" (referring to the lifewide learning of the learning society), which could legitimately be taken by critics like Bagnall (though he doesn't, in fact, mention them) to illustrate what the maximalist means by "institutionalization," is not reassuring.

What is in question in modern/postmodern societies, however, is not institutionalization but what kind of institutionalization, and for what purpose. Some styles and degrees of institutionalization and some normative theories of the learning society may be repressive, others less so, others not at all, and others still may be deemed emancipatory by their proponents. There is little if any obvious hint of repressive intent in the attempts to institutionalize the idea of lifelong learning and of the learning society by the European Union in the 1990s, and by Britain and Japan at the national level in the same period, which I have just referred to and which I shall describe in later chapters. In sum, one can have a mobilization of learning resources that is institutionalized as a learning society but not totalitarian. Illich's deschooled learning society is a theoretical example of this sort. Gabriel Frangiere (1976), one of those who argued for the "creative planning" of the learning society but recognized that it could be the agent of a totalitarian technocracy, suggested three policy criteria to prevent this: (1) it must not be total—it must embody only those decisions that affect the system as a whole and possess a long-term influence, leaving all else to individual initiative, encouraging pluralism and resisting anything making toward an alienating systematism; (2) it must not be authoritarian; its authority must be democratic; and (3) it must not be centralized—once the overall framework has been fixed democratically, all further decisions should be taken at the lowest level technically possible. Notwithstanding the reference to integration in the literature, the lifelong education writers pronounced themselves against "delegating educative power to one, single, vertical, hierarchical structure constituting a distinct body within society," and envisaged a learning society in which "all groups, associations, unions, local communities, and intermediary organizations must take over their share of educative responsibility" (Faure

1972:163). As we saw earlier, they suggested a partnership between the state and independent non-formal and formal agencies in setting it up. Their emphasis on the importance of these agencies and of the independent initiative of creative educators is another clear indication that theirs, at least, was not an intention to totalize. Henri Janne (1976:170), declaring himself strongly against all monolithic structures, says that the "decentralization of the greatest possible number of decisions is indispensable in a system founded on responsible choice, on individualization and education defined as 'learning' rather than teaching." Kurt Gestrelius (1979:283–284) identified detailed criteria developed in UNESCO projects for evaluating horizontal and vertical integration and noted the consistency with which these criteria are accompanied by: (1) a third set of criteria corresponding with the organization's commitment to self-education, criteria for "Autodidactic development of readiness for new learning and relearning" and (2) a fourth for "Directing studies towards creativity, flexibility and equality." And Colin Griffin's (1983:151–153) set of operational criteria for lifelong learning included, together with horizontal integration and vertical articulation, orientations to self-growth and self-directed learning, and toward democratization. Still, the totalitarian possibilities of integration are troubling me and need to be countered today with a politics of dissemination.

But I shall say more about this in later chapters. Here, as a final, rather different, remark, one needs to note that the decision to approach education from the perspective of the learning society rather than the more restricted perspective of schooling does not, of itself, commit one to the maximalist strategy for lifelong education. One could go for alternative, non-maximalist, operational definitions of lifelong education, "continuing" or "recurrent" are examples, or one could choose to restrict one's interest in the learning society to its formal learning agencies, as was once more usual among writers on education. It does, of course, follow that in adopting the notion of the learning society one is broadening one's interest in learning processes beyond those that occur in the school and are related to the ages of childhood and youth. In following Dewey and the lifelong education writers into the decision to include the informal dimension of learning, or learning "from life itself," the maximalist decides to take an interest in *all* kinds of learning at work in the learning society, not just the formal and non-formal. It also means that the sole criterion one admits as relevant to decide whether particular learning processes and activities are educative or not is their consistency with how one defines education normatively.

The Education Research Project

The distinction between the normative and the technical definition of education comes into sharp focus in the concept of an education research project, which I introduced in *PLE* where, believing strongly in its relevance, I first tried to come to grips with the lifelong education literature over the two decades or so previous to the writing of the book, hoping to introduce it into mainstream philosophy of education. I argued in the book that if one finds the pragmatic arguments for reconceptualizing education as a lifelong process persuasive, as I did, one could restate contemporary conflicting discourses about education—liberal, progressive, pragmatist, Marxist, and so on—as different competing projects of lifelong education. I thought at the time that this would also be a good way to rationalize the current philosophical discourse on education in a postanalytic world that recognized the contestability of the concept of education but seemed lost for an alternative research paradigm to work with. In other words, I worked with the idea that education theory could resolve itself into the articulation of a number of competing research projects alive in the modern world that could be identified fairly easily. I also assumed these projects not measurable against any general criteria of truth, justice, or whatever, but held that touchstone instruments *could* be negotiated con-versationally between the supporters of the different projects to avoid casting them as noncommunicating windowless monads. As Richard Rorty had observed in *Philosophy and the Mirror of Nature* (1980, henceforth *PMN*), which greatly influenced my writing of *PLE* in this particular respect, incommensurability does not mean incom-municability, or even incomparability. It was his conversationalist politics that mainly influenced me in Rorty. The idea of an education research project itself came to me from Kevin Harris (1979), who in turn was influenced by Imre Lakatos (1980).

While retaining the principle that the different projects were incommensurable against any external standard, I also held that they could each be judged individually on the basis of whether its state was progressive or regressive and degenerative at any given time of its existence. In this sense, following Lakatos, I distinguished three different ways in which a project could be judged: theoretically, empirically, and generally (that is theoretically *and* empirically). A project was *empirically progressive* if its problem-solving capacity was on the increase; *theoretically progressive* if it grew in consistency, openness to revision and change, in coherence, sophistication, and so on; and *generally progressive* if it was both. The model was a very liberal adaptation of Lakatos's model of a research project in the natural sciences. Adopting his terminology and structure, my education research project had a normative *inner core* and a pragmatic *protective theoretic belt*, with the former incorporating the project's most fundamental beliefs, values, and aspirations for the world (what one could call its ideology in the non-pejorative sense of a world-view), and the latter containing the operational theories that reflect the way these beliefs and aspirations are brought into contact with the actual world, in a heuristic, problem-solving way. To describe it more fully, the protective belt, fashioned by the operational definition of the project, would be a fluid, dynamic, and unstable instrument determined pragmatically as a set of policies, strategies, and practices established through negotiation with the world and its own normative core. It would be the zone where the aspirations of the normative core articulated by philosophy are rendered practical by being brought into contact with the world and translated into concrete policies and actions seeking a progressive response to the tension between the project's normative aspirations and the demands of reality. The project thus also required a sociology of the world to work with, while the core itself was its stable, ideological motor. The maximalist decision to reconceptualize education as a lifelong process, to adopt the learning society as its point of reference, to include informal learning, etc., was, as I explained in the previous section, a technical one made for the operational belt. Whereas for the writers of the movement, the normative core of their lifelong education project was, as we saw, a democratic form of scientific humanism.

I need to be precise on this. In accordance with what I have been saying, there could be, theoretically, any number of different lifelong education projects. Any education research project is a *lifelong* education project if, no matter what its normative core, the *technical definition* of its operational belt is one of lifelong learning. The different interpretations of "lifelong"— as recurrent, continuing, maximalist—determine the general strategic principles, policies, and practices of such a project. To repeat, the decision to adopt the notion of a learning society as a key strategic principle is not necessary to a lifelong education project but is the key operational feature of the maximalist project of lifelong education adopted by the writers of the movement. Other, non-maximalist, versions will operate with different operational principles; they may disagree with a lifewide interest in learning, for instance, and exclude informal learning altogether. Whether particular projects qualify as progressive or degenerative at any particular time depends on their current *state of health qua projects.* Certain projects may at a particular time be judged to be in a better or worse state of health than others, some may be in a state of bad health or decline, some may be moribund, while others still may be, temporarily (one can never say conclusively because the possibility of revival is, in theory, never lost entirely), dead. This means that, though they are not commensurable against external criteria or standards of truth, justice, or relevance, competing projects can be compared to one another on the basis of their state of health (or whether they are progressive or regressive on their own terms) at any given time, judged by the extent of activity they generate, the amount of support they enjoy, and the state of the project itself.[23] In this sense the old scientific humanistic project of the lifelong education movement of the 1970s could today, as I shall argue in the next chapter, be described as having become nearly defunct by the end of the 1980s.

Finally, there are a couple of things that need to be said about the normative core of a project before I close this account of the education research project for the time being. It will be recalled that I described the core of any particular project as incorporating the shared beliefs and commitments of its supporters; commitments that confer its "hardness" on it. It may (*will* if it is alive and healthy) modify itself, maybe even considerably, over time, but not usually against pragmatic arguments or considerations, and it must retain the fundamental normative principles and ideological commitments that make it identifiable for what it is—liberal, social democrat, Marxist, neo-liberal, neo-Thomist, humanistic, and so on. A project as a whole dies if its discourse is abandoned; if these normative principles and commitments no longer attract supporters. To give an example, when Paul Hirst (1974) redefined liberal education in terms of a curriculum that resolves itself into different forms of knowledge, he explicitly confirmed the continuity of his project with the ancient Greek ideal of liberal education, but specified significant departures from it, most notably the abandonment of its metaphysical justification. In other words, he was reworking the normative core of a liberal education project, which, though radically revised, continued to be recognizably liberal. The curriculum strategy and practices proposed by Hirst and other liberal philosophers, the decision to focus on the educated person (instead of a learning society, for instance) and forms of knowledge (instead of lifewide learning), enter into the debate about the liberal project's operational definition of education. They are operational decisions that are, like all operational decisions, just assumed; they are not, like the normative core, justified and defended theoretically. There is no philosophical work to be done on them.

Of course, this need not be how liberal philosophers themselves regard matters. Liberal philosophers of education have shown great reluctance in the recent past to recognize the relevance of sociological or historical factors for their education projects. Why? Because, for them, the question of what counts as *education* is a philosophical one impervious to empirical claims or considerations or to the state of the world such as it may be. It is determined by the universal qualities of rational autonomy, or being "educated," by the demands of educatedness *itself*, or by the "nature of knowledge." This is more or less, judging by his work, what Bailey was getting at in his remarks, referred to earlier in the chapter, that considerations of pragmatic relevance do not determine what one does in the name of education. With reference to my own remarks a few lines up that education research projects die or become moribund when they run out of supporters (even if they are always liable to be revived), this seems to be what is happening today with all the old modernist research projects, including that of the movement. The situation is a symptom of the current postmodern condition of the world, a subject I shall return to shortly. When I finished writing *PLE* with a final chapter on the learning society, my next project seemed indicated for me at once; namely to take the notion up, half baked as I left it there in that last chapter, and to develop an education research project with a maximalist operational framework and with a social democrat core that reflected my own political beliefs. But this book has turned out to be very different.

CHAPTER TWO

Death of the Movement: The Learning Society as Postmodern Myth

Problems with Utopia

The Faure report (1972:162, italics in original) summarized its utopia of a learning society by referring back to ancient Athens where *"education was not a segregated activity, conducted for certain hours, in certain places, at a certain time of life. It was the aim of the society. The city educated the man. The Athenian was educated by the culture, by paideia. This was made possible by slavery,"* it admitted, but *"Machines can do for every modern man what slavery did for the fortunate few in Athens."* This aspiration that "machines" can emancipate the modern world from the brutality of "slave" labor and cultural massification was a corollary to the movement's scientific humanism. It ignored other pessimistic accounts of a dominant instrumental rationality at work in the technologized modern world—expressed most famously by Weber, Adorno and Horkheimer, and Heidegger. Faure did acknowledge substantial difficulties in realizing its utopia: that people today were plagued by doubt and skepticism; that time-honored values had fallen into decay; that the latent threat of nuclear cataclysm had created an atmosphere of global doom; that people had lost the sense of emotional stability and security once provided by the close-knit community and were more prone to loneliness, anonymity, and helplessness than ever before; that the increase in material goods and their more equitable distribution had not decreased people's frustrations and their sense of alienation as they found themselves caught in the insatiable grip of the consumerist culture that produces a cycle of permanent dissatisfaction, setting up new needs as swiftly as it satisfies old ones, and so on.

But its tone was still optimistic, confidently reading utopian trends into the present world and its education systems and predicting the advent of a true if not perfect democratic regime, not built by bureaucrats and technocrats and other kinds of experts, or granted by the ruling caste, but created by its citizens. This would be a democracy whose social and educational structures would be remodeled on more humane lines and the privileges built into our cultural heritage reduced. Where restructuring would extend the field of choice widely to enable people to follow their own lifelong education patterns and paths through life. Where the subject matter of learning would be individualized, and learners made aware of their status, their rights, and their wishes, while authoritarian forms of teaching would be abandoned in favor of relationships marked by independence, mutual responsibility, and dialogue (1972:74). A democracy that would encourage commitment and vigorous action in all spheres of individual and social endeavor; in politics, in public affairs, in trade union activities, and in social and cultural life. One that would help individuals make authentic personal choices and fight the "omnipresent messages and temptations of the mass media" that threaten estrangement and "anti-education" (1972:104); that would study the use and abuse of leisure—a crucial dimension of human life, a source of new opportunities but also a site of diverse problems. And so on. The writers of the Faure report (1972:164), although they believed that the future looked auspicious, knew that this kind of ideal learning society would not come into being of itself and in the course of things. That one could not "confidently expect [it] to spring up one fine day, fully formed and equipped, shiny as a new toy, under the effect of ringing phrases." That it would have to be fought for and achieved through struggle. Today, "at the most," they reflected, "the call for a learning society may be one of the slogans on the banners in a rough political, social, and cultural battle, leading to the creation of objective conditions, a call for effort, imagination, daring ideas and actions," but little else. What has become of that slogan thirty years later? What has become of the report's dream of a utopian learning society? But first, what has become of the movement?

The post-Faure pragmatic writers emphasized their opposition to the representation of any one model of the learning society as one for other societies to imitate or copy. Gelpi (1984b) mentions the perception among critics of the movement of a plot to foist a Eurocentric model of the learning society onto the less economically developed societies in other parts of the world that was alienating progressive educators and activists in these countries. His faith in the struggle for education, contrary to that of the utopian writers, lay not so much in an adult education movement or in strong state involvement in sustaining a learning society as in the initiatives of "progressive individuals" working in the field of adult education in local settings, and in the initiatives of local communities. The pragmatists, in general, insisted on experimental action responding to the particular conditions, unique histories, experiences, traditions, cultures, and resources of such communities, always through popular participation. Gelpi (1984b) himself explained the shift in the approach to lifelong education that had occurred during this period. He described the interest in lifelong education in the 1960s and 1970s as twofold, the result "of a dialectic (a) in a context of educational policy, notably as between the school system and adult education, and (b) in one of social and economic policy for development, production and the inflexibility of educational structures" (1984b:79). The 1970s, he said, introduced "new and interesting features" of a social nature into the debate, notably about the participation and marginalization of adults in the formal educational system, and it came to be realized that "the priority for educational reform is to challenge the system as a whole and not merely to create parallel provision" (1984b:80). This shift, he continued, brought changes in perception over the identity, recruitment, functions, and training of educators that involved the inclusion of non-professionals in the category. Concurrently, another change of strategy brought a movement away from the construction of "lifelong education centers" toward action aimed at transforming the whole education system, as well as a movement toward creating new relations between formal and non-formal sectors. In some countries, Gelpi remarked, efforts were made to strengthen the cultural content of education and to grasp the educational dimension of non-working life.

Gelpi (1984b:80) remarked on the "provocative" nature of these developments and the obstacles to them created by the bureaucratic resistance of education systems and "the political elite." Suchodolski (1979:36–37), five years earlier and without elaborating, had already referred to the conflicting views and the contrary responses, optimistic and skeptical, both to lifelong education and to the idea of an "educative society" over the whole period of the 1970s. Some, he had said, greeted the official action on behalf of these ideals with enthusiasm as positive factors; others distrusted them and complained about too much pragmatism and the marginalization of different groups. Some, he had said, had a utopian vision and optimistic hopes for a new society; others foresaw "a society not very different from the contemporary one, that is to say, a society concerned above all with material success, consumption, politics, the mass media, and the enjoyment of leisure, and not at all concerned about the idea of an education which is lifelong and comprehensive, dignified and noble, but demanding" (1979:36). Still others questioned the very value of the ideal of an "educative society," claiming that "it is being used as a justification for different forms of manipulation of people, for enticing them to adopt doubtful values, and for shaping individuals according to arbitrarily established criteria which have already become part of a dead tradition, or only a mask for the interests of dominant groups or, in some cases, totalitarian states" (1979:37).

The utopian approach did continue to attract some support for a while, even outside the environs of UNESCO. Pierre Furter (1977:19) is a case in point. Working within the OECD's environs, he suggested that the criticism of the utopian approach may "well conceal the irritation of the supporters of the prevailing culture when confronted with attempts to interpret reality in another light or suggest other ways of organizing social life, even if only in an imaginary fashion," and took up the challenge of creating a utopian model for planning lifelong education. Furter (1977:20) rejected abstract representations of utopia for those "thought out by men of action on the basis of their experience and drawing on trends in real life which have either never been emphasized or which have remained unnoticed." His example of how utopian thinking can be turned into action was not the Faure report but the "red book" published in 1970 by the Council of Europe's Council for Cultural Co-operation. A book transformed from "an undertaking of pure utopian invention" into a strategy for action by B. Schwarz and his colleagues, approved by member states, and given the title *Fundamentals for an Integrated Educational Policy*. And which was to be followed by a "vast research and action program covering several years during which changes in the European systems of education will be put under the microscope" (1977:21). Furter was exceedingly optimistic that the strategy would be sustained and that these changes would materialize according to the program.

But utopian approaches grew increasingly anachronistic as the 1970s advanced and the world entered into deep global economic recession, bolstered by expansive monetary and fiscal policies and by the rise in OPEC oil prices, the growth of international terrorism, the renewal of tensions of the cold war, and so on. As I remarked earlier, by the 1980s the utopian idea of the learning society was already out of fashion among the pragmatists of the movement. At the beginning of the 1990s some, like Alan M. Thomas (1991:183), while conceding that it was still "obviously" only "a vision, something to be aspired to," believed that "the foundations for a true learning society already exist," but he did not specify what they were and in what form they existed. Nor did he say what he had in mind by a "true" learning society and whether he was suggesting that there was already a "false" or inauthentic learning society of some kind. At one point he hinted that the key to his optimism lay in the advent of the "so-called information society," which, he said, has shaken our faith in schooling and contributed toward a growing feeling of "disillusion and doubt about the efficacy of existing systems of formal education" (1991:xii). But the notion of the information society as a learning society is not without its problems, albeit that it has to be taken into account by any maximalist conception of the learning society today. Meanwhile, though the lifelong education movement continued to flourish in the 1980s, its fortunes went into rapid decline as the decade proceeded and it progressively lost the support and sponsorship of UNESCO, as the organization itself suffered political and financial crisis and practically packed up its lifelong education unit in Paris, which had been set up between 1966 and 1968. So that a sad and demoralized Gelpi, who had created and run it from the beginning, found himself fighting a long, drawn-out battle with the bureaucracy to save it and stave off the threat of his own redundancy. This turn of events, together with the loss incurred to the movement a few years earlier through Dave's retirement in 1989 from the UNESCO Institute of Education in Hamburg, which he had also headed for a long time (since 1979), was a lethal double blow to the movement that virtually marked its end, though Gelpi's lifelong education unit in Paris was not officially closed until the end of 1993, when his position there was finally terminated.

When the movement died, the notion of lifelong education, which it had worked with for nearly three decades, died with it. The situation is different with "lifelong learning," which had never, as I observed earlier, been limited to the confines of UNESCO or the literature of the movement. It has continued to be an important and vigorous notion in Europe, due largely, John Field (2001) has suggested, to its sponsorship by the OECD, and UNESCO has continued to work in the field. As Field (2001:6) points out, unlike UNESCO's literature on lifelong education, that of the OECD on recurrent education was, from the start, "couched more in terms of human capital thinking, albeit laced with a few dashes of social democracy." In its early years the OECD proposed paid educational leave as its leading instrument for the practical pursuit of recurrent education policies. Field (2001:8) notes, significantly as we shall see, that of the different intergovernmental agencies, "only the OECD's proposals appeared to have any concrete influence on governments possibly because," unlike UNESCO, "its remit was more closely focused on policy and partly because its membership was restricted to a small group of relatively like-minded countries." The OECD's literature was never, despite Furter, strategically based on the notion of the learning society, as was that of the movement in its earlier days. This changed, however, in the mid-1990s, when utopian thinking was suddenly back in vogue again and the debate about the future of the modern world was back on the agenda. With it returned the questions raised by Illich and by the lifelong education writers of two to three decades earlier about the contemporary relevance of modern education systems identified with mass schooling, and, after years in the wilderness, the notion of the learning society was back in vogue again. Before narrating that story I want to say something more about the postmodern world into which it was reborn to add to my description in Chapter 1. Meanwhile, the expression "recurrent education," with which the OECD worked in its earlier days, has suffered the same fate as "lifelong education"—nobody uses it any more. Indeed, it is even more conclusively obsolete than lifelong education, which continues to crop up unguardedly here and there. And this confirms my suspicion that it is the term "education" that has become problematic today rather than "lifelong education" as such.

The Postmodern World

Economic recession of the 1970s led to a restructuring of capitalism that changed the developed world dramatically. Industrial organizations reacted vigorously to the growing automation of their production systems induced by the introduction of new technologies and sought "new production lines and market niches, geographical dispersal to zones of easier labor control, mergers, and steps to accelerate turnover time of their capital" (Ranson 1994:37). The postindustrial society became a growing reality, replacing the old labor-intensive industrial society and creating new training needs for workers. What it signified, very briefly, was a transition from the type of mass production of standardized goods that had characterized the industrial past to more flexible forms of production, labor market segmentation and organization, and policies of "flexible accumulation." In the postindustrial world consumption achieves a new importance as against production, and the key word in production is flexibility. There is a progressive shift "into a service economy and a widespread rearrangement of activities, leading to sectorialization of the labour market, intensification of competition, and a rewriting of the culture of work" (Rinne 1998:110). The notion of the "labor society," as Arendt called it, where work is recognized as the central value and wage labor its normative form, becomes obsolete, as does the Keynsian notion of the welfare state with its homogenous workforce and its policies of full employment (Rinne 1998:115).

In the postindustrial world, "the pattern of the early modern, where occupation determined one's pathway through life, is being displaced" by different patterns of life-work, so that, Risto Rinne (1998:111) continues, quoting Beck, "'Normal' biography gives way to a biography of continual choices, of recurrent 'pastimes/occupations,' of threats and responsibilities, and of hiatuses (Beck 1996a:42)," that contribute in a key way to the creation of the "risk society." In this society the values of a consumer-oriented culture, growing in strength all the time, have changed people's perceptions and lifestyles, leading them to search for increasingly private and personal satisfactions, while business organizations are geared to respond to rather than regulate markets, and "are seen as frameworks for learning as much as instruments of control. Their hierarchies are flatter and their structures more open" (Ranson 1994:38). In short, the postindustrial world introduces trends toward reconceiving industrial and business organizations as *learning organizations*, a notion I shall return to presently. It also witnesses the growth of a sophisticated system of international finance, which, with the availability of computerized telecommunication technologies that have made global transaction easier, has grown increasingly indifferent to the constraints of time and space, creating the phenomenon of globalization both economic and informational. Globalization was made politically possible at the turn of the 1980s with the collapse of the communist economies, which internationalized the free market, established the dominance of liberal capitalism everywhere, and was celebrated with joy and a new feeling of optimism as signaling the birth of a brave new world by Western liberals. The Cold War, which many thought would last forever—or at least for their lifetime—was over and liberal democracy had won the day, while capitalism was confirmed as the only viable economic system available. True, the new world of the 1990s also witnessed the globalization of a set of pressing new issues, particularly environmental ones, while older ones tied to the politics of gender and sexuality remained on the agenda. But there was talk of the "end of history" or, at any rate, of the advent of a postmodern world where ideological conflict is "displaced by democratic reason and market-oriented thinking" (Hall et al. 1996:14).

The lifelong education writers never used the expression "postmodern" to describe the fast-changing world they saw emerging rapidly in the 1960s and 1970s; it was not yet in vogue. It started to become really popular in the 1980s after the appearance of Jean-François Lyotard's book *The Postmodern Condition: A Report on Knowledge* (1999, henceforth *PMC*), first published in 1979. With time "postmodern" has grown fashionable just like the expression "postindustrial" that preceded it. Not all writers like it. Some, like Giddens and Beck, prefer other expressions to describe the condition of today's world: "late modernity" or "reflexive modernity," for instance. I shall use "postmodern" nevertheless to go with the growing trend, always with the understanding that I take the term to signify an extension of the modern, *not* a radical break with it, as it is often used by apocalyptic writers.[24] Stuart Hall, David Held, and Tony McGrew (1996:2) refer to modernity as a "distinct and unique form of life which characterizes modern societies." I understand postmodernity (not to be confused with "postmodernism") similarly, as a "distinct and unique" but not discontinuous "form of life" characterizing postmodern societies. Hall et al. (1996:2) trace the origin of modern societies to the Europe of the fifteenth century, but they "could hardly be said to exist in any developed form," they say, "until the idea of the 'modern' was given a decisive intellectual formulation in the discourse of the Enlightenment in the eighteenth century" and became identified with the effects of industrialism and the sweeping social, economic, and cultural reforms it brought about. In the same way the emergence of postmodern societies reaches further back into the past than the intellectual formulation of the idea of the "postmodern" in contemporary discourse, and of postmodernism, which will be described in Chapter 6.

There are different theories about when the modern world started entering a postmodern condition. Steven Best and Douglas Kellner (1991) date it at the end of World War II when countries emerging from the war were forced to reconsider the future of the modern world on the basis of that experience, and were faced with the urgent task of reconstructing themselves socially, politically, economically, technologically, and in other ways besides. The main processes that had formed modern societies were the rise of the secular state and polity, the growth of a global capitalist economy, the creation of social classes and an advanced sexual and social division of labor, and the cultural transition from a religious to a secular mind-frame. The modern period saw the West shaping its identity and interests by conquering, colonizing, and exploiting the "other" that was the non-West, and by bringing into being a cluster of characteristic institutions to suit its purposes. These included an international system of nation states; a capitalist economic system both dynamic and expansionist and based on private property; industrialism; the growth of large-scale administrative and bureaucratic systems of social organization and regulation; the dominance of secular, materialist, rationalist and individualist cultural values; and the formal separation of the "private" and the "public" (Hall et al. 1996:2–3). Modernity progressively spread beyond Europe, becoming a global phenomenon. Postmodernity denotes a radicalization of many of these trends, mainly through the globalization of communication systems brought about by the technological revolution. Some have been diverted, or challenged, in some cases radically.

Existential disorientation and risk, which were already present to some extent in the modern world, become, as Giddens and Beck tell us, the outstanding features of the postmodern world. The world that began to emerge from World War II was one chastened by that war and its ravages, armed with potent new technologies, with a new international power structure marked by the emergence of the United States and the Soviet Union as world superpowers, and with the hardening of the world into two mutually hostile ideological and military blocs. The experience of "total war," of fascism and its death camps, of the Holocaust, of Hiroshima and Nagasaki, in short of the apparent moral failure of Western civilization, played a not insignificant part in the widespread disenchantment with modernity that followed and is the key feature of the postmodern mind, according to Lyotard. This disenchantment had already been articulated famously by Theodor Adorno and Max Horkheimer in *Dialectic of Enlightenment* (1992), first published in 1944, a bitter book reflecting the contemporary disenchantment of many intellectuals with the Enlightenment project. It was a project intended as a gift of reason and progress by the West to the whole of humanity but it interpreted "progress" in its own terms as "the subjugation, domination, exploitation, enslavement, and near-genocide of all those who are not the West," creating a heritage that is not easily set aside, one for which the once colonized still pay a hefty price (Bain 1995:4). The postmodern world went into a radically new phase with the collapse of global confrontation between West and East, state socialism, and liberal democracy in 1989, and with the advent of globalization, which has put nation-states, the political protagonist of the modern world, and their economies at risk, making interdependence between nations the new political reality of today and changing the face of politics.

Stephen Crook, Jan Pakulski, and Malcolm Waters (1992:39–40) point out how "the new conflicts" on the political stage "are more contingent and more conjectural," tending "to erupt around general values and lifestyles," and involving "status, situs and generational categories rather than socio-economic groups," while the concerns they represent "tend to be more ephemeral and global, undermining the old political divisions and transcending state boundaries." Globalization, however, has not equalized economic opportunity across the globe. It has created new sorts of colonialism and made the poor more dependent on the rich than they have ever been, due to the fast-widening technological and economic gap between them. It has signified the creation of cutthroat global market competition and of a new class of poor in the developed world itself, besides the growing degradation of the less developed, producing reactions of open revolt against its injustices in recent times, like those in Seattle and Venice. From the old world the postmodern has inherited the ecological abuses that threaten environmental disaster on a catastrophic scale. In short, the world today, in its postmodern condition, is scarcely a more just, safe, less violent, and more stable place than it was yesterday, as the events since late 2001, following the attack on the former World Trade Center in New York on September 11, have shown. The new confrontation today, fueled not a little by the Middle East crisis, is with fundamentalism and international terrorism, and between Christian and Islamic worlds. The United States is reaffirmed as the sole world superpower able to do pretty much as it pleases on the international stage. In Europe, the euphoria greeting the physical destruction of the Berlin Wall, symbolically representing the fall of communism, soon turned sour as a rising tide of racial and religious intolerance and savage civil and ethnic warfare quickly raised its ugly head in the newly liberated countries of Eastern Europe. However, the more recent growth and enlargement of the European Union as a major political—and not solely economic—reality to include these countries has rendered the likelihood of another major conflagration on this continent difficult. In Africa and Asia, however, wars and instances of ethnic violence have continued to be numerous, all occasioned, in large part, by the same old causes of the past: extreme nationalism, tribalism, ethnic hatred, religious fundamentalism, poverty, superstition, selfishness, intolerance, and greed. All of them ills targeted by the Enlightenment project for eradication at the hands of reason, science, and education, with the spectacular failure described by Adorno and Horkheimer.

Even where there is no war the poorer countries are still in a state of scandalous neglect, many racked by endemic and deep-ingrained political corruption, disease, gross socioeconomic inequality, and economic collapse. Human rights in most of them are a sick joke at best, and their perennial social and economic problems are frequently and dramatically exacerbated with natural disasters, often on a catastrophic scale. Circumstances all that cry out for intervention and redress by the wealthier nations in the name of global justice, but the billions are more available for war or for wars about "justice." Meanwhile, the economically developed, the rich world itself is not immune to problems as it struggles to make its way forward in a world of advanced technological progress and rapidly changing landscapes. It is afflicted with recurring periods of economic recession; with its own rising rates of urban poverty, unemployment, racial intolerance and xenophobia, urban squalor and escalating violence; and with the growth of the phenomenon of a disinherited underclass: a mass of deprived and marginalized people, many of them young, and often educated and qualified, whose composition, as Crook et al. (1992) point out, cuts across the traditional class. The Enlightenment agenda of optimistic adventure and faith in progress, transferred in this continent to the European Union, dampens before the reality of mass unemployment; seemingly irreversible social degradation; the scourges of drugs, poverty, and AIDS; environmental degradation; and so on, that are still visible in much of the continent today. In the United States, the most "progressed" of the economically developed world and most postmodern of the Western countries, things are no better. Peter MacLaren (1991:3) writes about "the ascendancy of a new post-modern institutionalization of brutality and the proliferation of new and sinister structures of domination accompanied by the insistent voices of the powerless and the marginalized," phenomena that have largely invalidated the reality of democracy in that country. And William Bain (1995:4) remarks, again about the United States, on how "we imprison a greater percentage of our population than any other 'developed' country and specialize in imprisoning poor people and people of color," and how "the disparity between rich and poor is growing" apace. How "xenophobia is on the rise in a nation of immigrants." How "we have 'progressed' so far that our prior visions of the 'end of history' are nuclear or ecological annihilation."

Within this scenario of the brave new postmodern world, MacLaren (1991:4) points to the rise to power and popularity of a new radical right that appeals to the popular culture, offering us a retreat into nostalgia and social amnesia. The left, on the other hand, he describes as being in a state of crisis, its economic alternatives largely discredited, its own critical work "held captive in the discursive grip of a neo-colonialist politics." The feminist movement is not in a much better state either. The early excitement over its radical intellectual and political challenge seems dissipated, giving way to internecine bickering and increasing self-doubt, and its growing preoccupation with its own internal theoretical and political difficulties has cut it adrift from what is going on in the rest of the "restructured" world. "It seems to be off in a space by itself somewhere," one writer observes wryly, "meanwhile something is burning and it's not Rome" (Kenway 1995:37). With the ascendancy of the new neoliberal right to power, the political government of the developed postmodern world is marked by a new realism in national and international politics, which recognizes little moral obligation toward the rest of humanity. At the same time, at home, it glorifies the old values of religion, hard work, health, and self-reliance; betrays a sentimental nostalgia for the past; and endorses an authoritarian populism playing on common sense and traditional values. Its attack focuses on what it perceives as threats to the bourgeois conception of the family (of which the housewife is re-projected as the moral center), on the "crisis" of traditional values in general, and on patriotism. And it is hostile toward the welfare state, which it charges with undermining self-confidence and perpetuating poverty. In the field of education it campaigns for a "return to the basics," for upholding the "traditional standards" and sustaining "excellence," for introducing management and quality control systems from the business world, for restoring the teacher's discipline and the practice of no-nonsense authority in the classroom, while targeting progressivism for its most acrid attacks.

The Information Society and Postmodern Culture

Postmodern societies are information societies. The postmodern world itself is very much the creature of "the globalization of information, communication, and technology (Giddens 1990, Harvey 1989, Menzies 1989, Naisbett and Aberdene 1990)" (Green 1994:51). Information revolutions "are among the most pervasive forms of social change experienced by the present generations." They, more than anything else, have taken contemporary societies into the postmodern age. Echoing Wexler, Rob Gilbert (1992:53) describes the media as providing "'the organizing concepts of a postmodern *administrative control apparatus*,' in a society 'semiotic at the cultural-consumption level, informational-production level, and at the communicative regulative or power level' (Wexler 1987:57)." John Gibbins and Bo Reimer (1999:37) observe that today we live "in a mass media-saturated environment. The mass media are all around us, from morning till night." Their effect on ordinary everyday life is everywhere and they are as integral a factor in the shaping of postmodernity as they were in the shaping of modernity (even if "surprisingly enough, the media are often absent in analyses of modernity" [1999:38]). "Of all the processes that characterized modernity," the authors continue, "the mediazation process is the one that more than any other continues to affect and change social life to even greater extents" (1999:38–39). They go on to highlight the way it impacts on the postmodern world and conclude that "no one can seriously question that the mass media have drastically changed people's everyday lives" (1999:42).

The information society has been fraught with controversy since it became an emerging reality in the 1960s. Optimists like Amitai Etzioni (1968) linked it with the advent of an "active society" where technological advance would be guided by normative values and controlled for the general benefit of humanity. Daniel Bell (1976), more guardedly, detected "dangerous" elements in the cultural change it was creating and the reaction it provoked, but he also regarded it with optimism and hope. Insightfully, Bell perceived within it the revival of a radical romantic strand in modernism with its typical revolt against everyday life, its antibourgeois, antinomic, and hedonistic impulses, and its extension into the social and cultural texture of Western countries. In short, the threat of "post-modernism"! The technological revolution he saw as an instrument by which these impulses would spread more deeply and rapidly, posing a serious threat to traditional values. Against it he called for a revivification of religious values echoed by many of today's conservatives. Meanwhile, progressive thinkers were immediately worried by other negative dimensions of the technological revolution that produced the information society noted earlier, such as the division it has created between those who possess its products and those who do not, individuals at the level of society, and countries at the global level; the haves and have-nots in the new global economy of information. And the atomization of society, the increasing search for private satisfaction, with individuals leading ever more private and secluded lives, content to interact more with machines than with other people, treating information as an item of consumption and entertainment rather than enlightenment and self-education. Asher Deleon (1984:36), among the pragmatist lifelong education writers, quoted Jean d'Arcy to complain about the "vertical, one-way flow from the top downward of non-diversified anonymous messages, produced by a few and addressed to all." This is a complaint echoed by Philip Elliott (1986) and others (notably Jurgen Habermas, as we shall see), who have pointed out that its main political victim is the public sphere, the Enlightenment's political and educational dream. Its progressive erosion of the public sphere, he says, produces a "shift away from involving people in society as responsible citizens of nation states towards involving them as consumption units in a corporate world" (1986:106).

Elliott concedes that there are both pessimistic and optimistic accounts of the information society, but he is not so sanguine as Bell that it could be the new Alexandrian library of the age available for the general benefit of the whole of humankind (there are many today who view the Internet in this same way). The advent of the media, he remarks, has created a mass international consumer society instead, "founded on an acceptable level of comfort, pleasure and control" in which people participate not as educated citizens but as unreflective consumers in a market (1986:106). Elsewhere, like Bell, Michael Peters (1996) traces this trend toward the marketization of information to the information society's early days, when the focus was on the changing role of knowledge production within the economy as societies were in transition from the industrial into the postindustrial. But Adorno and Horkheimer identified it even earlier in their description of the "culture industry" (discussed later in Chapter 4). Elliott points out how liberals, politically attracted to the information society as they link more information with more democracy, are blind to the threat it poses to the public sphere. Indeed, he doubts that transparent government and freedom of expression is what the information society delivers. Liberals, he argues, ignore the consequence of placing the production of information at the mercy of the market; what happens is that "information for which there is no market will not be produced" (1986:107). Besides, Elliott continues, the marketization of information destroys the very raison d'être of intellectuals, the lifeblood of the public sphere. And, to cap it all, it contributes to the negative growth of what he describes as the "twin features of the contemporary culture," namely "consumptive hedonism and anti-political repression" (1986:111). His conclusion to this pessimistic analysis of the information society is that far from the consummation of the liberal dream of transparency of information and international solidarity, it leads to the "further domestication of living functions and privatization of social life" (1986:107). In which circumstances "the public self and its masks are increasingly defined by a media-oriented culture in which youth, health, and sexuality have taken on premium values" (Denzin 1991:5).

This issue about the information society will be a central concern for me throughout the book because the future of the learning society in the postmodern world is intimately tied with the future of the information society. To put it more directly, the postmodern learning society is necessarily an information society. The information society constitutes the outstanding way that postmodern societies are mobilized for learning. The question of what kind of learning society it produces and to what ends—a matter of deep controversy as these introductory paragraphs show—will be taken up in the coming chapters, where I shall look mainly at the work of the Frankfurt theorists, Habermas, Jean Baudrillard, and Gianni Vattimo. Norman Denzin (1991:vii), influenced by Baudrillard, describes the postmodern media culture as "nostalgic," marked by a "conservative longing for the past, coupled with an erasure of the boundaries between the past and the present," by "an intense preoccupation with the real and its representations; a pornography of the visible; the commodification of sexuality and desire; a consumer culture which objectifies a set of masculine cultural ideals; intense emotional experiences shaped by anxiety, alienation, *ressentiment*, and a detachment from others." The postmodern imagination, Denzin (1991:ix) says, articulates itself as "a cinematic, dramaturgical production," as "'videocy,'" or "language of the visual, video image" and has achieved primacy over other languages or forms of communication (1991:8), displacing earlier forms of literacy based on orality and the print media, and thereby altering the individual's relationship to the "real" in a radical way. Denzin (1991:9) summarizes postmodernity, in general, as "a complex set of cultural logics" that turn on the meanings brought to five terms: the cultural object, the individual, family, sexuality, and work. As popular culture it is "conservative, consumer oriented, cinematic and visual to the core." In its many contradictory forms it is "a masculinized culture of Eros, love, desire, femininity, youth and beauty." A voyeur culture, "a looking culture, organized in terms of a variety of gazes, or looks (tourist, investigatory—medical, social science, television, religious, political—artistic, photographic and so on)." Homogeneity is what it lacks. To speak of "postmodern culture," he says, is "to make loose reference to a body of understandings which 'go without saying' in this complex, heterodox mass of shifting, conflicting, regional, cultural understandings that make up the cultural fabrics of the developed world" (1991:13–14). Not that these understandings are obvious to ordinary people. To the contrary, they are passed on in the form of a hegemonic cultural politics that stresses the overriding value of consumption, and has turned into the chief carrier of the state ideology.

The other outstanding cultural value besides consumption that postmodernity stresses, Lyotard (1999) tells us, is that of *performativity*, a term that, like postmodernity, has also come into popular use. Performativity is the other overriding criterion to which everything in postmodern societies is referred, valuing everything in terms of "the best possible input/output equation" (1999:46). Continuous with positivism, it projects power or mastery over things and people, or their effective management, as Lyotard says, as the only credible goal for politics. Its success lies in that it represents itself, and has all the appearances of belonging, to the technical language game, of being a purely technical criterion when, in point of fact, it is also, perhaps primarily, a "truth criterion," infiltrating our language of politics so that we come to identify the value of justice, like that of science, with effectiveness, with a technology of performance. "This is how legitimation by power takes shape. Power is not only good performativity, but also effective verification and good verdicts" (1999:47). The self-legitimation of performativity creates for it a kind of "context control," which ties it perfectly into the logic of digitized information societies. As Lyotard (1999:47) says: "The performativity of an utterance, be it denotative or prescriptive, increases proportionately to the amount of information about the referent one has at one's disposal. Thus the growth of power, and its self-legitimation, are now taking the route of data storage and accessibility, and the operativity of information." The culture of consumerism is tied into that of performativity because it feeds the illusion that the sheer possession of knowledge and information is an intrinsic good that should be pursued by all. MacIntyre (1981:71) captures the essence of Lyotard's concern over a performativist culture where "the whole concept of effectiveness is … inseparable from a mode of human existence in which the contrivance of means is in central part the manipulation of human beings into compliant patterns of behavior."

Denzin, like Elliott, addresses the question of the intellectual's role in postmodern societies, identifying journalists, politicians, and advertisers as the new intellectuals: "the new historians who have no sense of history, only meaning" (1991:9). In his novel *Immortality*, Milan Kundera (1991:127), describing the postmodern transition as "a gradual, general, planetary transformation of ideology into imagology," says the same thing. "Imagology" is the word he coins to describe the outlook of "advertising agencies; political campaign managers; designers who devise the shape of everything from cars to gym equipment; fashion stylists; barbers; show-business stars dictating the norms of physical beauty that all branches of imagology obey" (1991:127). The postmodern world, Kundera (1991:127) argues, is marked by "a historic victory" of these imagologues, and these image-makers or "spin doctors," as they are nowadays called in political circles (not ideologues) are today's "educators," the people who influence public taste and opinion. Their power lies in their ability "to fascinate the crowds" either through their own performance or indirectly by "educating" the crowds' political "masters." "Fascinated" is the way Denzin and Baudrillard describe the postmodern subject: "a restless voyeur, a person who sits and gazes (often mesmerized and bored) at the movie or TV screen," or, one could add, the computer screen (Denzin 1991:9). Dictators like Hitler, Kundera (1991:128) says, already had their secret imagologues, but these stayed in the background or hid their activity. Today, the imagologue "often even speaks for his politician clients, explains to the public what he taught them to do or not to do, how he told them to behave, what formula they are likely to use and what tie they are likely to wear." In short, she is the great puppet master of our times, who stands before the screen visible but glorying in her transparency, plying the craft openly and with impunity, while the silent masses, so Baudrillard contends, collaborate willingly with their own deception. Kundera (1991:129) describes public opinion polls as the chief tactical instruments of the imagologue's power, "because they enable imagology to live in absolute harmony with the people." Imagologues bombard the public with questions on all sorts of different things. They have, he says, opened up "a parliament in permanent session, whose function it is to create truth, the most democratic truth that has ever existed" (1991:129). Because the media is never at variance with this parliament of truth, and indeed creates it, it always "lives in truth," and this renders the power of imagologues indestructible (1991:129).

Kundera (1991:128) describes imagology as "stronger than reality," surpassing it in the same way that ideology was surpassed by reality. To illustrate, he compares his grandmother's world outlook in a Moravian village, where she knew everything and everybody directly—and undoubtedly also through the village gossip that she sat in on—who "had personal control over reality," and whom "nobody could fool" (for instance, "by maintaining that Moravian agriculture was thriving when people at home had nothing to eat"), with that of his Paris neighbor. This is a man who spends his time in his office for eight hours a day conferring with colleagues, then sits in his car and drives straight home, "turns on the TV and when the announcer informs him that in the latest public opinion poll the majority of Frenchmen voted their country the safest in Europe (I recently read such a report), he is overjoyed and opens a bottle of champagne without ever learning that three thefts and two murders were committed on his street that very day." Finally, in comparing the workings of ideology with those of imagology, he compares the former to "a set of enormous wheels at the back of the stage, turning and setting in motion wars, revolutions, reforms," while the latter's wheels turn subtly and secretly, silently, "without having any effect upon history." Ideologies fought one another and each ideology "was capable of filling a whole epoch with its thinking." Imagology, on the other hand, "organizes peaceful alternation of its systems in lively personal rhythms" that do not think. In Paul's (one of the central characters in the novel) words: "[I]deology belonged to history, while the reign of imagology begins where history ends" (1991:129).

The Return of the Learning Society

The notion of the learning society resurfaced again in the postmodern Europe of the mid-1990s, more than two decades after the Faure report, within the environs of the European Union (EU)—a very different proposition, as Field (1997) points out, from UNESCO. Through its

Commission, the EU possesses powers of initiative and decision-making at the European level that are unprecedented and growing with enlargement. For much of the 1980s international intergovernmental bodies had found relatively little to say, even on the topic of lifelong learning; "tackling unemployment replaced earlier preoccupations as the central task for adult education and training" during this period (Field 1997:9). Martin Yarnit (1997), tracing out the history of the key issues facing lifelong learning in Europe over the late 1980s and early 1990s and right up to 1997, divided it into three phases. In the first, covering the late 1980s to about 1992, after years of neglect the notion of lifelong learning gathered influence anew among governments and educationalists everywhere, or nearly everywhere. Yarnit contrasts the British government's "narrow utilitarianism," at the time, "which prompted vocationalism at the expense of traditional liberal adult education ways," and with a scarce interest in lifelong learning, with the strong leadership provided by the French government in the pursuit of lifelong learning policies and initiatives (1997:2). Interest in adult continuing education in Britain, he says, was only marginal, the education system fragmented, with schools and further and higher education separately planned and administered, and with a strict separation of the vocational from the academic, training from education. Government support for adult learning at the time, except in higher education, "required demonstrable contribution to the economy," and even then, he remarks, "the initiatives were rarely its own, while higher education in general continued to be constructed around elitist assumptions" (1997:3).

The EU itself only tentatively entered into the field of education policy-making in the mid-1980s, driven by two central concerns: the crisis in European economic competitiveness (which fueled the single market program), and expanding the EU's competencies in areas that had traditionally lain within national sovereignty, as part of its drive toward greater political integration (Field 1997:1).[25] But between 1992 and 1997, Field says, the policy debate on education and training acquired new momentum, as it was pressed firmly toward the center of the EU's integration strategy by the Delors Commission (1994), and the commitment to objectives tied to adult training relating to unemployment and industrial change grew. Yarnit himself dates this as the second phase, between 1993 and 1996, following the Maastricht Treaty, when, he remarks (as does Field), the debate about the future of the EU and especially about the social and economic reforms required for the successful implementation of the projected monetary union in 1999 grew.

Three key areas of educational debate, Yarnit says, developed around these reforms at the time: (1) over the concept of European citizenship, which developed alongside the issue of social exclusion; (2) over limited measures to protect workers' interests (which stemmed from the Social Chapter in the Maastricht Treaty); and (3) over the pan-European development of education policy and legislation. The Commission's white paper *Teaching and Learning: Towards the Learning Society*, which was the outcome of this debate published in late 1995, officially relaunched the notion of the learning society as an ideal for European societies. In tones mildly reminiscent of the Faure report of old in their enthusiasm, it proclaimed the advent of "the learning society of Europe." Its reception at the hands of the Council of Education Ministers is described by Field (2001) as "lukewarm," however, if not downright hostile. "Tomorrow's society," the white paper (1995:5) said, "will be a society which invests in knowledge, a society of teaching and learning, in which each individual will build up his or her qualifications, in other words, a learning society." In the very first paragraph of its introduction it set down the agenda of this learning society: It would address preoccupations concerning the future of the economy, social exclusion, and unemployment that were "major problems in all European societies" (1995:15). To add force and focus to the document, the EU declared 1996—the year following its publication— the European Year of Lifelong Learning.

With the publication of the white paper the expression "learning society" began to appear everywhere in EU documents, tied with the idea not of lifelong education but of lifelong learning. The difference does not escape the notice of the writers of an EU Eurydice Unit (2000) report on the contribution of education systems in the member states to the advancement of policies promoting lifelong learning. "The term 'lifelong learning,'" it says, "has now moved ahead of 'lifelong education,'" though there is still the same "lack of precision in the currently prevailing definitions and their often very abstract nature" that dogged the history of lifelong education (2000:8). Drawing on Boshier (1998), the report explains its preference for lifelong learning. "Directly implicit in the notion of learning," it says, "is the idea of personal responsibility for one's own educational development…. In order to remain employable, people, like consumers, have to be responsible for picking and choosing from what is available on the education and training market, in line with their requirements" (2000:8). It concedes that the individual's access to lifelong learning depends on the existence of appropriate social conditions, and that "bringing this about means that a government or other agency has to develop policies and grant resources which, ideally, relate to a context that is formal (and thus concerned with education and training systems), but also non-formal (separate from those systems but associated with organized bodies in society), or informal (any activities devised by individuals themselves)." But in the final analysis it lays the responsibility for lifelong learning ("education" and training) squarely on the individual cast in the role of free consumer in a learning and information market with employability as her first priority (2000:8). The change in the definition of "informal learning," which the lifelong education writers of the movement identified with experiential learning, is interesting. It coincides with this emphasis on the individual's responsibility for lifelong learning, which it identifies in the newer literature. Nor is experiential learning covered by the other kinds of learning, formal and non-formal, identified in the statement. In short, the old definition of informal learning as experiential learning or learning from life is abandoned, which is strange in a postmodern information society, and in times when education is fast disappearing as a normative concept, undermining objections like Bagnall's.

The Eurydice report (2000:8) does not suggest that we drop the expression "lifelong education," merely that we should tie it to "the need for ever-present public policies and regular determined action" that favors lifelong learning, rather than to a normative interest.[26] Lifelong learning, on the other hand, is the individual's personal responsibility. Frank Coffield (1996:1–2) argued that its "heavy concentration on the role of the individual" was matched by policies on the part of the EU Commission and the British government of the time, with regard to the learning society, that were "timid, narrowly conceived, and inadequate to the task," and reflected: (a) a conservative and timid acceptance of the necessity to decrease public expenditure on social welfare, (b) a reluctance to challenge the view of leading employers, (c) a comparative neglect of the role of institutions in change, and (d) a general willingness on the part of administrators and civil servants to serve up what they suspected would be acceptable to their political masters. Elsewhere, Bagnall (2000:21) describes them as "the product of economic determinism within a postmodern cultural context," articulated in the terms of human capital theory, where individual learning is evaluated mainly in terms of its earning capacity. He complains about the general vocationalization of adult "education" that the discourse of lifelong learning reflected, with the goal of occupational skill development uppermost on its agenda. He also complains about the overriding preoccupation with the efficiency of education systems, and the focus on outcomes and return on investment that haunts government policy. Finally, he identifies three "sentiments" that, he says, marked the discourse on lifelong education: individual progressive, democratic progressive, and adaptive progressive. He contends that they are gone. "Contemporary lifelong learning discourse," he concludes, "focuses strongly on the private benefit of education, with state involvement being reduced, ideally, to that of regulation, moderation, basic skills development, and safety-net welfare support" (2000:28).

These conclusions are confirmed everywhere in the research. Richard Edwards et al., in a Department for Education and Employment (DfEE) report on *Recent Thinking in Lifelong Learning* (1998), concluded that though "the threads of earlier meanings" remain as part of the debates about lifelong learning, "they have been powerfully supplanted by different concerns. Thus, while debates have tended to focus on the vocationalizing of post-school education, a more significant shift may actually be the individualizing of lifelong learning (McNair), and its reconstruction as part of lifestyle practices and consumer culture (Edwards and Usher 1997b), in which the identity of 'lifestyle learner' overlays and displaces that of 'educated person' in certain ways" (1998:15). The Eurydice report (2000) contrasts the approach to lifelong learning promoted within the EU countries not with the Faure report of 1972 but the more recent Delors report *Learning: The Treasure Within* (1996), describing the latter as Faure's follow-up. The "priority frame of reference" of the Delors report, the Eurydice report (2000:9) says, "is not that of good progress in working life. Instead it argues for a much more ambitious form of personal growth achievable by human beings." This statement, in fact, puts the difference between them in a nutshell. The Eurydice report (2000:9) continues to say that notwithstanding the widespread circulation of the Delors report (like the Faure report in its time), "it would appear that most public forums seeking to transform lifelong learning into an operational concept tend to take their cue from a definition that is close to sound progress in working life." This is the case with the EU, which takes its definition of lifelong learning from the OECD, not from UNESCO:

> This view of learning embraces individual and social development of all kinds and in all settings—formally, in schools, vocational, tertiary and adult education institutions, and non-formally, at home, at work and in the community. The approach is system-wide; it focuses on the standards of knowledge and skills needed by all, regardless of age. It emphasizes the need to prepare and motivate

all children at an early age for learning over a lifetime, and directs efforts to
ensure that all adults, employed and unemployed, who need to retrain or upgrade
their skills, are provided with opportunities to do so. (Eurydice Report 2000:9)

The report refers to amendments to the initial concept of recurrent
education in the OECD to include also informal learning engagements, but
we have already seen that these refer to personal initiatives by learners. The
report also discusses a new model of provision, management, and funding
of the system, which, it says, has displaced the reliance on public
authorities with a partnership between firms and learners. It notes too a "*de
facto* emphasis on post-compulsory and adult education and training, even
though the influence of basic education is acknowledged" (2000:11). Like
the Eurydice, the DfEE report (1998:15) emphasizes the power of this
new discourse:

Much of the literature contributing to the cause of lifelong learning is assertive
and prescriptive. The term "cause" is appropriate here as it signifies the power of
the discursive strategy to marginalize dissent and to unsettle pre-existing forms
of education and training. The policy discourse works hard to sustain a consistent
and coherent vision capable of attracting support from a diversity of
stakeholders, based on the twin requirements for economic competitiveness and
social inclusion. Lifelong learning then becomes a rallying cry capable of uniting
a diversity of interest groups behind a single banner proclaiming the need for
change.

The Employers' Agenda

The protagonists at the early stage in the second phase of the emerging
discourse of lifelong learning and the learning society distinguished by
Yarnit were not governments but a "wide coalition of interests, including
politicians, employers and educators" (Hughes and Tight 1995:290). Peter
Raggatt, Richard Edwards, and Nick Small (1996:6), in the introduction to
their jointly edited book *The Learning Society: Challenges and Trends*,
contend, however, that its main driving force was the European Employers
"influenced to a greater rather than a lesser extent by self-interest," with an
agenda that contributed only "coincidentally" to the goal of self-
fulfillment. This was not surprising because, as David Bradshaw (1995:14)
points out, the perception among many in business and training was that the
economic decline over the previous decades in evidence everywhere would
worsen "without commitment to become a learning society." Christopher

Ball (1995:18) remarked about how widespread "the claim that 'learning pays'" was, that it "embraces nations, organizations and individuals. It is commonplace and repeated worldwide," coinciding with the view, he continued (quoting from the 1991 report *America 2000*), that "the age of technology, information and communications rewards those nations whose people learn new skills and stay ahead."[27] In short, that we live "in a world that rewards learning." Not just individuals but business organizations and companies everywhere, he went on, have taken the message seriously so that they were taking the road towards becoming "learning organizations" (1995:20). He referred to examples of business's interest in the learning society, among them an initiative of the Economic and Social Research Council (ESRC) in Britain to set up a four-year, £2 million research project entitled *The Learning Society: Knowledge and Skills for Employment*—the subtitle of which was later reflected in the concerns of the EU's 1995 white paper (*Teaching and Learning: Towards the Learning Society*). A number of studies commissioned by the European Employers and followed by heavy investment in job training in many countries had, in fact, already concluded that "economic success depends on having a competitive 'hi-tech' industry, and that previous under-investment in vocational education and training have undermined European efforts to respond to changing economic conditions" (Edwards et al. 1998:19). In 1994, before publishing its 1995 white paper, the European Commission had published another entitled *Growth, Competitiveness, Employment: The Challenges and Ways Forward into the 21st Century*, where the challenges "were reduced to issues of employment and the economy" (Edwards et al. 1998:19), and where lifelong learning was already one of its cornerstones for future policies in these areas (Field 2001:9).

A good example of the early interest of Employers in lifelong learning and the learning society is found in the opening statements of a 1994 report published by the European Round Table of Industrialists (ERT), entitled (anticipating the title of the EU's white paper) *Education for Europeans: Towards the Learning Society* (Cornelis et al. 1994). In a sense, reading its opening statements creates a sensation of déjà vu. Like the Faure report, it refers to the urgency "to raise a *cry of alarm* to alert society to [the] educational gap" between the education that people need for today's complex world and the education they receive in schools (1994:6, italics in original). A similar "cry of alarm" had already been raised earlier across the Atlantic in the United States by the Carnegie Commission, in a report called *A Nation at Risk* (Superintendent of Documents 1983). Like the writers of the movement, the authors of the Round Table report complained that the standard schooling provision currently supplied by European educational systems is out of phase with the realities of the contemporary world and requires urgent revision. It referred to "dangerous gaps" in skills, curricula, and funding, "as they threaten Europe's ability to meet the new and complex challenges to today's world," particularly in economic competitiveness and democratic ideals, though unemployment and social marginalization were other negative trends (1994:14). It declared that industry must combat them by involving itself at all levels of the formal education system, by implementing relevant vocational curricula in schools, launching new European initiatives in adult education, innovating media production and management, and "re-motivat[ing] teachers." But it took good care to blunt its generally vocationalist tone with statements like: "The primary purpose of education is to develop each individual to become a whole human being, not just to become an economic resource" (1994:16). Such a statement would have been superfluous were it not for its recognition that its general tone could raise suspicions that its thinking was precisely along the latter lines.

Reassuring sprinklings of social democracy, as Field (2001) says, were in fact typical of the reports of the time. *Teaching and Learning: Towards the Learning Society* (1995:74) says that "the future of Europe and its place in the world depend on its ability to give as much room for the personal fulfillment of its citizens, men and women alike, as it has given to economic and monetary issues," and reminds its readers that Europe "is not simply a free trade area, but an organized political entity." While I do not question their sincerity, it is strange that these objectives of personal fulfillment and democracy could find no place among the five central objectives that the white paper identified as priorities for building the learning society of the future: encouraging the acquisition of new knowledge, bringing schools and the business sector close together, combating problems of exclusion (in the specific sense of creating more second-chance opportunities for the unemployed), encouraging proficiency in three Community languages for the purpose of labor transfer, and treating capital investment and investment on training on an equal basis; all of them priorities relating to the world of labor and human capital, i.e., to the interests of business and the economy. Even social exclusion is included, as Raggatt et al. (1996) remarked, as a problem related to employment rather than to democracy, personal growth or, indeed, social justice. And this bias is understandable since the white paper reflected perfectly the views of the mainly neoliberal governments in power in Europe at the time, who were scarcely interested in putting the issue of lifelong learning and of the learning society on their agenda differently, as part of a wider debate on social justice and welfare.

Indeed, so powerful was the Employers' economic agenda that skeptical commentators like Raggatt et al. and Hughes and Tight doubted the honesty of the references made in their reports to the other forces of change and disorientation at work in contemporary society also cited as the justification of lifelong learning. Their real purpose, for Raggatt et al. (1996:2), was to lend credibility and urgency to the economic agenda, and little more. As Edwards et al. (1998) noted, much of the operational vocabulary in the evolving discourse on lifelong learning and the learning society was continuous with that of the lifelong education writers in the 1970s. It re-proposed the maximalist project's central conviction that "'learning' in its *global* form" should be the "center point of discussion" and recognized its *lifewide* (a term that has come into fashion again) significance: that "it takes place in different settings—in the workplace, the home, in groups or alone—and not only, or primarily, in formal education settings"; it called for the mobilization of learning resources; referred to the same need for *self-directed* learning; and used the language of non-formal and informal learning (though the latter with the difference of meaning described earlier). What was essentially different was its agenda. Where the movement's writers resolved the tension between the wider cultural, social, and political goals that have traditionally been identified with education, and the vocational goals dictated by the labor market and the exigencies of new technologies, in favor of the former, the situation was now reversed. Now it was the vocational goals tied to the interests of business and the economy that achieved priority. Moreover, as Raggatt et al. remarked, in the mid to late 1990s, this agenda commanded considerably more "general and widespread recognition and acceptance" where it mattered, at the political level, than had the agenda of the radical educationalists of the movement thirty years earlier.

Of, course, not everybody regards this as negative. Apologists for the Employers' agenda deny that it should cause concern, arguing that as the economy becomes more information-based and the mode of labor shifts from manual work to knowledge work, it is reasonable to expect concern with the continuous growth and learning of employees to increase of its own accord. This is because it will be required by the conditions of work that will demand of employees that they should function well in groups, exercise considerable self-discipline, and exhibit loyalties at the same time as they maintain a critical outlook toward things and respect each others' rights—all virtues and characteristics required also by citizens in democracies. Indeed, some ESRC reports even attempted to articulate the business community's vision of a learning society with an explicit democratic agenda:

> A learning society would be one in which all citizens acquire a high quality general education, appropriate vocational training, and a job (or series of jobs) worthy of a human being while continuing to participate in education and training throughout their lives. A learning society, would combine excellence with equity and would equip all its citizens with the knowledge, understanding and skills to ensure national economic prosperity and much more besides... Citizens of a learning society would, by means of their continuing education and training, be able to engage in critical dialogue and actions to improve the quality of life for the whole community and to ensure social integration as well as economic success. (Hughes and Tight 1995:296)

One could hardly quarrel with an agenda like that. And Bradshaw (1995:8) is another who warns us not to demonize the Employer, who, he says, is by and large someone who recognizes her employees as persons and not just resources to be used and manipulated, and who encourages and sponsors learning that "is for the worker as a person as well as an employee."

But Raggatt et al. (1996:5) are skeptical of this language, complaining, on the basis of the contributions to their book, that the Employers' real agenda lacked any civic concern, while the state, completely insensitive to "the gaps developing in civic culture," withdrew its support from adult education and abandoned it to the market and the leisure industry. And, indeed, this is the picture that emerges from the contributions to their book: of a nonvocational adult education sector that had shrunk drastically in the early and mid-1990s due to underinvestment and neglect. Several of the writers in the book also specifically rubbished the view that postindustrial workplaces have a more democratic character than the industrial or are good places for cultivating the values and skills of democratic citizenship. Quicke (1997:143), elsewhere, contended the very opposite: that workers actually have less security and less possibility to be critical in the contemporary workplace. Quoting Green, he doubted "the extent to which new technologies and new work organizations have generated a high skill, reflexive workforce," and even more the extent to which workplaces have become more equal and democratic. To the contrary, "what has emerged in recent years," he said, "is a social differentiation which looks more like a new hierarchical structure rather than one where difference merely reflects diversity of occupation and life style. Workers," he continued, "may need to have higher skills and to be more cognitively engaged than previously but they have less security and less opportunity for being 'critical'" (1997:143). Rinne (1998:115), extending the metaphor of the risk society to the postindustrial scene, wrote about "a society of risk-prone underemployment, where people live under the constant shadow of the fear of losing their livelihood and the purpose of their lives." Where "persistent underemployment, a discontinuous working career, and straightforward unemployment move to the center of a life full of choices involving risk and risk-prone choices" (1998:116). And, for Christina Hughes and Malcolm Tight (1995:297), employers regard the learning society only as the answer to their own economic aspirations, and the way they actually prioritize economic over social goals "seems likely to marginalize the interests of individuals in pursuing learning for their own 'self-fulfillment,'" rather than otherwise.

Learning Organizations

One notion growing within the lifelong learning vocabulary of the 1990s and absent from that of the lifelong education writers is that of the *learning organization*. In its last page the European Round Table report (1994:32) echoed Ball's claim that "European companies are (or are rapidly becoming) learning organizations." There is a lot of literature about learning organizations today. Learning organizations are conceived as microlearning "societies." Their emergence coincides with the perception that *ad hoc* courses no longer serve the ongoing development of the organization's human resources adequately, and the postindustrial perception of the workplace as a place where knowledge is produced. Some, despite the rhetoric, contest the current reality of the learning organization, just as some doubt that learning societies actually exist; Hughes and Tight (1995:301), for instance, who believe that "the idea of the learning society has no current empirical reality ... in a country like the United Kingdom," though they concede the power of the "myth" that it does. Those who doubt the reality of a learning organization say similar things about it. For Alan Jones (1995:111), for instance, "much of what is considered to be a theory of a learning organization is simply anecdotal rhetoric. At best, the concept of a learning organization as currently understood and propounded," he says, "seems capable of acting as an initial rallying call throughout an organization to cascade mission and vision statements, but provides little clue as to its usefulness, other than perhaps to superficially knee-jerk the organization into considering training and development."

Others disagree, and recent years have seen the already substantial literature on the subject grow rather than decrease, to include examples of "actual" learning organizations. Contrary to Jones, Ruth Waterman, Judith Waterman, and Betsy Collard (1996), for instance, assessed the future of the learning organization positively, claiming, like Ball, to perceive a discernable trend for workplaces everywhere to develop toward increasing self-dependence and the ability to respond rapidly and effectively to unpredictable change in the industrial and service worlds. What is more important here, as with the learning society, is not whether learning organizations exist or not *as an empirical fact*, because this eventually turns on how one defines them, but that a growing number of people in industry believe that they do and perceive them as the way into the future, a target to aim for, an aspiration to have. Believing in something makes it real in the very important sense that people act as though it were real, and it conditions their thinking. So that, as Jones says, in the case of the learning organization the fact that they believe in it, whether that belief is justified or not, has "knee-jerked" industrial organizations everywhere into reconsidering their training and human resource development programs to follow its line of thinking. The importance of the notion of the learning organization from our point of view is that it provides us with a clue of what the learning society could look like with its agenda set by employers. Describing it theoretically, in fact, despite what Jones says, is not hard since there are several accounts of it going about. Early on, the 1993 Eurotechnet publication (Bradshaw 1995:108) described it as a setup in which "the process of learning is permanent not intermittent, holistic not segmented, problem centered, context related and includes all members of the enterprise. The learning organization," it continued, "brings the strategy, structure and culture of the enterprise itself into a learning system. Management development is transformed into a self-learning and self-management process. The transformation of the whole system for greater competitiveness is the goal!" In short, as with a learning society, the learning organization is mobilized for learning. Indeed, in this definition, it is a learning society with an explicit performativist agenda. One notes the reference to self-management, which, as we saw, coincides with the EU's lifelong learning literature.

One also notes that, as a model, it has already extended beyond the world of business and industrial enterprise into the world of education. Edwards (1997:143) has remarked that although it is still generally associated with the commercial environments where it originated, it "has come to have a wider applicability, partly as a result of changes in the public and voluntary sectors, wherein organizations have had to restructure to become flexible and entrepreneurial." And this applicability extends to educational "organizations" from schools to universities, where quality management and criteria of performativity are written into mission statements everywhere. Jerry Bamburg (1997:2), director of the Center for Effective Schools of the University of Washington, has argued explicitly for schools to become learning organizations on the grounds that the schools we need today are those that recognize the needs of tomorrow's workforce. We need schools, he says, that recognize that students need "to possess the knowledge and skills that will make it possible for them to access information, work harmoniously with those around them, and utilize the higher order thinking skills that are needed in a knowledge-based economy." Bamburg is making the same case for self-directed learning as in the Eurydice report (2000) quoted earlier, and as in Eurotechnet's definition of the learning organization, in the interest not of self-fulfillment but employability and the economy. In short, learning organizations encapsulate the philosophy of performativity very well and are tempting models for neoliberal governments (and neosocial democrat too, as we shall see in Chapter 5) that have already transferred the language and practices of business into the world of formal education, to harness the notion of lifelong learning and of the learning society to their policy-making too. Hughes and Tight, in fact, specifically identified the learning organization as one of the key concepts developing within the managerialist and vocationalist discourse on the two notions in the mid-1990s. In sum, a lifelong learning policy agenda linked with the vision of a learning society revolving around the requirements of the economy, modeled on the notion of a learning organization, reacting to individualist and managerialist philosophies, and answering to the dictates of performativity in the name of economic prosperity, is not that far-fetched. This is how Ball (Coffield 1996:3) outlined his vision of the learning society in 1996:

> My vision is for every individual to have a Personal Learning Plan (PLAN)...
> and every organization to become a Learning Organization... the key principle
> governing provision for and pursuit of learning in the future must be the primacy
> of personal responsibility for learning, encouraged and enabled by the support of
> the whole community... The focus of the campaign will be on individuals rather
> than on the providers of education and training.

Having or Being?

As we shall see later, this vision, shared by the Commission of Social Justice (see below and Chapter 5) proved attractive to the Labour government in Britain that came into power in the late 1990s. Here I want to elaborate on my earlier statement about the growing decline of adult education throughout the 1990s. It will be recalled that the lifelong education writers regarded this sector as the potential catalyst for radical change in education systems and hoped for a learning society resting on an alliance between a powerful and popular lifelong education movement and a state prepared to play the role of senior partner. In 1975 Lengrand (73) believed that even if "in most countries adult education is still a poor relation," such a partnership was possible. The "large-scale participation by the state" he believed necessary because "the resources that individuals and associations can bring together are and will always be far below the magnitude of the objectives set up for education" (1975:74). He saw the rise of an emancipatory adult education movement in the post–World War II era after generations of domesticated workers submitted themselves to the regimen of the evening class and the traditional teacher in their search for better conditions and to satisfy their desire for knowledge and understanding through instruction. Today's workers, he believed, recognized that regimen for what it was: an instrument of assimilation and conformity to a conservative bourgeois culture exalting the values of the past, of inheritance, and of order and security, at the expense of those of struggle, innovation, and openness. Their revolt took the form of a new, progressive kind of adult education born and nurtured away from the paths of school and the traditional university, in peoples' colleges and universities, organizations for mutual education, workers' cooperatives, associations for workers' education, and so on. In Lengrand's vision of things, from being subjected to education the adult would become the instrument of her own education, thus taking control of her life. Lengrand's optimism that such a movement was possible owed itself to his experiences of comradeship and cooperative organization in the French Resistance during the War, which he thought could be transferred to the struggle for education. He regarded the variety of experimental initiatives that were currently at work in the field of non-formal adult education, and in which he was himself much involved, as the first moves toward creating such a movement.

This kind of vision was in shambles in the early and mid-1990s when the only alliance neoliberal governments were prepared to enter into was with business and industry. The extent of the decline in adult education everywhere in Europe only just over two decades after Lengrand's book is described by Arthur Stock and Albert Tuijnman in different articles in Raggatt et al. (1996). Using various statistics, they show how in Britain and other European countries the consolidation and expansion of continuing vocational training had coincided with a sharp decline of provision for adult education. Raggatt et al. (1996:3) explained it by observing that in most European countries "adult education has never featured as a significant component of social policy and has only a weak statutory legislative base," and that in most European countries there was a "lack of any history of adult education as part of social policy" (1996:5). Thus, what Lengrand had optimistically regarded as its strength a quarter of a century before, its growing independence and experimentation, turned out in the 1990s to be its undoing. Even where a strong tradition of state investment in adult education had long existed, in the Nordic countries in particular, a number of authors in Raggatt et al. remarked that the trend was for private investment to surpass state expenditure in the sector, which went increasingly toward adult vocational training. Raggatt et al. also confirmed the growing tendency in the lifelong learning discourse to make the individual responsible for selecting what and where to learn (a trend that, evidently, discourages the idea of a movement), contrasting it with the thrust of earlier writing on the learning society like Lengrand's, which argued for the state's responsibility to provide lifelong learning resources for its citizens as their right, and as a welfare service. It was not the case, Raggatt et al. remarked, that the state was "absolved" from all responsibility for providing these resources, but the logic of the market, they argued, pointed toward this strong individualism, and the state was taking advantage of it.

Far from encouraging and aiding independent non-formal adult education agencies to grow, the neoliberal state minimized its responsibility for adult education and invested in learning needs intimately tied with vocational training, employability, and job retraining, otherwise leaving the learning society to take care of itself. Its general thinking was to decrease wastage and "the quality, internal efficiency and cost-effectiveness of adult education and training would improve." Which meant, in concrete terms, that adult education became increasingly "part and parcel of the commodity market, to be developed, bought and sold under conditions of competitiveness and profitability" (Tuijnman 1996:40). Raggatt et al. (1996:5), like Albert Tuijnman, discerned this same "shift in language" whereby "vocational activities [are] justified as 'investment' whereas non-vocational activities are rejected as consumption, a matter for individual decisions and choices." This was an occurrence that Lengrand and Suchodolski, as I said in Chapter 1, had predicted as possible in the 1970s. They had perceived a trend lurking within the market culture of advanced capitalism to project learning as a commodity, a possession to be had, an asset to be gained, rather than as a matter of self-fulfillment, of being. And writer after writer in Raggatt et al.'s book, referring to recent history, confirmed that trend, reflected also in the virtual disappearance of the concerns with equity and entitlement—which were historically integral to the growth of adult education everywhere—from the debate about lifelong learning. Not only that, Stock and Tuijnman, respectively, identified an equally troubling trend toward a massive decline over the years in the participation of various sections of the population in the vocational sector itself. Of older people in particular—despite the current reality of an aging society in most of the more economically developed countries of the world—but also of other sectors of the adult population: minority ethnic groups, the long-term unemployed, those in semiskilled and unskilled occupations, women (particularly, but not only, single mothers with dependent children), those living in rural and remote areas, and so on. Predictably, several authors in Raggatt et al.'s book also revealed trends in Europe that showed that those most at risk of not continuing with any further learning after compulsory schooling were those whose schooling experience was poor to begin with. These were the people least likely to benefit from the resources available on the learning market. Those caught in a vicious circle that allows no exit; whose learning needs or desires are not seen to justify "investment," who have few or no personal inducements and resources to go it alone, and are, therefore, in a no-win position.

This picture of gloom and doom in adult education, however, was not something everyone accepted. Strain and Field (1997:148), for example, responding to Hughes and Tight's (1995) gloomy assessment of the contemporary reality of the learning society, quoted data to support their claim that things were very different. The statistics emerging from different reports, they said, were positive, indicating increases in the numbers of adult learners in different countries. "It is relatively easy," in the economically advanced countries at least, they said, "to provide evidence of a significant societal shift towards patterns of lifelong learning" that make for a learning society. Numbers, however, do not tell the whole story. Tom Schuller (1998:13), for instance, argues that notwithstanding the expansion in numbers in higher education over the years, the student profile had remained largely the same, the mode of study (full-time/part-time) had not altered much either, and the main attraction of higher education was still that it pays in financial terms. In short, he suggested, it "has not altered its balance or shape significantly towards one of lifelong learning—in spite of the great increased numbers of continuing education students on short courses." Hughes and Tight's despondency over current adult education provision, despite the statistics, in fact, stemmed from the huge numbers who were left out because of the cultural, social, and economic obstacles they found in their path. The authors wanted to assess progress toward the learning society not in terms of the numbers in but of the numbers out, and of the social distribution of those in and out.

Strain and Field (1997:149) also reacted to Hughes and Tight's point about the marginalization of the motive of self-fulfillment in the current discourse of lifelong learning by observing that "the increase [in numbers] appears to be fueled in large part by precisely those concerns for individual growth which Hughes and Tight seek to define." But again, in this sense what worried Hughes and Tight is how growth, or self-fulfillment as they preferred to call it, is conceived and, again, its social distribution. While, for instance, the increasing number of individuals investing in their own personal growth through open or distance learning undoubtedly contributes to the creation of a learning society, what lies behind it, according to Field (1996:146) himself, is "commercial, technological and cultural trends [that] combine with one another to reinforce [its] appeal ... to a consumer market which currently shows every sign of growth without limit." Available on demand, well publicized, and in theory open to all, distance learning does undoubtedly, as he says, open access to new channels and modes of learning. It does create hitherto unavailable links between the educational and domestic worlds, opening up previously unavailable learning possibilities for the homebound, encouraging individual initiative, and creating a broad and varied choice of learning options for people. But it matters that its rationale is essentially consumerist, its mentality market-oriented, and that it represents knowledge as a prepackaged object that is bought, sold, and consumed; a consumer item among others. It matters that what is driving this culture of growth or self-fulfillment is not an interest in being and becoming but in having and possessing. It also matters, at least to me, and to those who are like-minded, that growth is available only to those who *really* have access to it; those culturally attuned to further learning, who can afford it financially, and who are alert to its value. Namely, those who already possess the right economic, cultural, and educational resources, or "capital," to begin with, and who are disposed to turn them into resources for their own further self-fulfillment or economic progress.

What is most worrying is the fact that, as Field (1996:140) admitted, it is not just open and distance learning that is prone to "display many of the classic characteristics of consumerism" but adult education, which is being cast as part of the leisure industry, in general. This does not seem to worry him overmuch, partly because he disagrees that "the cultural processes of communication which surround adult education are simply examples of 'consumer culture'" (1996:142). And partly because he believes that regarding adult learners as consumers is reasonable in economic terms, given the history of modern education with all its inbuilt prejudices in favor of schooling. Nor does he seem to worry that much of the latest growth in non-vocational adult learning is home-based and related to attempts at personal change rather than public and cooperative, and that the fact that it typically involves individuals reasonably familiar and confident with the communications media and relatively well educated, renders it the terrain of "the new petit bourgeoisie," as he says, and thereby elitist. He rejects the charge of elitism, in fact, arguing that the market of individual consumers had grown faster than anticipated and in unexpected and unpredictable directions, and that this fact makes hasty generalizations about elitism and consumerism dangerous. He also argues that, whatever may be the case with distance learning, there are always the more traditional settings of adult education (such as extramural classes) where learning continues to be cooperative and social and accessible to all. But whatever one thinks of his rejection of elitism, this last assumption is one he is not entitled to, given the pattern of neglect and decreasing investment precisely in this area. Indeed, it was the erosion of these settings more than the trend to invest in vocational learning that created the greatest concern for many advocates of adult education, who found a good part of its space eroded by the market-driven forces of open learning and by the new vocationalism (Taylor 1998:308).

But Field contests this thesis about market forces and the new vocationalism driving out adult education. He also assesses trends in open and distance learning toward employing forms that combine learning with entertainment positively. And, from a pedagogical point of view, he is right. But this is very different from casting nonvocational adult learning culturally as entertainment or akin to it, as falling within the ambit of the leisure industry rather than education. For this is the surest way to disqualify it from any state-supported assistance or public funding and render it strictly the individual's business, which is what the neoliberal governments did. Not to mention the fact that associating it with leisure justifies characterizing it as an instrument of the market, which is again what the neoliberal state wanted, since leisure today is perceived as yet another economic sector. It is therefore much more amenable to the rhetoric of enterprise and business than "to the age-old dream of free association, rest from work, play, a feeling of community and the creation of art and culture" that inspired the early ideals of the learning society (Worpole 1996:113). And this translates into "museum charges, savage cuts in adult education spending, residential college closures, cuts in extra-mural classes, local government cuts in public leisure provision, reduced opening hours (and in some cases, closure) for libraries, reduced spending on parks and gardens, no new government investment in public facilities, cuts in grants to voluntary arts organizations, legislation to make parents pay for educational visits and trips" (Worpole 1996:117). These are measures that "ensure that the private sector leisure industry will prosper and older traditions associated with the public realm will disappear and die" (Worpole 1996:117). Which is precisely what is happening in media broadcasting also, where "the public service tradition is being undermined in order to allow a deregulated and more profitable market to take over" (Worpole 1996:117). In short, the net result of associating it with the leisure industry is that non-vocational adult learning has been largely personalized and privatized, cast in the role of consumer item in the learning industry, consigned to the realm of the market, and rendered more inaccessible to the poor and the marginalized than it has ever been.

Considerations of this kind lead van der Zee (1996:165) to argue for the need to distinguish the learning society from the information society rather than to fuse them together as I do. It is not "the availability of information (i.e., knowledge), but the acquisition of knowledge" through active learning, he contends, that makes a learning society. He criticizes statements like Patricia Cross's that "the learning society is growing because it is a must" as careless confusion, and rebuts them with the remark that "an information society is still not an informed society" (1996:165).[28] Indeed, "the evidence is otherwise" today, he contends, where we find "a society in which the pressure from technology and the economy is so great that people, the users of the information, feel defeated," rather than informed, much less educated. "If we do not take action," he warns, "an inhuman, highly technocratic society lies ahead of us (see, for example, Martin 1988, and Roszak 1986)" (1996:164). This is because the missing element in the metaphor of the information society, van der Zee argues, is people; how they should link up with the information, and this is what a theory of the learning society must provide. The notion of the learning society, he contends, directs attention toward the dynamics of the relations between information and information technology on the one side, and the individual and the community on the other. He then proceeds to set out what he takes to be healthy criteria for the development of a learning society, which are virtually the same criteria as those defined by the lifelong education movement's writers of over thirty years ago. Namely:

(1) broadening the definition of learning to include education as a dimension of society, or lifewide learning;
(2) directing the goal of learning as growth toward individual "completeness," which, he acknowledges, cannot be defined except very generically as the pursuit of quality and all-around development;
(3) going beyond learning and instruction (by increasing collective competence, or the ability to act given the availability of support systems);
(4) fostering autonomy in learning (self-education, or self-directed learning, which includes learning to learn); and
(5) stressing a political approach to learning (or the right to learn). (1996:165)

Adult Education as a Welfare Right

This last condition, the lifelong right to learn, conceived not just as a freedom but as a welfare right, is what is conspicuously missing from the contemporary discourse of the learning society today. Dewey (1966a:51) made the case for it eloquently when he claimed that "a living creature lives as truly and positively at one stage as at another, with ... the same absolute claims," and "hence education means the enterprise of applying the conditions which insure growth, or adequacy of life, irrespective of age." One would be hard-pressed to put it better or more succinctly than that. Today, however, while the discourse about consumer rights grows stronger, the claim that lifelong learning can constitute a welfare right grows less and less credible. Part of the blame for this lies in the emphasis on self-dependence that underpins it, and in the current crisis of the welfare state, political, economic, and cultural. The latter trend puts the language of welfare rights in general under pressure, never mind the right to learn. Apart from other problems with the welfare state, as Robin Usher and Richard Edwards (1994) point out, focusing social policy on the needy and "disadvantaged" was unproblematic while the narrative of emancipation that lent it credibility was still powerful in the modern world, but this is no longer the case in the postmodern where the language of social justice has lost much of its power over people's imagination. The performativity criterion and the right to indefinite consumption is what persuades instead of social justice and needs satisfaction. Usher and Edwards (1994:178) contend that what drives the agenda of the learning society today is "the constant possibility for continuing education for the elite, but not necessarily for other groups, thereby perpetuating differences, if not injustices, depending upon the language game one is moving within." The truth, however, is that the case for adult education welfare rights has never been forcefully made in the public sphere with any sense of urgency or conviction, so that, despite Lengrand's hopes, there has never really been any acknowledgment of such a case by the general public. Nor has it—apart from exceptions like Dewey, the lifelong education writers, and R.W.K. Paterson (1979) (who argued for a right to a liberal education)—interested philosophers of education much.

The explanation of this last fact lies partly in the history of philosophy of education, and partly in the fact that the modern discourse about education has always been characterized as a discourse about mass schooling, a coercive practice that no society with liberal values would think of enforcing on its adults. So that the mention of adult welfare rights to education inspires suspicion that one means to put adults under the state's or some other agency's paternalistic supervision, and reinforces the view that the only educational rights for adults worth discussing are freedom rights. Paterson is a good example of this way of thinking. While arguing for the right of adults to a liberal education, he dismissed the suggestion that this right has anything to do with social justice. He also dismissed arguments that educational resources should be distributed on utilitarian grounds, or on the grounds of people's needs, or as compensation for opportunities denied them in their childhood, or to offset social or economic disadvantage. "We must," he insisted, in line with today's thinking, "expect the adult to be capable of taking charge of his own private life; we must treat him as essentially an autonomous agent" (1979:247). But he also regarded (as did Dewey and the lifelong education writers) the right to self-preservation, or survival, as the most basic of rights, so that assistance given to individuals in this respect is "among the most grave and binding duties of any society," an "inescapable" duty to help each of its members make the most of her life by acquiring knowledge of "who he is and where he is, what kind of a being he is and what kind of situation he finds himself in" (1979:232).[29] He just does not regard this knowledge as "education."

At first glance it seems surprising then that, in the climate of the mid-1990s, we find the Commission on Social Justice in Britain (1996) arguing that lifelong learning is a human right and that a moral obligation therefore exists to make it available to all. But, the Commission continued to argue, recognizing the state's obligation to assist individuals in their lifelong learning need not necessarily mean directly financing them. It could be represented as a right of *access* to credit from a "Learning Bank" instead, jointly funded by the state, the individuals concerned, and their employers, but managed by the *individuals*, who would draw on their account to pay for the services of public and private providers of learning themselves, rather than the state or some other funding agency. The scheme's main features would be: (1) to fund adult learning on an equitable basis, with no discrimination between different types of learning; (2) to build on a credit-based system of learning, allowing mobility and choice between formal courses and institutions; (3) to provide the flexibility of Individual Learning Accounts with which to fund education and training; and, last but not least, (4) to promote the joint funding of learning (Raggatt et al. 1996:200). Fully functional, the Commission claimed, the Learning Bank "would allow individuals, government and employers to fund lifelong learning in a way which attracts private capital, allows individual choice and flexibility, and promotes equity of access" (Raggatt et al. 1996:204). In 1996 Raggatt et al. (7) viewed this strategy positively, as the most equitable at the time. Despite the fact that it did not address the problem of those marginalized by insufficient initial formal education and financial resources, it relies, as they point out, "on individuals viewing personal investment as a realistic choice," nor does it cater to the unemployed. But it is obviously not a *human* right to continuing education at all, nor one based on social justice, but a conditioned right tied to one's status as an employee.

The authors highlight other, technical problems with the scheme: with accreditation and quality assurance, for instance. But its really serious problem, as I see it, is this sociopolitical one: the fact that it still puts the opportunity for lifelong learning beyond the means of the unemployed or unemployable. It is not an indiscriminate right to lifelong learning "from the cradle to the grave" but to continuing learning for so long as one is employed. Moreover, even among employees, its subscribers would most likely be those in relatively high profile jobs and positions; the educated employed who, as Raggatt et al. remarked, perceive investment in further learning as an investment in their career and life prospects. Not only does it fail to address, never mind redress, the situation of the unemployed, it also fails to address the problem of non-participation of the more vulnerable members of the risk society, those with no initial investment to make—economic, cultural, or educational—and who typically even lack the motivation to continue learning. In sum, notwithstanding that it was proposed by a "Social Justice Commission," the scheme has nothing to do with social justice as the left has understood it in the past, since the right to learn that it acknowledges depends not on a moral entitlement based on a just distribution that safeguards the needy (as befits social justice) but on one's membership in a Bank and the scale of one's investment in it. Also, although it does benefit some, possibly many, it perpetuates the culture of learning as a marketable good to be purchased with bank loans. Besides, though in theory there is no discrimination of the kind of learning that qualifies for the scheme, vocational and skills training are likely to receive special encouragement and priority, especially since the scheme's sponsors are, after all, employers and governments. Indeed, this encouragement is plainly seen in the British Labour Government's Green Paper (Department for Education and Employment, 1998), which eventually adopted it (see Chapter 5). Also, the scheme is clearly more appropriate for short-term vocational adult learning where the tradition of buying into short courses addressing specific and readily identified needs and demands has a long history and is synchronized with a business orientation, rather than a non-vocational learning that corresponds with the more long-term vision of self-fulfillment and personal growth.

Given this criticism, Illich's scheme of providing "edu-credit cards" on a once-for-all basis for everyone at the outset of their lives would seem to be more equitable. In Illich's eyes it would ensure that no one is disadvantaged from buying one's way into and through the system by lack of economic resources, and it would still be managed by the learner. It would also seem cleaner, more aboveboard, and simpler to operate, not subject to messy assessments or to the agendas or hidden pressures of employers or state bureaucrats. It would really put the choice of their learning into the hands of individuals. At the same time it would not be indefinite, as an economic proposition. It would exonerate the state from any obligation to finance the individual's learning beyond its initial outlay, though it would require a permanent counseling and advisory service, to assist people in the best use of their credit, which the state would presumably pay for. His system would again, however, leave the learning entirely to the mercy of the market, with experts acting like stock=brokers to advise one on the most advantageous investment of one's capital in the learning market that would replace formal schooling. It would not ensure strict equality of opportunity either. One would presumably have a right to supplement one's allowance from the state with further investment of one's own if one could afford it. This being the case, those who could afford it would still enjoy an advantage over those who could not, or those whose financial means were more limited. van der Zee (1996:178) has expressed skepticism over the idea of presenting educational vouchers to individuals, arguing that the system "does not lead to an enlargement but to a contraction of the opportunities for learning." His explanation is that social security arrangements in the welfare state in other areas of life using the voucher system have failed. And Michael Peters (1996:96), referring to a 1987 review by Boris Frankel, puts Illich among the "post-industrialist utopians" (Alvin Toffler, Rudolf Bahro, and Andre Gorz), who pictured education as the largest future industry requiring high levels of investment and advocated the radical decentralization of future educational systems and the need to move to demassified and "prosuming" forms of education. Peters criticizes these views for corresponding with free-market forms of decentralization within postindustrial society, which permit a diversity of "education" but at the expense of social inequalities between different income groups and regions. He is also concerned that the marketization of education in the demassified and decentralized form they envisage "is a recipe for increased social atomization, isolation and conflict."

Lynn Tett (1996:152) has argued, however, that lack of cultural capital may be a more significant factor behind educational disadvantage than the economic. Quoting McGivney, she contends that many adults fail to participate in adult education not because of cost or lack of time. These, she says, tend to be excuses fetched to "serve as a socially acceptable or face-saving reason" for non-participation. The true reasons are rather "because powerful constraints arise from cultural and social class divisions" that are replicated in schooling, and because of the influences of family background that condition one's value system. Although she acknowledges the practical reality of obstacles like lack of time, money, transport, daytime facilities, childcare, and so on, it is dispositional factors, she holds—namely attitudes, perceptions, and expectations—that constitute the most powerful barrier to adults learning. Tett's argument against deschooling is that deprived of an intermediary institution like the school to help them, families of the kind she describes have little chance of profiting by, or even making any sense of, the system proposed by Illich. The problem of adult non-participation in learning, in fact, is probably a combination of all the factors mentioned earlier by Tett and others, and there is probably no single solution to it. Tett (1996:156), quoting Edwards, remarks that the market model "'condemns us all to structures of inequality,'" and that these will remain with us as long as it persists, and she is certainly right. The question is whether there is any other model available today as the battering of the welfare state continues.

Finally, Charles Bailey (1988:123) has suggested an approach to solidarity with others in their lifelong education other than regarding it as a welfare right that could be more promising, based on a Kantian argument that begins by representing lifelong education as a duty one owes oneself as part of one's more general moral obligation to cultivate one's "natural powers (of the spirit, of the mind, and of the body) as a means to all kinds of possible ends," most particularly becoming autonomous. Bailey moves on to argue for a similar duty one owes to others to assist them with their lifelong education as an aspect of one's more general duty to help them lead an autonomous life. This description of moral solidarity avoids the difficulties of justifying adult education as a human or moral right. Besides, the claim that each of us has a moral duty to improve ourselves through learning is one many would consider more reasonable than the claim that adult education is a moral right that can be claimed against the state and the community. As we saw in the previous chapter, the lifelong education writers championed a learning society based both on the common recognition of this duty of self-improvement through learning and on the recognition of a mutual and joint responsibility of all its members to assist each other in their learning, though they also wanted to represent lifelong education as a right that could be pressed morally by individuals, not just as citizens against the state but also as members against the social institutions with which they mix their lives and of which they are themselves a product.

Counterdiscourse, Utopia?

Many in the mid-1990s, like Raggatt et al. (1996), were skeptical that the trends in adult learning described in this chapter would be reversed or even modified in any foreseeable future, or that any more humane model of a learning society, less economy driven than that emerging at the time, was in the offing. They were even pessimistic that any state initiative could achieve much or could be any more than a slow, fragmentary, and contested process. Nor was there any consolation in Hughes and Tight's (1995) claim that, in Britain at least, the learning society was still a myth with no empirical basis to it; an "initial rallying call" to action rather than a well-defined strategy, so that like the Faure Report, it would end up in the waste-bin of history; for rallying calls and slogans *can* have decisive effects if they are backed with the necessary political clout and initiative. The important consideration is whose slogan it is and who sets the agenda. And employers and the EU Commission, as Field pointed out, are a very different kettle of fish from UNESCO commissions where political clout is concerned.

The point I am driving at here is that a discourse that starts as a piece of myth-making or a slogan can become a reality if it succeeds in mobilizing enough support on its behalf and has powerful political backing. Hughes and Tight themselves acknowledged as much when they made it clear that by referring to it as a "myth" they were not thereby dismissing the notion of the learning society as so much pie in the sky. To the contrary, they warned that "myths can become very powerful for developing alternative visions, mobilizing rhetoric and leading people through change," when they "become organizing principles on which policy and practice are based" (1995:291). They are attractive because they offer "a superficially simple solution to what are manifestly extremely complex economic and social issues" (1995:301) and "despite (their) practical lack of achievement," they tend to extend their lives across generations, building on or recycling earlier myths, thus gaining the power of platitudes, "draw[ing] upon the energies of disparate power groups" and enabling them to create alliances (1995:302). Hughes and Tight (1995:302) recognized that the myth of the learning society going about at the time was "an ideological concept serving ideological purposes," not some harmless fantasy of a few theorists or radical writers, and that it gained credibility by drawing selectively on illustrative examples that appeal "to populist and commonsense reasoning" in order to render itself convincing. And this raised the question for them of what to do in these circumstances. How could one resist its ascendancy?

One obvious answer could be to create a countermyth or project, a different utopia or vision that would challenge the prevalent myth, a banner under which a movement could fight. This was what I was intending when I was planning to write this book—to take up the challenge of theorizing a counterproject for a learning society of social democrat inspiration, using the model of an education research project for my purpose. Aspin and Chapman (2000:13) disagree with this approach and propose a way forward instead that avoids being "bogged down," as they put it, in the debate between maximalists like myself and critics like Bagnall, namely, abandoning the paradigm of an education research project for a "pragmatic approach" where one looks "at the circumstances in which various theories and policies of lifelong education have been articulated, developed and applied," adopting them as our "objective referent" so that "we might attempt to see how, why, and in response to what pressures and quandaries the various versions of lifelong education have been developed or are in play and can be seen to be at work in the attention policy-makers devote to them, before attempting to assess how far these policies and practices have succeeded in addressing the problems that policy-makers are attempting to address." This "pragmatic" approach, in fact, satisfies part of the scope of the education research project, the empirical and explanatory but not the theoretical and constructive.[30] Indeed, my view in *PLE* was that the research project can be put to two uses: either as a tool with which to rationalize the actual competing education discourses as lifelong education discourses (which resembles what Aspin and Chapman suggest), or as a constructive tool to create utopian new ones. But Aspin and Chapman prefer to focus narrowly on particular running *programs* (the "objective referent"), rather than deal with them as part of all-embracing projects. In this way they can safely ignore the normative or ideological issues the latter holistic approach raises (unless, that is, the "pressures and quandaries" they intend are also ideological, but this seems unlikely), and simply measure the success or otherwise of the programs in terms of their problem-solving capacity. It sounds like Gelpi (1984b:85), who described the pragmatic turn in the "research into the subject matter of lifelong education, dominated in the past by theory and philosophy," and now centered "much more upon policies and strategies of education". Rendering philosophical work in the field redundant goes well with Aspin and Chapman's wish to abandon the normative dimension of "education". They, like Gelpi, would want to eliminate the notion of the learning society as a theoretical (though possibly not as a descriptive) notion. I am concerned, however, that evaluating the success of programs in terms of their successful outcomes set for them by the policy-maker smacks of performativity, when it is the criterion of performativity in policy-making that needs to be attacked today in the name of education.

Hughes and Tight (1995:303) themselves end their article with the provocative and ambiguous question, "What comes after the learning society?" Strain and Field (1997:142) read it to suggest, given their "potentially highly destructive critique," that the discourse of the learning society has "little but harm to bring to the project of human emancipation through education," and should be abandoned.[31] They disagree, however, that this is the case, arguing that the four composite "myths" of the learning society that Hughes and Tight had identified with that discourse—productivity, change, lifelong education, and the learning organization—could be combined within a humane rationale, a counterdiscourse to the dominant one that *could* be responsive to the concept of "an emergent 'risk' society," and emancipatory. This would be a job for an education research project in its constructive, utopian mode, perhaps referring back to Faure! Strain and Field (1997:141) observe that myths need not be negative. They "should not be confused with ideological distortion." The "fear that the project's aims might be subverted by interests hostile to humane educational values," they argue, "is insufficient reason for such skepticism" as Hughes and Tight showed with the project of a learning society. And Michael F.D. Young (1998:2) believes that, "despite the frequently ideological and rhetorical character that they have taken," the concepts of lifelong learning and the learning society (in some form or another) seem here to stay and cannot be ignored, so that we need to work with, not against, these concepts.[32] In Chapter 5, I shall complete my narrative of their fortunes in its third and final phase, starting with their appropriation by the new Labour government in Britain in 1997 with a very different policy approach and political agenda from that of its neoliberal predecessors, which is in line with the recent EU's policy initiatives at the turn of the century. These, in turn, have seen an important change as the concept of the learning society is substituted strategically with that of the *knowledge-based* society. When I set out to write this book in 1995, I was researching two philosophers—Alasdair MacIntyre and Jurgen Habermas—who I thought could help, because their work on the educated public, I thought, could be strategically useful for a project to restore the civic dimension to the learning society that I thought critical to my social democrat project. Habermas I identified as an important ally, MacIntyre an important opponent.

CHAPTER THREE

MacIntyre's Educated Public

The Crisis of Modernity

Significantly, both MacIntyre and Habermas are philosophers who have participated actively in the debate about the future of a modernity that is today nearly universally regarded as in crisis, with the world being in the postmodern condition sketched out in the previous chapter, the notion of education itself being its victim in the transition from the politics of mass schooling to the politics of the learning society. Postmodernity can best be described as modernity in crisis; a situation that cannot displease MacIntyre, who is, to put it mildly, not a friend of modernity. The interesting thing about MacIntyre, from our point of view, is that he addresses this crisis in education directly, not attributing it, however, to the postmodern condition of the world, but describing it as inherent in the project of modernity itself initiated with the Enlightenment. Namely, in the inability of the modernist project to reconcile the two tasks set for modern education systems: that of socializing the young into a functional role in society and that of rendering them individuals, reflective and independent members of their society and community.[33] This is because, he says in "The Idea of an Educated Public" (1987, henceforth *EP*), the project abandoned the notion of such a public. It is only where the notion of an educated public exists and induction into it is the clear goal of a society's education practices, he contends, that the two purposes become jointly possible. His discontent with modernity, however, runs through all his work and came to a head with *After Virtue* (1981, henceforth *AV*), which opened with a dystopian allegory about the state of the modern world that Oakes (1996:22) has compared with "the premise of Walter Miller's science-fiction novel *A Canticle for Liebowitz.*" In *AV*, MacIntyre (1981:1) imagines a series of environmental disasters that turn the public against the natural sciences:

> Widespread riots occur, laboratories are burnt down, physicists are lynched, books and instruments are destroyed. Finally a Know-Nothing political movement takes power and successfully abolishes science teaching in schools and universities, imprisoning and executing the remaining scientists. Later still, there is a reaction against the destructive movement and enlightened people seek to revive science, although they have largely forgotten what it was. But all that they possess are fragments: a knowledge of experiments detached from any knowledge of the theoretical contexts which gave them significance; parts of theories unrelated either to the other bit and pieces of theory or to experiments; instruments whose use has been forgotten; half-chapters from books, single pages from articles, not always fully legible because torn and charred.

These fragments are reassembled in a body of practices and discourses that are given the same names physics, chemistry, biology, and so on, though they are disembedded from the sociocultural context and intellectual culture that created them originally and gave them their meaning. Like the inhabitants of Plato's cave, MacIntyre's modern persons emerge from their cave with this new "enlightenment"—with the difference that as they "emerge into the light, what they see is not the Sun of Plato's ideal world but mere shards and fragments of the past with no coherent way of putting them together" (Oakes 1996:22). Because the discourses and practices they adopt, however, conform to the new canons of coherence and consistency, nobody, or nearly nobody, realizes that what they are doing is not natural science in any proper sense at all but a parody of it. MacIntyre uses the allegory to describe the state of our modernist moral language and intellectual culture and, by extension, of our discourse on education. Disembedded from their original contexts in Greek and early Christian culture, their languages are degraded and serve us not as tools of progress but as crude weapons to fight each other with.

MacIntyre (1981:11, italics in original) calls the *ethos* of modernity *emotivism*: "the doctrine that all evaluative judgments and more specifically all moral judgments are *nothing but* expressions of preference, expressions of attitude or feeling, insofar as they are moral or evaluative in character."[34] Emotivism is about "all value judgments whatsoever," not just moral ones. It "rests upon a claim that every attempt, whether past or present, to provide a rational justification for an objective morality has in fact failed" (1981:12). Its main features are a total disregard for historical context; a theory of conceptual incommensurability, which it sustains at the same time as its competing theories claim objectivity or impersonality for themselves; and a plurality of voices, which MacIntyre (1981:10) describes as "an unharmonious mélange of ill-assorted fragments," incapable of any harmonious resolution.[35] It appears in a great "variety of philosophical guises," including the work of Jean-Paul Sartre and Nietzsche (1981:21). In the English-speaking world emotivism first appeared in G.E. Moore's philosophy at the turn of the twentieth century (1981:9). Today it is firmly installed in our philosophical culture (1981:21). MacIntyre (1981:22) argues that every "moral philosophy—and emotivism is no exception—characteristically presupposes a sociology." He describes the social world seen through emotivist eyes as one where "any genuine distinction between manipulative and non-manipulative social relationships" is obliterated. The world of the aesthete, the bureaucrat manager, and the therapist, the stock characters of the modern world (recently [2002] he has added the bore), "moral representatives of their culture ... in which moral and metaphysical ideas and theories assume through them an embodied existence in the social world" (1981:27). Each is not so much a type as a role model who "morally legitimates a mode of social existence" (1981:28). All are manipulators *par excellence* in their relationships with people. Indeed, MacIntyre (1981:30) describes the *ethos* of the modern public realm, the "realm of the organizational," as manipulative generally; one "in which the ends are taken as given and not available for rational scrutiny" and the manipulators are the "elitist monopolies of managerial and therapeutic expertise."

In sharp contrast, he describes an anarchic "democratization of moral agency" in the private realm, "in which judgment and debate about values are central factors, but in which no rational social resolution of issues is available" (1981:33). The combination of the two, the manipulative public and the anarchic private, MacIntyre says, produces the kind of self described in the social psychologies of Jean-Paul Sartre and Irving Goffman. One that has "a certain abstract and ghostly character" about it that lacks "any necessary social identity, because the kind of social identity it once enjoyed is no longer available" (1981:31) as it once was to the premodern self, whose sense of identity was provided by her membership in a social group, an interlocking set of social relationships within which she inherited a particular space, together with a conception of a whole human life as a *telos*. "The emotivist self, in acquiring sovereignty in its own realm," MacIntyre (1981:32) remarks, "lost its traditional boundaries provided by a social identity and a view of human life as ordered to a given end," hence her sense of disorientation. He goes on to locate the emotivist *ethos* within liberalism, the cultural *imperium*, which has come to dominate, to assimilate into itself, the whole of Western culture, so that even objections to it are represented as debates within liberalism itself. What we call conservatism and radicalism today he describes as mere stalking horses for liberalism. Conservatives and radicals are really liberals of different hues. While emotivism itself puts everything up for grabs, the cultural tenets of liberalism itself are virtually unchallenged doctrine. Emotivism grounds itself not in reason but in "the generalizations of the sociology and psychology of persuasion" (1981:9). It replaces the search for truth with techniques of "psychological effectiveness" (1981:10).

Liberalism has remained the great enemy in MacIntyre's eyes over the years; an intrinsically degenerate, failed project that continues to prevail nonetheless, perhaps in an even more pernicious way than postmodernism. It has reduced public life to an arena of individuals who "pursue their own self-chosen conception of the good life" with no point of reference except a mythical and abstract law of nature (represented as a law of reason), protected by a state that maintains itself "neutral between rival conceptions of the good life for man," (1981:37) thus rendering itself "totally unfitted to act as moral educator for any community" (1981:39). Ancient and medieval societies, to the contrary, took the task of moral education seriously, he says, and performed it well. Indeed, they regarded creating virtuous citizens as a task of good government, "just as it is one of the tasks of parental authority to make children grow up so as to be virtuous adults" (1981:38). With their harmonious Christianized, Aristotelian culture and strong spirit of community they gave people a sense of solidity, direction, and moral purpose in their individual and collective lives that modern societies are incapable of, thanks to the malevolent influence of liberal modernism. Emotivism in particular, MacIntyre (1981:6) argues, precludes any mechanism for resolving serious disagreements rationally by working back to the premises, so that at some point "argument ceases and the invocation of one premise against another becomes a matter of pure assertion and counter-assertion." In other words, we are plunged into irrational quarrel and moral chaos, into "barbarism and darkness." In *AV* (1981:245), his remedy for this situation, the hope for "men and women of good will," is not to wait for some postmodern Godot but for a "doubtless very different" savior, a new St. Benedict, under whose guidance they could construct "new forms of community within which the moral life could be sustained" (1981:244).

Unsurprisingly, *AV* emerges as "not only a book of anger but of disgust, disaffection, and worse." The feelings that animate it are those of "an embittered prophet." (Kateb 1982:432–434). But MacIntyre's critique of modernism is not completely new. In many ways it echoes Max Weber's, with the difference that its tone in *AV* is also eschatological, "intended as a contribution to moral truth and hence to human salvation"[36] (Kateb 1982:434). Weber diagnosed the same instrumentalist, "means-end" rationality in modern life, identifying its beginning, however, with the mathematization of the external world and of the theoretical equipment created to come to terms with it. He also identified a certain "disenchantment of worldviews" at the heart of the modern technocratic *ethos* that preceded similar analyses by the Frankfurt theorists and, of course, Lyotard with his later account of the postmodern condition. Weber had warned that this trend toward rationalization was creating an "iron cage" of control and bureaucratization, resulting in the disappearance of civic society and a loss of meaning and freedom in public life. Moreover, he was pessimistic that it could be reversed or that the tensions it created could be resolved. Western societies, he believed, were already firmly imprisoned in the "iron cage," and he was skeptical that its grip could be broken, particularly since it had the powerful support of the positivist social sciences. All these themes became major concerns for the Frankfurt theorists who continued with Weber's analysis, as also for Michel Foucault, determining a certain pessimistic conception of the modern learning society in social theory, as we shall see, that is troubling. Adorno and Horkheimer, in particular, confirmed Weber's image of the "iron cage," referring to modern societies as "totally administered." Like MacIntyre, with his thesis of a failed liberal project, but much earlier in 1947, they noted "the collapse of bourgeois civilization" and the advent of a "new kind of barbarism" in the Western world, mocking the Enlightenment's claim that it was a world "entering into a truly human condition" (1992:xi). Their indictment of the Enlightenment project was harsh and unambiguous; everywhere today, they declared with heavy irony, "the fully enlightened earth radiates disaster triumphant" (1992:3). Martin Heidegger (1993) in "The Question Concerning Technology" (written in 1953) located the seeds of instrumental reason within the spirit of Western metaphysics itself from the time of the Greeks. Specifically in Plato, who first represented technology as an ordering, or setting upon, a management of both nature and "man." Inherently expansionist, Platonic metaphysics demanded total and exclusive mastery of all beings and things; their "enframing" (*Gestell*) within a unitary or comprehensive logic that represents and values them as mere availability, as a "standing reserve" or stockpile in its own service.

In short, Heidegger thought that Western metaphysics necessarily culminates in the hegemony of an instrumental rationality, so that the Greeks scaled the fate of the Western world long before the advent of modernity. The Enlightenment collaborated with it to set it on its final course, reappropriating the Platonic idea of "man" as a being with a "World View" and identifying itself as a humanism. Heidegger described technology as a form of *poiesis*, a mode of "bringing forth," of revealing and, hence, of truth, which becomes more and more hidden from us and invisible to itself the more successful it grows in the art of establishing its own hegemony, increasingly obfuscating other worldviews, culminating in the end of history as it completes itself. Performativity?! He discounted the possibility of going back on this destiny that we have only come to understand today, notwithstanding that it has been so long with us, because it is already more or less fulfilled. The best we can do, he came to believe, is open up the possibility of a postmetaphysical recovery of the Other as *self*-presensing, which is only achieved poetically. Heidegger's account of the metaphysics of technology, as I said earlier in the paragraph, connects with his attack on humanism also (characterized as its mode of being in the world as culture), taken up in his famous "Letter on Humanism" (1993) of 1947 (the same year Adorno and Horkheimer published the *Dialectic of Enlightenment*) where he responded to a series of questions set to him by Jean Beaufret in November 1946 based on Sartre's recent publication of *Existentialism Is a Humanism*. Humanists of all kinds distinguish theoretical conditions of existence that would render people's lives "truly human" from others that "dehumanize" them, and are typically dissatisfied with the current state of the world as it is, tending to highlight a persistent *haitus* within it between its inhumane existential conditions and an ideal, or truly human, potential, and to theorize some project of "emancipation" from the former into the latter.

While sustaining Marx's view in *Theses on Feuerbach* that there is no human nature as such and that 'man' is definable solely through 'his' action, which is to say "in connection with an *engagement*," Sartre also held that human freedom and human dignity are rooted in subjectivity, so that the Cartesian *cogito* is the point of departure for existentialism and the basis of its humanism. Heidegger disagreed. Leaving open the question of action, he strongly attacked the tradition of subjectivity and the Cartesian-inspired philosophy of the subject, which, in his "Letter," he identified as the fundamental point of origin of modernist humanism. Indeed, he rejected humanism in general because, he argued, it still bears the stamp and is cast in the mold of metaphysics, insisting at the same time that nihilism need not be the outcome of the rejection of metaphysics. With Nietzsche, he held that it is not the denial of humanist values but their installation in Western culture in the first place that raises the threat of nihilism, since the establishment of universal values anticipates their eventual disestablishment. I make this brief detour into Heidegger at this stage because of the powerful role his anti-humanism has played in the crisis of modernity, and because of its influence on poststructuralism, which will be the subject of Chapter 6. Adorno and Horkheimer are also important because of their influence on, or kinship with, Foucault (depending on whether one accepts his explanation of the resemblance between them or not)—the poststructuralist who interests me the most in this book—and their influence on Habermas. Before the publication of the *Dialectic*, the Frankfurt theorists were Marxist humanists with a utopian vision of a truly "rational" or non-totalitarian society yet to come. MacIntyre's humanism, on the other hand, though originally sympathetic with Marx, is Aristotelian.[37] In *AV* he proposed that moral communities founded on the medieval monastic ideal and guided by a strong leader could be the point of reference for "men and women of good will," their way out of our barbaric modern-postmodern world; learning communities where education can flourish.

Escathological Utopianism

MacIntyre was charged with having idealized and romanticized premodern societies in *AV*, attributing to them a kind of organic unity that they did not actually possess. But this was unfair since he warned in the same book against representing medieval society as having had "a unified monolithic Christian structure," and had even called this way of representing it "mythological." What unity it possessed, he had said, was "a fragile and complex balance of a variety of disparate and conflicting elements" (1981:55). George Kateb and John Caputo (1987), however, describe the book's tone as "escathological," the latter linking MacIntyre's approach with Heidegger's and warning that its kind of utopianism could be harmful to those who fall into its trap.[38] The escathological narrative begins with an account of a primordial utopia, narrates how that utopia fell into decline and eventual destruction, and anticipates the dawning of a new age when it will return, through the inspired direction of some enlightened figure, some philosopher or prophet (or budding saint, a St. Benedict in MacIntyre's case). Caputo (1987:241) anticipates the reader's surprise at seeing MacIntyre and Heidegger grouped together by referring to them as "otherwise unlikely bedfellows."[39] In fact, he argues, they have much in common. Besides being rabidly anti-modernist, "they both look to antiquity for light and a time of original solidarity; they both point their finger at the theory of "values," and specifically at Nietzsche, as at the heart of the modern ethical malaise; and they both leave us dreaming of a new dawn (while the forces of oppression ravage the land)." The problem with escathological narratives, Caputo remarks, is that they somehow always bring their believers to grief: "They plant the seed of discontent so deeply—in the loss of the ancient world, in a fall from primordiality—that nothing short of a miraculous renewal can save us. And, since miracles are beyond our individual and collective reach, they leave us dreaming of a new dawn, a wondrous transformation, even while they remain oblivious to the possibilities of the present."

Jeffrey Stout (1988) also charged MacIntyre with obliviousness to the present. Like Walter Feinberg (1991), he challenged MacIntyre's characterization of disagreement as the striking feature of contemporary moral utterance.[40] Stout suggested that the reason why there is radical disagreement among people of different moral opinion today, such as it may be, is that under conditions of relative freedom, public discourse tends to concentrate on controversial matters, the better to resolve them. "It would be more striking, and perhaps even disturbing," he went on, "if this ceased to be so and moral language came to be used in public settings largely for the ceremonial expression of widespread moral agreement" (1988:210). While agreeing "that complete absence of agreement on the good would render rational moral discourse impossible," and conceding that our modern agreement on the good does, in fact, fall "well short of perfect harmony" (1988:211), he insisted that "our disagreement about what human beings are like and what is good for us does not go all the way down," as MacIntyre suggests (1988:212). Indeed, it only makes sense to speak of disagreement because "we are prepared to recognize a background of agreement," of judgments of the good that we hold as platitudinous and that exist in any society, even if that agreement does not cover all matters of importance. "This line of reasoning," Stout (1988:213) continued, "suggests a picture of our society both more complicated and less dismal than MacIntyre's." No form of discourse, he went on to argue, needs to come up to the standards of rationality demanded by MacIntyre to function well. All it requires is the possibility of what John Rawls (1980) calls "overlapping consensus." Indeed, if the way we reach agreement exhibits "either philosophical foundations or means of resolving our most intractable disputes," Stout concluded, it deserves our rejection, not our approval. Agreements marked by overlapping consensus are usually enough to carry what moral reasoning we require to live together successfully, even if "we don't always know what to say to each other, how to keep the argument going in the face of someone else's bewildered stare or bewildered objections" (1988:215). In this connection, Stout rightly warned against letting our philosophical preconceptions set the standard of rational discourse unreasonably high (1988:215). MacIntyre, he argued, hasn't shown that rational discourse requires an established canon either. Habermas and Rorty provide us with perfectly credible descriptions of conversation that requires no canons to proceed rationally, only an honest commitment to its purposes by those engaged in it. "Don't we," in fact, in real life, "muddle through much of the time quite reasonably by appealing to areas of agreement with fellow citizens, by practicing immanent criticism on our opponents or on ourselves, by coming to terms with unfamiliar vocabularies in conversation, by using our creative powers, by confronting the moral imagination with instances of injustice and suffering, and by, in countless other ways, exploiting a culture too rich and complicated to be confined to a canon?" (1988:217).

Caputo (1987:242) criticized MacIntyre for seeming to think that "just by thinking through the modern demise, by telling a story on it, perhaps we will find the means to get the Christian-medieval tradition back on its feet and go after virtue again." In short, for seeming to think that one can retrieve a culture by recounting the narrative of its fall to people and demonstrating the high price paid for its loss. Susan Mendus (1992:90), who also charged MacIntyre with "nostalgia for the past" and succumbing to "the myth of the fall," made the inverse point. Quoting Williams, she argued that there is no narrative back to the premodern past, however it may have been. This is because modernity, she pointed out, has not merely changed the world; it has changed us, those who inhabit it. Moving into modernity meant, for those who came before us, moving "from a state of innocence to a state of reflection," and now that we are there, she said, "there is no going back ... without some form of suppression, and the unreflectiveness consequent upon suppression is quite distinct from the unreflectiveness consequent upon innocence" (1992:91). In short, barring catastrophes of the kind MacIntyre describes in *AV,* where the world turns on itself or is taken over by an irresistible movement, the project of returning to the cultural past is a non-starter. The really valid question today, Mendus argued, is not how one goes backward into the past but forward into the future. And we cannot begin to address it with any degree of adequacy without referring to our present, to our modern understanding of ourselves and of the contemporary world we live in (1992:92). In light of the work that followed these are all criticisms that MacIntyre seems to have taken, so that his point of reference in *EP,* for example, is not the medieval world but the eighteenth century.

MacIntyre's Challenge

MacIntyre's lecture on the educated public was given in London in the spring of 1985 as one of three public lectures held to honor the eminent British liberal philosopher Richard Peters, who was present for the occasion.[41] Peters, more than any other, had brought the liberal Enlightenment concept of the rationally autonomous "educated man" (later "person") to the fore in British philosophy of education, turning the philosophical debate on education toward the task of identifying the qualities of such a "man" and their incorporation into the general aims of school curricula. He had also been concerned that the political framework for the pursuit of these aims should be a democratic society marked by liberal values and by a great deal of active discussion by its members, and that the autonomous person should also be a good democratic citizen. And it was evidently with this agenda that MacIntyre was polemicizing in his lecture, though the provocation seemed lost on the audience present from what I could make out, and the subsequent publication of its text, unlike the publication of *AV,* made practically no impact on philosophers of education at all.[42] In making his case for the educated public MacIntyre was rejecting the liberal education project focused on the educated person based on the Cartesian/Kantian notion of the autonomous self, and proposing the project of the educated public in its stead.

An educated public requires: (a) the existence of "a tolerably large body of individuals, educated into both the habit and the opportunity of active rational debate, to whose verdict appeal is being made by the intellectual protagonists," and who "in their communication with one another ... must recognize themselves as constituting a public" (1987:18). Its other qualities are: (b) "shared assent, both to the standards by appeal to which the success or failure of any particular thesis or argument is to be judged, and to the form of rational justification from which those standards derive their authority (1987:19)," and (c) "a common body of texts, texts which are accorded canonical status within that particular community" (1987:19).[43] MacIntyre (1987:33–34) was not optimistic that the restoration of such a public was possible in the modern world because:

> ...both the persistence into our own time of the causes already at work in the larger society which destroyed the educated public of the Scottish Enlightenment, and the effects upon the academic disciplines of the disappearance of that public and of its counterparts, real or projected, at various times in England, France, the United States and elsewhere, ensure that the concept of an educated public has no way of taking on life in contemporary society. It is at most a ghost haunting our educational systems.

But he did not consider it to be dead either, because he described it as "a ghost that cannot be exorcised," an inheritance "so pervasive that we cannot rid ourselves of attitudes to the arts and sciences which presuppose that introduction into membership of an educated public of at least some of our pupils as one of the central aims of our educational systems" (1987:34). And indeed, it is not just MacIntyre among the philosophers who has kept the project of a public alive over the years—there are others, usually, unlike him, sympathetic to modernity, who have done the same. Dewey is perhaps the oldest and most obvious example, but the Frankfurt theorists—Hannah Arendt, Karl-Otto Apel, Habermas, and Hans-Georg Gadamer—are important others. Walter Feinberg, one of the few philosophers of education to react to MacIntyre's essay, criticized his view that the modern world is incapable of producing an educated public as excessively pessimistic. "A public that is more than simply a distributor or recipient of resources, more than simply an agent in a market and more than a cluster of individuals who happen to consume a common set of symbols," he contended, is still possible (1991:18). And Maxine Greene (1982:4) has expressed the same view, pronouncing the emergence of a public not just as possible but urgent, and arguing, like Dewey and Habermas, that the success of capitalism may be why there does not seem to be much interest in it today, notwithstanding the fact, she says, that it is more needed now, in times that clearly demand social renewal, than ever before. "Almost never" today, she complains, "is there an expressed concern about the public realm; there is silence about renewing the common world and about what that common world should be." She contends, like MacIntyre, that this lack of concern is itself a symptom of the growing fragmentation of society and of the alienation of people within it. A condition, she continues, that produces only "stasis, petrification, fixity," a palpable loss of freedom as people are frozen into indecision (1982:5). She also agrees that if the need for a public today is even greater than it was in Dewey's times, great as it was then, the current difficulties of creating it are much more formidable also, since "the vacuum" created by its absence "is filled by the messages coming from the media which, more often than not enhance the sense of givenness and objectification" that people experience in their everyday lives (1982:5). This conclusion echoes the assessment of the other critics of the modern-postmodern information society, as we saw earlier, including the Frankfurt School theorists and the early Habermas. MacIntyre, on his part, makes no mention at all of the media's part in producing the modern world, and this is certainly a lacuna in his sociology of that world. Greene (1982:9) ends her paper with an appeal for solidarity and commitment to recreate a public, for "each of us, from his or her own specialty or vantage point," to exercise our power to recreate a common world anew with others, "because we are together in speech and action, and because possibility spreads before us, and because there are boundaries to break through."

MacIntyre believes, however, that such appeals are not enough, that a model of an educated public is needed to frame and guide our action, and that this model existed in eighteenth-century Scotland. I shall describe this Scottish educated public shortly. First I want to say something about his earlier writing on education in *AV* where he introduced the important notion of a *practice*. After describing his educated public, I shall follow with a discussion of two of his books that followed the writing of *EP*, with some reference also to the other. Over this span of work we find the elaboration of an education project that outlines his plan of salvation for the barbaric postmodern world, and includes a pretty detailed account of a learning society that would install itself in it as a possibility for civilized living. In *AV*, where there is no mention of an educated public yet, his suggestion is that the twin tasks of enculturation and individuation can be harmonized in the notion of a *practice* embraced by a community, and the practice subsequently becomes the pedagogy of his educated public. He begins to describe it by citing Plato and Aristotle's view that becoming philosophers is "to embark on a *'techne'*" (1990:61) to be apprenticed to a craft, where the teacher "is the master-craftsman, the model of the person with *sophia*" (1990:61).[44] There is a clear suggestion here, as there is in Plato, that to become a philosopher is the high mark of being educated, and this is strengthened when he describes the education of the Scottish educated public as a philosophical one above all else. This view of a practice as a *techne*, he continues in *AV*, was later reappropriated by Aquinas and was much at home in the Middle Ages, where the institution of the craft guild gave it a suitable vehicle for extending into the contemporary society, to the extent that it was central to its life, crucial to the creation and sustenance of all human communities at the time—of households, cities, and nations (1987:175). Fundamental to the kind of apprenticeship a practice entailed was subordination to "a conception of rational teaching authority," invested in the master and embodied in the community's *telos*, which is also one's own (1990:612). "Faith in authority," MacIntyre (1990:64) argued, "has to precede rational understanding." He defined a practice, which he described as an entirely formal notion, comprehensively as:

> Any coherent and complex form of socially established cooperative human activity through which goods internal to that activity are realized in the course of trying to achieve those standards of excellence which are appropriate to, and partly definitive of, that form of activity, with the result that human powers to achieve excellence, and human conceptions of the ends and means involved are systematically extended. (1981:175)

MacIntyre compared initiation into a practice, or apprenticeship to it, to learning the game of chess, where the ultimate object is to develop the learner's skills in the game and attitude to the point where the joy of winning becomes a matter of secondary importance and love for the game and eagerness to excel in it become the primary object of playing it. Such an analogy closely resembles Dewey's in *Experience and Education* (1938), where he describes how pupils are initiated into democratic learning communities. Their love for the game produces a commitment to the skills and virtues that are required to play it well, and they come to understand that no game proceeds without rules, that the rules and regulations and some form of authority to interpret and enforce them are necessary to any game's practice. Like MacIntyre with a practice, Dewey describes the standards of a game (in his case the democratic game) and the goods it achieves, as internal to the game itself, not something imposed on it or sought from outside, or motivated by external purposes. Like

MacIntyre with a practice, he regards a game as a complex and dynamic "form of life," its rules and techniques permanently revisable and improvable. MacIntyre says about practices that they are dynamic in the sense that the standards and activities they pursue are open to ongoing internal criticism and change. As he puts it, "practices never have a goal or goals fixed for all time"; they are open-ended and subject to constant revision (1981:180). In both Dewey's and MacIntyre's views, the object of engaging in a practice or game for both teacher and student, as for the master and apprentice of old, is to raise its immanent standards of general excellence to ever higher levels. Not surprisingly, therefore, MacIntyre (1981:176) insists that the notion of "progress" is central to the description of a "practice," even if, as he remarks, "progress is rarely to be understood as straightforwardly linear," just as Dewey insisted that the notion of "growth" is central to the description of the game. The strong commitment to the standards of the practice required of teacher and pupil, master and apprentice, demands their common deference to its rules and regulations. It also requires "subordinating ourselves within the practice in our relationship with other practitioners," not just the master; recognizing what is due to whom; taking any necessary self-endangering risks on the way; and listening "carefully to what we are told about our own inadequacies and to reply with the same carefulness of the facts" (1981:178).

Finally, MacIntyre says, practices should not be confused with institutions, which are typically interested in external goods while practices are interested in internal standards of excellence. So that, though no practice can survive realistically without institutional support, virtues (defined simply as those human qualities required for the achievement of the goods internal to practices) are required to protect it from the corrupting power of the institutions that support it. The virtues that, in his view, every practice demands—though they may be characterized differently within different communities—are truthfulness (or honesty), justice, and courage. Describing a practice as an entirely formal notion means that it is "perfectly compatible with the acknowledgement that different societies have and have had different codes of truthfulness, justice and courage"—in other words, they have interpreted the virtues differently (1981:179–180). Later, in *Three Rival Versions of Moral Inquiry* (1990:72, henceforth *TRV*), he added *humility* to these three virtues, understood as deference to proper authority, describing it as "the necessary first step in education or in self-education" that is directed by one's own and one's community's *telos*. But the virtue of humility was already suggested in *AV*, where he made the strong emphasis, mentioned earlier, on the importance of submitting to a teaching authority. The sense of a *telos* is what, in MacIntyre's Aristotelian view, the modern self lacks. One's *telos* is what provides one with the sense of a life that has the unity of an unfolding narrative and takes the form of a quest for self-discovery within a community held together by its traditions and practices. No enduring community, he contends, can survive without such a conception of the self, and no such conception of the self can survive outside a community, which is why the sense of community is lost to the modern world.

The central pedagogical question that underpins this notion of education as self-discovery, in his view, is "Through what form of social engagement and learning can the errors which obstruct such discovery be brought to light?" One that exposes one to the possibility of dialectical refutation, he answers; an answer that anticipates the need for, and tells us something about, a public. "It is only by belonging to a community systematically engaged in a dialectical enterprise in which the standards are sovereign over the contending parties," he contends later, that one can begin to learn the truth about oneself and about one's limitations (1990:200). Such a community recognizes the mutual obligation of each to "inform the shared life of the community" to which one belongs through one's utterances and actions. MacIntyre describes this pedagogical model of dialectical self-discovery as "confessional" and credits Socrates with its invention, Plato and Aristotle with its refinement, and Christianity with its eventual perfection. In the kind of community "which shares this conception of accountability in enquiry," education, he says, "is first of all an initiation into the practices within which dialectical and confessional interrogation and self-interrogation are institutionalized" (1990:201). This initiation occurs in stages. First, in dialectical association with others, one obtains a good knowledge of the history of the formation and transformations of belief that have occurred over time through the practices that the community endorses, as well as of "the best theses, arguments and doctrines to emerge so far" in the process. Then one obtains the ability to rescrutinize these doctrines so that they become genuinely one's own through self-interrogation.

The Educated Public

MacIntyre's educated public existed in the first half of the eighteenth century, before Scotland was successfully Anglicized and brought into the modern world. This was a time when, having lost its political sovereignty, it found itself engaged in an internal struggle to redefine itself and its national identity. In this situation of national crisis an educated public was useful for its people "to provide a milieu for nationwide debate on its future development" (1987:18). And the lead was taken by the universities, which were themselves being reformed at the time. But the debate, MacIntyre (1987:23) says, spilled beyond and into the wider community, creating this broader public including not just the moderate clergy and the lawyers, but the "larger farmers and smaller gentry, the merchants, especially the more prosperous, and the schoolmasters, especially in the better schools." In short, it was "composed of the male middle classes, a spectrum that could range from the sons of the minor nobility to the sons of shopkeepers" (1987:24). What rendered the phenomenon nationwide was the fact that the universities shared the philosophy of common sense, developed by Reid and Stewart, and referred back to a common educational tradition that gave the professor of moral philosophy in the university preeminence and authority as "the official defender of the rational foundations of Christian theology, of morals, and of law" (1988:248). As MacIntyre puts it, the universities with their culture of philosophical debate and rational inquiry had displaced the medieval Church tribunals as adjudicators over moral and cultural orthodoxy. Moral philosophy was "to some degree the keystone of the curriculum, and it was moral philosophy of one particular kind" (1987:20) that steered a course between Hume's secular, rational anti-Christianity and the dogmatic appeal to a neo-Calvinist understanding of the scripture, which "is incompatible with the whole project of rational justification" (1987:21). Commonsense philosophy represented "the stance of the Presbyterian clergy of the moderate party and of their social allies" (1987:21). It was "at once secular and yet both consonant with and supportive of the Christian religion" (1987:20). It proceeded from first principles that were "seen" to be true and moved deductively from them. The established scheme of human knowledge this philosophy created was consequently a "unitary and more or less integrated" one, with the articulated disciplinary parts referring continuously to each other, and with both the unity and the differentiation of that scheme replicated in the curriculum of the university as a whole (1988:250).

The causes of the decline and eclipse of the Scottish public are important in the light of its present feasibility. One was fast change—political, social, economic, and demographic as well. Other equally fatal causes were immanent within the educated public itself from the start, particularly in the controversies that provided it with much of its intellectual life, and that were inevitable since, as MacIntyre (1987:26) points out, any kind of educated public "requires a degree of awareness of its own conditions which is likely to produce this result." Inevitably, with time, the philosophy of common sense lost its homogeneity and became more complex as it strove to deal with these controversies. It soon "ceased to be able to articulate a common educated mind," becoming a "plurality of 'minds'" instead, and this was fatal to the whole scheme of things (1987:26). Once it happened, the outcome was inevitable: "Within education itself, moral and theological truth ceased to be recognized as objects of substantive inquiry and instead were relegated to the realm of privatized belief" (1990:217). The modernist virus, emotivism, had set in. Scotland, in short, went down the same road already traveled, or about to be traveled, by many European societies, not just the English, with the growth of secular pluralism. One obvious way this could have been prevented from happening would have been to discourage critical debate from the outset. But "retreat from debate into assertion," MacIntyre (1987:26) rightly observes, would effectively have meant giving up on doing philosophy and returning to the old authoritarian dogmatisms of the past. Moreover, it would have been counterproductive to the existence of the educated public itself since, as he points out, it would have ruled out that sort of public from the start. Another suggestion would have been to create a multidisciplinary curriculum to cope with the new plurality. But whatever its other benefits, this sort of curriculum, he says, "cannot take us even one step towards the restoration of an educated public" (1987:30). What such a public requires for its intellectual coherence is to reason with one mind, nothing else will do. The challenge now for MacIntyre was how to restore it in a viable way to the modern world, which is irremediably pluralist, and this was a challenge he took up in *TRV*.

Before writing *TRV*, in his book following *AV* and published shortly after *EP, Whose Justice? Which Rationality?* (1988, henceforth *JR*), he developed the thesis he had already defended in *AV* that, as with our interpretation of the virtues, our notions of justice and rationality are rooted historically in our traditions and need to be understood as such, as products of these traditions. In *AV* he had rejected, notwithstanding his Aristotelianism, an Aristotelian metaphysical biology that identifies a single fundamental universal *telos* for all human agents. His argument in *JR*, as in *AV*, was that there is no philosophically persuasive way of reducing the competing rationalities and views of justice that have grown historically in different traditions to a single all-embracing one. From there it was a short step to the conclusion mooted in *TRV* that any scenario for the contemporary world would have to envisage not one but several competing notions of the educated public, all drawing on their different traditions. The enemy, however, is still the same: the pluralism of the modern-postmodern emotivist world, which he continued to think of as "an unharmonious *mélange* of ill-assorted fragments" (1981:10). The question *TRV* took up from *AV* and *JR* was how to redefine this unharmonious *mélange* as "an ordered dialogue of intersecting viewpoints" (1981:10). The answer, unless I am mistaken, came from a brief reflection left undeveloped in *EP* on John Stuart Mill's suggestion that a tolerant pluralism could be "founded on an agreement to disagree," provided that there is the same "allegiance to the purpose of the debate" *between* the disagreeing parties that they show to the purpose of the internal debate before their own publics (1987:32). What is different about the debate between opposing parties from the internal debate of a public is that it is not mainly dialectical but oppositional and combative, but it still needs to operate with preagreed rules. In sum, what MacIntyre envisages in *TRV* is a postmodern world rationalized by the existence of *different* internally homogeneous educated publics constituted on the general criteria of the Scottish public, coexisting in the public sphere in an atmosphere of intellectual rivalry and honest combat according to preagreed rules of ordered dialogue. To render this project practical, two things, he contends, are needed. First, to reconstitute today's universities on Scottish lines as internally coherent institutions able to take effective moral and intellectual leadership in the community such that educated publics would flourish around them anew. And to create those broader forums of interuniversity debate where the masters, the professors, or the intellectuals come together in the spirit that Mill suggested.

How feasible is this project that he sets up against the multicultural liberal university? He himself certainly supposes it is, perhaps because he thinks it possible to condense the significant rival intellectual traditions alive and healthy in today's Western world to just three. One, the Genealogist, did not feature among the moral and intellectual traditions he identified in *JR*.[45] The other two are the Encyclopaedist (a redefinition of the old liberal Enlightenment project) and the Thomist. Each, in his scheme of things, would have its own universities and educated public. And this rationalized complex of partisan universities would replace the modern permissive liberal university of today, which MacIntyre accuses of being incapable of intellectual coherence or moral leadership, since it does not have the internal homogeneity, the "single mind," "the type of agreement necessary to ensure the progress and flourishing of its enquiries" (1987:26). The homogeneity of a single mind is assured only if each of the competing partisan universities guards its own orthodoxy by taking suitable measures to protect itself from internal corruption. Otherwise, it could easily degenerate into the Babel of voices and intellectual chaos that, in his view, characterizes the modern liberal university. The measures it needs to take, in this respect, are three: (1) ensuring the existence of an academic community that is well knit intellectually, with a single mind, and able to work together to create a coherent curriculum for the university as a whole and for the public that feeds on it; (2) enforcing the exclusion of points of view that are too much at odds with this consensus; and (3) using preferments and promotions to reward those who uphold and advance the consensus, including those who extend, erect, or otherwise improve the standards of rational justification embodied in it, ensuring that they occupy the relevant professorial chairs (1990:224). Predictably, MacIntyre (1990:230) would also reintroduce something like the religious and moral tests and exclusions once typical of the medieval universities, as a further safeguard from the "fundamental dissent" that, he says, threatens the progress of any genuinely rational inquiry and, more especially, moral and theological inquiry. He admits that these policies and controls carry inherent dangers and are "liable to error and abuse, and to consequent injustice," if misused (1990:224). But, he argues, the liberal university is an unjust institution anyway. It lacks the inclusiveness its defenders hypocritically claim in its name, and marginalizes its most radical critics, among them Genealogists and Thomists, so that they "still cannot be heard in any authentic and systematic way" in its *fora* and are faced with the task "of continually trying to devise new ways to allow these voices to be heard" (1990:236). He also believes the "enforced and constrained agreement" in his university (1990:230) a much better intellectual climate for the pursuit of inquiry than the present climate of "increasing disarray" that marks the liberal university (1990:225). And though he admits that the partisan university is also exposed to the dangers of intellectual complacency, parochialism, and dogmatism, he believes that these dangers could be countered by keeping its intellectual and moral traditions alive and dynamic.

In fact, he lays down the parameters within which professors should operate to ensure that the partisanship with which their university operates does not degenerate in these ways. One is by taking account of conflicting readings, and ensuring that texts are read critically *against* each other, so that apart from advancing their inquiry within the tradition they support and exposing rival standpoints to analysis by reinterpreting them critically in order to expose their errors (thus expanding their own horizon of understanding), professors put their own theses on the line by exposing them to the objections of their opponents (1990:231). In sum, apart from its members safeguarding their internal orthodoxy, the university system would also need:

> … to uphold and to order the ongoing conflicts, to provide and sustain institutionalized means for their expression, to negotiate the modes of encounter between opponents, to ensure that rival voices were not illegitimately suppressed, to sustain the university—not as an arena of neutral objectivity, as in the liberal university, since each of the contending standpoints would be advancing its own partisan account of the nature and function of objectivity— but as an arena of conflict in which the most fundamental type of moral and theological disagreement was accorded recognition. (1990:231)

This means that, besides initiating students into the practice, the university professors would also have the task of initiating them "into conflict" in these "arenas" (1990:231).

Death of the Liberal University

MacIntyre is also confident that, all other considerations apart, the modern liberal university is in crisis, its future uncertain, perhaps even in its death throes, because it has lost its ability to provide society with the intellectual and moral leadership it needs, and is thereby already a largely discredited institution in everybody's eyes. Not just those of governments that regard it as a waste of money, and the general public that gets nothing from it, but also those of the academics who work in it. With these, he contends, it is now paying the price for its policy of permissiveness designed "to dissolve antagonism" and "to emasculate hostility," while behaving as though it were a single intellectual community. That price is its own cultural and social irrelevance and its general lack of success in justifying its existence and the privileges it has enjoyed as it comes under increasing social and political pressure (1990:219). With the crisis of the liberal university, MacIntyre (1990:221) sees spaces "opening up within the university system which may afford new points of entry for radical dialogue and new opportunities for recasting older genres, so that they may allow new antagonisms to emerge." This is a development that, he believes, Genealogists and Thomists will welcome and hopefully exploit, and that should ensure a receptive ear for his argument. His project to restore the model of the medieval and preliberal university could be made attractive on the grounds that, unlike the liberal, this university was able to function close to its community and to provide it with intellectual leadership because it was an internally coherent center of rational inquiry, and this rendered it a suitable hub for an educated public to grow around. Restoring this role and status to the university today, as a center of stability in a fast-changing world, would, he believes, justify the existence of the whole university system in the postmodern world.

How convincing is this argument? Its premise that the liberal university system is in crisis is not unique to MacIntyre; there are plenty of other voices around expressing this view. It follows from a postmodern *ethos* that is suspicious of the master narratives of modernity that created the liberal university, and that endorses the values of performativity. Not all those voices, however, are self-congratulatory as his are. Many are more alarmed than elated by the fact (if it is a fact), while those who are elated by it, as he is, may not necessarily be sympathetic to the alternative he offers. Besides, the signs are that the trend away from the liberal university such as it is points in a very different direction from the one he suggests it should follow. More than the desire to create coherent moral and intellectual centers or hubs for educated publics that serve communities with their moral and intellectual leadership, it seems rather toward reconstituting the universities as learning service centers: supermarkets offering wide and varied selections of prepackaged distance learning courses responding to customer demand on the lifelong learning market, and networking among themselves, rather than with the community. It tends towards a university system conceived as a market driven by consumer demands and answering to performativist criteria rather than one answering to the demand for community leadership or intellectual and moral guidance, *or education.* Performativist criteria not only define the development of postmodern universities, they extend to the schooling system, and as we saw in the previous chapter, to the adult education sector also. As Lyotard (1999:50) saw, the criterion of performativity is what drives the research and the teaching agendas of postliberal, postmodern universities and determines the kinds of graduates they produce, not some project to educate. Gone today is the old demand that the university "train an elite capable of guiding the nation towards its emancipation," he remarks in *PMC*. The new demand is to "supply the system with players capable of acceptably fulfilling their role at the pragmatic post required by its institutions" in the realms of the economy and the administration; "players," or graduates, who are professionally marketable human resources or a socially useful technical "intelligentsia." Otherwise the postliberal university's main concern is with job retraining and marketing courses to be chosen by adults "à la carte" for a variety of purposes, vocational, technical and "ethical." Jane Kenway (1995:47–48), who argues that Jameson's "key logics" of postmodernity apply to the universities, agrees with Lyotard that they "are certainly being redefined by the postmodern condition" by "reorienting themselves more and more in line with the demands of the corporate State and, in turn, with the needs of the service-based economy, capital's expanding global market and consumer culture." And Caputo (1987:230) agrees with Lyotard's other point that "the power exerted *within* the university" today "is dwarfed by the power exerted *upon* the university from without. For the university," he argues, "belongs to a technico-political power structure," and as such its free-play is severely curtailed, practically nonexistent. Caputo refers to Heidegger's concern that technology is the *Gestell,* the framework of rationality for today's world, and argues that preserving the life of protest, free play, and dissent is crucial if difficult in the university. "What we call reason today," he claims, echoing Heidegger, the Frankfurt School, and Foucault, "is a central power tightly circled by bonds of military, technical, and individual authorities which together make up the administered society" (1987:234).

These are not developments that MacIntyre can find encouraging. In fact, Lyotard (1999:50) himself concluded that new experiments in "discourse, institutions, and values" that qualify as education are driven today into "extra-university networks." While agreeing with MacIntyre that the modern university has brought many of its ills upon itself, by its remoteness from the community among other things, he saw in its contemporary state of crisis not an opportunity to relaunch the role of the Professor as an intellectual leader but a trend toward the "death of the Professor" at the hand of the expert technician operating learning technologies. In sum, if this analysis of Lyotard and the others is right, today's trend toward the death of the liberal university, such as it is, can give MacIntyre very little, if any, cause for comfort and would return him to the desperate hope he expressed in *AV* in the resurgence of something like the monastic movement in the Dark Ages under inspired leaders outside the universities. If Lyotard is right, the emerging rival that MacIntyre's new university system would have to contend with today is more formidable than the liberal university setup. It consists in an array of postliberal universities operating with digital communications technologies and driven by the demands of performativity and of a lifelong learning market that regards its students not as future members of an educated public, or even as persons to educate, but as clients for what they are able to market, pure and simple. These are virtual universities with virtual campuses, and with virtual rather than face-to-face academic communities, managed by technologists expert in creating and setting up interactive learning packages for distance learning that are efficient, rather than old style professors and students. Universities that measure their effectiveness according to quality indicators, often set externally, rather than on the basis of their ability to educate students and to serve a public or community. In this respect it is, unsurprisingly, not just the character of the institution and its experts that is changing but that of the student also. The new student is increasingly dissatisfied with being a full-time student attending a course designed for a class moving together over which she has little or no control, and more disposed to regard herself as a free agent, a client who buys into the curriculum of her choice and determines her own pace of progress. Lyotard himself had little sympathy with the liberal university and none with the postliberal, but he had too much respect for the growing power of the latter to see any real alternative to it in the future, hence his pessimistic remark about extra-university networks being the hope for education. This power is confirmed in the many conferences going about on distance learning and the future of university education, where the earlier concerns with the future of the traditional liberal university wear thinner all the time and the agendas turn more and more toward issues about effective technologies, quality assurance, marketing, and successful networking. And where more and more of the invited keynote speakers come from the world of business and industry rather than from the academic world.

In any case it seems unlikely, even without these trends, that MacIntyre's project would win the support either of Encyclopaedists or Genealogists.[46] The Encyclopaedist project is what originally motivated the rise of the liberal university, and he himself acknowledges that it has ceased to be a serious proposition in today's intellectual debate. Thus, even if there are, as he argues, reasons why its standpoint should continue to engage interest, they are not likely to attract much support for an Encyclopaedist university (1990:171). The Genealogist, on the other hand, though alive and kicking (thanks especially, as MacIntyre acknowledges, to Foucault's influence), would reject his model of a university, whatever difficulties she has had, and continues to have, with the liberal university. Indeed, a Genealogist university, one that took its inspiration from Nietzsche's and Foucault's texts and operated on the lines of MacIntyre's university, would be a hopeless contradiction, the latter being morally and politically repugnant to Genealogists, a betrayal of the value they place on difference and dispersion. Genealogists are unhappy that the liberal university promises pluralism only in principle; in practice it fails to deliver, tolerating divergent voices only very grudgingly or not at all, when, for instance, they find themselves rejected, snubbed, or marginalized by the philosophy departments for their lack of philosophical orthodoxy.[47] They struggle, however, for an authentic celebration of difference and plurality, not the more homogenizing perspective MacIntyre's university offers. The same is true of feminists, who have also found problems operating within the liberal university, especially with inserting Women's Studies into its general curriculum. Anna Yeatman (1994) contends that it was only the strength of the feminist lobby that eventually made it happen. But she acknowledges that most liberal universities now provide genuine space for the subject and for the development of feminist intellectual work in general, and she blames its ghettoization on the way the subject was represented by feminists themselves.[48] Martha Nussbaum (1997), on the other hand, has a very different story to tell about the fate of women, never mind feminism or Women's Studies, at Notre Dame, MacIntyre's old university. There, she says, notwithstanding recent improvement, "tension over women's role on campus" continues to be real, where "social relations between male and female students are far more tense and uneasy than at many other institutions," and where "the number of women, especially tenured women, on the faculty, is scant, although their numbers are growing" (1997:275).[49] In conclusion, MacIntyre's university scheme has one potential ally only, the Thomist, who, if she already works within a Catholic university like Notre Dame, knows his model of a university well and feels comfortable within it. Catholic universities already enforce the restrictive measures he identifies in *TRV* to preserve their intellectual unity and orthodoxy, but there is not much likelihood that either the Encyclopaedist or the Genealogist will endorse them.

MacIntyre's Politics

Of course, MacIntyre's dislike for the liberal university stems, as I indicated earlier, from a deeper dislike of liberalism in general that extends to liberal institutions and political values, and to the liberal political state. Democracy of course fits ill with the political culture of the Scottish public he so admired in *EP* and which, as we saw, was exclusively male and middle class and reflected one mind. In short, the class Aristotle would have consigned political power to rather than the people. The merit with the Catholic tradition, which MacIntyre has always admired as intensely as he has disliked liberalism, is precisely its internal cohesion, its cultural unity, its sense of itself as a community, its emphasis on virtue, and its historical obedience to a continuous and coherent body of texts authoritatively interpreted by the Pope and his moral theologians. The canonical texts of his own preferred public are those of Aristotle, Augustine, Aquinas, and the Popes in their encyclicals, all male Europeans and, apart from the first, Roman Catholic priests. It is not surprising that corresponding with his distaste for the neutral liberal state lies a sympathy toward a paternalistic state concerned with making its citizens virtuous. Having decided that the modern state is unable to play that role, he suggests in *TRV* that his type of university and its professors, feeding into educated public—and, as we shall see later in this chapter, homogeneous local—communities should take it up instead. A solution very different from Habermas's, who, though he also despaired that the modern state can be a moral educator, did so for very different reasons—namely that its institutions fail to emancipate its citizens. In his more recent work, Habermas has distanced himself from this view that the state's institutions should be emancipatory, a view he has described as "republican," associating democratic education exclusively (as did Dewey) with the communicative action of a critical public, but it was a view he held early on. Unlike MacIntyre, Habermas and Dewey accord democracy political priority over justice, Habermas (1996:136), and as we shall see later, Giddens (1998b), describing it as "the only postmetaphysical source of legitimacy." Democracy "makes it possible," Habermas (1996:136) says, "for issues and contributions, information and reasons to float freely; it secures a discursive character for political will formation; and it thereby grounds the fallibilist assumption that results issuing from proper procedure are more or less reasonable."

MacIntyre, however, is uncomfortable with everything that this statement values, with the idea that anything should float freely, with as undetermined a criterion for political and moral agreement as that of its reasonableness, and with fallibilist accounts of truth. True, he declares himself unsympathetic with totalitarianism also, describing it as "evil," so that it would be invidious to charge him with that sentiment, but he is certainly equally unhappy with unrestricted pluralism. And though this does not in itself render him antidemocratic, critics like Kateb have argued that the consequence of his thinking *is* antidemocratic, corresponding with the conservative prescription of "my station and its duties," and conflicts with the ideal based on the citizen's critical participation in the democratic public sphere. "I do not think," Kateb (1982:436) remarks, that "the democratic self, as proposed by the great American romantics, could live in MacIntyre's utopia." I have argued elsewhere myself, in a commentary on MacIntyre (Wain 1995:109), that a democracy that values plurality as "an ordered dialogue of intersecting viewpoints," as he does, rather than unrestricted plurality, sounds suspiciously like Lenin's Hegelian conception of democracy as a plurality of ideas within a "single will" with the state as its custodian. My example of the difference between this conception of democracy and that which leaves pluralism unrestricted is taken from the history of radio and television broadcasting in Malta, which was entirely state owned and supervised by an ineffective Broadcasting Authority until a Christian Democrat government in the late 1980s, reacting to the blatant partisanship it had suffered at the hands of the broadcast media in opposition, undertook to break this monopoly once and for all by granting licenses to privately owned radio and television stations. Its Socialist opponents, however, argued that private stations were not needed and that a plurality of viewpoints could be ensured *within* the state-owned media by putting it under the vigilance of a joint parliamentary commission instead of the Broadcasting Authority. The difference between the two sides, in essence, reflected very different political conceptions of democratic plurality, of the relation between state and media, and, ulti-mately, of democratic politics itself. What the Socialist opposition proposed differed from Lenin's conception of a "single will" in the sense that its custodian would not be state or party but parliament.

A parliamentary commission, the Socialists argued, would protect the media from corruption or abuse while ensuring that the plurality would not degenerate into permissive anarchy. And it is not difficult to project this sort of scheme in broadcasting onto MacIntyre's project of competing partisan universities, which would presumably have to operate under some sort of regulation, a university watchdog or some other regulator (a parliamentary commission for universities perhaps!) to ensure that the system remained intact and was not allowed to degenerate into the anarchy of unrestricted plurality that marks the liberal regime. Otherwise, how would its integrity be ensured? Certainly, an appropriate political infrastructure of laws and regulations would have to be created to control its growth and to ensure that the system stayed intact. Not necessarily by keeping the original structure of three kinds of universities, by excluding additions to it, but by ensuring that any addition was made in an organic, ordered manner and that it conformed with the basic institutional principles of the university as he identified them. But even the safeguards to internal orthodoxy that he describes could not guarantee that the kind of discord that tends to grow with time, even within the most homogeneous cultural entities (as he acknowledged happened with the Scottish universities) will not show its head within his universities unless that orthodoxy is safeguarded with regular internal witch hunts or other repressive mechanisms designed to unearth subversive signs of radical dissent and, having found them, nip them ruthlessly in the bud. This thought, by itself, is enough to terrify the democrat. Indeed, the question arises of why, once he proposes to adopt measures to exclude voices of radical dissent from the university, MacIntyre should not be prepared to extend this principle into the wider society to protect the rationalized pluralism he advocates. Why he should be averse to creating the same mechanisms at the level of the state to ensure that radical dissent is kept out of its other institutions and out of the lifeworld itself. The answer he gives to these concerns, as we shall see later, is that he is not interested in political entities of the size of the modern state, and that it would be a mistake to project his politics of community onto anything on that scale or of that kind. Meanwhile, the problem with the conception of democracy as a plurality within a single will, even if that will is the will of a democratically elected parliament that is supposed to represent the collective will of the people operating through a commission, is illustrated in the Maltese case by the fact that it was strenuously opposed by the smaller parties not represented in parliament. These supported the policy of total liberalization proposed by the government, arguing that a parliamentary commission would not represent the will of the people at all but that of the parties in parliament who could not be trusted not to use the commission to further their mutual interest to consolidate their collective hegemony. The Italians have a word for this distortion of democracy, *partitocrazia* (roughly, a regime of mutual accommodation of the parties, as distinct from *democrazia*, the rule of the people). The worry in MacIntyre's case is that the original tripartite structure of universities would with time be a collective hegemony on these lines, excluding those other voices it cannot encompass, creating a stranglehold on the university system, and consequently on the learning processes of society itself. A truly frightening prospect!

Whatever his views on democracy, predictably, he strongly attacked rights-based theories of justice like those of the early Rawls and Nozick, criticizing both for excluding any criterion of desert and for their "universalist" approach, "applying across all societies, or at least all of a certain level of development" (Taylor 1994:24). In *JR*, he defined justice in Aristotelian terms as the "disposition to give to each person, including oneself, what that person deserves and to treat no one in a way incompatible with their deserts" (Taylor 1994:23). Against Rawls's Kantian belief in *A Theory of Justice* (1980) that a definition of "pure justice" from an Archimidean standpoint of "disengaged reason" is possible, he insisted on a standpoint that is thoroughly historicist. The "belief in reason disengaged as such," MacIntyre argued in response to Charles Taylor's defense of Rawls, "is a philosophical illusion," and, "just because it is an illusion, to tie important beliefs about human dignity to it, as Taylor credits liberalism with doing would be to cast needless doubt on those beliefs" (1994:289). Insisting on regarding its traditions as the basic explanatory matrix for the history of Western justice, he casts liberalism itself as one of these traditions, as a set of beliefs, institutions, and practices to be explained historically. MacIntyre's other problem with the Rawls of *A Theory of Justice* (and even more so with Nozick) is that, like all contract theories, it lies within the liberal tradition of radical individualism that he himself evidently disowns. Rawls's "original position," he points out, is an association of individuals pursuing their own personal goals who are forced together in Hobbesian fashion by the exigency of common and mutual protection rather than for moral reasons. Against it he presents his Aristotelian view, later amplified in *Dependent Rational Animals* (1999, henceforth *DRA*), that no form of human association can be rendered intelligible if its members do not share some conception of a common or human good that binds them together as a community. The desert-based conception of justice this kind of communitarianism produces, as Taylor points out, is based on the intuition that "in any common attempt to achieve the good, all genuine collaborators benefit from the contribution of others. They are in a sense all in each other's debt. But since some will make a more signal contribution, the mutual debt may not be entirely reciprocal"

(Taylor 1994:37). This being the case, it demands that the principle of equality in the distribution of benefits is not absolute but "proportionate" so that some will be recognized as having greater merit, others less, than the rest. MacIntyre's is "a practice-defined notion of desert." It must "be taken to refer to the specific forms of desert that a particular practice at any moment takes to correspond to its notion of excellence" (Miller 1994:255). As he points out, the acquisition of certain virtues is central to this account, since it is what enables the members of the community to safeguard its practice from the distortions it could suffer from the society's institutions that would make it unjust. Namely, when the goods or benefits they distribute do not, through the particular institutional arrangements in force, "assign(s) to each what is her or his due, in virtue of her or his contribution and place in the practice and in the community" (MacIntyre 1994:289). This role played by the virtues, MacIntyre (1994:290) replies to feminist critics like Elizabeth Frazer and Nicola Lacey, "is itself sufficient to provide a standard for identifying and condemning the deformations and distortions to which practices may be subjected and the consequent injustices to women and others."

While affirming his communitarianism, however, MacIntyre (1994:30) "strongly disassociates" himself from those contemporary communitarians who "advance their proposals as a contribution to the politics of the nation-state." Indeed, any nation-state that projects itself as a locus of community, he contends, "in whatever guise, is a dangerous and unmanageable institution" (1994:303). He thus registers his agreement with liberals who hold "that modern nation-states which masquerade as the embodiments of community are always to be resisted" (1994:303). For Aristotelians like himself, he says, the nation-state "is not and cannot be the locus of community" (1994:303). The claim that it can, he agrees with liberals, is indeed a recipe for totalitarian and other evils. Which means that, as Taylor says, he is not interested in questions of justice at the level of the nation-state. Liberals are mistaken, however, he continues, when they go on to conclude that "any form of political community which embodies substantive practical agreement upon some strong conception of the human good" must perforce be totalitarian (1994:303). This need not be the case with smaller communities, with "genuinely Aristotelian conceptions of the polis," which, "for a variety of reasons has to be a relatively small-scale and local form of political association. And when practice-based forms of Aristotelian community are generated in the modern world, they are always, and could not but be, small-scale and local" (1994:302). Problems, however, arise with defining justice as desert even at the level of the local community in that it excludes from any benefits those who do not or, even more significantly, *cannot* deserve according to its criteria, either because they cannot make any contribution to the community's progress at all, or can only contribute to it, through no fault of their own, in an exceedingly small or insignificant way. MacIntyre addresses this problem and the ethics and politics of the local community in *DRA*. They will be the subject of the next section and constitute the last piece of the picture I am building of his views on education (which started with my description of his notion of a practice in *AV*), a picture I shall bring together in the last section of this chapter.

Dependent Rational Animals

In *DRA*, MacIntyre (1999:x) recants his view in *AV* that Aristotelian biology is irrelevant to the purpose of constructing a moral theory. He instead holds that no account of the goods, rules, and virtues that define our moral life is possible without an explanation of "how that form of life is possible for beings who are biologically constituted as we are," and how it can flourish in a human environment. He approaches his subject with a premise that is key to his account: "that the facts of vulnerability and affliction, and the related facts of dependence (are) central to the human condition." He also assumes that flourishing in human terms is always flourishing *in virtue* of possessing characteristics "that involve applications of the more fundamental concept of good (to flourish translates *eu zen* and *ben vivere*)" (1999:65). Most fundamentally, he defines human flourishing as that in which one benefits oneself and others, "both *qua* human being and also characteristically *qua* the exemplary discharge of particular roles or functions within the context of particular kinds of practice" (1999:65). To flourish in this way human beings "need to understand themselves as practical reasoners about goods, about what on particular occasions it is best for them to do and about how it is best for them to live out their lives" (1999:67). Everything, he argues, that threatens or damages the exercise of such reasoning is a threat to human well-being itself. He then goes on to trace out the practices, all of which, evidently, have a strong pedagogical basis, through which human infants are nurtured into practical reasoners of this kind, activities that involve, in true Aristotelian fashion, the cultivation of a range of intellectual and moral virtues.

Rendering affliction and dependence the key characteristics of the human condition—and thereby fundamental to moral and political relationships between individuals in a community—evidently challenges the liberal representation of society as a set of relationships between individuals in which the freedom of each, rather than their mutual dependence, is the key assumption. But, MacIntyre argues, dependence is a simple social and biological fact. We are first dependent on others; then, with the passing of years, the position is reversed as others (who may include those on whom we were once dependent ourselves: parents and other members of the community) become dependent on us. The object of our upbringing, in his view, should be to render us "independent practical reasoners," a goal that we achieve through our "participation in a set of relationships to certain particular others who are able to give us what we need" (1999:98). The independent reasoner is one who is "able to give to others an intelligible account of one's reasoning," about means that may be theoretical or practical (1999:105). The ends are given, since fruitful debate with others in a community presupposes some agreement already about the relevant ends, but the debate about these ends falls outside the ken of the practical reasoner and within that of the educated person (one assumes), which, it is hoped, a sizeable number of former will become to form a public. Social relationships based on dependence produce an ethics of giving and receiving within which "I have to understand that what I am called upon to give may be disproportionate to what I have received and that those to whom I am called upon to give may well be those from whom I shall receive nothing. And I also have to understand that the care that I give to others has to be in an important way unconditional, since the measure of what is required of me is determined in key part, even if not only, by their needs" (1999:108). This ethics of needs is, evidently, the exact opposite of that of desert. "It is only," MacIntyre (1999:109) contends, "insofar as it is need that provides reasons for action for the members of some particular community that the community flourishes." He goes on to define the community in this most basic sense as a network of givers and receivers who recognize these reciprocal relationships of dependence and are practical reasoners engaging in ongoing debate about the common good that constitutes the community's flourishing. A third ethical principle arises from this, one of "conversational justice" that presupposes certain conditions of truth and economy for the debate: "first that each of us speaks with candor, not pretending or deceiving or striking attitudes, and secondly that each takes up no more time than is justified by the importance of the point that she or he has to make and the arguments necessary for making it" (1999:111).

MacIntyre rejects two kinds of ethical relationships for his community: bargaining relationships designed for and justified by the advantages of the parties involved in them, and those of sympathy that are spontaneous and therefore not subject to the direction of reason. Both, he argues, fail to consider the set of relationships of giving and receiving that typify social life and that should determine what is involved in different kinds of affective relationships, including our market relationships. Against them, borrowing from the Lakota custom of *wancantognaka* (and sounding, as we shall see, like Bataille and Derrida), he proposes an ethics of generosity to others through "acts of uncalculated giving," which, because it is owed, is demanded of one in the sense that failing to exhibit it is failing in respect of justice (1999:120). So, MacIntyre introduces yet another concept of justice, besides those of desert and conversational justice, one based on generosity in response to the needs of others. The virtue of just generosity, he continues, citing Aquinas, stems from a moral duty "to act from attentive and affectionate regard for (the) other" (1999:122). When the other is outside our community, such regard takes the form of hospitality (another Derridean concept), a form of generosity that extends to the whole of humanity and implies the virtue of *misericordia*: "grief and sorrow over someone else's distress ... just insofar as one understands the other's distress as one's own" (1999:125)—a virtue Aquinas described as one of the effects of charity. But MacIntyre argues that though just generosity requires a kind of giving that is, in principle, uncalculating, it also requires the virtue of temperateness, or prudent calculation, otherwise the principle becomes self-defeating since uncalculating profligacy leaves us with nothing more to give. Moreover, the virtues of giving, he continues, are complemented by the virtues of receiving, which require from the recipient "a truthful acknowledgement of dependence" (1999:127), namely "knowing how to exhibit gratitude, without allowing that gratitude to be a burden, courtesy towards the graceless giver, and forbearance towards the inadequate giver" (1999:126).

Turning to the politics of the community that embodies these relationships, MacIntyre (1999:129) says that they must satisfy three conditions: (1) "they must afford expression to the political decision making of independent reasoners on all those matters on which it is important that the members of a particular community be able to come through shared rational deliberation to a common mind," by affording them institutionalized forums for deliberation and procedures of decision-making that are generally acceptable, "so that both deliberation and decisions are recognizable as the work of the whole"; (2) the established norm of justice in these forums will be consistent with the virtue of just generosity that corresponds with Marx's notion of justice in a socialist society (1999:129), construed in a way such that it is characterized "both by effective appeals to desert and by effective appeals to need, and so by justice to and for both the independent and the dependent" (1999:130); (3) the political structures must "make it possible both for those capable of independent practical reason and for those whose exercise of reasoning is limited or nonexistent to have a voice in communal deliberation about what these norms of justice require," by giving a formal place to the role of proxy in the political structure (1999:132). These are not, he argues, conditions that can be satisfied by either the modern state or the family. The former—though it cannot, he again says, masquerade as a genuine community and guardian of the common good without rendering itself "ludicrous or disastrous or both"—cannot be ignored because of its massive resources, its coercive powers, "and the threats that its blundering and distorted benevolence presents, and because the security it provides is a public good" (1999:132). While insisting that the modern state cannot "provide a political framework informed by the just generosity necessary to achieve the common goods of networks of giving and receiving," he concedes that its "blundering" could bring some benefit in providing the means to remove some of the obstacles to humane goals that we want to achieve (1999:133). But the advice he gives is to approach it with prudence and suspicion; "to weigh any benefits that can be derived from it against the cost of entanglement with it" (1999:132).

If the political framework of just generosity required to sustain the community of givers and receivers cannot be the state, it cannot be the family either. It needs something larger in scope that incorporates the family, "some form of local community" within which "the activities of families, workplaces, schools, clinics, clubs dedicated to debate and clubs dedicated to games and sports, and religious congregations may all find a place" (1999:135). At its heart will be a willingness of each to learn about the common good and about one's own good from the other, including the badly disabled. Neither our common nor our individual good is ever learned without an attentive care and respect for the disabled, which requires us to stand in proxy for them, not primarily by theoretical reflection but "in everyday shared activities and the evaluations of alternatives that those activities impose" (1999:136). Such learning can be obscured by three things: our inability to detach ourselves from and stand back in judgment of our own desires, our lack of adequate self-knowledge, and our failure to recognize our dependence on others. Our encounters with the disabled for whom, in the spirit of friendship that the ethos of just generosity requires, we stand in proxy, are practically valuable to us in this sense because they contribute to our self-knowledge. They bring to light hitherto unrecognized sources of error in our own practical reasoning and teach us what it is for someone to be wholly entrusted to our care. In this way they help us reform our collective practices. The proxy's role, MacIntyre (1999:139) says, is to speak for the disabled "in just the way that that particular disabled individual would have done so for her or himself, had she or he still been able to speak." This is recognizing the political right of the disabled to have their voice heard in the community's deliberation. This participative politics of the community, which dwells on the perception that doing politics, as practical reasoning, is an activity every adult is capable of, is very different, he emphasizes, from the politics of the modern state, which only requires the political activity of a small minority against what are usually largely passive majorities. Revolutionary political struggles of the past that broke down the barriers to achieving modern citizenship, like abolishing slavery and extending the suffrage, he argues (confirming my earlier suspicions that he has little if any sympathy for democracy), involved degrees and forms of effective political participation "that are quite as alien to the democratic forms of the politics of the contemporary state as they are to non-democratic forms" (1999:142). But the obverse to the "communitarian mistake" that infuses the politics of the state with the values and modes of participation of the local community is to think that local communities are good things as such (1999:142). What we need, he concludes, somewhat as Dewey says about democratic forms of life, are comparative studies of different communities that will help us choose from the best practices around.

Similarities with MacIntyre

Something that struck me as interesting in MacIntyre's paradigm of competing university-educated publics in *TRV* was its resemblance to my own paradigm of competing education research projects in *PLE*.[50] Both are about wanting to rationalize the contesting voices in a pluralistic world into a coherent framework that would render them accessible to theory and permit them to communicate with each other without suppressing their plurality. My aim in *PLE*, as I remarked earlier, was to create a descriptive matrix within which the lifelong education movement's humanist educational philosophy with its notion of the learning society could be represented as an education research project in its own right competing with other projects that were about at the time, especially the liberal. MacIntyre wanted essentially the same thing in *TRV* for his ideal of a Thomist university and his notion of an educated public. In *JR* he asked a question raised in *AV* and left waiting in abeyance, namely, "How ought we to decide among the claims of rival and incompatible accounts of justice competing for our moral, social, and political allegiance?" (1988:2). This was a question I had also raised with respect to competing rival and incompatible education research projects when I wrote *PLE*. My answer then was that there is no way to measure them against each other, other than by referring to their state of health at any given time. Being healthier does not mean either being more just or true, or even better, nor does it necessarily constitute a good reason for offering a project our allegiance; otherwise we would all be supporting the neoliberal performativist project of lifelong learning and the learning society described in the previous chapter. I emphasized in *PLE* that embracing a politics of incommensurability need not, and in my case certainly did not, imply hermetic non-communication between the different projects, and that rules of touchstone could be negotiated between the competing parties to bring dialogue between them. But that was as far as I was ready to go.

Looking back on that paradigm now, in the light of my reading of MacIntyre, I acknowledge a fundamental error in it; by concerning itself with the touchstone conditions for dialogical conversation between adherents to the competing projects, it ignored the fact that any open exchange between them would be bound to be agonistic and conflictual also, as MacIntyre rightly emphasized. I understood these touchstone principles at the time the same way as MacIntyre, as mutually agreed-upon conditions for civil exchange that would enable the systematic exploration and charting of differences between the competing points of view, *but* within the spirit of consensus-seeking rather than combat. MacIntyre is right in insisting that the best political framework for describing the meeting together of different viewpoints keen to retain their difference and, probably, to affirm their ascendancy over one another, is one of conflict and combat, and that the framework of communication to be sought by the contending parties is not an ideal one of consensus-reaching but one of constraint and an agreement to disagree on fundamentals. In his commentary on *EP*, Graham Haydon (1987) raised questions about how philosophy is done today and how philosophers communicate among themselves, about (a) the extent to which philosophers themselves actually constitute a public, and (b) the extent to which philosophy is or can be the well-ordered dialogue of a public. I was sympathetic with his suggestion that philosophers should form a public at the time I wrote *PLE*, and that they should be looking around them to see why this was not the case; whether, as he wrote, the amount of skepticism and dogmatism going about at the time was not what was making the task impossible. MacIntyre himself does not believe so. He believes that the root problem lies in our modernist philosophical culture, which prevents philosophers from operating with a "single mind" (as they did when the dominant paradigm was analytic philosophy). His solution to this situation is, as we saw, to recognize that there are different minds in our pluralist modernist culture, principally Thomist, Encyclopaedist, and Genealogist; to accept it as an irreversible fact; to give up on the idea of a single all-encompassing mind; and to work within the culture of combat and competition just referred to. One could visualize both a Thomist and an Encyclopaedist education research project. In fact, MacIntyre's work on education over the years has been to create an education project of the first, Thomist, kind. The model of the education research project, however, as I shall argue in Chapter 6, does not suit the Genealogist, who would have fundamental objections to representing her philosophical outlook as friendly to a project of this sort, though she would not deny the need for or value of one.

Otherwise, apart from this difference I have pointed to, our respective criteria for identifying a project as internally progressive at the theoretical level, namely (to use his words), "only if and insofar as it is able to transcend the limitations and failures of that earlier stage, limitations and failures by the standards of rationality of that earlier stage itself" (1990:180–181), were essentially similar. It was when he went on to talk about commensurability, about being able to establish "the rational superiority" of a tradition over other rival traditions, that we parted, and still part, company. He believes that such superiority can be shown if a particular tradition has the "capacity not only for identifying and characterizing the limitations and failures of that rival tradition as judged by that rival tradition's own standards, limitations and failures which that rival tradition lacks the resources to explain or understand, but also for explaining and understanding those limitations and failures in some tolerably precise way" (1990:181). This criterion, however, runs into serious difficulties if rationality is acknowledged, as it is by both of us, to be relative to traditions, so that there are no Archimedean points from which to examine the pluralistic world. For, this being the case, bringing standards or criteria of rationality to bear on some other tradition is always bringing one's own standards to bear on it. One's judgment has no force behind it other than that. Or at least no force that those within the tradition being judged will acknowledge. This being the case, I cannot see how, if the tradition being judged lacks the resources to explain and understand its own "limitations and failures," one can get its supporters to acknowledge that they exist; once those same resources, whatever their weaknesses in the eyes of an outsider, are the resources that are available to them and the only resources that they will recognize as legitimate. Moreover, the fact that one has the resources to detect internal inconsistency within a rival project to which its holders appear to be blind does not render one's own project superior to it except in one's own eyes. How can one assume that there are not blind spots within one's own project, perhaps even more serious ones, that have as yet to be pointed out and that one is still unconscious of? Anyway, "tolerably precise" is not a good enough criterion of measurement to serve the purpose of objectivity, since what is "tolerable" is also defined differently between traditions. In short, this attempt to smuggle a rational criterion of commensurability between competing rationalities into his paradigm fails. It probably stems, as his modified biological approach to theorizing in *DRA* indicates, from a lingering unhappiness with the idea that his own preferred model cannot be claimed as somehow more "rational," humane, or progressive than the others.

I agreed, on the other hand, with MacIntyre regarding the role he would assign to philosophy and philosophers (or philosophically trained intellectuals) in a particular project or tradition, as he refers to it. He criticizes both today for offering ordinary people little or no moral or intellectual guidance, which is not available to them either from "more or less organized communities of shared belief, such as churches or sects, religious and nonreligious, or certain kinds of political association" (1988:3). The best academic philosophy can do, he says, is help articulate the differences and issues for us without helping us resolve them. And when people turn to churches, sects, and so on, "they put their trust in persons rather than in arguments," and thus "cannot escape the charge of a certain arbitrariness in their commitments" (1988:5). He worries that this state of affairs doesn't seem to concern ordinary people unduly, laying this indifference down either to a cynical fideism on their part or to a distrust of intellectuals. The latter owes itself, he says, to a suspicion they harbor, often founded, that the intellectuals in their midst, the lawyers, academics, economists, journalists, and so forth, favor rational argumentation because this is where they are skillful and where they can use their power best. This suspicion leads them to perceive the discourses of these intellectuals not as sincere expressions of a disinterested rationality but as "weapons" of manipulation, the techniques for deploying which furnish a key part of their professional skills. Such weapons they use to "dominate the dialectically unfluent and inarticulate" (1988:5). Reassurance, he believes, will come to ordinary people only if they come to perceive their intellectuals as operating within the same practice, the same intellectual and moral tradition as themselves. And I would have had no problem at all when I wrote *PLE* in going along with this conclusion. In the specific case of philosophers of education they would, I thought, work at the research project they support, maintaining it in a theoretically progressive state and critiquing its practice, and regarding themselves as conversational partners with other non-philosophers (theorists, policy-makers, educators and educationalists, members of its educated public, of the general public, etc.) who share their allegiance to it, so that a kind of community of inquiry would grow around it. In fact, in essence, I believed, like MacIntyre, that an education project requires a public—though did not use the term "public" at all in *PLE*—to debate it and keep it under critical review, and a community to make it operational. Influenced as I was by the Rorty of *PMN*, however, I regarded the status of the philosopher of education within the community differently from that envisaged by MacIntyre. I saw her as a fellow conversationalist with the other partners in the education project, with the special task of keeping the project's conversation going, rather than setting its agenda, or worse still, regarding oneself as the guardian of its orthodoxy.

MacIntyre's Learning Communities

It is not difficult to see a well-defined Aristotelian education project with a Thomist core emerging in MacIntyre's work over the span of his writing from *AV* to *DRA*, of which the formal notions of practice, virtues, educated public, partisan university, and community are key operational features. This project addresses the learning society not on the broad national scale described in Chapter 2 but on the smaller, more manageable scale of the local community. In valuing the community as the locus of the learning society, MacIntyre points to the danger of conceiving learning societies on the scale of national communities. More importantly, he contends that the modern state cannot engineer a learning society that educates. Indeed, any learning society it engineers can, from his point of view, only strengthen its totalitarian tendencies. Today, well over a decade and a half after his Richard Peters lecture of 1985, his view is that the situation with education has worsened and things have become even more difficult than before for teachers working within the formal educational structures, the schools and the universities, who wish to educate (MacIntyre & Dunne 2002:1). In his interview with Dunne, he adds two "major threats" to education to the ones he identified then: underresourcing and "the baneful influence of an idea of schools, colleges and universities as engaged in activities the measure of which is productivity" (2002:4). These are the "threats" that were, more or less, identified in the previous chapter of this book, where, however, I wrote about the underresourcing of adult education rather than the schools, but performativity was identified as the measure of progress for the whole education system. The question now is whether, once MacIntyre recognizes the reality posed by the threat of performativity to the universities I described myself in this chapter, he still has any hope that his radical new politics for the university system in *TRV* can succeed. If he gives it up, he also gives up on the idea of an educated public as he conceived it and, from his point of view, he is left with one remaining hope in the postmodern world, the original one expressed in *AV*: recalcitrant local learning communities expressing one mind, compact havens of enlightened learning and centers of hope and humane solidarity (as he describes them), with their own partisan schools that conform with that mind, fighting against the postmodern current.

What he says about schools, on the general principle that parents should have the right to choose their children's education, is, "Where there are rival traditions within one and the same local society, it may well be best for each tradition to have its own primary and secondary schools" (2002:12). This is logical, of course, consistent with his view that rival traditions should have their own universities. So that the general education project that emerges from his writing is one in which communities of like-minded people, belonging to the same moral, religious, and intellectual tradition, would set up their own denominational schools within their local society where their children would be taught and prepared for entry into matching universities to become members of an educated public that provides them with their intellectual and moral leaders, and that sets the lower intellectual targets of independent practical reasoner or just, on a lower scale, practical reasoners, for those who do not make it to the universities. In this same interview with Dunne, MacIntyre insists constantly, not only with reference to the universities but to the schools also, that partisanship should not mean an inward-looking indoctrination or parochialism. Children should learn "at some early stage" that there are other and rival traditions and what some of them teach, so that they understand how fundamental disagreements about the human good arise (2002:12).[51] But he seems to disregard the risk these communities run, nevertheless, of developing a fortress or siege mentality where the object becomes that of keeping the barbarians with whom we, and our children, mix at the moment, firmly at the gate, and that this mentality easily degenerates into one of fear and prejudice rather than hospitality toward the other. The kinds of traditions he mentions at the level of the school are religious, Protestant, and Catholic within the example he uses (the local societies in Ulster), and, presumably, others also, including Moslem and Jewish, if they are present in some particular society—very different traditions from those into which he separates the universities. So the question arises, why didn't he envisage Muslim, Jewish, and other denominational universities also in *TRV*?

On reflection he might. Indeed, he would reasonably expect to receive more enthusiastic support for his project from these quarters than he would from Genealogists and Encyclopaedists. On the other hand, while Encyclopaedist schools have been advocated by liberals, Genealogist schools would be impossible.

MacIntyre's education project qualifies as a project for a learning community because, as we saw, it is not confined to formal learning institutions like schools, colleges, and universities. In *DRA* he devotes as much, if not more, care in describing the non-formal and informal pedagogy of the community itself in terms of its upbringing practices, or its practices of enculturation—intended to produce independent practical reasoners—as he does in *AV* in describing the process of educating, tracing out in detail the transition from the state of total dependence of infancy into adulthood and the acquisition of independent reasoning in three stages. The first involves the transition from merely having reasons, which is our situation in early childhood, to being able to evaluate them as good or bad, thereby deciding on whether to act on them or not. The second is the ability to stand back from our present desires so as to be able to evaluate them, as a necessary condition for engaging in sound reasoning about our reasons for action. Neither of these transitions is made alone and a number of obstacles could stand in their way: physical, social, and psychological. Other people enter their history by providing the resources (nursing, feeding, clothing, nurturing, teaching, restraining, and advising), and by helping us avoid encountering and falling victim to disabling conditions; to obtain needed, often scarce, resources; to discover what ways forward there may be; and to stand in our place from time to time, doing for us what we cannot do for ourselves (1999:73). The move from being aware only of the present to one in which one's view is informed by an imagined future is the third and final stage of the transition and completes the process of becoming independent practical thinkers: persons who are able "to understand ourselves as directed to a range of goals that are more or less remote from our present situation and to order our desires accordingly" (1999:76). MacIntyre describes the relationship between the three stages as complex but interdependent and contributing toward a single process of development, so that failure at any one stage compromises the others. He completes his account by outlining the virtues of independent practical reasoners, and also those of caring and teaching that the enablers who make essential contributions to the process need, and how they relate to the virtues of the practical reasoner (1999:77). Just as the virtues are exercised in the whole range of our activities, they must also be learned in the same range of activities and contexts of practice in which we learn from others how to discharge our roles and functions within the home, the school, and later according to our calling.

Accordingly MacIntyre distinguishes different teachers, their roles, objects, methods, and virtues, operating in different learning contexts with different relationships to the learner, starting with the parents, the mother especially, who play a leading role in bringing their child to the point where it is educable by other teachers. These teachers take over then and teach the elements of various practices; namely the skills each one of them requires and how to recognize the goods internal to each practice, especially those in terms of the achievement of which its excellence is defined. The virtues these teachers need are those of risk-taking and patience, courage, justice in assigning tasks and praise, the temperateness required for discipline, and the cheerful wit of an amiable will (1999:92). At this second stage of growth, MacIntyre says, the object is not to encourage children to question the goods internal to the practice but to teach them how to recognize these goods and respond rightly to them. The goal is to help them identify what the harms and dangers are in each situation, and what the virtues require them to do by way of response (1999:93). Also, as we saw earlier, to acquaint them with different ways in which these goods are understood in different cultures or traditions and the practices they give rise to. Knowing how to act virtuously, however, involves more than simple rulefollowing; it needs the other elements of practical reasoning also, namely reasoning skills and self-knowledge (as distinct from self-discovery, which is the task not of enculturation but education), and other kinds of knowledge as well; otherwise we are unable to imagine the range of realistic alternative futures open to us in our circumstances. Honesty is the virtue that makes possible the achievement of self-knowledge and the ability to resist self-deception. It remains important for self-discovery where, in addition, one requires humility, courage, and justice.

Throughout his account MacIntyre keeps emphasizing that we do not become independent practical reasoners on our own; we need the support of others who are able to give us what we need for the purpose and to continue to sustain our efforts to remain so and improve ourselves later in adult life, as we grow older. These others are our parents, family, and members of our household to begin with, then they could be "farmer workers or carpenters or teachers or members of a fishing crew or a string quartet" (1999:89) our friends, coworkers, and so on. Our interaction with these various sorts of people we live with on different occasions and in different places, in family settings, workplaces, schools, churches, clubs, and so on, enables us to continue to develop our skills, exercise our virtues, and acquire significant knowledge. In short, he also recognizes the value of lifewide learning, and not simply that which comes from one's interaction with other members of a like-minded community but also that which comes from one's interaction with members of the broader society. There is in his account of the joint responsibility for the upbringing and continuing growth of members of the local community the kind of mobilization of its human, spatial, and institutional resources in the service of cultivating independent practical reasoners that qualifies it as a microlearning society. This reminds us of similar accounts by the lifelong education writers of the movement, who also encouraged a collective responsibility of the community to ensure the lifelong education of its members. MacIntyre's view is that, with proper initial upbringing in the family, an appropriate schooling, and the willingness of different members of the community to contribute their part to the process, the quality of independent practical reasoning is within everyone's grasp. To go a step further, however, beyond the independent practical reasoning one needs to engage actively in the life of the community and its politics and to become a member of the educated public, one requires a university education. Here, at the university, what is required of teachers is not the kind of generous relationship with students captured by Aquinas's account of *misericordia* that motivates the community's sense of duty toward its members, helping them to grow into independent practical reasoners, but a very different kind based on the magnanimity that marked Aristotle's *megalopsychos*.

In sum, MacIntyre's learning community, as I have called it, which is small and local and more intimate and morally and intellectually coherent than a local society, has three kinds of members: educated, independent practical reasoners, and dependent. The first reason about ends, the second about means, and the third reason through the proxy of the other members. This creates two levels of discourse in his learning community within a single tradition or common mind: that of the philosophically trained, educated public gravitating intellectually around the university and debating about ends, about "the ultimate human good"; and that of the independent practical reasoners in the community debating about the means of converting the theoretical ends into the practices of everyday life. The discourse of the former is theoretical, regulated by the criterion of truth within practices; while that of the latter is pragmatic, regulated by criteria of conversational justice. Then, besides these publics, there are the dependent of various categories, infants and very young children and the disabled generally, who do not constitute a public at all but whose voices are heard in the pragmatic deliberations of the community by proxy through the voices of others who speak for them in matters of justice. The university education of the members of the educated public will include hermeneutic skills that will enable them to assess other traditions from within their own and absorb from them that which is useful and good, in order to ensure that the practice they subscribe to does not become solipsistic or unduly self-absorbed. But it will also include initiation into the art of conflict, as they will be required to test and defend their beliefs and arguments against those pushing the interests of these rival traditions. At the same time, while recognizing the fact of conflict and difference with other points of view as important, MacIntyre insists that we should not be blinded to those large areas of potential agreement that allow us to come together with them, and that disagreement, where it occurs, should be kept civil. Thus, while the conversation within a practice will be contained by the rules and the *ethos* of the same practice, conflict with others requires the negotiation of rules of fair combat institutionalized in a forum of conflict. Fighting fairly in this case, he argues, requires us to keep our partisan viewpoint but to be loyal to the rules of conflict and to the purposes of the encounter.

CHAPTER FOUR

Habermas: The Rational Society

Habermas and Education

One striking omission from the set of intellectual traditions that MacIntyre identifies as alive and kicking in the late modern world in *TRV* is the Marxist. This may be why he shows no interest in the Frankfurt School, in Adorno and Horkheimer in particular—who were, like himself, critical of modernity and its project and interested in restoring a rational public to modern societies. Neither did he show interest in Habermas, the critical theorist who has been a key protagonist in the debate about the future of modernity on both sides of the Atlantic more recently, the very debate that, as we saw in the previous chapter, lies at the heart of MacIntyre's own writing.[52] MacIntyre could not, at the time he published *TRV* (in 1990), have regarded Habermas, even remotely, as a Marxist.[53] The dismissive comments he has frequently made about Marxism in more recent times, could not, therefore, have applied to him. My own interest in the Frankfurt School theorists when I was writing this book evidently stemmed, like my interest in MacIntyre, from their interest in the notion of the "rational society": a utopian society that Horkheimer represented in his earlier writing as the true, just, and virtuous order of things. One, as he put it, that achieves the true unity of theory and practice and gives rise not to exploitative but to authentic "labor." But it started with an interest in Habermas, who also took up the subject of the rational society in his early work, rather than the other way around. Habermas, I knew at the outset, was politically close to Dewey and a social democrat. I therefore expected him, unlike MacIntyre, to be on my own political wavelength, an ally. I read him with the hope that, like Dewey, he could be useful in my attempt to theorize my learning society, while I read MacIntyre from the first as a potential opponent.

Contrary to MacIntyre and like Dewey, Habermas is sympathetic toward both social democratic liberalism and modernism. He believes that the Enlightenment project of modernity, though needing radical revision, was basically right and disagrees that it should be rejected outright.[54] With Dewey, on the other hand, he shares distaste for the capitalist brand of individualism. Both he and Dewey are for retaining and revising the fundamental liberal values that they take the capitalist *ethos* of the modern world with its "rugged individualism" (as Dewey calls it) to have distorted and disfigured beyond recognition but not entirely eclipsed (they are also specters that continue to haunt our modern/postmodern world), though they both tend politically toward social democracy. Both are strong democrats convinced that these liberal values can be recovered through the reconstitution of a critical public sphere. Moreover, both identify the practice of democracy with the conditions of communicative action. Habermas has said less directly about the subject of education than MacIntyre, even where, as his critics point out, it seemed particularly appropriate for him to do so. But his reception at the hands of philosophers of education has not been nearly as cold as MacIntyre's. More generally, as one commentator has put it: "Habermas has not directly addressed education as a social practice. In the few instances in which Habermas directly mentions education, he mentions it as an example rather than as a main topic. For this reason, the significance of Habermas's work for education is best viewed from the perspective of the educational literature that applies Habermas's theories and concepts," rather than that of his own work (Ewert 1991:346). The literature Ewert refers to is mainly critical pedagogy, such as written by Michael Apple, Henry Giroux, Robert Young, and Peter MacLaren, all of whom have extended critical theory's central interests in the ideological underpinnings of everyday practices and problems into the area of the curriculum, the school, and the classroom, and into the politics of teaching and of the text.

In the mid-1980s, while Habermas's star was in the ascent among these writers, one commentator observed that in Europe "the era of emancipatory or critical pedagogy seems to have come to an end" (Masschelein 1985:95). Brian Connelly (1996:242), however, has remarked about Habermas's increasing influence on adult education theory in the first half of the 1990s, thanks largely to Mezirow's work on perspective transformation, on "transformative critical reflection on the constraining psycho-social assumptions which inform our identity," linked with emancipatory action.[55] Schaller does not amplify on his remark about his dwindling influence in Europe, which may have been prompted by the rising influence of "postmodernism," which Habermas himself saw as his future enemy, much as MacIntyre saw his enemy in liberalism. But Joseph Masschelein (1991:95–96) opines that it could be due to an excessive focus on the methodological and meta-theoretical aspects of his work and insufficient attention to his theory of social action. He suggests that "the meaning of Habermas's notion of 'communicative action' for the conceptualization of education has not sufficiently been taken into account." Masschelein argues that Habermas's account of intersubjectivity in his theory of communicative action is, indeed, a significant and fruitful territory for educators, since linguistic interaction is, as another commentator remarks, "surely both central and basic to any educational practice," leading as it does "directly and quickly into concern with learning processes at both the individual and social level" (Blake 1995:355).

Connelly (1996:245) points to a number of areas of Habermas's work that are fertile for adult education theory but generally ignored by those who have used his work: "One such theme is the systems-lifeworld thesis (Habermas, 1988) where Habermas argues that the economic and political institutions increasingly dominate the lifeworld of lived experience and the private world. This distortion of the lifeworld also involves the 'colonization' of education (Habermas, 1987b)." This is evidently a thesis that is fundamentally interesting to the debate on the learning society, suggesting an analysis of the learning society as something produced in the tension between systems and lifeworld. Indeed, Habermas's sociology of the modern/postmodern world, his work on the rational society and the politics of the public sphere, became relevant to the 1990s when the notion of the learning society came into focus again, and when interest in lifewide learning was resumed. Over the years, in fact, he has provided an in-depth analysis of the learning mechanisms of our modern-postmodern societies, contrasting their ideological distortions with the emancipatory possibilities of communicative action in ideal speech situations. In this way he has not only described the way our societies learn, he has also proposed a normative criterion against which to measure them as democratic learning societies, namely that they must satisfy the universal conditions of ideal speech, though, as we shall see, his understanding of this notion has suffered drastic modifications with time (as have those of enlightenment and emancipation). Systems he reminds us, teach, or *steer* the lifeworld in different ways. Theirs is the business, to put it in his language, of "will-formation" (a more brutal, but perhaps more precise, term than enculturation), and it occurs not only directly through the activities of formal educational agencies but also through the colonization of the lifeworld by the system. One recalls his terse judgment on institutionalized "adult education" four decades ago in 1962, in *The Structural Transformation of the Public Sphere*, (1989a, henceforth *STP*), that it is simply one of the ordering agencies of the contemporary system, created to substitute, not to produce, critical debating publics. And his response to this state of affairs later is to encourage a dose of anarchy from the lifeworld and originating outside the systems of institutionalized adult learning.

In sum, Habermas's sociology of the modern-postmodern world, his theory of social action, his theorization of an emancipatory society founded on communicative action that responds to the conditions of ideal speech, are important when education needs to be reconceptualized in a context where the focus of discourse shifts from schooling to the learning society. Habermas has, like MacIntyre, explored the possibility of reconstituting a critical, rational public sphere at the interface of system and lifeworld to respond to the technocratic rationalization of the lifeworld he describes in his sociology and to the false publicity of the media. In the early stage of his writing, as Robert Young (1990) remarks, his preoccupations were mainly epistemological, about the nature and validation of knowledge, however, then he changed focus and, like Dewey, became interested rather in the kind of knowledge that is produced by the social ontology of the modern world. Young (1990:472) observes that with this change of focus epistemological questions are "set *within* a theory of knowers as social beings" rather than in the abstract where they are made to refer to the nature and justification of knowledge. This crucial shift toward a pragmatic epistemology, he remarks, is what enables both Habermas and Dewey "to focus on the epistemic politics of the knowing community," or learning society as I am calling it (1990:473). The two philosophers actually complement each other in this respect in that while Dewey focuses more narrowly on the epistemic politics of schooling communities, Habermas focuses on the broader society, the systems and lifeworld. He thus, in point of fact, takes on a task before which most self-styled educational theorists have balked: that of describing, like his Frankfurt predecessors, how modern societies learn, how they are learning societies, and how they could learn if they were interested in emancipatory rather than performativist outcomes and turned into "communicative communities." In sum, if, as Helmut Peukert (1992:121) remarks, "the basic task for a theory of education as well as a theory of democracy remains to develop a critical concept of communication which would be able to describe the structure and goal of transformatory educational processes and, at the same time, to establish the regulative ideals for communication in collective non-ideological decision-making," this is what Habermas gives us as his contribution to a theory of a democratic learning society or learning democracy.

The Rational Society

In the late 1930s, Horkheimer's disillusionment with the modern world and his loss of faith in the working class movement's development into a revolutionary force that would emancipate society from the evils of capitalism led him to develop his critical standpoint on lines more and more independent of it. Critical theory, he came to believe, must have its claim to "objectivity" justified otherwise than by a Marxist point of reference. "The rational organization of society" was what it "set itself to elucidate and legitimize" (Held 1980:195). The goal of a truly rational society, in his view, is not set ideologically but given anthropologically in human beings as such as potential; in interests lying "immanent in man," in "his" yearning for emancipation.[56] This representation of emancipation as a fundamentally human interest echoes in Habermas's writing for a long time, providing him with scope for a restatement of critical theory that is optimistic in the possibility of a rational society after the gloom and doom of the *Dialectic*. The early Habermas was also to share Horkheimer's view that the concept of the rational society could be gained only in praxis, *ex negativo*, pointed to by immanent critique and attained by freedom from the contradictions of the existing order, not through ideological utopianism. Horkheimer was prepared to say little, if anything, concrete about what this rational society could be like, contending like Marx that its conditions could emerge only in *praxis*, in the struggle for the future conceived of as an emancipatory struggle. Critique, he held, was necessary to assess the actual contemporary potential for its coming into being, but it could not take us beyond that. Concrete political action required it to be linked with some actual historical movement and program. Without such a movement, he believed, the critique itself had no credibility. His optimism in earlier years that such a movement was possible was backed up with the observation that collective struggle was historically a part of the experience of many people. So there was nothing preposterous, he believed, about the idea that it could occur in modern times. His loss of faith in the clear-sightedness of the proletariat, in its ability to recognize its own real self-interest as a truly revolutionary movement, however, and his inability to see any alternative revolutionary force anywhere on the horizon, together with his actual experience of the contemporary flourishing of totalitarianism everywhere in Europe in the years preceding World War II, eventually led him to the total pessimism with the modern world he shared with Adorno, which produced the *Dialectic*. This pessimism was reaffirmed in their joint introduction to the 1969 reprint of the book nearly a quarter of a century after the war was over, and it led them both to withdraw from doing social theory and from their former political interests and to retire into different intellectual interests and activities.[57]

Their pessimism was not shared, however, by Herbert Marcuse, who published *An Essay on Liberation* (1969), a work dedicated to the young militants, the student intelligentsia, of the 1968 Paris revolts at about the same time. Marcuse (1969:11) saw in these revolts—together with Marxist-inspired guerrilla-based revolutions sprouting in different parts of the globe—a sign of a "great refusal" of Western capitalism everywhere, exposing the weakness of its powers of containment, despite the "threatening homogeneity" described by Adorno and Horkheimer and despite the fact that its "so-called consumer economy and the politics of corporate capitalism have created a second nature of man which ties him libidinally and aggressively to the commodity form." In his *Essay* Marcuse (1969:viii) defended utopian thinking, insisting that it was not only in order but necessary. Looking into the space beyond the limits of the Establishment where a new and free society can be constructed, he argued, "necessitates an historical break with the past and present." His dream, echoed in Suchodolski and others of the utopian strain of the lifelong education movement, was of a new type of man coming into being in a type of socialist society that would respond to "his" real "needs" and create a social environment for "him" different from the present "context of violence and exploitation" that characterized advanced capitalism. It would be a utopian society where a newly formed consciousness or sensibility and "a desublimated scientific intelligence would combine in the creation of an *aesthetic ethos*" (1969:24, italics in original) and where "the abolition of poverty and toil terminates in a universe where the sensuous, the playful, the calm, and the beautiful become forms of existence and thereby the *Form* of the society itself" (1969:25, italics in original).

Marcuse recognized the difficulty of achieving this utopia in practice within the "general framework of repression" of contemporary capitalist society (1969:29). Had he not, after all, written his own dystopian account of this society, *One-Dimensional Man* in 1964, only a few years before?[58] Still, in 1969, he was confident that that repressive framework could be infiltrated by subversive "collective practices" taking "surrealistic forms of protest and refusal" (1969:30). He also saw a new potential for revolution in the languages of black militant groups and hippie subcultures, which created a rupture from the language of domination, and which he interpreted as "a systematic linguistic rebellion, which smashes the ideological context in which the words are employed and defined" (1969:35), as well as in contemporary manifestations of "anti-art," which involved the "destruction of syntax," the "fragmentation of words and sentences," and the "explosive use of ordinary language, compositions without score, sonatas for anything" (1969:41–42). He admitted that the Establishment had partly "absorbed" this rebellious aesthetic "in the art gallery" (1969:42), just as it had harnessed science and technology into its bureaucratic infrastructure. Marcuse (1969:45), however, alternates respectful awe before an Establishment "whose capabilities defy the imagination" and whose resources to combat its own "negativity" are limitless, typical of the Frankfurt School, with this optimism that it can be infiltrated by radical aesthetic impulses, by newly emerging subversive subcultures and lifestyles, and by *avant garde* art which, as we shall see, later influenced Habermas. His dream of a socialist utopia is the dream of a society where "free men (or rather men in the practice of freeing themselves) shape their life in solidarity, and build an environment in which the struggle for existence loses its ugly and aggressive features" (1969:46). In the *Essay* Marcuse (1969:52) expressed confidence that, cut loose from the middle classes and from "the organized working class," the student movement and the ghetto populations were capable of such "spontaneous solidarity," and described the late 1960s optimistically as "the period of enlightenment prior to material change—a period of educa-tion, but education which turns into praxis demonstration, confrontation, rebellion" (1969:53). He recognized the limitations of the student movement, however, in that as a revolutionary force it could not take up the mission of the proletariat, because it had no mass backing. It could not seize power and take society into the brave new world of his socialist utopia.

Its rebellion could only "lead to an extension and development of consciousness which would remove the ideological and technological veil that hides the terrible features of the affluent society." It could only, in short, serve the purpose of education, or consciousness-raising, of unmasking the contemporary society and, he hoped, encourage the proletariat to take up the revolutionary cause spontaneously. At the same time it was this potential to perform its educative task, Marcuse (1969:61) believed, that made it so feared and hated all around, including by the official left, the workers' movement.

Unsurprisingly, Marcuse (1969:61) defended the "politicization" of the university in this period against those who opposed it in the name of "the pseudo-neutral features of academia," describing struggle as the very "internal dynamic of education," required for the "translation of knowledge into reality, of humanistic values into humane conditions of existence." Conceived in this way, as *praxis*, he argued, education must be taken "beyond the universities, into the streets, the slums, the 'community'" (1969:62). The "unorthodox" nature of the current struggle, its lack of a class basis, which gave it its instinctual, strange, antinomian, anarchic, even non-political appearance was its strength. "In the face of the gruesomely serious totality of institutionalized politics, "satire, irony, and laughing provocation become a necessary dimension of the new politics," he remarked. "The rebels revive the desperate laughter and the cynical defiance of the fool as a means for demasking the deed of the serious ones who govern the whole" (1969:64). As we shall see, this dimension of ludic aestheticism that Marcuse detects and praises in the student revolt, in *avant garde* art and militant subcultures, was inherited not by Habermas, who continued to aspire lingeringly for the rational society and who was put off rather by this aspect of the student revolt, but by a postmodernism also influenced by Nietzsche. Marcuse (1969:89), on his part, praised the "strong element of spontaneity, even anarchism," in the revolt, "the aversion against pre-established leaders, apparatchiks of all sorts, politicians no matter how Leftist." In this way of doing politics, he observed, "the initiative shifts to small groups, widely diffused, with a high degree of autonomy, mobility and flexibility," waging an intermittent guerrilla warfare against the system. Powerful shades not of Habermas but of Foucault! Habermas, like the lifelong education writers, has been more inclined to favor the more stable and organized strategies of social movements. But it is important to remember with respect to Marcuse, that although he regarded the infiltration of society by an anarchic, nihilistic, ludic element as an indispensable factor of struggle against domination, he also held that this spontaneity could not itself be the basis of the new society, which had to be a rational society. Elsewhere, in fact, he warned that "the less a society is rationally organized and directed by the collective efforts of free men, the more it will appear as ... governed by 'inexorable' laws," and prone to totalitarianism (Held 1980:172).

Erich Fromm, another veteran of the old Frankfurt School, took an altogether different line on capitalism from Marcuse's. He began *The Sane Society* (1971) in 1956 with a typically negative analysis of the modern Western world's state of "sanity," gauged on published rates of suicide, homicide, and alcoholism (today he would undoubtedly have added drug abuse and AIDS to the list), which echoed Adorno's view that modern Western societies showed no signs of any moral progress over earlier societies at all. He held the Marxian view that alienation is "the central issue of the effects of Capitalism on personality" (1971:120). Like Horkheimer he held that "needs like the striving for happiness, harmony, love and freedom are inherent in ['man's'] nature" (1971:81) and represent dynamic factors in history that render it potentially permanently revolutionary even if frustrated by current actualities. Unlike Marcuse, however, whose negative attitude toward capitalist societies was total and uncompromising, Fromm (1971:207) identified progressive elements in them, pointing, as Habermas did later, to "a humanistic tradition alive" in them that alienation has not destroyed, and that resonated with his communitarian socialist beliefs.[59] He pointed to "millions of people" in America involved in authentic "informal" learning who "listen to good music in concert halls or over the radio, an ever-increasing number of people paint, do gardening, build their own boats or houses, indulge in any number of 'do it yourself' activities." And formal adult education "is spreading, and even in business the awareness is growing that an executive should have reason and not only intelligence." Fromm's argument, like Habermas's later, uncongenial to Marcuse, was that the ideals and norms of Western civilization are positive and that impressing them on people should be the task of education. What is "woefully inadequate," he complained (like his Frankfurt colleagues), are our institutional agencies, which continue to aim "at the usefulness of our citizens for the purposes of the social machine," rather than their education (1971:345).

Fromm (1971:347, italics in original) urged the promotion of non-formal adult learning programs in "collective art," which require us "*to respond to the world with our senses in a meaningful, skilled, productive, active, shared way.*" Programs of this kind, he argued, would play a key role in the "transformation of an atomistic into a communitarian society" by creating "the opportunity for people to sing together, walk together, dance together, admire together," again, "together, and not, to use Reisman's succinct expression, as a member of a 'lonely crowd'" (1971:349). At the same time, however, aware of the limitations of these programs, he observed that the "sanity and health" of our societies "can be attained only by simultaneous changes in the sphere of industrial and political organization, of spiritual and philosophical orientation, of character structure, and of cultural activity" (1971:271). In the world of industry on "the idea of workers' participation and co-management, on decentralization, and on the concrete function of man in the working process" (1971:327). In politics on the replacement of an anonymous mass-voting atmosphere with intimate face-to-face encounters in the public sphere. Still, this is very different from the unrelenting pessimism of the authors of the *Dialectic* and from Marcuse's revolutionary optimism. Fromm suggests that a rational, or sane, society is still recuperable in the current reality of liberal democratic, capitalist societies, and so did Habermas.

The Culture Industry

A crucial part of the Frankfurt School theorists' critique of the modern learning society, ignored by Marcuse and Fromm but not by Habermas, focuses on the media. Adorno and Horkheimer created the expression "culture industry" in the *Dialectic* and introduced the concept of a "mass culture" and of a "mass society" for the purpose of their critique. Their basic thesis was that, finding itself in crisis or at least under severe pressure, the modern capitalist state harnesses the considerable powers at its disposal, including the cultural, for its self-preservation, projecting culture, infiltrated with the ethos and mentality of the market, as an "industry." As Adorno (1989:129) put it so well later when he wrote about it alone in 1967, "the entire practice of the culture industry transfers the profit motive naked onto cultural forms." It serves as the tool for the economic arm of capitalism, banking and finance, to infiltrate society with new, suitable, aesthetic standards that accord with the financial logic of the marketability of a product, and that emphasize the value of presentation and public relations. According to this logic, culture ceases to be the expression of genuine human demands and becomes a marketable commodity instead, interchangeable like any other; the logic of possession, of "having" as Lengrand would put it, rather than that of "being," which is the true province of education. In short, the culture industry is an important dimension to the "learning industry," a notion that has become as much a part of our lifelong learning vocabulary today as learning organization, and that is fundamental to the description of today's learning society. Only, while the notion is problematic for Adorno, it is simply accepted as part of the natural landscape of today's learning society in the lifelong learning discourse.

In his essay Adorno (1989:128–129) explains that he and Horkheimer had replaced the expression "mass culture," which they had originally thought of using, with "culture industry" in order "to exclude from the outset the interpretation agreeable to its advocates; that it is something like a culture that arises spontaneously from the masses themselves, the contemporary form of popular art," and to confront it with the real "planned" nature of the "industry," which, far from liberating the creative energies of the masses, as the term "mass culture" could suggest, studiously turns them into "an object of calculation, an appendage of the machinery." However, "the expression *industry*," he continues, "is not to be taken literally... It is industrial more in a sociological sense, in the incorporation of industrial forms of organization even where nothing is manufactured—as in the rationalization of office work—rather than the sense of anything actually produced by technological rationality" (1989:130). It is its style that renders the culture industry industrial rather than what it actually produces, which may not even be a product. Far from educating, the culture industry, Adorno (1989:129) says, "misuses its concern for the masses in order to duplicate, reinforce, and strengthen their mentality, which it presumes is given and unchangeable." The term "mass media," he remarks, was "specially honed for the culture industry" in order to misrepresent itself as normatively neutral or harmless, when through it the Establishment appropriates culture and denaturalizes it by stripping it of its revolutionary potential and turning it into a commodity, thereby "debasing" people in the process. And he leaves no doubt as to the thoroughness with which it commodifies culture: the "cultural entities typical of the culture industry are no longer *also* commodities, they are commodities through and through." As the profit interests that originated it "have become objectified in its ideology," he continues, the capitalist state has turned the culture industry into its instrument of public relations; (1989:129) an "ordering factor" for the Establishment, Adorno (1989:133) calls it, that "extols order *in abstracto*" as an unqualified good, and "hammers into human beings" the concepts of order, which "are always those of the *status quo*." The "consensus which it propagates strengthens blind, opaque authority" (1989:134).

While "thorough research has not, for the time being," he concedes, "produced an airtight case proving the regressive effects of particular products of the culture industry, it can be assumed without hesitation that steady drops hollow the stone, especially since the system of the culture industry that surrounds the masses tolerates hardly any deviation and incessantly drills the same formulas of behavior" (1989:134). The cumulative outcome is beyond doubt: A learning society is created where adults are systematically informed and equally systematically disempowered, since they are only as "ripe" for emancipation and empowerment "as the productive forces of the epoch permit" (1989:135). As I said earlier, Adorno and Horkheimer had no doubt that what guides the productive forces in modern life is an instrumental rationality, which makes for the "total administration" of the whole of society. The culture industry was, for them, one of its instruments. Adorno identifies two equally dangerous contrary attitudes toward the culture industry that, he says, should be avoided: either taking its influence lightly or being overawed by its power. The latter tendency, he says, is often manifested by "servile intellectuals" as well as by its consumer customers. These are people, he continues (in a statement that strongly recalls Baudrillard, notwithstanding the differences in their respective social analyses), who "are not only, as the saying goes, falling for the swindle, if it guarantees them even the most fleeting gratification, they desire a deception which is nonetheless transparent to them" (1989:132). In short, they are people collaborating in their own deception.

The Bourgeois Public

Habermas (Dews 1986:175) took up both concepts, those of a rational society and of the culture industry, in *STP*. In an interview he gave in 1984, referring to "the centralization of organizations which privilege vertical and one-way flows of second- and third-hand information, privately consumed" in the media and "an increasing substitution of images for words, and also that intermingling of categories such as advertising, politics, entertainment, information," already criticized by Adorno, he argued that the latter's "critique of mass culture should be both extended and rewritten." A 1968–69 collection of essays, *Toward a Rational Society: Student Protest, Science and Politics* (1970, henceforth *RS*), had the term "rational society" in its title. As it indicates, the essays, like Marcuse's on liberation, were inspired by the student unrest in the late 1960s. His stance toward that unrest, unlike Marcuse's, however, was polemical rather than supportive. The general question he took up in the book, an issue raised also by Marcuse, was the politicization of the university. The essays raise issues he had discussed already in *STP* in 1962 but go far beyond. In both books, *STP* and *RS*, Habermas was concerned, like his Frankfurt School predecessors, with the penetration of an instrumental rationality into the lifeworld, the growing scientization of politics and public opinion, and the loss of democratic power for ordinary people. He showed no sympathy, however, with Marcuse's dream of revolution and of a "great refusal" of capitalism, and the idea of revolution has remained uncongenial to him over the years. His opinion of the students' disturbances at the time was that they "have the advantage of obtaining rapid publicity," but "bear dangers, which students themselves have observed: the danger of diversion either into the privatization of an easily consolable hippie subculture or into the fruitless violent acts of the actionists" (1970:26). In short, while regarding the students' actions as important provocations engendering a public debate on the long-standing issue of the politicization and democratization of the university and of the wider society, he worried about their degeneration into escapism or mindless violence.

A key question Habermas raised in *RS*, like Lyotard later in *PMC*, concerned the relationship between the knowledge produced by the university, particularly in the human and social sciences, and the lifeworld: "the relation of technology and democracy." Namely, "how can the power of technical control be brought within the range of the consensus of acting and transacting citizens?" (1970:57). Here is a question that is crucial for democracy, following his argument in *STP* that the social sciences and the culture industry have combined forces to substitute democratic, face-to-face, opinion-making encounters with controlled methods of opinion formation of the media, which have obliterated the need for a critical public sphere. He also described the inversion of the old power relationship between the expert and the politician, in which "the latter becomes the mere agent of a scientific *intelligentsia*, which, in concrete circumstances, elaborates the objective implications and requirements of available techniques and resources as well as of optimal strategies and rules of control" (1970:64–65). And how bureaucratic power has appropriated organized research in the university, so that "the client at the gates is now no longer (at least immediately) a public engaged in learning or discussion," but "a contracting agency interested in the outcome of the research process for the sake of its technical application" (1970:76). More broadly he wrote about the "bureaucratized exercise of power" over information flows that "has its counterpart in a public realm confined to spectacles and acclamation" (1970:75). In sum, Habermas argued, "the specialization of large-scale research and a bureaucratized apparatus of power reinforce each other only too well while the public is excluded as a political force," so that "we can no longer reckon with functioning institutions for public discussion among the general public" (1970:79).

This bleak outcome is confirmed in the pessimistic final essay of his book, where he retold a Weberian–Frankfurt School narrative of modern disempowerment through the predominance of a technocratic public consciousness, reflecting not just "the sundering of an ethical situation but the repression of 'ethics' as such as a category of life." Such disempowerment is also reflected in a positivist mentality that creates a frame of reference whereby interaction in ordinary language is rendered inert and favorable for domination and ideology to arise under conditions of distorted communication. It is a mentality that legitimates the de-politicization of the mass of the population at the same times that it encourages "men's self-objectification in categories both equally of purposive-rational action and adaptive behavior." A mentality that, migrating into it in the shape of "reified models of the sciences," gains "objective power over the lifeworld's understanding." The ideological nucleus of the technocratic consciousness is the elimination of the distinction between the practical and the technical. "It reflects, but does not objectively account for, the new constellation of a disempowered institutional framework and systems of purposive-rational action that have taken on a life of their own," beyond democratic public control (1970:113). In *RS*, Habermas believed that the situation required the politicizing of the university and the lifeworld, and the reconstitution of a critical public at the interface between lifeworld and system. A public already described in *STP* where, as MacIntyre did with the Scottish public, he returned to eighteenth-century Europe for his model, to the time when a liberal bourgeois public emerged, mainly in England, France, and Germany.

In the same book, like MacIntyre also, he discussed the rise of this public, its political features, and the causes of its eventual decline and disappearance, and followed with his views about how to reactivate it in the contemporary world. Otherwise there were very significant differences between the liberal bourgeois and Scottish publics, which were also bourgeois but not liberal. The liberal publics did not grow around the universities, and convened informally in the coffeehouses and salons of Europe, and were completely secular in their inspiration. Unlike the philosophical Scottish publics, they were literary publics, that grew with the development of capitalism, and were related to the emerging bourgeois political class that created it. The political space they occupied was different from that of the Scottish public, since they inserted themselves not in the lifeworld but in the interface between the lifeworld and the state system. Their political purpose was very different also, challenging the old classical, totalitarian sense of publicness in which the ruler's power was merely represented *before* the people with a democratic sense of publicness in which the state's authority was monitored through informed and critical discourse *by* the people in different ways. In simpler words, the bourgeois public wanted to submit public authority to the standards of reason and the law, standards that liberals everywhere proposed as the standards of democracy. Unsurprisingly, Habermas traced its historical inspiration to the ancient Greek democracy, where the citizen's life gravitated between two spheres: the public and political, where he was an equal among equals, and the private and domestic, the sphere of the household, where he was master. In the former, Habermas says, "life" was reproduced in dialogue, in the latter through the labor of the slaves and the service of the women.

Habermas (1989a:47) regarded this separation of public and private spheres as crucial to the creation of a democratic public. In modern times he noted its replication in the sense of privacy that marked the emerging bourgeois family, the notion of subjectivity as the innermost core of the private that was turned into an ideal of "emancipation ... of an inner realm, following its own laws, from extrinsic purposes of any sort." This bourgeois notion of subjectivity, in turn, nurtured the ideal of autonomy as a reason-guided faculty accessible to all. The bourgeois public sphere emerged "as an expansion and at the same time completion of the intimate sphere of the conjugal family," with its own "institutional criteria," however (1989a:50). These were: (a) the preservation of a kind of social intercourse that did more than presuppose equality of status among its members—it disregarded their social status altogether; (b) the problematization of areas of discourse and action, cultural and political, which until then had gone unquestioned; and (c) a policy of inclusiveness, at least in principle. In reality the autonomy of its members was socially guaranteed by property and its membership, therefore, restricted. Moreover, the fact that it was rooted in the world of letters meant that, besides property, it required, as with MacIntyre's public (and every other educated public, of course), the qualification of education. (1989a:85). While pointing out these realities, subsequently exposed as politically problematic by Hegel and Marx, he says, Habermas regards the ideal of inclusiveness itself as critically important to the development of our conception of a democratic "public opinion," a conception that received its first classic formulation in Kant's writings, where the critical public sphere is conceived as the method of enlightenment interpreted in terms of the achievement of individual liberation from a "self-incurred tutelage" to others, and of a collective progress toward the realization of a perfectly just social order. Kant's critical public would include scholars, particularly philosophers, and its realms of competence were those that are subject to the authority of reason alone, morals, politics, and culture, although this fact did not render them merely academic or private matters.[60] Indeed, as matters of general concern about which there are varied opinions and conflicts of viewpoints they should, he believed, concern all and be debated publicly by scholars and philosophers, to challenge and instruct the government but also to model popular debate, to encourage ordinary people to use their reason as "scholars" in their own right. There was a certain ambiguity in this relationship between philosophers and public; it assumed a public "under tutelage and still in need of [their] enlightenment, while, on the other, it already claimed the maturity of people capable of enlightenment" (1989a:105). But its democratic ideal was unambiguous and, going along with the Enlightenment ideal, cosmopolitan: "each person was called to be a 'publicist,' a 'scholar' whose writings speak to his public, the world" (1989a:106), not just "to the more restricted affairs of the commonwealth" (1989a:107). In the *Critique of Pure Reason*, Kant added to this idea of the citizen as publicist, the idea of a pragmatic test that defines truth in terms of public agreement under specific conditions. These ideas have influenced Habermas greatly, though he cited Hegel's and Marx's criticism of Kant's idealized view of a public sphere as intrinsically classist.[61]

The liberal public sphere, in fact, eventually fell victim not to socialist or proletarian revolution but, to some extent, to the internal logic of the capitalist system itself in the shape of the culture industry, with which it quickly came into tension. The popularization of information and proliferation of press and propaganda material by the industry as the nineteenth century advanced soon cost the public its exclusiveness and its life (1989a:132). The principle of publicity stopped being controversial, the problematization of specific political issues lost its importance, and the issue of electoral reform, of "the enlargement of the public" (1989a:133), moved to the center of political debate. A new specter raised its head in the consciousness of democrats like Mill and Tocqueville, who welcomed this enlargement of the public sphere but worried that it could be "more a compulsion toward conformity than a critical force"(1989a:133); more a means of creating a tyrannous majority opinion than of liberating public opinion without distinction. In short, the question was now how to ensure that the power of public opinion did not swallow up all power in general. The fear of this eventuality converted Mill to the idea of representative government that would filter public opinion, which now necessarily included a mediocre and largely uneducated element. Tocqueville, Marx, and Mill, however, as Habermas (1989a:155) points out, also shared a common fear of the danger posed by the growing power of the modern state as its function changed from maintaining order to assuming "formative functions" in the lifeworld; "the functions of upbringing and education, protection, care, and guidance—indeed, of the transmission of elementary tradition and frameworks of orientation." So that its institutions and the societal ones fused into a single functional complex that could no longer be differentiated according to criteria of public and private (1989a:148), while the family was transformed "ever more into a consumer of income and leisure time, into a recipient of publicly guaranteed compensations and support services" (1989a:156). Add to this the commercialization of the media through the culture industry, turning the "culture-debating" public into a "culture-consuming" one (1989a:162) with orchestrated sites of "so-called debates, formally organized and at the same time compartmentalized as an element of adult education," and the picture is complete (1989a: 163–164).

Habermas (1989a:164) contends, like Adorno, that contrary to any other impression we may have, the media today are purely a consumer item and have lost their former publicist function. Shifted from the sphere of education to that of the leisure market, they are driven by a single logic: "achieving increased sales by adapting to the need for relaxation and entertainment on the part of consumer strata with relatively little education" (1989a:165). In making cultural goods cheap and accessible to an ever-larger public, the culture industry levels down, "lowering the entrance requirements" and producing suitable material for every taste and ability, rather than upgrading the abilities of those previously excluded from it (1989a:166). The process began in the nineteenth century with the appearance of mass newspapers and of literary styles that broadened popular access but commercialized and depoliticized the public sphere's content in the process. "By means of variegated type and layout and ample illustration, reading is made easy at the same time that its field of spontaneity in general is restricted by serving up the material as a ready-made convenience, patterned and predigested" (1989a:169). This technique of the print was easily extended to the broadcast media. In sum, Habermas's (1989a:171) critique of modern publicity, following that of Adorno and Horkheimer, is that the industrialization of the media conspired to put the public under "tutelage" once more, this time to a different political master: the modern capitalist state and its publicists. "The world fashioned by the mass media," today, he warns, "is a public sphere in appearance only." While it perpetrates "the illusion of an untouched private sphere and intact private conditions," whose basis actually disappeared a long time ago, its emphasis on its "advertising" functions betrays an intention to manipulate public opinion rather than enlighten it. A task it manages "scientifically" and with extraordinary success, thanks to a thriving "public relations" machinery that is engaged in "opinion management," in the "engineering of consent," for which purpose it employs techniques of mass entertainment and commercial advertising that have been transferred also to the world of politics.

Habermas's comment on the educational implications of these developments is scathing: "[T]he consumption of mass culture leaves no lasting trace; it affords a kind of experience which is not cumulative but regressive" (1989a:166). In other words, it is the antithesis of the process of education, which, as Dewey tells us, is a process of progressive cumulative growth, while the infiltration of the culture industry into the public sphere has created a situation where "the public is split apart into minorities of specialists who put their reason to use non-publicly and the great mass of consumers whose receptiveness is public but uncritical" (1989a: 175). Thus, "the institutions of social-convivial interchange" that bourgeois publics once were, and that once "secured the coherence of the public making use of its reason lost their power or utterly collapsed" (1989a:202). Their space is now occupied by administrators, special-interest associations, and partisan political parties, whose power depends more and more on their management of public relations, on the service of Kundera's imagologues, who recruit the collaboration of the mass media to their cause. Political parties in modern democracies, Habermas (1989a:206) tells us, have seized on the new science of publicity and public relations to further their ends. Parliamentary debate and procedures (which are further affected by direct media publicity) are modeled to suit its purposes, and it has been transferred into the realm of legal proceedings and trials also. In all these realms "publicity loses its critical function in favor of a staged display, even arguments," he remarks wryly, "are transmuted into symbols to which again one cannot respond by arguing but only by identifying oneself with them." In short, the media has restored to the political arena the same "aura of personally represented authority... as an aspect of publicity" (1989a:200) that characterized power in premodern societies before the rise of the liberal public sphere. It has enabled a "refeudalization of the public sphere in yet another, more exact sense" (1989a:195)—"the public sphere becomes the court *before* whose public prestige can be displayed—rather than *in* which public critical debate is carried on" (1989a:201).

Critical Reactions

STP drew conflicting responses, friendly and otherwise, from a variety of quarters and perspectives when it appeared in English translation in 1989. Criticized for its "close adherence to a Marxist framework," which tied it "too narrowly with economic forces and issues" (Zaret 1992:213), and for partiality and lack of historical accuracy, it was praised as "an indispensable resource" for theorizing the limits of democracy in late-capitalist societies and for "circumventing some confusions that have plagued progressive social movements and the political theories associated with them" (Fraser 1992:109). While judging his critique useful for contemporary feminisms, Nancy Fraser (1992:110) remarked that Habermas's account of the public sphere needed "some critical interrogation and reconstruction if it is to yield a category capable of theorizing the limits of actually existing democracy" (1992:111). Aligning herself with the recent revisionist historiography of critics like Joan Landers, Mary Ryan, and Geoff Eley, who objected to Habermas's idealization of the bourgeois public sphere in that it "rested on, indeed was importantly constituted by, a number of significant exclusions" (1992:115), she acknowledged that Habermas had recognized as much himself, but criticized him for having failed to examine or even consider other non-liberal, non-bourgeois publics that were also in existence at the time: women's, for instance, but not women's only. Echoing the question raised by other commentators like Eley, Baker, and Garnham, she asked whether, instead of the idea of *a* public, we do not need the notion of *multiple* publics, their discourses sometimes overlapping, sometimes distinct, sometimes contending and competing with each other, to describe the modern world.

Dewey had suggested something similar in *The Public and its Problems*. Since modern societies are irreversibly pluralistic, he observed, it is dangerous to think of them as homogeneous wholes, as we tend to do. "As a matter of fact," he said, "a modern society is many societies more or less loosely connected" (1997:21). He also attempted a typology of these connections, beginning from the more "intimate" level of the household with its immediate extension of family and friends, extending outward to the village or street group, business groups, clubs, and so on. The variety of these societies, he observed, can be bewildering in a modern city, never mind in larger national entities "like our own," meaning the United States, where "in spite of its nominal political unity there are probably more communities, more differing customs, traditions, aspirations, and forms of government and control, than existed in an entire continent at an earlier epoch" (1997:21). Far from being a homogeneous society, the United States, Dewey pointed out, is formed by a variety of races, religious affiliations, and economic divisions. And the same is true of most Western societies today. This being the case, the individual could be, predictably is, a member of many different publics in which she plays different roles in different ways. In sum, Dewey represents modern societies as heterogeneous networks of microsocieties, some with their own publics, within a larger mega-society, which is the national society with a broader public, if it has one, and which is more amorphous and fragile than the focused local publics of the microsocieties. Evidently, if we were to apply this typology to the Europe of today, and if we were to consider the experiment that is the EU as an even broader European learning society than the national, as the EU 1995 white paper suggests, we would have to be thinking of something even more amorphous, complex, and fragile, and the concept of a European public would be even harder to conceive.

Fraser's (1992:117) criticism of Habermas continued on the grounds that revisionist historiography proposes a much darker picture of the bourgeois public sphere than the one he presented in his study. Seyla Benhabib (1992b:94) questioned the desirability of the strong separation of the public from the private sphere underpinning it and traditional liberal politics, raising the standard feminist objection that it belongs to a discourse that legitimizes the institution of the patriarchal family and the domination and exploitation of women at the hands of men. Both she and Fraser, however, feel that feminists should "not only criticize Habermas's social theory but enter into a dialectical alliance with it." Habermas himself had little difficulty accepting most of this criticism. In fact, so many years had passed since he wrote the book that he had long freed himself of many of his former influences. So it was not difficult for him to acknowledge that his idealization of the bourgeois public had been a mistake he put down to the "ideology-critical" approach to his book at the time (1992:441). He also acknowledged that a very different political picture of the historical period emerges if *from the very beginning* one admits the coexistence of competing public spheres and takes account of the dynamics of (these) processes of communication that are excluded from the dominant public space" (1992:425, italics in original). He itemized the voices of the proletarian society, of women, of the "plebian culture," and ethnic and other minorities within the same society, as examples. He also admitted to the more general point, made earlier, that his perspective in *STP* was conditioned by the "now questionable notion that society and its self-organization are to be considered a totality," which, he agreed, had led him to adopt an "all-too-handy parallelization of action systems and action types," and which, he now acknowledged, "produced some nonsensical results" (1992:443), notably a two-tiered concept of society as lifeworld and system with considerable implications for his theory of democracy and, one could add, for his analysis of the modern learning society.

More recently, he has described system and lifeworld as dynamically interactive and interdependent rather than as separate and hierarchical entities. He also admitted that, on deeper reflection, the remedy to the situation he described in *STP*, the only one, he said, he could imagine at the time, of promoting internally democratized interest associations and parties as vehicles of critical publicity, runs into several difficulties. What he had hoped for when he wrote *STP*, he said, was the restoration of a public sphere, which, unlike the eighteenth-century liberal sphere, "cannot be denounced as an ideology," and which brings the idea of Enlightenment embedded in the ideal of the rational society to fruition (1992:235). In *STP* he had thought of the rational society in terms of creating structures and practices for rendering transparent, publicly available, and truth-seeking the discourse and affairs and activities of political parties, special interest groups, and so on. In short, he still thought of the rational society as a "fully transparent society."[62] In *STP* he showed how remote we are from this ideal by describing the way the run up to elections and the electoral process in democracies are manipulated by the media, by public relations, and by the opinion-forming experts, the spin doctors, of the contending political parties. At this stage he had been unable to go beyond a rather vague hope for enlightened reforms within the current political institutions that would somehow generate a participatory mentality and a commitment to forms of discursive transparency, favorable toward serious critical political involvement. The first "historical" and analytic part of *STP*, in fact, as Calhoun (1992) observes, was more successful than the theoretical second part, where he passed on to propose these remedies.[63] And Habermas conceded this point also in his reactions to the critics of the English version of his book and in his later work.

By the time he wrote his reply to the critics of the English version of *STP*, Habermas, in fact, had not only changed his way of doing theory completely, he had also lost his former enthusiasm for the liberal bourgeois public sphere. Later on, in a comment resembling that which MacIntyre made about his own early attraction to medieval society, he described it as "a category that is typical of an epoch. It cannot be abstracted from the unique developmental history of that 'civil society' (*burgeliche Gesellschaft*) originating in the European High Middle Ages; nor can it be transferred, ideal typically generalized, to any number of historical situations that represent formally similar constellations" (1992:97). Irrespective of its pros and cons, he maintained, one cannot just uproot it, or any other social phenomenon from the past, and transfer it to the contemporary world. As far as his way of doing theory is concerned, he had long since abandoned "the attempt to ground critical social theory by way of the *theory of knowledge*," which, "while it did not lead astray, was indeed a roundabout way" (1982:233). His famous "linguistic turn" had long occurred; he had long since exchanged his former epistemological critique with one based in the pragmatics of language. He had also long given up on the Cartesian-Kantian philosophy of the subject and replaced it with one of communicative action. By that time also he had long abandoned the tendency in his early work to project the basic tenets of historical materialism, with its emphasis on human labor, as the source of the social and historical constitution of the whole of reality. Politically, he had turned more and more into a social democrat. Marx and Freud were important to him early on for "incorporating in their consciousness an interest which directs knowledge, an interest in emancipation going beyond the technical and practical interest of knowledge" (1974:10). But in *Theory and Practice* (1974), written in 1971, he was already rejecting the emancipatory potential of the Freudian-Marxian strategy of applying the psychoanalytic paradigm of self-reflection on a larger scale and to larger groups, which involved transferring the therapist/patient relationship of the paradigm to the relationship among the Communist Party, the party intellectuals, and the masses. What remained of their influence was his interest in emancipation, which he defended fiercely against opponents like Gadamer, whose philosophical hermeneutics otherwise exerted an important influence on his theory of communicative action, identifying it, in the tradition of the Frankfurt theorists, as a fundamental human interest, anthropologically rooted in strategies for interpreting human life experience.

In *Theory and Practice* Habermas (1974:3) held that the processes of an authentic public discourse, which "cannot be denounced as an ideology, can only be translated into processes of enlightenment which are rich in political consequences when the institutional preconditions for practical discourse among the general public are fulfilled." This is a position he has continued to hold since. Identifying those preconditions and the conditions under which validity claims made by the participants in the discourse can be verified became the key project of his political writing. Starting by identifying "the restrictive compulsions, that is, the inhibitions to communication which have their origin in the. structures of the system" (1974:3), the object of his critique became to unfold the elements of a universal ideal speech situation rooted in our emancipatory human interests and defined as "a systematically relevant mechanism of learning for a given society," and to describe the democratic procedural preconditions needed to make it possible (1974:26). The difference his linguistic turn made to it was that, though, as Calhoun (1992:32) observes, "the public sphere remains an ideal" he does not abandon, "it becomes a contingent product of the evolution of communicative action rather than its basis." Which meant, as Habermas (1982:235) himself said in another reply to his critics in the Thompson and Held volume of 1982, that he abandoned the idea of a rational utopian society that is fully transparent. This is confirmed again in a 1984 interview where he states that in his view an emancipated society is not "'one where communication is free from domination'" (Dews 1986:180). In sum, over time, Habermas changed position as his interest shifted away from seeking out the properties of a model public sphere that is a rational society toward amplifying the conditions for communicative action, which make the existence of publics possible, and rejecting the notion of a rational society conceived of as an "emancipated society." "The theory of communicative action," he says, "intends to bring into the open the rational potential intrinsic in everyday communicative practices," rather than impose some model of rationality on them (1992:442). This is why it starts with the pragmatics of language rather than with a model.[64] Politically, it means moving from the idea of seeking a revolutionary "political praxis" grounded in an *avante garde* toward promoting an interactive "social praxis'" embedded in the communicative potential of the lifeworld and active at the interface between system and lifeworld in the old form of a deliberating critical public.

The Publics Compared

One could argue that Habermas's narrative in *STP* strengthened Feinberg's case against MacIntyre that a public *is* possible under modern conditions. Indeed, Habermas's point in *STP* was that bourgeois publics were *characteristic products of modernity*, incorporating the liberal-democratic political vision of the Enlightenment in concrete form, and that restoring them in some form is not beyond us. MacIntyre (1981:36–38) himself actually acknowledged their historical existence in *AV*, referring to them as typically northern European phenomena with "outposts" outside northern Europe. Like Habermas, he pointed to Kant as the philosopher who gave them their "theoretically fully developed form" (1981:96), and he identified them with the Kantian "project of an independent rational justification of morality" (1981:38). This renders puzzling his contention that modernity is incapable of producing an educated public. He could have argued that the aspirations of the liberal public were fatally flawed from the start, as Habermas conceded in a certain sense when he put its failure down to the principle of democratic openness and inclusion that lay at its heart, but this is different from saying that it is impossible in the modern world. This was also true, in fact, of the Scottish public, which degenerated partly because of changing historical conditions (as did the liberal public), but also because its aspirations were fatally flawed initially—since, as a *philosophically* educated public, it could not have been expected to continue to articulate "a common mind." In any case, the fact that the Scottish public had also failed historically did not prevent MacIntyre from reviving it again as a model for our time with the argument that the notion of an educated public had not been laid to rest, which is, no doubt, what Habermas thought also when he wrote *STP* to repropose a different kind of public.

I have already hinted at some of the differences. The bourgeois public had no ambition to articulate a common mind, nor did its literary nature predispose it in this way. Also, the two publics served contrary political purposes in their respective societies. The Scottish were concerned to preserve the country's cultural integrity and national identity in the face of threatening political change; the liberal to advance the causes of democracy and political change and to keep the growth of the modern state under critical review. Habermas was worried about the progressive infiltration of the lifeworld by an all-engulfing instrumentalist rationality, about the role of the technocratic expert in this process, and about the state's progressive colonization of the private realm, which he regarded as a realm of freedom crucial to the existence of the public sphere. MacIntyre was concerned instead about the anarchic impulses the culture of modernity has injected into the same private realm, blaming its permissive individualism for making any sort of public impossible in principle. The difference between them, in short, is a difference of political perspective; the one, as I said earlier, being a social democrat with strong liberal sentiments and a modernist and the other a conservative with strong antiliberal sentiments and an antimodernist. Habermas sets a lot of store on the liberal values of freedom and pluralism and disagrees with both MacIntyre and Adorno and Horkheimer that the Enlightenment was a recipe for disaster. For a long time, as we saw, he cherished the possibility of achieving its authentic embodiment in the modern world in the shape of a rational society. Like Marcuse he believes the capitalist state to be perpetually open to challenge and prone to different kinds of legitimation crises, including crises in its own motivation and credibility (1989b). His view about the Enlightenment project is that it should be revised, drained of its positivist elements, and exorcised of its fatal attachment to the philosophy of the subject—which is what, in his view, has rendered it vulnerable to the lure of atomistic individualism—not that it should be fought and abandoned.

There *are* some elements that the respective publics, MacIntyre's and Habermas's, hold in common. For instance, both envisage a membership qualification—education—and this renders them both, in principle, intrinsically exclusive. But the literary qualification of the liberal public, which eventually signified its downfall at the hands of the culture industry, rendered it more open and accessible in principle than the Scottish public, which required training in a particular philosophy. The liberal public was animated by politically progressive ideals of free speech and equal citizenship, and its accessibility was also positively affected by the fact that it grew outside the universities in the salons and coffeehouses of Europe, while the Scottish public was self-consciously formal, sectarian, and conservative, grew around the more rarified air of universities, and had professors rather than salon intellectuals as its protagonists. Unsurprisingly, given the time when they flourished, the members of both publics were bourgeois and male, but while the Scottish public seems to have regarded its class and gender bias as unproblematic, the liberal public was, by Habermas's account at least, uncomfortably self-conscious of its class (if not its gender) bias. MacIntyre himself made no fuss about either bias, but Habermas was profoundly unhappy with both. He sought to comfort himself with the thought that, whatever else might have been the case in practice, in theory at least the bourgeois public was committed to the principle of openness and inclusion, and that this was politically important, since that principle could always be appealed to or even demanded in the name of consistency by the excluded. MacIntyre's view that the public need only be "tolerably large"—providing its members are self-consciously committed to its purposes—suggests that inclusiveness was not what he gave priority to. It is ironic that when, in Habermas's account of things, learning spread it did not happen through the growth of a wider and more inclusive educated public but by its degeneration into a consumer public. His analysis here may have been lopsided. Calhoun remarks that Habermas failed to acknowledge the positive contribution of reforms that opened schooling more to the masses among its effects.[65] But the role he assigns to the culture industry in the destruction of the critical public is crucially important, even were one to reassess its impact against the advent of mass schooling, which need not have been motivated by the wish to educate either. MacIntyre, who argues that mass schooling has failed to educate, neglects the role of the culture industry and the media in general in the making of the modern world, and this is a minus point for his project. A distinct plus, on the other hand, is the attention he gives to the pedagogy of upbringing in the local community that would create the independent practical reasoner, which Habermas, on his part, shows no interest in, just as he shows no interest in the contribution of mass schooling to the modern learning society.

Habermas locates the need for a "universal," or nationwide, public at the interface of system and lifeworld, while MacIntyre locates his publics in and around universities. The difference between them here is that MacIntyre, as we saw, is politically uninterested in the modern state of which he disapproves, while the opposite is true of Habermas, who has devoted entire volumes of his writings to it. MacIntyre's interest is not even in the lifeworld, in the society as a whole, but in local communities within it that can be rendered close-knit learning communities in the way described in the previous chapter. It is in these communities that he pins his hopes for the future of education in a postmodern world, while Habermas is interested in the lifeworld of the broader society. He defines the lifeworld as "a culturally transmitted and linguistically organized stock of interpretive patterns" (1989a:124), the "horizon within which communicative actions are 'always already' moving," and that is "limited and changed by the structural transformations of society as a whole" (1989a:119). It supplies its members with a shared background of conventional values and convictions, "prejudices" as Gadamer calls them, "platitudes" as Stout refers to them, that set the boundaries within which all social communication and understanding is shaped. "Communicative actors," Habermas (1989a:126) says, "are always moving within the horizons of their lifeworld; they cannot step outside of it." In this sense, he points out, lifeworlds could be referred to as "forms of life," "cultures," or "language communities"—with the difference that the concept of a lifeworld captures more than any one of these concepts (1989a:138). While the lifeworld "is established by normatively secured or communicatively achieved consensus" between actors, the system is held together more anonymously "by a non-normative regulation of individual decisions that extends beyond the actors' consciousness" (1989a:117). The lifeworld "remains the subsystem that defines the pattern of the social system as a whole," in the sense that "systemic mechanisms need to be anchored in the lifeworld: they have to be institutionalized" (1989a:154), so that societies need to be conceived of as *both* systems and lifeworld simultaneously and interdependently.

This observation sets the parameters for a Habermassian approach to the learning society. He quotes Luhmann's observation that modern societies are prone to the "uncoupling" of the two when, from the lifeworld's perspective, the system appears ever more "objectified" or remote and "assimilated to external nature," while it feels itself "pushed back behind media-steered subsystems and is no longer directly connected to action situations, but merely forms the background for formally organized interactions—into 'society'" (1989a:155). And when the system's "increasing complexity" and "the rationalization of the lifeworld" reaches a stage where "action oriented to mutual understanding gains more and more independence from normative contexts," and gets "overloaded in the end and replaced by delinguistified media" (1989a:155). Habermas believes that this is happening now in today's world. Hence, the urgent need for a public realm at the interface to restore the normative dimensions to discursive communicative action, functioning, "so to speak," as "the transcendental site where speaker and hearer meet, where they can reciprocally raise claims that their utterances (objective, social, or subjective) fit the world, and where they can criticize and confirm those validity claims, settle their disagreements, and arrive at agreements," as the case may be (1989a:126). The conditions of ideal speech function regulatively in this context, as do the conditions of a practice in MacIntyre's account of dialogue. In either case, ideal speech situation and practice constitute the embodiment of their respective publics' notion of what constitutes rational discourse. The one, in terms of the universal conditions of communicative action, requires the discursive competence of its members; their willingness to tell the truth; their possession of democratic virtues; and their willingness to submit to the rules, procedures, and ethics of ideal rational speech. The other, in terms of the historical conditions of communicative action laid down by a tradition that also sets its own conditions of truth and competence, similarly requires discursive competence, honesty, and a willingness to submit to the rules, to the ethics of rational speech, and so on.

The later Habermas recognizes not only the need to acknowledge a plurality of publics and the inherent instability of the modern-postmodern lifeworld, but also the desirability of this state of affairs; of new publics arising spontaneously from the lifeworld, often reactive to a systemic crisis of credibility, or some other kind, as a permanent possibility. These are publics that grow around causes and issues and emerge in a combative spirit, or spirit of contestation, and sometimes crystallize into the stability and endurance of social movements that could have a national, or even international, agenda. But he still also recognizes the more stable, nationwide site of deliberative politics, where intellectuals and others communicate interactively before the citizens, within the apposite institutions or outside them, as an indispensable part of the mechanism of national democracy. Both, for Habermas, should ideally be publics of the democratic kind in the sense that their debate follows the procedures of democratic exchange and is governed by the normative conditions of a communicative ethics with emancipatory intent. Unlike MacIntyre, he does not intend any of these publics to be exclusive and self-contained, or protected by a "socially integrative pre-understanding" (1998b:296). To the contrary, he wants them, like Dewey's publics, to be "porous to one another," to "permeate and intertwine with one another," in a search for common areas of consensual collaboration (1998b:111). In short, Habermas distinguishes two political levels of communicative action for his learning social democracy: (a) that involving democratic institutional discourses within formal or non-formal structures that are defined by the general civic and political culture of the society, and (b) that involving a lifeworld that is permanently instable and capable of generating ever new, spontaneous, "wild" experiments in living and communicating. In either case the procedures establishing the rational norms of discourse are collaboratively made and openly negotiated in an ongoing way by the members. The spontaneous publics serve to keep the lifeworld dynamic and protect it from suffocation by the encroaching systems and, at the same time, to sensitize the system to the agitations within the lifeworld when they occur.

Utopia

In 1962 when he wrote *STP*, Habermas (1989a:235) was optimistic that the interest in emancipation "can today no longer be disqualified as simply utopian." Whatever the negative sociopolitical conditions that are actual, he believed, the old liberal principles of freedom that inspired the bourgeois public still survive, even if only as unfulfilled ideals or specters, because they are "natural" to human beings. He also claimed to detect a widespread support today for genuine communication, as opposed to the "*staged and manipulative* publicity displayed by organizations over the heads of the mediatized public." In short, he believed a genuine critical public sphere possible. "To the degree to which it preserves the continuity with the liberal constitutional state," he declared, "the social-welfare state clings to the mandate of a political public sphere according to which the public is to set in motion a *critical* process of public communication through the very organizations that mediatize it" (1989a:232). There is, he insisted, obviously with Adorno and Horkheimer in mind, no *a priori* or historical reason why this mandate need be regarded as impossible, no intrinsic "impenetrability or indissolubility," no "irrational relations of social power and political domination" such as would render it hopeless. He acknowledged that there was no guarantee that it would be taken up either, or that the ascendancy of critical over manipulative publicity would feature in the future (1989a:235). What was important, he felt, was to keep the utopian energies immanent in the emancipatory project of modernity connected with the future of the welfare state, alive and well, and he still thinks so today, though the world has changed radically from what it was in 1962, and his views on emancipation and the welfare state have changed also. For this reason, like Marcuse he believed in the strategic necessity of utopian writing, and has written a lot about utopia over the years.

In "The New Obscurity" (1994a:50), he described approvingly its "modern rehabilitation" at the hands of Ernst Bloch and Karl Mannheim "as a legitimate medium for depicting alternative life possibilities that are seen as inherent in the historical process itself." More required today when, he said with some concern in a 1984 interview with Andersen and Dews, "we manifestly suffer from an apparent retreat of utopian energies" (Dews 1992:206), which could mean that social theory is itself in crisis, since social theories "live from their connection with these utopian contents" (Dews 1992:206). A utopian thrust, he believed, is necessary for social progress, though he qualifies this by contending that "the only utopian perspectives in social theory which we can straightforwardly maintain are of a procedural nature," not those that project a substantive form of life. Which may be why, he acknowledged in reply to an observation to this effect by his interviewers, the discussion of socialism was always marginal in his writing (Dews 1992:184). Much of his more recent work has, in fact, focused on the features of a procedural democracy that tries to perfect the conditions of ideal speech. He also regarded utopias as having "a practical function to the extent that they enter into social movements in the form of orientations" (Dews 1992:144).[66] Insofar as they conjure up concrete goals, he held, they have always been "necessary constituents of movements which have any effect on history at all. Everything else, by comparison, is re-working and stasis" (Dews 1992:145). He acknowledged the fact that not everybody shares his positive attitude toward utopian writing. And MacIntyre (1990:233) did the same with respect to the type of university system he envisioned for the future in *TRV*, anticipating that it would be greeted as "an academic cloud cuckooland, something incapable of existence," and replying by pointing out that it had already existed at least once before, in the eighteenth century. But this is, of course, no argument that it can exist today, for what may have been possible then may be impossible now.

MacIntyre (1990:234) defended utopian writing in general. More usually than not, he remarked, it is denigrated by those "who pride themselves upon their pragmatic realism, who look for immediate results, who want the relationship between present input and future output to be predictable and measurable." Those who are, as he puts it, "enemies of the incalculable, the skeptics about all expectations which outrun what *they* take to be hard evidence, the deliberately shortsighted who congratulate themselves upon the limits of their vision." The charge against utopianism, he concluded, somewhat like Furter, "is sometimes best understood more as a symptom of the condition of those who level it than an indictment of the projects against which it is directed" (1990:236). But Habermas has taken it more seriously and so have philosophers like Benhabib (1992a:48), who holds that the problem with utopian writing today is not its association with repression, as may have been the case some years ago, but its association with "extreme irrelevance." Though this is true of rationalist utopianism, she argues, we can steer a course between it and political realism, because we possess the "political imagination as well as collective fantasy, to project institutions, practices and ways of life which promote non-violent conflict resolution strategies and associative problem solving methods." She cites Habermas's paradigm of communicative ethics to her aid, arguing that it can help us by supplying "our minds with just the right dose of fantasy such as to think beyond the old oppositions of utopia or realism, containment or conflict" (1992a:49). Feminists in particular, Benhabib (1992a:152, italics in original) believes, need to articulate "an *anticipatory-utopian critique* of the norms and values of our current society and culture, such as to project new modes of togetherness, of relating to ourselves and to nature in the future." And she regards the alliances with postmodernism suggested by some feminists as unhealthy precisely because they have produced a "retreat from utopia" within feminist theory that, she argues, has been generally debilitating, if not outright disastrous, for the cause of women in general.

Habermas shares this criticism of postmodernism, which he started to engage critically with in 1981 in an essay entitled "Modernity versus Postmodernity." There he located its roots in the romantic movement that grew antithetically to the rationalist Enlightenment project from the beginning in the form of an "aesthetic modernism," attacked today's postmodernists as "young conservatives," anarchists, and irrationalists, and argued that postmodernism is unable to establish anything of political substance (1981:13). And he has over the years continued to regard it as a dangerous enemy to the critical outlook, more dangerous even than positivism, the Frankfurt school's old nemesis, which seems to have sunk into oblivion nowadays. In *The Philosophical Discourse of Modernity* (1990a), first published in 1985, he took on an impressive, full-scale evaluation of the French postmodernists, particularly of Foucault, whom he has consistently treated as their most interesting and valid exponent and, therefore, his own most valid antagonist. Postmodernism he has described as the "new obscurity" that reflects the negative state of Western culture's self-confidence today and undermines its utopianism (1994a:51).[67] It tries "to show how the very forces that make for increasing power, the forces from which modernity once derived its self-consciousness and its utopian expectations, are in actuality turning autonomy into dependence, emancipation into oppression, and reason into irrationality" (1994a:51). He dates the suspicion of utopia, however, back to Hegel, who first denounced "the supposedly unavoidable marriage of utopia and terror," and insists on retrieving "the utopian dimension of historical consciousness and political debate"—minus the "illusions," however, that "cast a spell over the self-understanding of modernity" and have encouraged its enemies (1994a:69). "As utopian oases dry up," he warned, "a desert of banality and bewilderment spreads" everywhere (1994a:68).

For both Habermas and Benhabib, the most serious problem utopianism meets with today is that with accepting its universalism, which must be re-established differently. Benhabib (1992a:153) calls for the replacement of the *substitutionist* model adopted by philosophers from Hobbes to Rawls, "identifying the experiences of a specific group of subjects as the paradigmatic case of the human as such," with an "*interactive* universalism" that "acknowledges the plurality of modes of being human, and differences among humans, without endorsing all these pluralities and differences as morally and politically valid." Interactive universalism, she says, recognizes plurality *as an element of utopia* rather than something the utopia is invented to eradicate, but it still operates with universal moral and political concepts and criteria of truth and justice. Discussing socialism with Beck, Habermas (Dews 1992:145) similarly declared himself against "theoretically-based utopias" that suggest "whole forms of life, whole life-histories, whole areas of life in their concretion," that "can be politically realized," and disagreed that socialism should be represented in this way. It should, he believed then, be represented more modestly as "an attempt, in the historical conditions in which one finds oneself, to indicate the necessary conditions which would have to be fulfilled in order for emancipated life-forms to emerge." We must avoid the "methodological illusion," which he admitted having been guilty of himself in the past, of embracing a utopianism "connected with projections of a concrete totality of future life possibilities." In this respect he described "the utopian content of a society based on communication" as one "limited to the formal aspects of an undamaged inter-subjectivity" no more, and concluded that "even the expression 'the ideal speech situation' is misleading" to the extent to which it suggests a concrete form of life. What can be outlined normatively are only "the necessary but general conditions for the communicative practice of everyday life and for a procedure of discursive will-formation that would put participants *themselves* in a position to realize concrete possibilities for a better and less threatened life, on *their own* initiative and in accordance with *their own* needs and insights" (1989c:69). We must, he concluded in the same 1984 essay, avoid confusing "a highly developed communicative infrastructure of *possible* forms of life with a specific totality, in the singular, representing the successful life" (1989c:69).

Habermas and the Welfare State

The ideal of a welfare state based on social justice that followed World War II, with "its power to project future possibilities for a collectively better and less endangered way of life" (1989c:54), which "crystallized around" and was "nourished by a utopia of social labor" (1989c:52), Habermas (1989c:53) argues, has failed to keep the capitalist system under control as was intended, and has failed, in particular, to use its political power to promote and safeguard emancipated forms of life that have truly human worth. Worse still, it "has lost its point of reference in reality."[68] Far from living up to the expectations of its pioneers, it is now linked, he says, echoing Foucault, "with a practice that isolates individual facts, a practice of normalization and surveillance" (1989c:58). He thus appeals for the "closing off" of this old debate about "the utopian contents of a laboring society," and for a redefinition of the welfare state, which need not be radical since, he believes, notwithstanding the criticism it has received, there are no serious threats to this welfare state's key structures (1989c:68). Even if they have never stopped being controversial, he argues, they have proved durable and are in no immediate danger of collapsing, even if, with time, they have developed as "compromise structures," further and further removed from their original reformist ideals and more and more entangled with the agenda of "neo-conservatism." This agenda, on its part, lives with its own dilemma: namely, while it supports the economic and political ethos of advanced capitalism, it is nervous about capitalism's permissive culture. The "new conservatism" supports a supply-side economic policy and is willing to accept relatively high unemployment rates at the same time as it emphasizes the importance of governance and of political realism, discredits intellectuals and the universalist morality of the Enlightenment, and emphasizes the values of traditional culture and the stabilizing forces of conventional morality: the values of patriotism, bourgeois religion, and folk culture. Habermas's (1989c:63) political quarrel with the "postmodernist dissidents" is that, while they perceive these threats well enough, they "remain caught in the fundamentalism of the Great Refusal and offer no more than a negative program of dedifferentiation and a halt to growth."

This is not an evaluation I agree with. Nevertheless, to continue, the dilemma confronting us today, Habermas (1989c:59) says, is "that the developed forms of capitalism can no more live without the welfare state than they can live with its further expansion." In his 1983 interview with Beck, he observed that the social democrats in Germany had no answer to it; having strongly defended the welfare state with their right hand for three decades, he says, they "intensif(y) the neo-conservative critique of the welfare state" with their left, unable "to counterpose a productive answer to the false prescriptions of the other side" (Dews 1992:134). This was long before the advent of the "Third Way" view of social democracy to be described in the next chapter, and he confessed that he shared that dilemma at the time (Dews 1992:134). He referred to the collapse of neo-Keynsian economic policies, no longer sufficient to ensure the growth required to sustain full employment and to inhibit conflicts over social distribution, on the one hand, and the problem taken up by the Greens and other social movements of "the costs of capitalist modernization, and the breakdown of a policy of war-prevention based on strategic calculation rather than on the generalization of consensus," on the other. (Dews 1992:135). With the social democrats pulled in different directions, their alternatives were ultimately reduced to two: either to justify a defiant continuation of old welfare policies or to find "a productive answer" that avoids being sucked into the "Reaganomics or Thatcherism" of the new conservatism. (Dews 1992:136). Habermas's choice (anticipating the Third Way social democrats) was the second: to engage with the welfare state "on a higher level of reflection" (1994a:66).

In the same interview with Beck, supporting his remarks about the contemporary irrelevance of the utopian model of social labor, Habermas (Dews 1992:140) quotes Ralf Dahrendorf's contention that "work is disappearing from the work-based society." That we are experiencing its end and moving toward a "'split' society, with a productive core of the employed, and an expanding margin of the poorly fed and neglected, who are forced into subcultures and ghettos," those Dahrendorf labeled the underclass (Dews 1992:141). We may, Habermas (Dews 1992:141) contends, have come up against "a critical limit" in our ability to transform "traditional domains of activity into organized occupational systems with monetary rewards," and in the state's ability to organize services in educational, social, and even political sectors without "deliver[ing] up the lifeworld even more to the clutches of experts." It may well have to be left to local initiatives by tenant associations, neighborhoods, or communes "to arrange the collective life of different generations—for example—in such a way that the negative effects of nuclear family structures, whose advantages we would not wish to abandon, could be compensated for—in relation to the elderly, to children, to the handicapped and frail, to those afflicted by loneliness, and so on" (Dews 1992:142). Perhaps we need to rethink local communities on the lines proposed by MacIntyre for the purpose! We are also in a society, Habermas says, whose members find themselves needing to reevaluate their activities because of the increase in free time both on a day-to-day basis and across their life span. Habermas (1994a:66) thinks that a new energy for the welfare state is necessary *and possible* if we take the focus off labor and conceive it in terms of "a newly found balance between money, power and solidarity," which are the steering resources of modern societies. This we can do by shifting the balance more toward regulation through solidarity, and if we mobilize "the subtle communication flows [that] determine the form of political culture and, with the help of definitions of reality, compete for what Gramsci called cultural hegemony."

Habermas (1990b:18), in fact, assumes that the struggle for the welfare state today is not primarily one about money but about "definitions," about articulation, publicity, and education. The core problem is not mainly economic but one of rearticulation: to redress the legalistic and bureaucratic tendencies that "have robbed the supposedly neutral medium of administrative power through which society was to exert an influence on itself, of its innocence." A problem of "social curbing" on the interventionist state in favor of a newly conceived politics of solidarity, with "the potential for reflection necessary for such an undertaking" lying "in the topics, arguments and proposed solutions of free-floating, public communication," of critical publics that alone in a democracy can curb the abuses of interventionism and reanimate the welfare state through the discovery of a new consensus. Functioning critical publics that constitute "a dynamic of self-correction" based on "a combination of power and intelligent self-restraint that could make the self-regulating mechanisms of the state and the economy sufficiently sensitive to the goal-oriented results of radical democratic will-formation" (1994b:xxvi). This dynamic, Habermas (1990b:20) has continued to believe, "cannot be set in motion without introducing morality into the debate, without universalizing interests from a normative point of view."

Emancipation, Democracy, and Justice

Habermas's key notions of ideal speech and emancipation, which he originally identified firmly with the progress of socialism, have been radically reworked over recent years, and he has also rethought the nature and use of theory and its relation to practice. The recent Habermas is light years away from the Habermas of *STP* and of the 1960s and 1970s on all these topics, even distant from the Habermas of the 1980s. Commenting in his foreword to *The Past as Future* (1994b), Peter Hohendahl (1994b:xxiii) remarks that comparing Habermas's essays from the late sixties with his views in the interviews in the book, one is struck by two things: "first, his later statements are considerably more cautious when they address the nexus of theory and practice; second, and more importantly, the emphasis itself has shifted. Whereas the debate of the 1960s focused on the political application of a theory that was more or less taken for granted, the debate of the 1990s questions the feasibility of and the need for theory." The latter, undoubtedly, owes itself to his entanglement with postmodernism. He disagrees with Hohendahl's suggestion that we should give up on theory, but his notion of theory has changed radically since *STP*. "I do not," he explains, consistently with what he says about utopianism, "force anything into one theoretical frame, and I don't assimilate everything into the basic concepts of a holistic master theory" (1994b:114). Distinguishing himself from Rawls and Nozick, he denies any ambition "of sketching out a normative political theory... I don't design the basic norms of a 'well-ordered' society on the drafting table" (1994b:101). Pressed with the view by Michael Haller (1994b:99), on a different occasion, that theory may be out of fashion today, that we are observing "a certain weariness with theory itself; a kind of theoretical exhaustion intoned with resignation, particularly by sensitive people," he concedes that too much may have been expected from theoretical work in the past, and that theory is not something one does for its own sake, but he warns that announcing its death may be premature since its popularity fluctuates with the mood of the times, and its fortunes may change. Today, he says, his own interest in theory is limited to the reconstruction of the actual everyday conditions of communicative practice, an approach that is complemented by his political attitude toward democracy.

Habermas, in fact, declines to work with either the liberal or the republican models of democracy and, like Dewey, goes for a procedural model where democracy redefines itself pragmatically in an ongoing way. Likewise, though he continues to think the notion useful and important, there are radical shifts in the way he now defines the "ideal speech" condition. He no longer views it as "an ideal rooted in the universal presuppositions of argumentation and able to be approximately realized" (1998b:322), but more modestly, as a "thought experiment"; "a small bit of ideality [which] breaks into our everyday lives" when conflicting validity claims arise and need to be settled. This "idealization," he says, has nothing "to do with ideals that the solitary theorist sets up in *opposition* to reality; I am referring only to the normative contents that are *encountered* in practice, which we cannot do without, since language, together with the idealizations it demands of speakers, is simply constitutive for socio-cultural forms of life" (1994b:102, italics in original). This revision of the notion of ideal speech inevitably brings with it a reassessment of his views on enlightenment and emancipation reflecting changes in his political orientation. Enlightenment he now defines as "a reflex of self-experience in the course of learning processes," no longer as a collective experience of societies or entities. Emancipation builds on it "because in it processes of self-understanding link up with an increase in autonomy" (1994b:103). A truly startling reappraisal of both notions, particularly of the latter, given the energy of his old polemics on the subject with Gadamer and others.[69] Indeed, where it was once the most prominent of his political concerns, he now downplays the importance of emancipation in his political thinking. "I am rather careful these days," he now says, "about using the expression 'emancipation' beyond the realm of biographical experience." Other notions, he says, matter to him more, "bare notions" like "reaching understanding" and "communicative action," for instance. Concern with procedural notions like these, he confirms, has moved to the center of his thinking today. Their merit being that they "have a more trivial significance" than the "grandiose-sounding" emancipation, and that they refer to what goes on in ordinary everyday practice "without the poetic or false-romanticizing luster of being somehow *extraordinary* experiences" (1994b:104, italics in original). He goes further. "The 'emancipated society'" (rational society in old Frankfurt school parlance), he now says, "is an ideal construction that invites misunderstanding. I'd rather speak of the idea of the undisabled subject" (1994b:112). Not even the "empowered" subject! Shades of Foucault again?! In the interests of being "foolproof against all misunderstanding," he continues, we must—if we use the term emancipation at all—understand it semantically rather than normatively, as something that "makes humanity more independent, but not automatically happier." Once we do this, it "no longer comes with a promise of happiness," but with the promise of democracy (1994b:105).

There is no doubting, of course, his continuing commitment to the European style of democracy. "Despite all the talk of postmodernity, there are," he asserts, "no visible rational alternatives" to it. Our political task is "to search out practical improvements *within* this form of life," not to undermine it with revolution or anarchy (1994b:107). We must guard against "both *revolutionary self-confidence and theoretical self-certainty*," not only "because bureaucratic socialism has turned out to be a worse variant of what was to be fought against" (1981:222), but because of the "risks" arising from "the incalculability of interventions into deep-seated structures of highly complex societies," such as Western societies, and because of "a fallibilistic consciousness on the side of theory" itself, which needs to be recognized (1981:223). Later, he explained the nearly universally positive reaction to the fall of the communist empire in Eastern Europe as a sentiment stemming from the growing tradition favorable to democratic institutions assimilated into European political culture over the centuries. A sentiment, he remarks, taking a dig at Foucault, that militates "against all the repression of a ghostly surveillance state," and that justifies optimism in the future of democratic institutions (1994b:105). This assimilation by Europe of democratic culture is the only sense, he says, in which one can speak today of a history of political emancipation. In *Between Facts and Norms* (1998b), first published in 1992, he distinguishes his own conception of the democratic state both from the liberal state, which regards itself simply as the guardian of an economic society, and from the old republican concept of an ethical community institutionalized in the state, criticized by MacIntyre, which operates with "the notion of a social whole centered in the state and imagined as a goal-oriented subject writ large" (1998b:298).

Rejecting both the republican view of the citizenry "as a collective actor that reflects the whole and acts for it," and the liberal, where citizens are individual actors operating blindly and anonymously, producing "aggregated but not consciously formed and executed, collective decisions," as grounded in the *philosophy of consciousness*, he proposes a discourse theory that demands a *"higher-level intersubjectivity* of processes of reaching understanding" (1998b:299, italics in original). Taking elements from both the other models, discourse theory casts democracy as "an ideal procedure for deliberation and decision making," from which "reasonable or fair results are obtained insofar as the flow of relevant information, and its proper handling have not been obstructed." In this conception of things, "practical reason no longer resides in universal human rights, or in the ethical substance of a specific community," but "in the rules of discourse and forms of argumentation that borrow their normative content from the validity basis of action oriented to reaching understanding," and that "arise from the structure of linguistic communication and the communicative mode of sociation" (1998b:296–297). It signifies the disappearance of "the 'self' of the self-organizing legal community ... in the subjectless forms of communication that regulate the flow of discursive opinion- and will-formation in such a way that their fallible results enjoy the presumption of being reasonable" (1998b:301). Quoting Dewey as the one who pursued this view most "energetically," Habermas (1998b:304) refers to the discursive level of public debate as the key criterion of democratic quality. On the other hand, he rejects Joshua Cohen's democratic proceduralism because it is silent about the relation between decision-oriented deliberations regulated by the institutionalized democratic procedures, and the informal, unregulated processes of opinion-formation active in the lifeworld. A relation that, as we saw earlier, Habermas (1998b:307) regards as fundamentally important for democratic theory, and that he takes up himself, describing the first realm as a *"context of justification"* and the second as a *"context of discovery"* from which emerge the "wild publics"; the "open and inclusive network of overlapping, sub-cultural publics," with their "fluid temporal, social and substantive boundaries" that "develop more or less spontaneously," and form "a 'wild' complex, with its pros and cons, that resists organization as a whole."[70] On the "con" side, they render the lifeworld "more vulnerable to the repressive and exclusionary effects of unequally distributed social power, structural violence, and systematically distorted communication than are the institutionalized public spheres." On the "pro" side, their unrestricted and informal nature enables them to take on new problem situations and issues more sensitively. In the process they articulate collective identities and need interpretations more freely than they are within the institutionalized spheres (1998b:308). Habermas (1998b:308) points out that the procedurally regulated, institutionalized public sphere relies on a supply of this free informal public opinion to keep it active and dynamic. While the unregulated spheres, on their part, require "the support of a societal basis in which equal rights of citizenship have become socially effective."

In the final analysis, Habermas (1998b:308) wants to promote a society that is egalitarian, dynamic, and disposed toward cultural pluralism. A society that "no doubt abounds just as much in conflicts as in meaning-generated forms of life ... a secularized society that has learned to deal with its complexity consciously and deliberately," in which "the communicative mastery of *these* conflicts constitutes the sole source of solidarity among strangers—strangers who renounce violence and, in the cooperative regulation of their common life, also concede one another the right to remain *strangers*." Working with the idea of a Habermassian education research project, this could be a summary of its normative core. Recently he refers to its political outlook as a "Kantian Republicanism" to distinguish it from other older sorts of republicanism and from Rawls's political liberalism, which begins, he says, with the intuition that realizing private autonomy is the basic preoccupation of democratic politics:

> Kantian Republicanism, as I understand it, starts from a different intuition. Nobody can be free at the expense of anybody else's freedom. Because persons are individuated only by way of socialization, the freedom of one individual cannot be tied to the freedom of everyone else in a purely negative way, through

reciprocal restrictions. Rather, correct restrictions are the result of a process of self-legislation conducted jointly. In an association of free and equal persons, all members must be able to understand themselves as joint authors of laws to which they feel themselves bound individually as addressees. Hence the public use of reason, legally institutionalized in the democratic process, provides the key for guaranteeing equal freedoms. (1998c:101)

There are again some shades of Foucault here, as we shall see in Chapter 7. Meanwhile, Habermas talks about freedoms in the old way, not only in terms of private but of "public autonomy" also and dismisses the contrary fallacies of either setting the individual against the social or imagining her to be "simply *at the mercy* of the lifeworld" (1998c:101). In his conception of things, "private and public autonomy mutually presuppose each other in such a way that neither human rights nor popular sovereignty can claim primacy over its counterpart" (1998c:261). Reacting to the long-standing debate in political philosophy about which is prior, "the good" or "the right," he argues that "the good that is relevant from the moral point of view shows itself in each particular case from the enlarged first person plural perspective of a community that does not exclude anyone" (1998c:30). In other words, our individual conception of our own good must depart from our understanding of ourselves as members of a comprehensive and inclusive moral community, where "the good that is subsumed by the just is the very form of an inter-subjectively shared ethos in general, and hence it is the structure of membership of a community, though one that has thrown off the shackles of an exclusionary community" (1998c:30). This community requires its members to think of themselves "in terms of the Rousseauian model of self-legislation," where one extends the maxims by which one would regulate one's own life to the community as a whole as laws. Thus, in the question of justice as against ethical-existential questions, one asks not "what is good for me, or good for us, or good for them," but rather "what is *equally good for all*?" (Dews 1992:248, italics in original). "The 'moral point of view,' constitutes a sharp but narrow spotlight, which selects from the mass of evaluative questions those action-related conflicts which can be resolved with reference to a generalizable interest; these are questions of justice" (Dews 1992:249). But Habermas downplays the moral priority given since Plato to justice; ethical-existential questions, he argues, are usually far more urgent and equally important. And "justice is nothing material, no determinate 'value' but a dimension of validity" (Dews 1992:249). Accordingly, there are, in his view, different principles of distributive justice possible (needs-based, desert-based, and egalitarian), any of which may apply in any situation, and no one overriding the rest. Which principle to adopt is decided in each particular context within "discourses of application." In other words, pragmatically on the grounds of which fits the situation after all the relevant factors are taken into account in the process of democratic discussion and will-formation.

In *Between Facts and Norms*, Habermas (1998b:322) still refers to communicative action in the spirit of the Kantian public as "a process of argumentation in which those taking part justify their validity claims before an ideally expanded audience ... without limits in social space and time." A process, in other words, where the participants "presuppose the possibility of an ideal community 'within' their real social situation." In short, he still assumes that authentic communicative action requires participants to think of themselves as members of an "ideal communication community." While ideal speech, in the form of a "thought experiment," enables its members "to transcend the provinciality of their spatio-temporal contexts that are inescapable in action and experience" (1998b:323). In other words, it remains an adaptation of the Kantian transcendental standpoint, with the difference that "essentialist misunderstanding is replaced by a methodological fiction." But not a fiction in the sense of operating in the abstract. Ideal speech does not, he insists, "abstract from the 'finitude' of communicative social relations," but functions as "a foil against which the substratum of *unavoidable* societal complexity becomes visible" (1998b:323). The law and the procedural concept of democracy are, similarly, methodological fictions that permit communicative action (1998b:326).

Finally, "conservatism" and the agenda of technocratic rationality have remained constant political targets for Habermas's writing. Postmodernism he regards as either nihilistic or collusive with the contemporary impulse toward conservatism. Its aestheticization of politics he describes as, at best, a type of "compensation" for the pressures of the hyperrationalized institutionalized systems of late capitalism. Not only does it not threaten them, however, it actually has a system-stabilizing effect insofar as it provides "apparent outlets for frustration while leaving the technical-political infrastructure of the system itself essentially untouched" (1994b:xxv). At the same time as he has been its critic, as I showed earlier, he has remained a consistent supporter of the welfare state, worrying about its failures, about the way it has been targeted politically and economically by neoconservatives, and about the absence of a coherent social democratic answer to its ills and political weaknesses. The fall of communism, which forced him to reassess his early commitment to socialism and to address the question of the left's future, led him to the unequivocal conclusion that "a welfare state compromise that has established itself in the very structures of society now forms the basis from which any politics here has to start," albeit that today its future needs to be subjected to an urgent public debate on the lines described earlier" (1990b:17). Meanwhile, even his self-perception as a universal public intellectual has changed. Though he continues to pronounce himself in interviews and on the media on a number of general issues ranging from German unification to the Gulf War to, more recently, nationalism and the EU, he has grown increasingly sensitive to the criticism Foucault and others have made of the universal intellectual's stance. Today, he "sees the intellectual in a supplemental function, as someone who counters and subverts the hegemonic discourse" (1994b:ix). But still insists that "when intellectuals, using arguments sharpened by rhetoric, intervene on behalf of rights that have been violated and truths that have been suppressed, reforms that are overdue and progress that has been delayed, they address themselves to a public sphere that is capable of response, alert and informed," that they still "count on a recognition of universalist values," and "rely on a halfway functional constitutional state and on a democracy that for its part survives only by virtue of the involvement of citizens who are as suspicious as they are combative" (1994a:73). The last bit about citizens being "as suspicious as they are combative," though not the rest, resonates with Foucault yet again, as we shall see later.

Habermas's Learning Society

Habermas's relevance to the debate about the learning society is self-evident. His earlier work contains a dystopian description of modern society as a learning society, where the steering mechanisms of the system are operated by a technocratic rationality that extols "order" *in abstracto* as a good, draws on the social and human sciences for its legitimation and self-perfection, and signals "the repression of 'ethics' as such as a category of life," continuous with the social analyses of the Frankfurt School. What emerges from this analysis is a lifeworld tightly, but not totally, administered, and subjected to an alarming degree of colonization by the system of areas that formerly fell under the influence of family and neighborhood and were, therefore, to some degree autonomous of it. And of a public sphere that should be under the democratic influence of citizens but is similarly colonized by the system's bureaucratic institutions, by the state's experts, and by a culture industry that operates not in the interests of enlightenment or emancipation but in the commercial interests of the market. This culture industry "transfers the profit motive naked onto cultural forms," infecting them with its *ethos* of consumerism, which works in the interests of the administration. A lot of this description of the culture industry coheres sociologically with the growing trend in adult learning today, described in Chapter 2, to cast adult *education* as an aspect of leisure and to represent it in the same way as culture, as a product, a commodity that is packaged, advertised, bought and sold, and consumed on the open market. In short, the culture industry has itself been recast as a learning industry, and it is operated by business concerns that answer not primarily to the law to educate but to the law of flexible and efficient delivery of information that ensures profit in a competitive market. Adorno had, in fact, remarked on how the culture industry does not simply invite us to see things as commodities *among other things* but turns them into commodities *through and through* so that, in our eyes, they are nothing but commodities. The learning industry today replaces the intimate face-to-face relationship of educator and learner—once typical of adult education encounters—with one between a faceless technical expert delivering a service and a faceless consumer receiving it from a distance. More generally, adults are increasingly encouraged to regard their self-fulfillment in the same way that they regard their leisure and private entertainment, namely as the self-satisfaction of consumers of information and knowledge, and nothing more.

Habermas is concerned by the way the media have trivialized culture and education, distorting the notion of publicity. In addition, they have appropriated the realm of truth production and meaning for themselves in different spheres of life (not least the political), and measure their success not ethically (in terms of their power to enlighten and emancipate), but in terms of the effectiveness with which they deliver their messages and produce "suitable outcomes" that are not the outcomes of education. He is concerned by the way the public sphere is colonized by the media and by the demise of the intellectual within it—replaced, as Elliott pointed out, by expert communicators and opinion formers whose object is not to educate or engage in debate, critical or otherwise, but to spin information. They are Kundera's imagologues, who reduce publicity to a "staged display" conducted above the heads of the public, as it was in classical times. Habermas also worries about "reified models of science" that "migrate into the socio-cultural lifeworld and gain objective power over the lifeworld's understanding," and about the power of that other type of expert typical of the modern world, the technocrat, whose manipulative mentality and sense of order is transferred into the lifeworld as it is colonized by the system. Technocrats have distorted the original meaning of the welfare state just as imagologues have distorted the meaning of publicity and democratic communication. In short, he worries about a situation where "the public is split apart into minorities of specialists who put their reason to use non-publicly and the great mass of consumers whose receptiveness is public but uncritical." Though he is no longer tempted by the project to revive the old eighteenth-century bourgeois public in some form, he continues to instigate the democratic reanimation of the public sphere with critical publics that will open up political spaces between system and lifeworld, and within the lifeworld itself, where the utopian thrust of modernity is kept alive, repoliticizing it and restoring the relevance of the intellectual as one who "counters and subverts the hegemonic discourse"; including, in our case, that of lifelong learning and the learning society.

Education was for Kant, and for subsequent liberal thought, an instrument of liberation from one's "self-incurred tutelage" to others, a process of increasing self-governance whereby one passes under the tutelage of an impersonal universal reason. Kant called this process enlightenment and its outcome autonomy. Habermas, as we saw, rejected the Kantian view that the subject of the universal law of reason is the free-floating, reflective, autonomous self, and located it and the ideal of self-legislation instead in the reflective practices of a communicative community, a public, guided by the democratic principles of "conversational justice" (as MacIntyre calls it), framed by the conditions of ideal speech. This is where, for Habermas as for Dewey, education is produced: in participating in the activities of such a public. The later Habermas, as we saw, no longer thinks that the efforts of a reflective public can produce anything as "grandiose-sounding" as individual and collective emancipation, not even self-fulfillment, but it can give us the "undisabled subject," MacIntyre's "independent practical reasoner." However, in Habermas's view this is a notion that has nothing to do with morality, where "we want to know what is equally good for all," but with freedom, with "the subject's relation with itself," and "refers to discontinuous transformations in the practical self-relations of persons," which is how, in his view, personal autonomy should be reconceived (1994b:104). This conclusion is reflected in his reformulation of enlightenment and emancipation as notions to be interpreted within "the realm of biographical experiences" and not properly applicable to the idea of a collective subject. While he now looks at enlightenment and emancipation in this way, as something self-reflexive, he grows increasingly convinced, like Rorty, that in the sphere of morality—that is, in the sphere of justice and the public good—"despite the talk of postmodernity, there are no visible alternatives" to the form of life that has developed in the post-Enlightenment West, and that what is left for us is "to search out practical improvements *within* this form of life" (1994b:107). So that, instead of theorizing a utopian "emancipated society," the discourse-theoretical approach to the learning society "allows a critical relationship with the self-understanding of familiar political cultures, existing institutions, and recognized legal systems, with the goal of fully tapping their potential for self-transformation stored up within them" (1994b:110). This requires us to "shake up the interpretations of existing states of affairs—prepared for the most part by experts," with a "critique that operates with better grounds" (1994b:109). For sure, one should "never imagine the addressees of social theory, or even society itself as a subject writ large, whose eyes are to be opened by the social theorist" (1994b:101). Apart from "shaking up the interpretations of existing states of affairs," the social theorist/intellectual enters into the battle for cultural hegemony, for definitions, including the political and social definitions of the learning society.

Aligning with these views, Habermas (1994b:113) maintains that he does not "correspond with the traditional image of the 'philosopher' who explains the world with one thesis." Also, he distances himself from professional philosophy and the work of productive scientists that is "completely absorbed into the anonymity of the research process," that communicates badly with contemporary experiences, and that still "appears withdrawn, cocooned in esotericism" (1994b:118). He describes himself instead as engaging with "separate, already 'disassembled' problems that have their place in very different contexts," in speech act theory, moral theory, legal philosophy, political theory, and so on, making contributions "to this or that issue" and tackling them within their different theoretical discourses (1994b:114). Unlike his earlier work, which was, as we saw, concerned with articulating the conditions necessary for creating a rational democratic society with a socialist agenda, this approach does not, on the face of it, go well with the theoretical work of articulating the normative core of a project of a learning society I envisaged for philosophers in *PLE*. His work on communicative action would, on the other hand, be an important contribution to the conversational politics internal to a project whose adherents operate with the self-perception of members of a communicative community committed to reaching a democratic consensus on the project's agenda. This is, in fact, how I envisaged things in *PLE*. The fact, on the other hand, that Habermas regards master narratives of justice and emancipation, and the temptation to theorize them, as unacceptable, tilts him to some degree toward the postmodernism whose relativism and historicism he nevertheless continues to reject.

CHAPTER FIVE

The Learning Society and the Third Way

The Learning Democracy

Habermas's work (interestingly enough with some borrowings from MacIntyre), has encouraged Stewart Ranson, in some cases in collaboration with other writers, to articulate a politics of a learning social democracy. Articulating this kind of politics as an education research project was also, as I wrote earlier, the original project of this book. Had I kept to it I would probably have finished years ago. My serious engagement with postmodernism in the early 1990s, however, particularly with Foucault's and Rorty's work, caused me to suspend the project and to reconsider, putting its future in doubt and leaving me uncertain as to how the book would turn out. Obviously it has not turned out as it was originally planned. And it is impossible for me to say to what extent my account of a social democrat learning society would have coincided with Ranson's, though Habermas would have been an important influence on it also. In any case, Ranson's account of the learning social democracy is important because the project to create a learning society with social democrat politics was, as I said earlier, on the British Labour Party's agenda in the later half of the 1990s. This coincides with the third, and last, part of my narrative of the fortune of the learning society, suspended temporarily from Chapter 2, which covers the late 1990s and the beginning of the new millennium. Meanwhile, social democracy itself was redefined in Britain and elsewhere following the collapse of the Soviet Union in the early 1990s, which had the European left struggling to redefine itself and come to terms with a Western world that had been governed for years by neoliberal politics. The outcome was the politics of the so-called "Third Way," which will be described later in this chapter. This was the political background against which Ranson theorized his learning democracy, and it is interesting to see how his project fits the Third Way social democracy in Britain. In the next chapter I shall take up the question of how the left has reacted to postmodernism and how postmodern writers have, themselves, come to terms with the left.

But my first concern in this chapter is with Ranson, who unlike Hughes and Tight and, again, like myself at the outset, and like the writers of the lifelong education movement, regards the promotion of a learning society as an outstanding challenge for policy-makers today. "It is only when the values and processes of learning are placed at the center of the polity," he argues, "that the conditions can be established for all individuals to develop their capacities, and that institutions can respond openly and imaginatively to a period of change" (Ranson 1994:106). Ranson also believes that a learning democracy needs a framework of national governance and the promotion of strong local communities. He agrees with Habermas and its other critics that the left must revise its thinking on the welfare state, which, he says, has encouraged the view that "the good society or educated public" is best delivered by "knowledgeable specialists," when it should be lived and created by the public with specialist support. In a paper written with Jane Martin and John Dixon (1997:117), he also points to the left's task to challenge the key organizing concepts of the neoliberal public domain— those of choice, diversity and equity—with a different set: those of *civitas* (citizenship), difference (democracy), and equality (justice). The authors implicate the former set of concepts in creating "a public domain that reinforces rather than resolves the predicaments facing education and society." Apart from objecting to the political morality of the market, they argue that the market model of the learning society cannot resolve problems that derive from the transformations of the times we live in. Particularly those that stem from environmental erosion, the fragmentation of society, and the unrequited demand for opportunity for all, which raise deeper "questions of identity, well-being, rights, liberty, opportunity and justice." These are problems, they argue, that cannot be resolved by individuals acting in isolation, "nor by 'exit' (see Hirschman 1970), because we cannot stand outside them." "Only the public domain," they continue, people who "learn how to act together more effectively" (1997:117), "can solve the physical problems of the environment, or the dilemmas of reconciling different cultural traditions" (1997:120) and keep the growth of the learning society under democratic scrutiny. Thus, public choice conceived by neoliberals "as an aggregation of self-interest," is replaced by "the public good of voice, deliberation and collective judgment" (1997:121). And a return to "a commitment to the politics of equality ... based now upon redistribution of outcomes as well as inputs to ensure equal dignity" replaces "the neo-liberal thin view of equity." In the public domain, "in place of an emphasis on diversity of goods is a valuing and reconciling of differences of cultural traditions and identities: a growing awareness of the need for a new politics of 'equal recognition' (Taylor, 1992)." Finally, "underpinning and enabling this remaking of the public domain are the values and institutions of democratic citizenship (Nixon et al., 1996; Ranson, 1994)." Indeed, the learning democracy "makes the agency of citizens central to personal and social development (Clark, 1996; Deem et al., 1995; Turner, 1993)" (1997:121).

In *Management for the Public Domain*, written with John Stewart, Ranson (Ranson & Stewart 1994:78) goes further along these last lines, describing citizenship as *"the ontology, the mode of being"* in the learning democracy, and referring to the need for a comprehensive theory that brings together the goal of private self-creation and the public world of justice. Meanwhile, he contends, the learning democracy must have two basic organizing principles: first "that its essential structure of *citizenship* should be developed through the processes of *practical reason*" (Ranson 1994:106, italics in original) as Habermas suggests, and second that it should be guided by a set of new values and conceptions of learning "at the level of the *self* (a quest for self-discovery), of *society* (in the learning of mutuality within a moral order) and at the level of *the polity* (in learning the qualities of a participative democracy)" (Ranson 1994:107, italics in original). These principles again assume that "there is no solitary development or learning; we can only create our worlds together" (Ranson et al. 1997), that we only grow individually and collectively, as Dewey and Habermas suggest, in interaction with others. They assume that we "regard each other as citizens with shared responsibility for making the communities in which [we] live" (Ranson et al. 1997:121) and in which "mutuality and thus the conditions for learning can flourish" (1997:122). In his book with Stewart, Ranson (Ranson & Stewart 1994:122) acknowledges Habermas's notion of a communicative community (and some debt to Gadamer too) as his inspiration for this model of a learning democracy based on the preconditions of a good polity, justice, participative democracy, and public action. Its existence, the authors argue, requires political structures, institutions, and forms of life that create the conditions for communicative rationality and for the growth of its appropriate virtues: "Intermediary institutions, forums for participatory democracy, and structures of justice which establish what Rawls calls 'the basic structure of society' in its fair distribution of fundamental rights, duties, opportunities and 'advantages from cooperation' (1971:7)," and which work "as an inclusive network in which all citizens may voluntarily associate" (1997:122).

Ranson, Martin, and Dixon (1997:122) also insist that, like that of Habermas, theirs is not a "bounded community reliant upon cultural homogeneity ... but rather an inclusive community or inclusive communities in an associative democracy," in which "private meets public; a public sphere where private interests are reconciled in the context of the public good," and the civic virtues are incorporated within a "tradition" (Ranson 1994:81). Where the institutional arrangements "recognize different interests and accommodate cultural diversity," and "strengthen the public sphere through an active democracy (Martin et al. 1996)" (1997:123). Within these kinds of communities, Ranson (Ranson 1994:105) writes, citizens develop a much firmer sense of their *agency* (where the concept of agency is understood, again as with Habermas, as involving "the reflective subject in action"), than they do now, "both in the creative development of the projects that are to define the unfolding of their lives and their active contribution to the social and political life of the community as a whole." This sense of agency, he continues, goes well with that of MacIntyre, who in *AV* defines it as a process of self-discovery through a life perceived as a unity that acknowledges itself as made in relation to others (Ranson 1994:107). Thus, the set of conditions that will provide the self with a sense of purpose within society is the cultivation of the civic virtues, active participation in creating the moral and social order with others, and a capacity for interpretive understanding (depending on the acquisition of hermeneutic skills) (Ranson 1994:109).

Ranson (Ranson 1994:113) goes on to write that the learning democracy requires reform in the structure of government itself. It requires as well the abolition of private education: "the government of the learning society needs to begin by celebrating education as a public good and challenging the enclaves of private power to take down boundaries," he says. It also requires avenues that enable citizens, through their membership in publics, to contribute to the development of their society through processes of democratic and cooperative planning, where the choices made are sensitive to diversity. This means, he says, a progressive decentralization of the power of national government to local forms of government, and importance given to the principle of subsidiarity, where decisions are always taken at the lowest level commensurate with efficiency. "We need a theory of power and authority that analyses the distribution of powers to different tiers," to the center, the local authority, institutions, and the community, he says, "to fit their proper responsibilities and tasks," and that restores the ideal of polycentrism and partnership (1994:114). The "center," as he describes it, should be able to promote a national policy for the learning society, to develop the infrastructure, to develop strategic planning and resourcing, to commission research, and to evaluate the quality of learning. His criticism of the welfare state is aimed particularly at the way it has cultivated the key idea of professionalism, fomenting the illusory promise of universal welfare and, as we saw, the view that "a just and open society to improve the well-being of all its members could be *provided* and, as it were, 'handed down' to the public," by the state and its experts. The way it has cultivated the fantasy that "the good society or an educated public were to be *delivered* by knowledgeable specialists rather than lived and created by the public with the support of professionals." In short, the idea of the state creating the learning society as a "welfare provision" means that the public is encouraged to surrender the initiative to the providers; namely the state and its experts, hence, today's predicament, where the rapid transformations of the times fail to be addressed by an active public domain (1994:102).

The solution, for Ranson (Ranson 1994:102–103) as for Habermas, "is to recreate, or create more effectively than ever before, a public and an educated public that has the capacity to participate actively as citizens in the shaping of a learning society and polity." But, surprisingly, he identifies not Habermas's but MacIntyre's critique of contemporary society in *AV* and his complaint that the educated public has been replaced by a heterogeneous set of expert specialized publics, as the influences on his thinking in this respect. However, like Feinberg, he criticizes MacIntyre for the unnecessarily pessimistic view he has of citizenship in the public domain today. Habermas, as we saw, is as much concerned about the control of the public realm by experts as MacIntyre, and has certainly written more on the subject than the latter. Moreover, where MacIntyre limited himself to some remarks about the manipulation of the public sphere, Habermas's critique, particularly in his earlier work, is a deep and analytic sociology of the colonization of the lifeworld by the system and its experts. So one does not see Ranson's need for MacIntyre, especially since MacIntyre apparently inspired him only with the *idea* of an educated public; he does not use the Scottish public as his model. It raises the question of whether he was aware of Habermas's more relevant and richer work on the subject. Habermas would have led him to consider the role of the media and the culture industry in general in shaping the social reality of our times, and how its impact on people affects the possibility of a learning democracy. Also, his reference to "the good society or educated public," which is clearly of MacIntyrian inspiration, is confusing. Habermas does not equate the two. Ranson gives the state perhaps too strong a role in the creation of the learning democracy for Habermas, who has pronounced himself against the notion of a social whole centered on the state because it is inspired, he says, by "the philosophy of consciousness." From this point of view Ranson's suggestion that private education should be abolished is especially worrying because he makes it not in the context of schooling but that of a learning society, and could be taken to suggest a blanket abolition of all initiatives in learning other than those of the state. One recalls the importance Habermas ascribes to spontaneous initiatives in the lifeworld independent from the state or system in this respect, the emergence of "wild" publics that challenge both and that he regards as necessary for democracy. Thus, rather than *constructing* "intermediary institutions, forums for participatory democracy," Habermas emphasized the value of an "undisabled" lifeworld capable of these wild initiatives. Otherwise, Ranson's model of a social democrat learning democracy is clearly in line with Habermas's general democratic politics of communicative action. It is not, however, in line with the thinking of the Third Way social democracy, which, as we shall see, emphasizes the value of individual self-dependence rather than that of collective action.

The Welfare State Reconsidered

Before I describe Third Way politics I need to take up the question of the welfare state and its future, which, as both Habermas and Ranson point out, is fundamental to the social democrat left and to the question of what kind of learning society one has. It raises critical questions about the financing and resourcing of adult learning in the learning society in a way that is socially just and restricts the power of state experts to dictate its politics. The writers of the lifelong education movement, as we saw earlier, believed that lifelong *education* (not just learning) could be claimed as welfare right for all in the learning society and part of the provision of the welfare state. But in Chapter 2 we saw a contrary trend in adult learning today, and noted the weak position of anyone who wants to claim either lifelong education or lifelong learning as a right. It was a claim clearly impossible to make politically under neoliberal regimes. Theoretically, a social democrat regime committed to creating a learning society with social justice at its core, should be a different proposition. The problem here is, again as Habermas and Ranson point out, that social democrats also have problems with the welfare state and its ability to deliver on social justice. Ranson argues that experts should merely *support* the welfare state, not provide it, but that it should otherwise continue to operate within the principles of social justice based on needs. There is, however, clearly a clash here with the strong self-responsible individualism promoted by the EU in its discourse on lifelong learning and the learning society that was evolving at the same time that he was making his arguments and that he does not consider. Nor does he describe how the role of the market and the employers, strong as we have seen under the neoliberal regime, would be redefined in a learning social democracy.

Giddens (1998b:112), today a leading exponent of the thinking of the Third Way social democrats, raises the same questions as Habermas and Ranson with regard to the welfare state. He also refers to its "problematic history"; its negative image today as essentially antidemocratic and unfriendly to autonomy, "depending as it does upon a top-down distribution of benefits." Other familiar charges he echoes are that it is "bureaucratic, alienating and inefficient," static, and completely unequipped to cover new-style risks like those arising from rapid technological change, social exclusion, and newly emerging family patterns (1998b:113). Far from responding adequately to these problems, he argues, the welfare state encourages moral hazard, serious benefit dependency, and fraud. Habermas, as we saw, as far back as the 1980s, felt that the welfare state was fast losing "its power to project future possibilities for a collectively better and less endangered way of life" (see Chapter 4) and that its socioeconomic and political ideals fail to harmonize with today's reality. Neoliberal critics, like Robert Nozick (1984), have, of course, long argued more fundamentally that the welfare state is immoral, that it involves an illegitimate use of the state's coercive power to rob Peter in order to pay Paul. The criticism of feminists like Yeatman (1994) has been different. Yeatman argues that the issue about the welfare state is an issue about citizenship, about power, rather than about morality, and that the debate should be about the form citizenship will take for the future. She describes the exclusions generations of women have suffered historically as "inherent rather than accidental features" of the modern discourses of citizenship that have created the welfare state. Predicated on the idea of a civic community as "homogeneous and monocultural (monorational, if you will)" (1994:81), they identify the model citizen with the formal individuality "of a rationally-oriented, freely contracting subject," bracketing out other representations of individuality (1994:85).[71] The welfare state's concept of citizenship, she contends, generates "a dualistic distinction between those who can achieve independent status as freely contracting individuals via market activity, and those who for various reasons are unable to achieve this status, and for whom, therefore, special provision must be made." And it casts women among the latter, disabling them and impressing on them, as on others cast in this role, "their client status, their lack of contractual freedom, of choice" (1994:85). Yeatman (1994:86) also identifies an assimilationist intent behind the welfare state, exemplified by the progressivists' argument for the extension of welfare resources to culture in the 1920s, on the grounds that the lack of "cultural capital" can be as serious and disabling as the lack of economic capital. This kind of thinking, she argues, contributes to social citizenship's invention of "its other as those who are constituted as 'special' because disadvantaged, deviant, in relation to a norm."

Zygmunt Bauman (1996:243–244), however, sounds a strong note of warning against this welfare state bashing. Reminding us that there are two welfare models, the European and the American, distinguished by the fact that, at its inception, the former "wisely, institutionalized *commonality* of fate," and encouraged a moral *ethos* based on solidarity, while the latter institutionalized a safety net for protection against absolute poverty and destitution, "the *diversity* of fate," instead of its commonality. So that where the European welfare state philosophy makes "tangible the bond between public and private—community and individual, and casts the community as the pledge of the individual's security," in the United States, it is "the taxpayer's privations that are balanced against someone else's, the benefit recipient's, gain." In this way public and private interests are set against each other, and the welfare state is cast "as the individual's burden and bane," while the nation is divided into the "premium payers and the benefit recipients." In short, the U.S. model "recasts 'being for Others,' that cornerstone of all morality, as a matter of accounts and calculation, of value for money, of gains and costs, of luxury one can or cannot permit." Bauman shows how European neoliberal governments turned toward this model in the 1980s with the slow but steady retreat from general to "means-tested 'focused' assistance for 'those who need it.'" Thus, where in Europe it was originally conceived "not as a charity, but as a citizen's right, not as the provision of individual handouts, but a form of collective insurance," it has become "the stigma of the impotent and the improvident," of the needy who are "vilified for being a drain of 'taxpayers' money,' associated in the public mind with sponging, reprehensible negligence, sexual laxity or drug abuse," the contemporary version of the wages of sin, whereas it was previously seen as insurance against the effects of "capital which could not stay solvent without enormous social costs in shattered existences and broken lives." Now in full tranquility and without fear of any public outcry, the state can refuse responsibility for the ill fate of these people, and send out the message that there is "no more collective insurance against the risks; the task of coping with the collectively produced risks has been privatized," in a world where their number is growing (1997:37).

The "self-propelling and self-accelerating" tendency to abandon the moral purposes of the welfare state, Bauman (1997:42–43) remarks, has signaled an inevitable deterioration of collective services. He sees rising criminality and growing police forces and prison populations as the price already paid for it in many countries. In the United States, he mentions the restoration of the death penalty, which, he remarks, is reserved overwhelmingly for the poor and marginalized. This is because "the 'problem' of the poor" is "recast as the question of law and order," and funds which the welfare state would have earmarked for the rehabilitation of the temporarily unemployed, for instance, are shifted instead into the construction and technological updating of prisons and other punitive/ surveillance outfits (1997:60). On the other hand, the ordinary citizen is cast as a satisfied customer in a society that is there for her to seek and find satisfaction for her wants, a "permanent tourist" for whom "the social space is, primarily, a grazing ground, the aesthetic space is a playground. None allows, nor calls for, moral spacing." One is "free to do his or her own aesthetic spacing and forgiven the forgetting of the moral one" (1996:244). Bauman (1997:23) describes this "switch from the project of community as the guardian of the universal right to decent and dignified life to the promotion of the market as the sufficient guarantee of the universal chance of self-enrichment," as one that "deepens further the suffering of the new poor—adding insult to their injury, glossing poverty with humiliation and with denial of consumer freedom, now identified with humanity." It aggravates risk, since "livelihood, social position, acknowledgement of usefulness and the entitlement to self-dignity may vanish together, overnight and without notice." The situation is rendered worse by the fact that "the other safety nets, self-woven and self-maintained, these second lines of trenches once offered by the neighborhood or the family, where one could withdraw to heal the bruises left by the marketplace skirmishes," are considerably weakened if they have not fallen completely apart.

Bauman is pessimistic of any possibility that these trends can be reversed, and Avishai Margalit (1996) shares his pessimism. Margalit's narrative goes back further than Bauman's. He describes the moral advance the welfare state made on the "charity society" that predated it, where the motive for solidarity was pity rather than justice; a motive he castigates, quoting Nietzsche, as humiliating. In principle, he points out, the welfare society canceled out the humiliation of the weak by projecting welfare as a matter of entitlement, of "right" rather than charity. We seem now, however, he remarks like Bauman, to have regressed to the "charity society" again. Like Bauman and its other critics he blames the modern state for mishandling the project of the welfare state from the start. Theoretically, he argues, it was justified to set up its structures as the mechanism to enact a fair or just entitlement to welfare rights and contribute to justice and self-esteem, but the paternalistic attitude of its officials toward its beneficiaries has tended to humiliate people. Put differently, the welfare state inverted priorities; the bureaucracy became the end and the welfare of the needy became the excuse to sustain it. Humiliation follows, Margalit points out, when the recipients of welfare are treated as recipients of charity rather than justice. The argument is sometimes made, by Robert Nozick (1984) for instance, that a charity society dependent on the benevolence of its members and based on the principle of voluntary giving is morally superior to one where the giving is enforced by the state's coercive intervention. The point being that what is coerced has little or no moral value. One could also argue, in defense of the charity society, that unlike the welfare state it is not at the mercy of the state. But from a recipient's point of view, living in a charity society means being at someone's mercy, and the recipient's point of view counts from the standpoint of social justice. Social justice is not about creating moral opportunities for potentially charitable members but about a fair distribution of benefits and burdens according to need. Moreover, depending on other people's sense of charity is risky for the recipient, who must depend on the means at their disposal, their priorities, their moral conscience—in short their favorable disposition.

Margalit (1996:238), like Bauman, is not uncritical of the welfare state. As we have seen, he argues, like many of its other critics, that it perpetuates the culture of dependency; it impairs the autonomy of the needy placing their destiny irrevocably into the hands of the officials of the state. Yeatman (1994:109), like Ranson, blames this outcome on the welfare state's culture of needs definition, "in which expert professional opinion guide[s] the way that policy-makers frame[d] needs and the services responding to those needs." She describes it as "a centric culture of scientifically informed needs formation which preempt[s] an open politics of needs formation in favor of professional expertise." A culture that favors the political rhetoric of rational consensus, where the consensus is defined by the professionals in terms of objective needs based on their scientific research, and finding active support on the part of "a number of left, masculinist commentators" who argue that the professionals who laid the foundations for the welfare state had thereby succeeded in undermining the classical picture of a neat division of private from public to the advantage of the domestic sphere. Yeatman (1994:107) argues that no such thing has happened. Instead the compromise between the two spheres "has maintained a principle of patriarchal determination of needs, now expressed on behalf of a corporate representation of households—the state—and, in due measure, involved a transfer of rights from individual heads of households to the state in respect to the members of the households." Against this old rhetoric of the welfare state that vests the power to determine needs in professionals, she argues for "a rhetoric of negotiated needs settlement where the principle of user rights provides guidance towards achievement of an effective and practical compromise" between the perspectives of experts, professionals, and of the needy person.[72] A politics of needs satisfaction where the rhetoric of rational consensus is replaced with a rhetoric of difference, beginning with a recognition of the principle of user rights, such that needs are not identified for all collectively by the state through its experts but by the needy themselves in collaboration with experts and professionals. Yeatman argues that this rhetoric is more amenable to the postmodern mentality, with its skepticism toward master narratives, than the old rhetoric. In short, what she suggests is the retention of a discourse of welfare rights cast politically in a different way, as user rights, with an emphasis on the fact that they are recognized as *rights* for all, not as aspects of state or any other charity.

In Chapter 2 we saw that the Commission for Social Justice in Britain in the mid-1990s represented the right to lifelong learning as a right to *access* the resources of a Learning Bank, driven by the individual's initiative, and involving a partnership with the state and employers. The virtue of the arrangement, which envisaged a contribution by the user, as the Commission saw it, is that it attracts private capital, allows individual choice, flexibility and control, encourages self-dependence, and promotes equity of access. As I shall show presently, the British Labour Party went for the model when it won power in the late 1990s, thus also accommodating the trend in the EU toward self-responsibility for lifelong learning by the individual. The Commission recommended that the Bank should not just finance training needs but also those broader needs that fall within the domain of self-fulfillment, should the users wish. This was a move that has the benefit, theoretically at least, of making funds available for the purposes of non-vocational adult learning in a situation where state funding of this sector was drying up. But this trend toward self-dependency and the personalization of initiative, as I said in Chapter 2, exacerbates the division of society into those self-directed learners who are active members and creators of the learning society, and can, if they so desire, regard non-vocational learning as part of their self-fulfillment, and those who are not; who may, for different reasons—such as being unemployed or having low-profile jobs and insufficient funds available to invest in their own learning, or not perceiving the value of such investment, or not even knowing what the stakes are—be outside the learning society. The question is what the state should do about their situation, if anything at all. The government of a learning social democracy would, theoretically at least, adopt aggressive policies to ensure that they should be the fewest possible, and this could involve actively seeking out the marginalized and working with them in the sort of personalized partnership suggested by Yeatman, extending the notion of needs to *learning* needs. Maybe, it could be argued, equality of opportunity is better achieved with a universal voucher system supported with appropriate guidance and counseling services, as Illich suggested. The need for such services was, as we saw, emphasized by the lifelong education writers, who stressed the importance of motivation, of cultivating a culture of learning, for the learning society. But it would put the whole burden of financing back on the state and would add to rather than diminish the problem of economic viability that plagues the current welfare state.[73]

What is the profile of the needy in today's society? Raggatt, Edwards, and Small (1996:4) identify the "psychological consequences of living with instability which bear most heavily on the least skilled and most vulnerable adults," as the most pressing problem for today's learning society, which must lie at the heart of the contemporary issue of social justice. And Jansen and van der Veen (1996:125) argue that this class of "vulnerable adults" has grown and changed dramatically in recent years and under postmodern conditions, and that they cannot be identified any more with a particular social sector. The risks that postmodern societies produce, they say, "not only threaten the life chances of socio-economic de-privileged groups, but the quality of life of society and even the survival of mankind." Referring to Beck throughout and sustaining that problems of social inequality and marginalization are sharpened in today's risk society, they argue that these no longer coincide with traditional class boundaries, so that the question of social welfare needs to be redefined differently from how it was in the past. Today, they say, social chances are increasingly determined by "age, sex, race, i.e., pseudo-biological hallmarks, in combination with the level of qualifications and occupational branches" (1996:125). In the risk society, individuals are expected more than ever to take responsibility for their own lives and make the right kinds of decisions while they become increasingly dependent on conditions that lie beyond their control, conditions that they can hardly even see through. In this context, the authors see adult education more as an instrument of a broad cultural policy tackled at the community level than as an instrument of social policy tackled at the level of government as an aspect of the welfare state. A community-based cultural policy that attacks existential problems as well as new forms of social inequality at their source (1996:134) and promotes adult education as a broker in problem-solving networks, they argue, is more effective today than the more cumbersome social engineering of the state (1996:130).

Adult Welfare Rights Revisited

Of course, the language of rights, as moral entitlements, finds its objectors in the shape of utilitarians, postmodernists, and others who object that any such rights can derive from something called a "universal human nature" and are justified in terms of something called a "universal human reason." "Fictions," MacIntyre (1981:67) calls them, on a par with unicorns and witches. It would appear, therefore, that anyone who wants to retain the notion of a human or moral right has a problem on her hands, namely that of accounting for the *source* and *subject* of such rights. MacIntyre's (1981:67) case against them is that there is nothing "out there" to which they correspond. This objection, however, depends on one's endorsement of the correspondence theory of truth or meaning; it holds no water for those who deny it. MacIntyre suggests that the credibility of what one believes depends either on its self-evidence or its correspondence with our intuitions, while ignoring the fact that both criteria, along with the correspondence theory of truth, have also encountered serious objections at the hands of philosophers. Thankfully, however, problems of justification of theories are problems for philosophers, not for ordinary people. The latter, including those among them we designate as "educated," converse seriously with fictions, myths, and metaphors all the time, not the least that of human rights, with no inkling at all of the preoccupations of philosophers. MacIntyre, as we saw, is dismayed by this fact and thinks it unfortunate; others, like Rorty, celebrate it. The fact is that, with or without the support of philosophers, the language of human and moral rights is popular and widespread. Ordinary people use it all the time when they want to make a strong claim to something, and it grows ever more central to our moral, legal, social, and political vocabulary. Moreover, such rights are still popularly regarded as universal and inalienable, so that their political and moral weight is considerable and especially important and meaningful at the level of international politics where they are appealed to, to put pressure on totalitarian regimes and defend people subjected to inhumane treatment. Whether people still think of them as proceeding from an underlying human nature or reflecting something "essentially" human or not is important only to the extent that they may attribute a status to them that cannot be sustained on philosophical grounds. But here I am with the poststructuralists, who discourage us from thinking that moral language needs philosophical justification or foundations, and the same can be said for politics, which Rorty describes as a matter of pragmatic adjustment. On the other hand, the fact that something does not require philosophical justification does not mean that we should accept it without question. While the language of human and moral rights is mostly sustained today not by its metaphysics but by its social and political currency, it still owes its popularity to the historical success of liberal modernism. In other words, it owes its popularity, as Foucault argues, to the power of the West, not to philosophical persuasion.

Once this is understood, the culture of moral and human rights can continue without recourse to the fiction that it has some grounding in natural law or in something out there. In this sense the adjective "human" describes not the source of these rights but their status in the eyes of their users, as applying to all human beings indiscriminately—thereby giving them greater moral force, and their legal and political enforcement greater credibility. Apart from his questionable assumption that truth is some sort of correspondence between language and something existing outside it in the "real" world, MacIntyre's reasoning is flawed by the assumption that acknowledging something to be fictitious is a good reason to reject it. The alternative Wittgensteinian view, supported by poststructuralists, is that the value of a language lies in its *use*, not its *truth*, as accuracy of representation. With respect to unicorns and witches, though most people today acknowledge that they do not exist, this does not stop them from using the words meaningfully; i.e., in a way others understand. There are narratives we tell about unicorns and witches, and they have been described or depicted in imaginary forms by storytellers, illustrators, and cartoonists. This is how they are brought to life in the imagination of people through narrative or illustration, the way people in the historical past of whom we have no original picture are brought to life. Santa Claus corresponds with nothing more substantial than the images we have created of him over the centuries in the Christmas tradition, within which he has acquired a more or less consistent form. Nor has the Bible lost its influence on many who acknowledge it to be fiction, a myth. The conclusion of our discussion of the "myth" of the learning society, as Hughes and Tight referred to it, in Chapter 2, brought out the usefulness and value of myths, their power not just in the world of the imagination but in that of concrete policy-making and practice. In short, one does not need to show or even to believe—with reference to words or expressions—that they correspond with anything out there in order to use them meaningfully; all they need do is cohere with a language game people play or are ready to play. A later MacIntyre, in fact, acknowledges this when he argues that truth, like reason and justice, is always relative to some tradition or language game.

If we sustain that our moral and political discourses need have no deeper sources of support than their current popularity, then the language of rights is truly well supported. Whether it deserves to be is another matter. MacIntyre proposes a better way of promoting solidarity with others as a moral obligation than by making recourse to the language of rights: that of promoting the recognition that we are all dependent creatures, and as such have reciprocal duties toward each other. But is grounding a moral language in an anthropological metaphysics a better way? Is it not a betrayal of the historicist outlook he defends in *AV* and elsewhere? MacIntyre links this solidarity with a sense of *misericordia* and describes it as an effect of charity (1999:124), a gift that we extend beyond the circle of our immediate community to others outside it (1999:126). But I am as unhappy as Margalit with a politics of solidarity represented in this way, as an effect of charity. Not only for the reasons given earlier but because what is at stake here, as the critics of the welfare state I cited earlier have argued, is the not inconsiderable matter of the recipient's dignity, self-respect, and sense of freedom. The *ethos* of our modern—and even more of our postmodern—world is individualist; it teaches people to be proud of their autonomy and self-reliance, and to regard dependence with shame. It is hostile to the representation of any help to others as charity, a ring of humiliation in the modern use of the term. The sense of dignity that is often ascribed to poor people is one that makes no claims on others, that bears poverty as an unfortunate cross. There is the proud poverty of those who live without hope but ask for nothing as a gift. Feeling that one is *entitled* to something as a matter of justice, on the other hand, allows one to look the other in the eye while receiving it. Charity is a gift that may be withdrawn at any time by the giver without any right of protest by the receiver. This is the case with all kinds of gifts, even if they are given in the unconditional way described by Derrida as a call to responsibility. This is why a feeling of entitlement goes together with dignity in the receiving; when one feels entitled to something one does not feel that one is at the mercy of others, as one does when one receives their charity.

A Japanese "Postmodern" Model?

What may have won the British Labour Party over to the argument for lifelong learning and the learning society in the late 1990s was its determination to bring its policies in line with the real demands of the political, economic, and social realities of the postmodern world, to "modernize" Britain. Or it may simply have been a decision to bring its policies in line with the EU's thinking. In any case, it decided that the learning society in Britain could not be left to grow in a *laissez faire* manner; that, as Ranson suggested, it required a framework of national governance. A model approach to the governance of a learning society was already available in a very different part of the world, namely Japan, which anticipated Europe by nearly a decade in its interest in lifelong learning and the learning society. But there is no evidence that the British looked at the Japanese model; indeed their model is very different. The Japanese government shared the same perception that the fundamental changes that had taken place in Japanese society over recent decades had created serious socioeconomic and political problems for the country and had to be addressed. The country's social system was rapidly changing, the emphasis on the development of a strong work-force supporting economic growth was weakening, and so were the homogeneous values of the past, and the old belief in, and passionate commitment to, the nation. Japan was threatened by the same battery of forces that were challenging Western societies at that time: inter-nationalization, an aging society, the coming of the Information Age, and changes to the employment system in the new information-based industrial structure. All these factors had led it to rethink its educational system radically as far back as the late 1980s, even though the advisory organs of the Ministry of Education had been urging toward policies of lifelong education even earlier, since the early 1970s in fact (Makino 1997). After the spadework carried out by the *ad hoc* Council for Educational Reform (*Rinji Kyoiku Shingikai* or *Rinkyoshin*) between 1984 and 1987, Japanese national policy for the creation of a learning society was officially placed in the hands of a National Lifelong Learning Council by parliamentary legislation in 1990 (the Lifelong Learning Promotion Act, July 1).

This was not all, however. The Japanese government also adopted the policy of supporting and encouraging independent initiatives at local levels, in *ad hoc*, or non-formal, learning situations, through exemptions, financial assistance, tax breaks, and other policies. "The primary point of departure" for this policy, Gunther Dohman (1996:69) observes, was to advance "non-formal learning within the context of everyday life" in Japan "called *shakai kyoiku* which literally means social learning and learning within society." Dohman (1996:68) describes these policies as a "success" and attributes it to the single-mindedness with which they are pursued. The key principle the Japanese adopted from the start, in line with the maximalist model of the learning society, is that all forms of learning, not just those pursued in more traditional learning institutions, should be incorporated into an overall network of learning opportunities and learning aids throughout Japanese society. The "main players" operating the non-formal part of the network, Dohman (1996:70) says, were the 17,000 *kominkan*, or community learning centers, already active before government intervention. But he also refers to the growth of a booming industry in learning businesses that work with public institutions, private companies, publishing houses, broadcast stations, and other entities to develop new learning opportunities, learning magazines, and media programs for a broad spectrum of lifelong learners. In addition, there was the near-effortless incorporation of modern information and communications technologies, and the creation of public and private telecommunications centers which, on the style of Illich's hubs, offer open access to electronic information networks, so that Japan became "the world's most comprehensive model for a nation-wide lifelong learning society in recent years" (1996:68).

Dohman stresses that the soil for these initiatives was already fertile because of a cultural tradition that attached great importance to the use of one's leisure time for continuous self-improvement, for the development of the quality of one's life, and for the enhancement of one's satisfaction with one's life; because of a tendency in Japanese society to attribute these outcomes—self-improvement, quality of life, and happiness—to the pursuit of learning. "The Japanese understanding of learning as an ongoing activity that is as much a part of life (and offers just as much pleasure) as eating and drinking," he remarks, "is unusually broad compared to Western thinking." In keeping with it, he says, "the Japanese feel that all social institutions and all spheres of life can be places of learning: not only libraries, museums, theatres and cultural centers, but youth clubs, sports facilities, cinemas, organizations, hobby rooms and bars as well." Which is not the same as the growing trend in Western societies, described in Chapter 2, to cast education as a consumer good in the entertainment market. The Japanese cultural outlook is that learning is to be valued everywhere and is as much a feature of the outing, the bus trip, the place of work, the privacy of one's garden, the hospital, the watching of television, as the formal setting of classrooms, lecture halls, and so on (1996:70). Given this outlook it is not surprising that the lifewide mobilization of the learning society, which the lifelong education movement dreamed of as utopia and which many of its members and adherents tried to actualize in their local communities, and which died a swift death in the Western world in the late 1980s, found ready resonance in Japan. Dohman (1996:71), in fact, identifies the existence of the very popular "lifelong learning movement" in Japan that failed to materialize in Europe, attributing its popularity "to its propinquity to leisure time, recreation *joie de vivre*, social life, contentment with life, and even festivals and exciting contests—and its remoteness to school performance pressure, control, qualification processes, career, competition, selection processes and the like."

The National Lifelong Learning Council of Japan, he observes, is restrained in its initiative of governance from controlling this movement by the principle that politics should not channel the direction taken by people's learning needs and activities, that "lifelong learning must spring spontaneously from one's life, personal experience and interest" (1996:71). But he also admits to problems here; namely, that the "zesty" growth of the movement, its spontaneity and lack of focus, creates difficulties for educational reformers who want a more critical and focused approach toward learning needs examined from the perspective of "the oppressive problems that affect our future such as pollution, demographic trends, women's rights, etc." (1996:71). These educational reformers, in short, perceive lifelong learning policies as instruments of social reform and problem-solving and argue that, left to itself, to spontaneous or market forces, the learning society will ignore the national agenda that the state wants to address, and exclude the voices that are, for whatever reason, not articulated by those forces. Moreover, the harmonizing of the formal education system and its institutions with the mushrooming non-formal lifelong learning initiatives promoted by the lifelong learning movement would not happen by itself. Dohman (1996:72) remarks that with the Council's intervention it may not happen anyway. "The incorporation of learning institutions into a broad learning network as more or less fixed, stabilizing nodes appears to be rather difficult," he says, "because of the dissonance between formal stress-filled learning and informal leisure-time learning in Japan," since no relenting of the "stress-filled" formal learning in schools and other learning institutions seems to have occurred. Notwithstanding these tensions, however, he believes that the result of government intervention is a successful new concept of the learning society that avoids being either meritocratic and formal or one geared to the definitions of the market economy. It comes close instead to what he refers to as "the 'postmodern' model of an open learning-network society and constitutes a special variation of it," in the sense that, while it "encourages the learning society to develop freely 'on location,'" the model also "uses centralized planning to coordinate these developments and makes use of organized aids to stabilize and develop them" (1996:74). Making sure, in turn, that this planning avoids turning the learning society into a well-developed "'educational realm' or rob[bing] it of its 'joie de vivre dynamic' through formal regulations and bureaucratic approval and control procedures" (1996:74). Its policy is to permit learners to move about freely within the learning society and according to their own wishes, on the understanding that this approach not only satisfies individual demands but is also better suited to promote the country's economic strength than policies that are specifically geared to establish vocational qualification and competence. Which is radically different thinking from the European, as we have seen.

But Dohman's evaluation of the experiment may be too enthusiastic. Atsushi Makino's (1997:16) is more cautious. He prefers to describe the results as "mixed" and worries that the central education administration has, in fact, become too powerful and intrusive, destroying the balance. He worries about the trend toward increased centralization of responsibilities, and about the role played by the private sector, threatening "the relative autonomy and freedom of local education administration." Remarking that "local autonomy and the individual needs of the people must be recognized and incorporated into any model" of a learning society, he hints that this may not be happening to the extent suggested by Dohman. Whether real or not, his fears raise the central issue with state governance or administration of the learning society; namely, how strong should it be? What kind of "partnership," if this is what is contemplated, should there be between the state, the non-formal sector of free, independent, and spontaneous learning and initiatives (whether or not it is coordinated as a movement), and the market forces that control the information society and its learning agenda? How can it work in a way that guarantees and safeguards a free and equitable access to the available learning resources, the freedom of all to learn in their own way and for their own self-fulfillment, and, at the same time, satisfies the state that its investment is relevant to its broader social, political, and economic tasks and aspirations? Balancing these factors, not capitulation to market forces, is the challenge facing governments with a social conscience, such as that of the social democrat are supposed to be. So what kind of conscience is the social conscience of the new Third Way social democrat?

The New Left

Like the Japanese, the British Labour government that came into power in 1997 pledged a strong commitment to policies of lifelong learning and to turning Britain into a "modern" learning society; "a Britain equipped to prosper in a global economy of technological change; with a modern welfare state; its politics more accountable; and confident of its place in the world" (O'Brien 1999:2). This was in marked contrast with its predecessor neoliberal governments. Yarnit (1997:4) said of them that "the triad economy, society and citizenship—so fundamental to European policy since Maastricht—has found almost no echo with the outgoing Conservatives." And Richard Taylor_(1998:304) comments that Thatcherism "saw education and training as properly having two essentially ideological purposes: first, to provide 'relevant' education and training—relevant, that is, to wealth creation and to the specific skills necessary for an increasingly sophisticated economy. Secondly, education and training should induct people into the culture of populist capitalism." The perception of Conservative governments, Taylor (1998:304) says, was that the root cause of economic decline in the UK was the country's "persistent, anachronistic liberal approach, which gave primacy to the arts, high culture and the old professions at the expense of engineering, technological skills and, above all, the business culture." In November 1998, Richard Edwards, Peter Raggatt, Roger Harrison, Ann McCollum, and Judith Calder, in Research Report No. 80 of the Open University, published for the Department for Education and Employment, with the title *Recent Thinking in Lifelong Learning* (already mentioned in Chapter 2), reviewed the key points in the recent and current lifelong learning literature and related issues, especially where it revealed thinking in areas related to policy. Where "recent" was understood as following on the Maguire report *Factors Influencing Individual Commitment to Lifetime Learning* of 1993. The opening judgment of the Research Report (1998:8) was also that in these years "lifelong learning has largely developed as a policy strategy to support the wider aim of economic competitiveness" and that in its evolution as a concept it had discursively displaced "conventional front end notions of education ... even if actual practices have a long way to go to catch up."

The report (1998:8) confirmed a situation where "rather than providing a policy framework for the reform of education and training provision, lifelong learning becomes itself 're-formed' by its adoption and translation into pre-existing institutional structures with management and professional cultures and agendas of their own (a familiar finding of studies of policy implementation—Bates 1998)." Not surprisingly, therefore, it described the notion of lifelong learning as still "in the making" (1998:9). a conclusion that the Eurydice report (also mentioned in Chapter 2) confirmed two years later in 2000. Those "making their voices heard" in its making were "the pre-existing influential stakeholders within the economy," while the missing voices were those of "the learners themselves" (1998:8). The report (1998:8) noted that a "greater emphasis is being placed on individual self-reliance to cope with change," a trend also confirmed in the Eurydice report. It also reported the trend in the literature to emphasize skill development, competencies, and capabilities as the relevant learning goals, and that "the notion of employability has moved to the fore." Although the "concern for the availability of employment and appropriate opportunity structures," it said, tended to be deemphasized, with the language turning more toward individual self-dependence, "a notion of a learning society which sees inclusion mediated through participation in employment" seemed to be emerging which, though providing opportunities for many, "itself produces other exclusions" (1998:9). Meanwhile, the report noted that following the EU's white paper of 1995, another priority had been added to the agenda of economic competitiveness; that of social cohesion. On this the report expressed the fear that, as had happened with the notion of the expansion of opportunity, when the notion of participation is reframed within the discourse of lifelong learning, the old notion of participation in liberal democratic structures and civil society "may be displaced by concepts of a learning society, in which as long as one learns, one is not excluded and to learn is interpreted in the widest possible sense" (1998:9).

Notwithstanding its pledge to modernize Britain, the new Labour government's manifesto qualified its political approach as nonradical. "Some things," it said, "the Conservatives got right. We will not change them. It is where they got things wrong that we will make change" (O'Brien 1999:1). Politically, as Giddens (1998b:26) put it in his book *The Third Way: The Renewal of Social Democracy*, the government aimed "to transcend both old-style social democracy and neo-liberalism" with a politics that—as the title of Giddens's earlier book, published in 1994, put it—was *Beyond Left and Right* (1998a). Giddens (1998b:26) argued that the Third Way new Labour had emerged from the necessity to react with pragmatism to "a world which has changed fundamentally over the past two to three decades," not at the hands of the left but of a neoliberal right bent on rolling back socialism. These changes, Giddens argued, those of globalization, a new individualism, the apparent collapse of the traditional left and right framework of modern politics, the problem of political agency or the future of democracy, and of how to deal politically with ecological problems, have left social democrats with no way back and with a number of political dilemmas to cope with. One, as we saw, is the welfare state whose future existence, he held, is not at issue, but would need to be rethought, no longer on the lines of dependence but of empowerment with responsibility, the language of the EU's lifelong learning policy documents. So what's the difference from neoliberalism? The difference, Giddens (1998b:45) says, is that though the Third Way speaks the language of self-dependency, it does so without abandoning its traditional politics of social justice. This qualifies it politically as center-*left*, which is not "an innocent label"; the word "left" is still politically significant. The new social democracy is "left of center, because social justice and emancipatory politics remain at its core." But these concepts must be recast in terms that render them relevant to the changed world and the changed political perceptions and attitudes of people today that reflect the permanent victories of neoliberalism. "Center left," he insists, means not a "moderate left," or "the middle" understood as compromise between right or left. The center, he says, must be rethought and its substance based on "philosophic conservatism."

The expression is explained in detail in *Beyond Left and Right*. While arguing for "the exhaustion of received political ideologies," Giddens (1998a:10) denies what, he says, postmodernists say, "that the Enlightenment has exhausted itself and that we have to more or less take the world as it is, with all its barbarities and limitations." We still need a radical politics, he contends, but today this can "only be loosely identified with the classic orientations of the left." Philosophic conservatism refers to a "philosophy of protection, conservation and solidarity." It "must recognize that confronting manufactured risk cannot take the form of 'more of the same,' an endless exploration of the future at the cost of the protection of the present or past." The Green movement emphasizes this point in its politics of conservation, restoration, and repair, but it "falls prey to the 'naturalistic fallacy' and is dogged by its own fundamentalisms" (1998a:11). Distinguishing different "conservatisms," Giddens (1998a:28–29, brackets in original) identifies the "philosophic" strain with Michael Oakeshott's, Roger Scruton's, and Gadamer's thinking, with "its critical attitude towards ideals of human perfectibility," and toward "the superiority of 'universal' solutions to problems," and its emphasis on tradition and the importance of embedded practice as sources of authority. "Traditions relate allegiance to authority, storing up as they do the sedimented wisdom of earlier generations. In the political sphere the state brings authority, allegiance and traditions together, 'in order to define the citizen as subject' [quote from Scruton]." Giddens notes the reluctance with which Scruton acknowledges democracy but leaves it unremarked. Finally, he concurs with Oakeshott's emphasis on the fact that traditions "are never fixed or complete and they do not have a changeless essence in which understanding can be anchored" (1998a:30). They can, he says, referring to Gadamer and this time, Rorty, and quoting from Oakeshott also, be best described as an ongoing "conversation."

What a "radical politics" means in this context is "being prepared to contemplate bold solutions to social and political problems" (1998a:49–50). Radicalism is not, Giddens (1998a:50) says, "here valued for its own sake but instead is tempered by that awareness of the importance of continuity on which philosophic conservatism insists." What it suggests is that the emancipatory politics of the old left be replaced by a "life politics," meaning that a concern with life chances becomes a concern with "life decisions." It contends that decisions on issues that press themselves on us, namely on what to do and how to do it, are decisions that we as individuals must learn to take. It is this commitment to "life politics"—the politics of self-reliance, Giddens (1998b:44) says—that renders the new social democracy "a politics of choice," but, at the same time, of "identity and mutuality" also. Rejecting the old socialist collectivism, it strives to "weave" alliances "from the threads of lifestyle diversity" (1998b:44). Its "overall aim" is "to help citizens pilot their way through the major revolutions of our time: *globalization, transformations in personal life* and our *relationship to nature*" (1998b:64, italics in original). In short, preserving a "core concern" with social justice but abandoning socialism, it seeks "a new relationship between the individual and the community, a redefinition of rights and obligations" in which *"no rights without responsibilities"* becomes its "prime motto" (1998b:65, italics in original). A motto that, clearly, clashes with the old idea of welfare rights as unconditional claims registered on the basis of needs that require no further justification than the fact that they are needs. Rights must now, in this redefinition of social justice, be justified and traded against the evidence of "responsibility," against the willingness to try for self-dependence, to help oneself first before the state steps in; in short they must be earned. Giddens draws a distinction between this definition of welfare rights and that of the political right, which restricts them to the poor and needy. The Third Way left, he says, applies this principle to everyone, thereby retaining the spirit of commonality of the old European politics of the welfare state.

Another key precept he defines for the new social democracy is *"no authority without democracy"* (1998b:66, italics in original). Democracy, he argues, must be particularly valued because "in a society where tradition and custom are losing their hold the only route to the establishing of authority is through democracy" (1998b:66). Giddens (1998b:73) remarks on the democratization of today's world; on the changed nature of the nation state, a "state without enemies," through the advance of globalization and the retreat of large-scale war; and on a growing distrust of politicians. And he refers, obviously with the EU in mind, to a "double democratization" that calls for a concurrent trust toward globalization and decentralization, or devolution, of power built on the principle of subsidiarity, as "the way to construct a political order which is neither a super-state nor only a free trade area, and at the same time clothes the nation with renewed influence." "To retain or regain legitimacy, states without enemies," he says, "have to elevate their administrative efficiency," they have to learn from business, not the least to reassert the effectiveness of government in the face of markets (1998b:74). They need especially to be able to manage risk and to involve ordinary citizens in its characterization, assessment, and management. The distrust of politicians requires the expansion of the public sphere through "constitutional reform directed towards greater transparency and openness, as well as the introduction of new safeguards against corruption" (1998b:73). In short, it requires the state to bring itself under greater public scrutiny, thereby making itself more moral in the eyes of citizens. Governments need to reestablish more direct contact with citizens, and viceversa, through "experiments with democracy" that take the form of local direct democracy, electronic referenda, citizens' juries, and so on.

Giddens writes about the importance of regenerating solidarity based on the idea of oneself as member of a national community, and on the idea, mooted also by Ranson, of a common morality of citizenship. In fact, he identifies the new social democracy with a reassertion of the nation-state as a stabilizing force in today's global world to balance out its cosmopolitanism, and refers to the fostering of an active civil society as fundamental to Third Way politics. "Government can and must play a major part in renewing civic culture," he says (1998b:79). In this respect, "the theme of community is fundamental to the new politics." At the same time, the politics of community should not, he insists, be cast in the old sentimental terms of "trying to recapture lost forms of social solidarity," but as a practical means of furthering the social and material refurbishment of neighborhoods, towns and larger local areas" (1998b:79). In this respect he refers to research in Britain and the United States indicating the growth of "a burgeoning civil sphere" even as the modes of civic engagement and association have changed and are changing fast. To the "small group" movement in the United States and to the expansion of the voluntary sector as examples of this phenomenon, and suggests that these experiments be harnessed to serve wider social ends. "Significantly," he adds, "most of the increase in civic activity has happened among the more affluent strata," there is the need to renew and recover poor and deprived local communities through economic enterprise; through partnership between government and business, using participatory techniques and meeting community organizations for the purpose (1998b:82). The general principle is to encourage "bottom up decision making and local autonomy" (1998b:84), and this requires an open public sphere and the opening of public space. What the government should address are questions raised by these politics; about the handling and distribution of power, about conflict, about identity and membership. Referring to the family as the most basic form of community and a basic institution of civil society, "the meeting point of a range of trends affecting society as a whole," (1998b:89) he advocates cultivating the idea of the "democratic family" as a general aim for social democrats as against the old right's appeal to the state to restore traditional family values. The democratic family, he says, shares characteristics similar to those of the democratic public sphere; namely, formal equality, individual rights, the public discussion of issues free from violence or threat, negotiated authority, and a shared responsibility for child care, or co-parenting, all drawn up as a contractual commitment.

Giddens (1998b:66) summarizes the values incorporated into the politics of the Third Way as those of equality, the protection of the vulnerable, the expression of freedom as autonomy, the principle of no rights without responsibilities, that of no authority without democracy, a cosmopolitan pluralism, and philosophic conservatism. He reinvents the welfare state as a "social investment" state that recognizes the need for new partnerships between the state and different agencies within civil society and that promotes individual self-dependence. (1998b:70) "Social democrats," he argues, "have to shift the relationship between risk and security involved in the welfare state," toward a relationship between risk and responsibility, in order "to develop a society of 'responsible risk takers' in the spheres of government, human enterprise, and labor markets" (1998b:100). This means that the issue of equality and redistribution, on which the notion of social justice is defined, has to be rethought and the mixed economy reformulated, so that social justice includes meritocratic principles. The social investment state must not, however, be a meritocratic society *tout court* since this would create deep inequalities of outcome that are socially divisive, and a great deal of downward mobility, which would ultimately "be as threatening to social cohesion as would the existence of a disaffected class of the excluded" (1998b:102). In any case, the idea of a meritocratic society, he argues, is unrealizable in principle and self-contradictory. To guard against the negative aspects of meritocratic principles, equality must be defined as inclusion, and inequality as exclusion. Both merit and inclusion, he continues, should be principles related to citizenship, civil and political rights and obligation, and to opportunities and involvement in public space, particularly with reference to work and education. Giddens distinguishes two types of exclusion: one suffered by those who are cut off from the mainstream of opportunity; the other involving the voluntary withdrawal of affluent groups who choose to live apart from the rest of society (a phenomenon he refers to as the "revolt of the elites"). Neither, he says, is socially acceptable. "Exclusion at the top is not just as threatening for public space, or common solidarity, as exclusion at the bottom; it is causally linked to it" (1998b:105). Later, on the same subject, he remarks that "a society that separates older people from the majority in a retirement ghetto cannot be called inclusive" either (1998b:120). He therefore proposes abolishing the fixed age of retirement and regarding older people as a resource rather than a problem, arguing that the same principle should be applied to them as to the other members of society. Retirement shouldn't be seen, he says, "as a time of rights without responsibilities," though he acknowledges exceptions to this rule, namely "the frail elderly, people who need continuous care" (1998b:121).

The fundamental difference between the welfare state and the social investment state, Giddens says, is that what the latter redistributes is not wealth but "possibilities." It denotes a shift of emphasis from the economic meaning of welfare to the psychic, where it has to do with general well-being. The investment of the new social investment state will be in its citizens' learning rather than in direct economic support, and it will involve the activity of localized third sector, or voluntary, agencies. In low-income neighborhoods it will be an investment in community-based programs, emphasizing the value of support networks, self-help, and the cultivation of social capital as means to generate economic renewal. Besides being effective, Giddens (1998b:110) argues, this approach permits more democratic participation. The Third Way's inclusive society involves a politics of inclusion in the work force and provision for the basic needs of those who cannot work. He has remarkably little to say directly about education for someone who observes that "education and training have become the new mantra for social democratic politicians" (1998b:109). While he acknowledges that investment in education today is "imperative," and a key basis of the "redistribution of possibilities," he has no faith or expectation that it can reduce or redress inequalities in any direct way. These inequalities, he argues, should be tackled at the source, at the social level, rather than through education policies. He does say that "governments need to emphasize *life-long education*, developing education programs that start from an individual's early years and continue on even late in life," but does not amplify any further (1998b:125, italics in original), leaving the how to Labour's policy documents on education to define.

New Labour's Learning Society

The British Labour Government's Green Paper, or consultative document, *The Learning Age: A Renaissance for a New Britain* (Department for Education and Employment 1998), published soon after its election to power and with the end of the millennium in sight, is the policy document where one would expect the political agenda for a learning society to be translated into specific policies. It was preceded by three earlier related reports, two commissioned earlier than 1997, but all published over that year: the Kennedy Report, *Learning Works: Widening Participation in Further Education*, commissioned by the Further Education Funding Council (FEFC) in December 1994; the Dearing Report, *Higher Education in the Learning Society*, commissioned by the Conservative government with the support of the opposition parties in May 1996; and the Fryer Report, *Learning for the Twenty-first Century*, published by the National Advisory Group for Continuing Education and Lifelong Learning (NAGCELL), commissioned by the Labour government itself in June 1997. The Kennedy Report made the point that further education should be defined lifewide, as occurring not only in colleges but in other locations too, "including the home and the workplace, training and enterprise councils, and schools and community centers, where people expand their horizons and extend their capabilities" (Tight 1998:475–476). It reaffirmed the European Union white paper's view that "learning is central to economic success and social cohesion," and argued that drawing "those who are not fulfilling their potential" or "have underachieved in the past," into "successful learning" is crucial for these purposes. The Dearing Report referred continuously and directly to the learning society and tied its advent with the expansion of higher education, which it identified as a key priority for government in the next twenty years. Fryer, on the other hand, spoke about the need to develop the culture of lifelong learning for all if Britain is to respond to the challenges of the new century, in the economy and the labor market through the radical and far-reaching transformations afoot in the world of technology, information, and communications; and in the social sphere, which is experiencing wide-ranging changes in the realms of family, relationships, communities, people's aspirations, and identities. Fryer also addressed the issue of the "learning divide" between those who possess qualifications and learn actively and who are in a relative minority, and the majority, who are under- or non-qualified, who have had little systematic learning since leaving school, and have little or no motivation for more (Tight 1998:474).

Malcolm Tight (1998:478) observes that all three reports accepted the forcefulness of the arguments for lifelong learning without question and argued for its extension throughout society. He also notes their sectorial interest, with none making any direct reference to "anything that happens before the age of 16," so that the model of lifelong learning and the learning society they assumed was not the maximalist one.[74] All three reports identified developing partnerships and using new technologies as important strategies for creating the learning society. Kennedy and Fryer both emphasized the key role government needs to play "in 'leading a campaign' or establishing a 'strategic framework' for the learning society—and all stress the importance of progression routes and learning pathways" within it (1998:478). *The Learning Age* (Department for Education and Employment 1998) brought the three reports together and, in the process, also reflected the policy objectives on lifelong learning and the learning society of the 1995 EU white paper discussed in Chapter 2 (*Teaching and Learning: Towards the Learning Society*). The Secretary of State for education opened it as follows: "Learning is the key to prosperity—for each of us as individuals, as well as for the nation as a whole. Investment in human capital will be the foundation of success in the knowledge-based global economy of the twenty-first century" (1998:7).

The priority of his government, in short, was to be no different from that of his neoliberal predecessors. His foreword to the document identified "two initiatives that will exemplify our approach" to lifelong learning; the introduction of individual learning accounts (possibly inspired, as I remarked earlier, by the Commission on Social Justice) "which will enable men and women to take responsibility for their own learning with support from both government and employers," and the setting up of a University of Industry, which will "offer access to a learning network to help people deepen their knowledge, update their skills and gain new ones" (1998:8). Both priority areas are connected with industry and the economy rather than with social purposes.

The Green Paper (Department for Education and Employment 1998:10), however, also has a political vision: "Our vision of the Learning Age," it says, "is about more than employment. The development of a culture of learning will help build a united society, assist in the creation of personal independence, and encourage our creativity and innovation," all priorities identified in the sociopolitical agenda defined by Giddens for the new social democracy, and consistent with the lifelong learning agenda in the EU 1995 white paper. The Labour Government, it says, aims to promote "social cohesion and foster a sense of belonging, responsibility and identity" among people. It goes on to describe its education policies as lying at the heart of the government's welfare reform program, which, it says, would attack the problem of widening social inequality through empowerment, breaking "the vicious circle of under-achievement, self-deprecation, and petty crime" among young people by rebuilding their self-confidence and independence. There follows a list of projected or actual government-sponsored initiatives to achieve this, to create the learning society: getting more young people at postschooling age into further training and higher education, creating "the University for Industry," setting up individual learning accounts for people who want to continue to learn, attacking the problems of basic literacy and numeracy at an early stage, widening people's access to and participation in adult education programs, raising standards across teaching and learning, setting and publishing clear targets, working with business, employees and trade unions, and building a qualifications system that gives equal value to vocational and academic learning. Finally, confidence in the success of these initiatives, the Green Paper says, stems from the fact that the country "has a great learning tradition," and that it possesses "the superb universities and colleges which help maintain our position as a world leader in technology."[75]

Tight (1998:481) observes that the document "uses similar language and arguments to its precursor reports" and includes most of their key recommendations. Like them, he says, it "fails to make any significant linkage between lifelong learning and compulsory education," so that, again, "the implications of this for pre-16 compulsory education remain unconsidered" (1998:482). Moreover, Tight (1998:482) notes the "tendency to elide the broad view of lifelong learning for all with a narrower perspective on vocational education and training," which ties lifelong learning in closely with the interests of the economy, and he remarks further that it fails to provide the vision for a learning society compatible with the broad social targets it sets itself. In fact, in Tight's view, despite the political rhetoric, a lot seems to have remained exactly the same as it was before 1997, with the difference that the Labour Government, unlike its conservative predecessors, had decided to take a more active role in making policies for lifelong learning. However, the Green Paper does have a social agenda expressing a commitment toward creating a more reassuring, more inclusive learning society that sets a high premium on social cohesion and self-identity, and announces a policy of recuperating young dropouts, to balance the emphasis on self-dependence, even if its policies in these areas were vague. Tight (1998:483), however, is even suspicious about the government's concern with non-participation in the learning society and its commitment to inclusion, and critical of the way it deals with these issues in practice, describing it as "off-putting and unrealistic," a case of "victim bashing" and "stigmatizing," of "effectively blam[ing] non-participants for the 'learning divide'" by charging them to "'fulfill their potential,' 'modify their behavior' and personally invest in the future." Which is, of course, more than a mere attack on its lifelong learning policies, an indictment of the way the government has interpreted the philosophy of the social investment state with its emphasis on self-dependence and self-sufficiency.

Finally, Tight (1998:483), like the Open University report of 1998 quoted earlier, describes the Green Paper as reflecting the "apparently compulsive aspect" of lifelong learning as the imperative of our times, the trend to take it for granted as the guiding principle for policy-making. Later in this chapter I shall refer to more recent initiatives in the EU that continue to consolidate this outlook explicitly. The trend worries Nigel Blake, Paul Smeyers, Richard Smith, and Paul Standish (2000:2), who quote the sentence in the opening paragraph of *The Learning Age* that says, "In an era or change, the only thing certain is change itself," and remark that what usually follows immediately on statements of this kind is something about the importance of managing change. So one of "the nostrums" of our time is that since, as things are, "all is in flux substance can be ignored and more power given to managers immediately." This may or may not be what is happening in their experience but, of course, a different implication can be drawn from the observation that all is in flux. That is that power should be disseminated with the flux to ordinary people, not to the managers, by giving them the skills to manage their own lives, by teaching them to live with the flux, and to regard risk and uncertainty positively as a challenge to their creative powers, in the way described by Lengrand in Chapter 1, rather than negatively and with fear. As we saw, the lifelong education literature of the 1970s and 1980s placed a lot of emphasis on the value of self-directed learning and managing one's own life and, as I have been saying, the more recent literature on lifelong learning, and the Green Paper itself, emphasize on self-dependence and self-management, which is reflected also in the thinking of the Third Way social democracy. I made my own remarks about the appropriateness of adopting lifelong learning policies as a response to change earlier in Chapter 1, replying to Bailey's rather similar objection. I continue to believe that lifelong learning policies are the appropriate policy response to unremitting change, that the need for self-dependence should be emphasized on people, and that self-directed learning should be a chief target of schooling. What worries me is not that lifelong learning is represented as indispensable for survival in the postmodern world but that it is defined within a performativist culture and, notwithstanding the rhetoric, identified with the instrumentalist outcomes of performativity. What concerns me, to return to the point once more, is that the dimension of *education* is being phased out and self-fulfillment translated into the satisfactions of the consumer, a matter of having rather than being and a purely private matter like one's leisure, and beyond the policy concerns of the learning society. More importantly, that education, which is a matter of being, is not recognized as being in any sort of crisis, so that it is not even debated as an issue anymore.

As we saw in Chapter 2, it has been argued that this state of affairs, where education is deprived of its normative dimension, need not be a bad thing in itself. Dewey's insistence that all we need do is to define education operationally as growth could even be seen as a vindication for it. But I replied to this argument in Chapter 1, where I argued that although he was only prepared to give an operational definition of education because he was against being overdirective and describing common aims for everyone,

Dewey indicated democracy as the appropriate environment for growth, for the classroom, school, and, eventually, the learning society, and that this description of a desirable environment for growth gave his account of education a normative dimension. So that the whole question of education from a Deweyan point of view reduces to one of providing, or struggling for, a democratic society that would have the same sort of features, roughly, as Habermas's and Ranson's learning democracy based on the communicative action of citizens in the public sphere through the formation of publics. Dewey thought similarly in terms of dynamic democratic communities marked by open and unrestricted communication of all kinds, both internally and between different communities. Growing as an active citizen capable of experimenting and managing change and risk intelligently or creatively in a communicative environment of this sort is what Dewey understood as education and as self-fulfillment. So that the self-dependence he recognized as crucial to individuals was not of the rugged "economic" kind, that of the pioneer, the individualism translated into the *ethos* of late capitalism, which he regarded as "superficial" and chaotic. Concerned mainly as he was with social reconstruction, he wanted not an extension of this kind of individualism to more and more persons but a reformulation of individualism, a "new" individualism, the creation, as he put it, of "a new psychological and moral type" whose beliefs and values are "the spontaneous function of a communal life in which he shares" (1930:14).[76] The kind of individualism that is served up in the literature in the name of self-dependence today, to the contrary, celebrated both by neoliberalism and the new social democracy, is precisely the kind Dewey disliked.

The Civic Learning Culture

The problem in the contemporary Western world where the promotion of a civic culture of learning is concerned is that it lacks a tradition like that of the Japanese. The lifelong education theorists of old could only dream of such a culture, just as they could only dream of the creation of a popular "movement" to create and sustain it. The qualities Dohman identifies with the Japanese, the importance they attach to one's continuous self-improvement, to the quality of one's life, to enhancing one's satisfaction with life, and their approach to leisure as an investment in one's learning, do not by themselves explain the phenomenon of a civic culture of learning in their country. All these qualities and ambitions can just as well be pursued privately in an atomized society, as by all accounts they are today with numerous individuals living in the Western world. What is missing today, notwithstanding Fromm's optimism, is Dewey's adage that "living together educates," the dimension of learning as a social, collective act; the promotion of self-conscious initiatives in collective learning at the community level. Something writers and activists of the lifelong education movement like Joan Bofill, Mustapha Haddab, George Papandreu, and Alberto Melo wrote about and struggled for in their different countries two to three decades ago: the activities and experiments in collective learning and participation in the communities of Catalunya, Algeria, Greece, and Portugal (see Wain 1984). Initiatives and struggles long dead, from what I was able to ascertain some two or three years ago from Gelpi, that Dewey, Habermas, and Ranson would have been happy to support but that are not contemplated in the Third Way's thinking, notwithstanding Giddens's statement that "the theme of community is fundamental to the new politics" of social democracy. Giddens, as we saw, dismisses the idea that we should try "to recapture lost forms of social solidarity" fundamental to the thinking of Bofill and the others and describes social solidarity instead in terms of cultivating social capital and taking practical steps to further the social and material refurbishment of neighborhoods, towns, and larger local areas as means to generate their economic renewal.

Lengrand's confidence in the possibility of a non-formal lifelong education movement emerging in the Western world in the early 1970s stemmed from the urgent demand for lifelong learning created by the challenges to individual and social growth in a fast-changing world, by the growing sociopolitical aspirations of workers at a time when the argument for workplace democracy and the self-management of workers was strong, and by the examples of solidarity he and others had experienced in the not remote past when faced with urgent challenges, the kind of comradeship in the resistance movements in France and other countries in Europe during World War II. Lengrand's lifelong education movement would, therefore, with its overt sociopolitical agenda, have been very different from the Japanese. Chapter 2 described how dreams of this kind, shared by other writers of a movement that never became a popular movement, came to grief in the 1990s when the policies taken in the field of adult learning in Europe—influenced by a powerful lobby of employers and their neoliberal political allies—were oriented more and more toward the interest of industry and the economy, and the major concern was to maximize adult learning as an economic and industrial resource, rather than with issues of adult *education*. In the 1990s adult learning was cast into two dichotomous sectors: that of vocational training and human resource development answering to the dictates of the economy, with the learning organization as the ideal learning model; and that of self-fulfillment left to private, individual initiative, and closely linked, like culture, with the leisure market and the culture of consumerism. What suffered irremediably was the possibility of promoting a culture where people learn together for their own collective self-fulfillment, spontaneously or as publics. And what emerged against this background in the late 1990s was not an independent lifelong education movement to fill this gap and promote a culture of this kind, but the accession to power of social democrat governments committed to governing the learning society rather than letting it grow in its own way, as it had more or less done under the neoliberals.

This was, of course, in character with the traditional social democratic belief that social justice needs engineering; it cannot take care of itself. Ranson, who, as we saw, advocated it, tempered his advocacy of such governance by also advocating the devolution of power from the state through the principle of subsidiarity (a politics of "bottom up decision-making") supported by Giddens, and by encouraging experiments in local democracy, also echoed by Giddens. Apart from supporting Dewey's view that democracy must be the form of life, not simply the mode of governance of the learning democracy, Giddens also emphasizes the importance of creating a political ethos favorable to transparency of government and political accountability, and the need to regenerate the public sphere and to open public space, though he makes no mention of any need for a critical public. Measures such as these, theoretically at least, do much to allay one's fears that the new social democrats are after centralizing political power over the learning society in the state. On the other hand; the fact remains that their political outlook, at least as it is described by Giddens, laced as it is with a strong sense of economic and political realism adopted from neoliberalism, does not project a social *ethos* that is any more conducive to the emergence of a more convivial learning democracy than the neoliberal. To the contrary, as we have seen, against the old left's emphasis on collective action, they place the same tactical emphasis as the neoliberals on the self-dependent individual as the learning society's protagonist. And they redefine the old left's political goals of emancipation and social justice, the former as the promotion of individual life chances based on self-dependence, the latter as social investment in the self-dependent. In the process of emphasizing the values of self-dependence, independent action, and the social cohesion of mutuality over those of collective responsibility and solidarity that were emphasized by the old leftist writers, and by projecting self-dependent responsible choosers and "risk takers" as the heroes of the learning social democracy, they redefine the welfare state on American lines.

It is in its heroes, in these kinds of individuals, that the social democratic state cast as a social investment state will mainly invest its resources, not in community-based action for the sake of the powerless. Thus, the Third Way replaces the old left's concern with needs and life chances with a more robust neoliberal concern with wants and life decisions, and speaks the tough language of *no rights without responsibility* (Giddens himself italicizes the expression for emphasis). The concerns of solidarity and needs satisfaction seem remote from this kind of language. Rather than promoting the sense of learning to *be*, theirs sounds, their critics say, more like an injunction to learn or else, or to learn to have. Unless, that is, one is disabled to the degree of being incapable of responding to such injunctions; then the safety net comes up. But even here fears have been expressed in Britain and elsewhere over how the disabled are identified, how the free riders are separated from the genuinely needy. European governments are accused of discrediting and destroying the standard practice of classifying the needy in terms of *a priori* categories: single parents, the elderly, the disabled, and so on, and, following the American welfare model, individualizing need instead. Of course, not in the sense that Yeatman describes! The "victim bashing" that the British government is accused of follows the trend to place the onus of proof of genuine helplessness on individuals. An approach that is hostile to the left's traditional politics of needs identification and suggests the politics of means testing characteristic of the neoliberal attitude toward welfare rather than that of solidarity. One problem here is that it is easy to pass from the view that the onus of proof in the matter of welfare entitlement lies with the individual to the general principle that the onus of proof *always* lies with the individual, even in matters, say, of freedom in the political sphere (where one would need to *justify* one's freedom), and of justice in the legal sphere (where one would need to *prove* one's innocence). And the outcome of that would be the general collapse of the liberal values of freedom and legal justice themselves.

In the political sphere a strong *ethos* of self-responsibility produces a meritocratic view of justice. And this is what Giddens, unsurprisingly if guardedly, advocates for the social investment state; though as we saw, he distances himself emphatically from a full-blown meritocratic society as unfair and socially divisive. In any case, the basis of the Third Way state's investment in the learning society is not need or right but initiative, the readiness to help oneself. You will be helped if you help yourself first, is its declared motto. One needs to earn the right to learn to receive support to learn. It is not one's human entitlement, or one's entitlement as a citizen. And this line of thinking *can*, in turn, as its critics say, lead to a cynical definition of inclusion in the learning society, where people are forced to learn and penalized if they don't. The fact that the politics of inclusion that Giddens describes are about attacking the two kinds of disillusioned in the postmodern world, at the two opposite ends of the social scale—those who are cut off from the mainstream of opportunity, from the work force, and from the learning society by their circumstances, and those who cut themselves off deliberately, the affluent who choose to live apart from it— confirms the motive of social cohesion in Third Way politics over that of social justice. This seems to be the main motive behind the politics of mutuality he advocates: the programs of social and material refurbishment for communities, the economic renewal of neighborhoods, towns, and so on; the expansion of the voluntary sector; the setting up of support networks; and the cultivation of social capital. These measures seem largely to stem from a concern over the threat Giddens perceives to individual and social self-identity in today's world, and over the results of social exclusion of all kinds, rather than from the concerns of social justice as such. Echoing the 1995 EU white paper, it evidently follows his own and Beck's analysis of the risk society undertaken in their respective sociological work, their common concern over the destabilizing and fragmenting joint effect of globalization and risk, and of other postmodern forces. As we saw, he responds to it by attributing to the state a fundamental task "to help citizens pilot their way through the major revolutions of our time; *globalization, transformations in personal life,* and our *relationship to nature,*" and by placing these concerns at the heart of the social democracy's agenda for the learning society.

As a final remark, there are substantial differences between the learning society emerging in Britain under the government of the Third Way social democracy and the Japanese. Notwithstanding the boldness with which it projects a new modernizing vision and its discourse on empowerment, self-dependence, responsibility, and choice, the thinking of the former appears defensive and protective; of the nation, the community, the economy, individuals at risk, national identity and social cohesion, and its solutions formal and institutional. The Japanese also worry about the loss of social cohesion, the disappearance of a homogeneous value system, and changing life conditions and existential perceptions that challenge people's sense of identity. But in Japan, as we saw, the initiatives of the local communities, their experimental responses to these problems, even if at the cost of some social instability and of living in a far from easy, perhaps even precarious, tension with the state's efforts to govern and stabilize the learning society has created a *modus vivendi* that is foreign to the British or any other European country. It may well be that there are signs of increasing regulation and control on the government side in Japan, and that the government's initiatives to formalize lifelong learning policies were instigated by these motives. It seems a fact that the Japanese government's initiatives to create a formal structure within which the learning society would grow was inspired by the wish to regulate the flourishing but anarchic phenomenon of spontaneous learning communities. Whatever may be the case it would appear that the non-formal, community-based movement will always—because it has a long tradition to support it—be a formidable force in the Japanese learning society, a constant source of instability and experiment, able to hold its own against these initiatives. A tradition, on the other hand, that the Japanese do not have and that is typical of the Western world is the very different one of a critical public. Giddens advocates the expansion of the public sphere as a counterbalance to the power of the government, achieved through more direct contact with citizens, through experiments in local democracy, electronic referenda, and so on. The ideal would seem to be, as Habermas suggests, to have *both* these critical publics of justification, and those wild ones, like the Japanese, of discovery.

The Present

This last part of my narrative of the fortunes of the notions of lifelong learning and the learning society takes me to the beginning of the new millennium and coincides with important initiatives taken by the EU toward a continental harmonization of both, communicated to its member states and the "candidate countries" for the new enlargement of the Union, in the form of a "memorandum" and "working paper" circulated for their guidance and reaction in 2000. In its introduction, the memorandum refers to the European Council held in Lisbon in March 2000 as the new "decisive moment for the direction of policy and action in the European Union" after Maastricht (Commission Staff Working Paper 2000:3; the boldfaced parts that follow are all in the original text). The conclusions of that Council, it says, "confirm that the move toward **lifelong learning must accompany a successful transition to a knowledge-based economy and society.** Therefore, Europe's education and training systems are at the heart of the coming changes. They too must adapt." The Commission's prescriptive tone is familiar; they *must* adapt. The memorandum invites "'the Member States, the Council and the Commission ... within their area of competence, to identify coherent strategies and practical measures with a view of fostering lifelong learning for all'" throughout the European continent (2000:3). This is mobilization at a level undreamt of by the lifelong education writers and beyond the wildest aspirations of UNESCO. In doing so it responds, it says, to the mandate of the Council to "**launch a European-wide debate** on a comprehensive strategy for implementing lifelong learning at individual and institutional levels, and in all spheres of public and private life" (2000:3). To this end, it continues in a manner that is reminiscent of the statements emanating from UNESCO in the late 1960s, "**lifelong learning** is no longer just one aspect of education and training; **it must become the guiding principle** for provision and participation across the full continuum of learning contexts" over the first decade of the new millennium, to ensure that all living in Europe 'have equal opportunities to adjust to the demands of social and economic change and to participate actively in the shaping of Europe's future" (2000:3). It invites the member states to lead the debate on this strategy, which "should take place **as close as possible to citizens themselves**" (2000:3). Reactions to the memorandum were requested from member states and candidate countries and were later published in a report in autumn 2001.

The document itself is divided into four sections: the first stating the familiar case for lifelong learning; the second identifying (as with the 1995 EU white paper) the promotion of active citizenship and employability as the central policy aims; the third arguing that the changes in "all kinds of teaching and learning" responding to current economic and social change should be put under the "umbrella" of lifelong learning; and the fourth highlighting six key messages, which collectively suggest "a comprehensive and coherent lifelong learning strategy" for Europe, and which would guide the debate (2000:4). The key strategic messages were:

- to guarantee universal and continuing access to learning for **gaining and renewing the skills** needed for sustained participation in the knowledge society;
- to visibly **raise levels of investment** in human resources in order to place priority on Europe's most important asset—its people;
- to develop effective **teaching and learning methods** and contexts for the continuum of lifelong and lifewide learning;
- to significantly improve the ways in which learning **participation and outcomes** are **understood and appreciated**, particularly those of non-formal and informal learning;
- to ensure that everyone can easily access good-quality **information and advice** about learning opportunities throughout Europe and throughout their lives;
- to provide lifelong learning opportunities as close to learners as possible, in their own communities and through ICT-based facilities wherever appropriate.

The sociopolitical objectives of these strategies were also clearly announced:

- **to build an inclusive society which offers equal opportunities for access to quality** learning throughout life to all people, and in which education and training provision is based first and foremost on the needs and demands of individuals;
- **to adjust the ways in which education and training is provided**, and how paid working life is organized, so that people can participate in learning throughout their lives and can plan for themselves how they combine learning, working, and family life;
- **to achieve higher overall levels of education and qualification** in all sectors, to ensure high-quality provision of education and training, and at the same time to ensure that people's knowledge and skills match the changing demands of jobs and occupations, workplace organizations and working methods; and
- **to encourage and equip people to participate more actively** once more in all spheres of modern public life, especially in social and political life at all levels of the community, including at European level. (2000:4–5, all highlighted parts in original text)

The strategic messages containing the operational definition of this project correspond with the assessment made by Edwards et al., in their

Open University report of the trends and emphases in the lifelong learning literature up to the end of 1998. Namely, (1) that the discourse has developed largely as a policy strategy, and that, this being the case, the notion of lifelong learning that emerges from the memorandum has been reformed by that discourse rather than forming it; (2) that it constructs lifelong learning as something inevitable and compulsory from which there is no escape; (3) that it emphasizes the importance of skills and competencies over other kinds of learning and motivation, and, in general, speaks the language of performativity, emphasizing the objectives of certification and human resource development, effectiveness, quality assurance, qualification, and so on; (4) that it continues to emphasize individual initiative notwithstanding its social objectives. Analyzed as an education project, its normative core is left predictably vague, given that it needs to accommodate the political vision of governments both left and right as these may succeed each other in the different member states of the Union. All it commits itself to in normative terms is the creation of a more inclusive society and a more actively participatory public sphere. The language of justice and emancipation are completely absent from it and, strangely, so too is democracy, though it does emphasize that decisions should be made as close to the citizens themselves as possible.

And this is not surprising, since it was prepared predominantly by bureaucrats rather than by educators. In stark contrast with the manifesto-like Faure report, where considerations of justice and democracy are uppermost, the memorandum reads like, and has the format of, the mission statement of a company or business organization, with its bullet form, flat unemotional language, and economy of style. The list of aims that refer to the need of governments to tackle exclusion, to achieve higher overall levels of teaching and learning, to work as closely with the citizens in devising policies and actions as possible, and so on, all find an echo in the British Labour Government's policies described earlier and in those of its European counterparts, and indicate the degree to which these have adapted to the Commission's efforts to harmonize policies. Indeed, what is politically important about the document as a whole is its intention to stabilize and harmonize lifelong learning policies across the much-enlarged EU. This gives it a political profile of unprecedented power as it is proclaimed the *guiding principle* of policy-making in all manners of teaching and learning across the European continent, and the motor of political, social, and economic change in these countries. Finally—interestingly from our point of view, and significantly—the expression "learning society," prominent in the 1995 white paper, is missing from the memorandum, which emphasizes a very different expression, "knowledge-based society," instead. To be precise, the document refers to **"a successful transition to a knowledge-based economy and society."** Economy *and* society! The order of precedence cannot be insignificant, and with this latest twist in its history the term "learning society," although it is still used occasionally at conferences and in other forums, seems to be returning to oblivion once more to be replaced by the newer, and more focused, term "knowledge-based economy and society." The substitution signifies, as in the case of that of lifelong education by lifelong learning, an instrumentalist learning agenda with very precise concerns, not with the more humane general flourishing of societies and their members, as was the agenda of the Faure report, but with making societies more efficient and effective in producing and managing knowledge and their human resources. The postmodern transition is thereby complete and the agenda for Europe set for the future; from lifelong education and the learning society of the 1960s to late 1980s we have now moved to lifelong learning and the knowledge-based economy and society of the new millennium. The implication is clear: the policy targets now (nothing so quaint as aims of education), for our postmodern world, are to create skillful, competent, self-dependent learners who can manage risk in their lives, and produce and manage knowledge effectively in the knowledge-based society, whose main targets are economic competitiveness and social cohesion, and where the learning organization is the model for future institutions.

These targets are confirmed in a communiqué by the European ministers for higher education issued on 21 May 2001 subsequent to their meeting in Prague with the subject "Towards the European Higher Education Area." The document starts with the usual premise that "lifelong learning is an essential element of the European Higher Education Area. In the future Europe, built upon a knowledge-based society the challenges are the challenges of competitiveness and the use of the new technologies and to improve social cohesion, equal opportunities and the quality of life" (2001:3).

The *Journal of Lifelong Learning in Europe* (LlinE) announced its fourth conference in Helsinki in September 2001 entitled "Creating Human Capital: *Lifelong Learning for the Knowledge Society*." The way it advertised the conference in the literature was with an impressive list of keynote speakers, all with strong reputations in the field of adult education.

But it offered the following inducement for attending, captured in a mock question-and-answer:

Qs. "Why come?"
Ans. "Everybody talks about KM—knowledge management, human capital, creativity, etc. Do we really know what we are talking about?"

The first object of the conference, the leaflet announces, is the clarification of these and other concepts.

Qs. "Best practices?"
Ans. "The participants will have the opportunity to see and hear about practices in some big companies and consultancies like Nokia, ACCENTURE, Arthur Andersen and Tieto Enator, small companies, NGO and *even* educational institutions (University of Helsinki, Helia Polytechnic)." [my italics]

Note the implied order of importance and priority: big companies and consultancies, and *even*, as though this were some strange or unusual thing, at any rate an *added* inducement, educational institutions.

Qs. "Use of it?"
Ans. "The Conference, after all the information we have collected during two days, will end up in the Finnish Parliament to hear about the relation of learning and society, the future, and what Parliament itself has done to promote knowledge management."

Who is it addressed to? "You and your company, institution or organization will certainly benefit from the offerings of the Conference."

This seems to be the agenda for the future as defined by the most powerful players in the field in the name of lifelong learning. A postmodern agenda in which the term "education," having, as we said earlier, lost the currency and meaning it had in the modern world, finds itself ousted by the ethically neutral term "learning," in turn governed by the postmodern operational norms of effectiveness and efficiency, performativity in one word, and guided by sociopolitical objectives that list self-dependence, social cohesion, and employability as their priorities. Unsurprisingly, in this climate, education theorists, not excluding philosophers of education, have been encouraged more and more to turn their attention to policy-relevant questions and to avoid asking the unfruitful questions of the past such as, what is education? These past questions, which are abstract and not, apparently, urgent, are further discouraged by two other developments (besides the collapse of analytic philosophy of education). First, the postmodern collapse of the politics of left and right, of the grand narratives of socialism and conservatism, into an indeterminate fluid center (which some have labeled euphemistically as the end of ideology). The creation of this center renders agreement between social democrat and neoliberal governments on the objective of learning institutions easy: to cultivate self-dependent, responsible choosers and risk takers, who contribute positively toward the performance of the economy, who are not a burden to the state, and who regard their self-fulfillment as they regard their leisure—as a private matter. The second development, in the field of philosophy and educational theory itself, is the advent of postmodernism, which also discourages questions of this kind. Its critics insist that among the many "deaths" that postmodernism celebrates is the "death" of education, the advent of an era of posteducation.

In the next two chapters we shall examine the extent to which this is true. At this point an intriguing question arises: To what extent can the Third Way's attempt to relaunch social democracy into the postmodern world, as outlined by Giddens, be itself described as postmodernist? Clearly the substance of postmodernism is there in the decisive abandonment of ideology, or socialism, in exchange for a pragmatic outlook identified with a center that is not the synthesis of the old left and right but their radical, amorphous, fluid, and inconclusive deconstruction. True, it claims to retain the old normative concerns of the left but charges them with new and very different meanings that are unrecognizable as reinterpretations of either emancipation or social justice. In this way it has followed the neoliberal right, which did the same "postmodern" deconstructing job on its politics earlier on in the 1980s, leaving traditional conservatism behind much in the same way as the new social democrats have left socialism. What unites the two, the new social democracy and the new neoliberalism, is this decision to put pragmatism before ideology. Liberalism, with its suitable fluidity, has become the political center of both, with the Third Way social democrats tempering their pragmatic liberalism with a politics of reassurance, of philosophic conservatism, as Giddens calls it, which gives it its leftist tone. Of course pragmatic calculations are what encourage a performativist outlook to which both claim an allegiance, though the terms of that allegiance seem, in theory at least, to be less radical with the social democrats. The social democrats, in fact, still have a strong reformist and interventionist agenda, a strong program of government, compared with the neoliberal. Beneath his often bizarre-sounding language, this situation where the left and right implode into a fluid center may be what Jean Baudrillard seeks to articulate in his work. Neutralizing ideological struggle in this way, in fact, brings politics as a contested terrain, a terrain of struggle for justice and democracy, to an end, and produces a consensual center where the political contest is one about efficient administration, and the silent, apolitical masses Baudrillard describes in his work.[77] Effectively, Baudrillard pronounces the death of both politics and education. His reaction will be examined in Chapter 7. The next chapter reengages with philosophy and takes us from the antimodernism of MacIntyre and the promodernism of Habermas into the troubled terrain of postmodernism.

CHAPTER SIX

The Politics of Hope

Postmodernism: The Objections

What is postmodernism? At the Paedeia Conference in Boston in 2000 I heard Daniel Dennett describe it as a virus fatal for our civilization. Habermas, as we saw, agrees and so do many others of its critics. A distinction needs to be made between the postmodern *condition* of the world, whose description by different social theorists was summarized to some extent in Chapter 2, and postmodernism as an *ism*, signifying, as with all *isms*—socialism, feminism, liberalism, Protestantism, Marxism, Catholicism—a faith, a worldview, an ideology, a program, a commitment, and so on. In this sense, *postmodernism* (outside the arts, at any rate) is really a misnomer, since it does not declare itself in any substantive way. It is simply, in the standard sense we have adopted from Lyotard, an attitude of disenchantment with modernity as such, with Western reason, which Dennett and others distrust as nihilist, as a negative and destructive influence because, while it rejects modernism's grand narratives of justice or emancipation in politics, and progress in science, postmodernism proposes nothing in their stead. Indeed it is suspicious of all master narratives and embraces none of its own, leaving us, as its critics say, without a cause to fight for, a banner to fight under.[78] Those usually referred to as postmodernists are Jacques Derrida, Lyotard, Foucault, Gilles Deleuze, Felix Guattari, Jean Baudrillard—all French, and, on the other side of the Atlantic, Rorty. In effect, there are four different kinds of critics of postmodernism: (a) those who go along with Habermas and Dennett and object to it on all counts, political and philosophical; (b) those who disagree with it philosophically but are sympathetic toward its social critique of the modern/postmodern world; (c) those who think it philosophically sound and agree with its critique but find it politically and ethically sterile; and (d) those who describe it as philosophically right but disagree with its social critique and regard it as "politically silly" (Rorty 1992:43).

Unsurprisingly, these positions are reflected in the field of education. Barry Kanpol (1995) summarizes, more or less, the reaction in the critical pedagogy camp to the idea of a postmodern politics of education. Postmodernism, he says, leaves critical pedagogy without an agenda for social transformation within schools, and without the possibility of a politics of solidarity. Like most critical theorists influenced by Habermas, and like many feminists, Kanpol (1995:155) believes that only social movements with clear emancipatory agendas, with programs incorporating clear counterhegemonic strategies, and with "a sense of community dialogue and inter-subjectivity that bind people together despite their sundry differences" can provide educators of the left with an agenda for transformative action. What the left needs, he says, is not postmodernist pessimism but "the hope that Jurgen Habermas brought to our attention within his unified communicative subject position" (1995:153). Andy Green (1994:74) warns that "taken to extremes," postmodernism can "only lead to moral nihilism, political apathy and the abandonment of the intellect to the chaos of the contingent." That in education its logic "points towards an individualistic educational consumerism in many respects similar to that advocated by the free-marketeers of the new Right" (1994:76).

Not all assessments of postmodernism, however, have been so negative. Landon E. Beyer and Daniel P. Liston (1992:371), for instance, describe postmodernist critiques of modernity and of modern institutions, including schools, as important because they draw attention to the marginalization and exclusion of particular social groups and minorities in postmodern societies. But they feel that the value of the critiques is undone by the postmodernist distrust of all forms of commonality and emancipatory discourses, and by its emphasis on the need to engage in local struggles rather than global ones. While conceding that local struggles may be fruitful in some circumstances, the two authors argue that abandoning the idea of global struggle "makes problematic significant contributions to alternative social and educational actions," and undermines the kind of collaborative social action that alone makes change or reform possible, or impacts the public realm, including action in favor of the marginalized. Finally, they argue that because postmodernism's "radical relativism" undermines the notion of moral responsibility, it cannot be recommendable to the educator "for whom both intellectual engagement and transformative practice are mandatory." Rob Gilbert (1992) agrees. Postmodernism, he says, allows for two alternative moral responses, nihilist or narcissist, neither of which is acceptable for educators. While Paul Standish (1995), commending the way it problematizes the kind of socialization individuals are exposed to in modern society, argues that postmodernism makes it difficult to identify the subject to be educated, since the self it proposes is a centerless, seamless web of experiences. This way of viewing selves, Standish claims, as beings living fragmented lives, conflicts with the customary way educators are encouraged to view them, namely as *whole persons*, and could justify turning the aims of education to purely instrumental purposes.

Inspired by Hall, Gilbert (1992:55) notes other possibilities in "postmodern writings," on the other hand, that are positive. Their celebration of the "pluralization of social life," he points out, "expands the positionalities and identities available to ordinary people (at least in the industrialized world) in their everyday working, familial and sexual lives," making for an altogether richer social world. He again, however, emphasizes postmodernism's political dangers; the way, he believes, it threatens the very notion of democracy and renders both the idea of citizenship and that of citizen education problematic (1992:52). Not just because of its general distrust of consensual discourse but also because, he argues, like Stanley Aronowitz and Henry Giroux (1991), the idea of democracy requires certain master narratives; of representation and of a sovereign "people," for instance, the validity of which postmodernism denies. In a similar vein Wilfred Carr (1995:77) expresses his preoccupation that by undermining the Enlightenment vision of democratic societies peopled by rationally autonomous individuals, postmodernism encourages descent into irrationalism. Carr (1995:78) adds another common related concern that postmodern arguments lend theoretical sophistication to what he describes as a "reactionary drive to jettison the last vestiges of enlightened educational theorizing under the banner of a neo-pragmatic, anti-intellectual education ideology, that has raised commonsense beliefs to the status of self-authorizing truth." Aronowitz and Giroux (1991:19), however, have also claimed to identify an "emancipatory postmodernism" that shares with modernism a critical reflexive approach to knowledge, and which they have contrasted with a "right-wing postmodernism" that (as critics say of postmodernism in general), "verges on a nihilistic renunciation of engaged intellectual and political activity."

They argue that the project to restore an emancipatory democratic public sphere must be achieved "within (rather than in opposition to) the existing conditions of the postmodern world" (1991:59). This is a view Carr shares. Carr (1995:81) argues that the challenge today is to "devise a way of thinking about the relationship between education and democracy which is 'modern' in the sense that it does not abandon emancipatory ideals but postmodern in the sense that it abandons the Enlightenment narrative within which these ideals have hitherto been articulated." He suggests a "postmodern educational strategy" (which is different from a postmodern politics of education) that satisfies a number of conditions, namely that it: (1) no longer pretends that the emancipatory values it seeks to promote could be justified by an appeal to *a priori* philosophical foundations and recognizes the historical contingency of our values; (2) does not assume eventual success guaranteed by some inexorable law of human nature and regards "human nature" itself as socially constructed instead; (3) does not regard democracy as the embodiment of a universally valid social order but as a contingent human project, without, however, giving up the Enlightenment language of emancipation and empowerment, or the epistemological notions of objectivity and truth. The basis for such a strategy, Carr (1995:82) believes, lies in the unexploited theoretical resources "to be found in the philosophy of John Dewey." Rorty, as we shall see, says something similar, but he takes the very different political view that we should drop the language of emancipation and empowerment altogether. Otherwise he would agree with Carr that we should recognize the historical contingency of our values and of democracy, and the social construction of the self. Mustafa Kiziltian, William Bain, and Anita Canizares (1990:353) have argued similarly to Carr that the postmodern condition is the condition within which we must devise today's educational strategies. "As an institutional constellation of a variety of practices (e.g., teaching, disciplining, testing, tracking, etc.)," they argue, contemporary education "largely intersects with the broader society," and must respond to challenges the broader society faces in a postmodern world that constitute a radical threat to our modern education systems, challenging the existing concepts that we have, and the structures and hierarchies of knowledge we operate with.

These are also the assumptions that underpin the writing of this book and that I obviously share. Assumptions the writers of the lifelong education movement shared also in the 1970s and 1980s when they made their case for lifelong education. Though they didn't use the term, the essence of what they said was that a postmodern world needs a radically revised approach to education; one that is relevant to and responds to the challenges it poses to the modern world. They, however, assumed the old emancipatory norms of the left for their project, the norms of scientific humanism. Though they saw that modern education, in the shape of mass schooling, was in crisis, they did not see that modernism itself was in crisis. They failed to see the implications of the rapidly changing conditions of the world *for modernity itself* as a relevant sociocultural, political, and ethical point of reference. They did not see that the postmodern condition of our world threatens the status of everything within it, not just of schooling—of politics, philosophy, intellectuals, culture, and education itself, and the way we write about them—raising fundamental questions about their future meaning that run through the chapters of this book. The problem with postmodernism for Kiziltian et al. (1990:355) is that it has no answer to them; that while "disclosing education's inwrought partiality and exposing the fragility and the insubstantiality of its epistemic and metaphysical presuppositions," it offers nothing in return, and "radically threatens" the very possibility of public education. Usher and Edwards (1994:25) have argued that public education *is*, in fact, sensitive to the postmodern moment, to its profound challenges and uncertainties. Such that increasingly, they say, "debates over the curriculum, pedagogy and the organization of education, resonate with the challenges of the postmodern," but usually "without the reflexive understanding of a postmodern position," and "resistant to the postmodern 'message'" (1994:2), understandably since the curriculum of public education has been the vehicle through which modernity's grand narratives and ambitions have been transmitted in the world. "The very rationale of the educational process and the role of the educator" in public education, they point out, is founded on modernity's self-motivated, self-directing, rational subject, capable of exercising individual agency" (1994:2), which is a rationale postmodernism denies together with the need for educational theory of which it teaches us to be skeptical because educational theory is still founded on modernity and its self-understandings, so that there can be little, if any, hope of help from that quarter (1994:25).

None of its critics agree with Aronowitz and Giroux, and Usher and Edwards, that there is a postmodern message that educators and policy-makers could find positive. The most Green (1994:74), for instance, will concede to postmodern writing is that contributions like those in Stephen Ball's (1990) book, which bring Foucaultian discourse analysis to bear on education practices, could be a "useful tool for decoding ideologies, policies and power relations at the macro and micro levels" of school and classroom. Otherwise, his view of "postmodernism proper (i.e., as propounded by Lyotard, Baudrillard, et al.)" is that it has "so far contributed little that is distinctive or theoretically fruitful and it seems unlikely that it will" (1994:74–75). Aronowitz and Giroux (1991:70) contend that apart from raising crucial questions about the hegemonic aspects of modernism reflected in contemporary schooling, postmodernist thinking offers the more radical promise of deterritorializing modernism and redrawing its political, social, and cultural boundaries, while affirming a politics of racial, gender, and ethnic difference. They further argue that it has the power through deconstruction to resituate us within a world that little resembles the one that inspired the old grand narratives of Marx and Freud, and calls attention to the shifting boundaries related to the increasing influence of electronic mass media and information technology, the changing nature of class and social formations in postindustrialized societies, and the growing transgression of the boundaries between life, art, high and popular culture, and image and reality. Insisting at the same time, against the basic postmodernist belief to the contrary, "that the notion of totality be embraced," even if as "a heuristic device rather than an ontological category." Green (1994:75), however, dismisses this view as seeking "to annex some of the ideas of postmodernism to the unashamedly modernist project of radical democracy and social justice," and he questions postmodernism's resources to "extend 'critical discourse,'" as the two authors suggest, "when it rejects the very rationalist foundation on which critique is built." These are difficulties that seem to have come home to Giroux, he remarks, in his next book, *Border Crossings* (1992), where his claim "to have made a political and theoretical shift into 'post-Marxism'" is more modest.

Peter MacLaren (1995:88), however, rejects even this move for critical theory, claiming that the main pillars of Marxian social analysis must remain intact if resistance to capitalism through organized political action is to be maintained. MacLaren (1991:10) subscribes to the bleak picture of the world postmodernism describes but dissociates himself from its "politics of retreat or despair." He argues that postmodernism is unneeded because the last few decades have produced "vivacious new developments in critical social theory that have brought with them important new ways of understanding the relationship between the process of schooling and the reproduction of economies of power and privilege in the wider society," which have profited from various theoretical strands of feminist discourse, the influence of continental philosophy, cultural studies, and critical pragmatics. Against postmodernism MacLaren supports an alliance of feminist and critical pedagogy, creating "an arch of social dreaming" (1991:12), to which Foucault's theoretical program could provide a key contribution as a tool for uncovering the way power works, how the modern personality is produced, and how disciplinary matrixes are legitimated and objectivity defined in education sites. Neither Foucault nor postmodernism, however, MacLaren argues, can deliver on a politics of solidarity and emancipation, which is what the left wants. The left cannot be content with social critique only, he says; it requires "an ethical imagination" besides, as Benhabib puts it, "a regulative principle of hope" (1992b:111), a utopia, or "postmodern imaginary" (1992b:117). What MacLaren supports is a politics of experimental praxis that begins with a critical reading of experience and could include some postmodern contributions, but no more. Kanpol (1995:149) suggests that these contributions could be postmodernity's basic tenets about difference, multiple-subject positionality, and identity confusion. The left could concede the failure of the old master narratives of modernity, Kanpol (1995:150) contends like all the critics of the left, but cannot abandon master narratives of emancipation completely. Instead, it should create a new one "loaded with both modern and postmodern tendencies, and particular and universal generalities."

Feminists have had similar problems with postmodernism. Many, like Benhabib, are also reluctant to surrender the emancipatory narratives that have sustained feminism to the postmodern moment. Not all, as Usher and Edwards (1994:20) point out, accept the need to radically challenge modernism, because feminism is itself located in the legacy of the Enlightenment tradition. Many worry that alliances with postmodernism threaten their transformative agenda. Linda Hutcheon (1989:168) echoes the common complaint that it has "no theorized agency; it has no strategies of resistance that would correspond with the feminist ones." And Linda Alcoff (Singh 1995:196) writes that reducing gender to a social construct raises the question of what one can demand in the name of "women." Benhabib (1992a:229) argues that though feminists can endorse a postmodernist critique made from the margins that exposes the exclusionary nature of the logocentric discourses of the Western tradition, they have to insist on the gendered quality of the subject, of history, and of reason rather than pronounce them dead as, she claims, postmodernists do. Any alliance with postmodernism, she concludes, can only be one of "partial and strategic solidarity," otherwise its "retreat from utopia," which has attracted some feminists, should be resisted. Without utopia, neither morality nor social transformation is thinkable. Moreover, feminist social criticism, she contends, needs to posit "the legal, moral and political norms of autonomy, choice and self-determination" for its struggle (1992:16). Christine DiStefano (Nicholson 1995:80) agrees, and asks suspiciously, "Why is it, just at the moment in Western history when previously silenced populations have begun to speak for themselves and on behalf of their subjectivities, that the concept of the subject and the possibility of discovering/creating a liberating 'truth' becomes suspect?" While Parlo Singh (1995:195) complains against poststructuralist (not postmodernist, an important variation we shall see) feminists that because of their celebration of difference and their focus on the local and the specific they "fail to examine the uniform structures of state-education systems across the world today." "It seems paradoxical," she remarks, "that when capitalism is restructuring the State across national boundaries in new structures of international education, that social educational theorists attempt to avoid political and theoretical imperialism by speaking only for the 'self'" (1995:196).

Like other critics, Singh (1995:196) criticizes the poststructuralist response to education as a "retreat response," from speaking for others into the narrow confines of personal experience. Yeatman (1994:13), however, who argues that an interest in postmodernism is unavoidable for feminists once the postmodern appears to be the discursive terrain on which the politics of difference is currently being played out, argues that an emancipatory politics with "postmodern revisionings" (not an emancipatory postmodernism) is possible. Impressed with the way postmodernism treats difference as an extension of its epistemological politics of representation, she contends that it "permit[s] feminist theory to investigate the materiality of the discursively interpellated female subject, and therefore open up the significance of difference in embodiment for the politics of difference" (1994:15). She emphasizes that postmodern does not mean "anti-modern" (an important point made by many so-called "postmodernists"). To the contrary, the "post" indicates continuity with, maybe even dependence on, modernity—possibly a stage at which it is possible from a vantage point to create a critical perspective on the modern.

But other feminists have judged postmodernism's politics of difference differently. Jean Anyon (1994:120) remarks that the shift in discursive terrain noted by Yeatman should not be regarded as an endorsement of postmodernism. Though she confesses to being "moved and instructed by the postmodern/poststructural critiques," because they have "taught me a respect for ambiguity—an appreciation of partial theories and of the complexities and possibilities of an attempt to assess local networks," as well as "a healthy respect for the power of discourse—and of totalizing narratives—to influence subjectivity," thus helping her gain "a new understanding of the uncertainty that must attend reliance on any one discourse," she is nevertheless also skeptical that they can "constitute a reliable guide to emancipatory practice" (1994:121). Carol Nicholson (1995:21) remarks that several feminists turn to postmodernism because it enables them to step outside the dualisms that characterize modern discourse, within which women and the concepts and values associated with them have been positioned "as negative reference points in relation to the privileged positioning of masculinity and men," but she voices the concern that its opposition to universality tends toward a cynical relativism.

Nicholson notes that though the feminist interest in postmodernism stems partly from the reading of writers like Lyotard and Foucault, it also grows from a new sensitivity to difference among feminists themselves. Marianne Marchand and Jane Parpart (1995) argue that feminists concerned with the marginalization of Third World women and women of color in the North are attracted to postmodernist approaches, while those working within liberal and Marxist traditions, both embedded in Enlightenment thinking, show greatest resistance to them. Liberal feminists, they say, generally write as if postmodern critiques have little or no applicability to their work, while Marxists regard them as politically dangerous. Feminists of both kinds attack postmodern anthropology with the argument that it is profoundly sexist and operates in favor of Western male power; "they believe that feminism, with its openly political stance and its grounding in actual differences among women, has more to offer anthropology and the search for sexual justice than postmodernist theory" (1995:5). But feminists active within socially deprived groups or poorer countries, they say, respond to these concerns with the argument that they are typical of the interests of middle-class feminists in the richer countries who they accuse, in turn, of creating a new colonialist/neocolonialist discourse essentializing "woman" to their own image and likeness. In this situation, Marchand and Parpart (1995:17) feel, postmodern thinking provides new ways of thinking about women's development, welcoming diversity, acknowledging previously subjugated voices and knowledges, and encouraging dialogue between development practitioners and their "clients."

Poststructuralism

In this text I differentiate between the terms postmodernism and poststructuralism.[79] Also, though it is economic to band the different writers labeled postmodernists—or, indeed, poststructuralists—together, this obscures the differences between them, particularly the political. None but two of the thinkers listed in the previous section, namely Baudrillard and Lyotard, would agree to being called postmodernists, and none would declare themselves as antimodern like MacIntyre. The appearance of a postmodern outlook is dated differently by different authors, but Best and Kellner (1991:15) observe that it became consistent in the 1950s, coinciding with the feeling that an old era had somehow come, or was coming, to an end—and consistent with a sense of being confronted by a novel historical situation and by new choices.[80] Some greeted this prospect positively, as holding out new hope for a world exhausted by two world wars, others negatively as a threat to civilization so that "by the 1980s the postmodern discourses were split into cultural conservatives decrying the new developments and avante-gardists celebrating them." French thought's long association with romanticism, the authors remark, rendered it open to postmodern suggestions. A spate of social theories emerging in France after World War II, to articulate its rapid modernization, imported the key concepts of "postindustrialism" and the "postindustrial society" from the United States for the purpose. The nihilistic roots of French postmodernism, however, lie not in American social or cultural theory but in the French romantic literary tradition, in Sade, Bataille, and Artaud mainly but also in Baudelaire and Rimbaud. The genius of the French postmodernists lay in introducing Nietzsche and Heidegger into this romantic stream to create a highly potent cocktail; dynamite, as Nietzsche would call it, a deadly virus for our Boston philosopher, Habermas, and its other critics.

Habermas perceives not one but two political streams in postmodernism, not those, however, identified by Giroux and Aronowitz, but the neoconservative and the aesthetically inspired anarchist (1990a: 4–5). He uses the expression "poststructuralism" just once in *The Philosophical Discourse of Modernity*, defining it as a revitalization of Nietzsche that reflects "moods and attitudes ... confusingly like those of Horkheimer and Adorno" (1990a:106). However, in his introduction to Habermas's book, McCarthy (1990a:vii) describes "French poststructuralism," not "postmodernism," as the real "point of departure for these lectures." To describe poststructuralism simply as a revitalization of Nietzsche, however, does little justice to the complexity of the term, which indicates connections also with structuralism (its theory of language and thought), and is influenced by other thinkers besides. Like structuralism, of which it is "post"—a continuation—it projects language as a rule-governed system of signs that are purely social in their origin, and the subject as no more than a social and linguistic construct. It also denies the need to postulate the Cartesian self as a constituting consciousness (a subject of thought that is subject to thought through introspection or self-analysis), a coherent unity, and as authentic or inauthentic in some way. Instead it projects the self as a shifting bundle of experiences, a more or less loose and dynamic network, which is socially constructed but not bound together by any inner structure of either thought or language, as also the Cartesian notion of language as a transparent vehicle of thought, or intermediary between thought and the outside world. It is not, in their view, "thought" but language that is our point of contact with the world, to the extent that the world is *made*, not represented or mirrored, by language. Unlike the structuralists, however, and like Nietzsche, poststructuralists represent language as saturated with power, and they reject the view that it is processed within the structures of a universal grammar or mind, or universal pragmatics of speech, holding instead that it is processed in language games with different rules. They also distance themselves from structuralism's "scientific" pretensions, and they take the anti-humanist elements found in structuralism much further, criticizing it for not having broken with humanism decisively enough and for continuing to be metaphysical, retaining the key humanist notion of an intrinsic, unchanging human nature in different guises.

The poststructuralist challenge to humanism has been usefully condensed into a number of platforms, all of them, in one way or another, installed into philosophy by Heidegger but originating with, or at any rate foreshadowed by, Nietzsche. The rejection of metaphysics, of a "universal essence" of Man or Reason, is one. The rejection of the idea of human history as a linear process, the unfolding of some inherent historical purpose, or as driven by predictable dialectical necessity, about which we should ask the truth, or "what really happened?" (rather than, how have we come to tell the story in this way and how can it be told differently?) is another. Poststructuralists are struck by Heidegger's powerful thesis that the heart of humanist metaphysics is "technological" and that the intrinsic logic of technology is to reduce everything to a "standing reserve." They resist Plato's agenda for philosophy, restated in modern times by Descartes and Kant, to ground the truth about the world or the mind in epistemology. It is a project that invests philosophy with the hegemonic status of "guardian of culture," as Rorty (1980:10) put it, with the authority to "underwrite or debunk claims to knowledge made by science, morality, art, or religion ... on the basis of its special understanding of the nature of knowledge and of mind." Magnus Bernd (Peters 1996:4) has identified seven affinities between poststructuralists, all of Nietzschean influence: perspectivism; the diagnosis and critique of binarism and of the metaphysics of presence; the substitution of genealogical narratives for ontology; the diagnosis of the power-knowledge connection, as well as the structure of ideological domination; an erasing of the boundaries between philosophy and literature; the disarticulation of the self; and a resorting to the self-consuming, self-deconstructing character of Nietzsche's discourse and categories.

Apart from two political streams, Habermas (1990a:97) also identifies two philosophical paths from Nietzsche into the postmodern world, one via Bataille, within which he places Lacan and Foucault, the other via Heidegger, which, he says, produced Derrida. The distinction is oversimplified but useful nevertheless (Foucault, for instance, acknowledged a great debt to Heidegger, and one finds traces of Bataille in Derrida). It corresponds with Hans Bertens's (1995) account of a two-stage evolution of poststructuralist thought that saw first the prominence in the early 1980s of a *deconstructionist* phase influenced by the work of Roland Barthes in addition to Derrida, followed, roughly in the middle of the 1980s, by a *genealogist* phase influenced by Foucault and, to a lesser degree, Deleuze and Guattari. Deconstruction's complete absorption with the task of exposing the self-reflexivity of language limited its interest to texts and intertexts and opened it to the criticism that it was politically sterile. "In its firm belief that the attack on representation was in itself an important political act," Bertens (1995:7) says, and "content to celebrate the so-called death of the subject," it ignored the important political difficulty that the proclamation of such an event raises: that "in the absence of transcendent truth," the subject becomes vitally important, "it matters, more than ever, who is speaking (or writing), and why, and to whom?" Kanpol (1995:152) refers to a "pure ludic deconstruction by bourgeois theorists who impose bourgeois suavities [and] simply exalt theory as a type of travelogue, a form 'of fatal attentiveness to difference and infinite heterogeneity.'" Things were different, however, with the genealogical phase that followed, as deconstruction began to lose popularity because of the increasing politicization of the debate on modernity to which it was perceived to have nothing to contribute. This second phase corresponded with the ascendancy of Foucault's star as his influence "materialized almost imperceptibly until it is suddenly very much there, like a fine drizzle that to your surprise has managed to get you thoroughly wet after an hour's walk" (Bertens 1995:7).

Foucault introduced political relevance into poststructuralist discourse by shifting the emphasis from language and the constitution of the text to power and its constitution of the modern subject. Merquior (1985:14), an otherwise hostile critic, describes him as "the man who tried to place post-structuralism on an ethico-political ground at a far remove from the textual navel-gazing of 'deconstruction.'" Merquior (1985:70) judged the impact of Foucault's thought on continental philosophy as "unfortunate" because of its revolutionary, "spontaneist," anti-utopian character and because it was interested only in particularist combats, dismissing him as a neo-anarchist who distrusted all institutions, even a "bad anarchist" because he distorted the notion of "power" that is "the very kernel of anarchist theory." Foucault has, in fact, been criticized for his self-conscious political elusiveness, dismissing the labels that critics had fixed on him as tiresome, typical of their yen to categorize (or "normalize") everything and everyone, and as being of no interest to him whatsoever. Critics have labeled this declaration of his intellectual freedom as irresponsible. Derrida, on the other hand, was described as utterly indifferent toward politics. From a different point of view, both Derrida and Foucault have been charged with being irrationalist.[81] There is in fact no truth in either of these charges. Foucault's irresponsibility, according to his critics—not just Merquior but others also of the weight of Habermas, Nancy Fraser, Michael Walzer, and Richard Taylor—stems from this refusal to identify himself with any positive political or ethical project or tie his allegiance to some master narrative of justice and democracy. This attitude, they argue, leaves one with no answer to the question, "What ought to be done?" so that resistance to injustice, for example, becomes a matter of blind transgression.[82] Honi Fern Haber's (1994:90) apt answer to this criticism is that "this is a worry only for those operating within a certain set of traditional expectations," not for Foucault. Foucault himself repeatedly declared his determination not to be blackmailed into surrendering to these expectations. They were, as Fern Haber (1994:92) argued, "trying to force him to conform to their notion of what a concerned social critic must be—but he does not want to fit that mould." This is the first thing that one needs to understand about Foucault—his intellectual independence.

Otherwise, a televised argument with Noam Chomsky in 1971 illustrates his differences with his critics and tells us something about his approach to politics. Chomsky readily answered their host's question of why they were interested in politics; Foucault, however, refused to do so, regarding the answer as trivial and obvious. "Why are you interested in politics?" he replied, is not the interesting question. The interesting question is, "How is one interested in politics?" And in his case it is certainly not by providing some theory of a just social order or some general principles of justice to apply to our present conditions. He wanted rather, he said, to focus on power, on how it works within specific institutions and practices, especially those claiming to be neutral and independent of power interests, in order to expose or unmask their political violence and fight it. Fight it in the name of what, and what for? came Chomsky's predictable reply. The question has been echoed over the years by Foucault's critics, who, as we saw in the previous section, find it hard to accept the general poststructuralists' rejection of master narratives. We fight political violence, Chomsky argued, because it is unjust, and we cannot determine that anything is unjust without knowing what is just, without principles or criteria of justice of some kind. Without a theory of justice we are lost. Foucault's answer? The idea of justice, he conceded, is a useful political invention, a good strategic instrument for conserving political and economic power, but useless when the object is not to conserve but to "overthrow the very fundaments of our society." Doesn't the anarchist also, however, need a theory of a better society? Otherwise anarchism is blind and chaotic. This was a time when Foucault was politically close to the most dynamic *gauchiste* Maoist and anarchist groups that had spawned in Paris after the 1968 student revolt, particularly the *Gauche Prolétarienne* (Macey 1994:217). In his debate with Chomsky he was rehearsing Thrasymachus's argument in *The Republic* that power precedes justice; that justice *is* how the Establishment's power is defined, and that it is power, therefore, that is struggled for, not justice. These were conclusions denied by a scandalized Chomsky, who retained the classical view that justice precedes power and needs to be defined separately as an ethical concern.

The problem with Derrida was different. At the beginning of the 1980s he was criticized by such critics as Nancy Fraser (1984:127–128) for "deliberately, consistently and dexterously" avoiding politics.[83] Fraser accused him of unwillingness to take a position in relation to Marxism notwithstanding his regular promises to encounter Marx's "text" deconstructively. A more sensitive Thomas McCarthy (1989–90:151), though he echoed the concern of other critics that it is seriously disabling where a positive approach to politics and ethics is concerned, noted behind the "essentially iconoclastic drive" of deconstruction, a "Heidegger-inspired" ethico-political impulse, which could be interpreted as commitment "to bear witness to the other of Western rationalism: to what has been subordinated in hierarchical orderings, excluded in the drawing of boundaries, marginalized in identifying what is central, homogenized or colonized in the name of the universal" (1989–90:154). John Caputo (1988:60) agrees and contends that "the notion of responsibility, of responsive-ness," goes "right to the heart of the deconstructive project." Deconstruction, he argues, is "set in motion by the rights of the different… It does not heed the mainstream call of Being, presence, the same, but keeps its ear peeled to the call of the other" (1988:67). Again, as with Foucault, the question is how one describes responsibility. In an interview with Ewald (Derrida & Ewald 1995:291), remarking that deconstruction is not a philosophy, Derrida himself insists that "this does not mean that the deconstructive experience is not, does not practice, or deploy within itself any responsibility, nor even any ethico-political responsibility. I would say that by questioning philosophy on its treatment of ethics, politics, and the concept of responsibility, deconstruction aligns itself with the concept still *higher* than responsibility." Caputo points out that Derrida took up the notions of responsibility and responsive-ness already in "The Principle of Reason: The University in the Eyes of Its Pupils" (1983), where he discussed Heidegger's argument that "the principle of sufficient reason," the *arche* that "every being has a reason," which has the modern university tightly in its grip, needs to be shaken off. Like Heidegger before him, Caputo (1988:61) points out, Derrida's rationalist critics accuse him of irresponsibility for putting this traditionally uncontested principle on the spot. But for Heidegger and Derrida, he argues, not only is this project not irresponsible, it derives from a "higher responsibility" to examine the status of Reason or Science itself. Particularly in the light of what Heidegger has shown us, and Nietzsche before him, that the principle of reason is inextricably tied with the will to power.

For Derrida, Caputo points out, the charge of irresponsibility is more appropriately made against those who are not similarly exacting, who take Western Reason for granted and do not open themselves to the call of its Other. Deconstruction's "double gesture" allows us to operate both *within* the principle of reason and *outside* it, at its limits or margins. In the case of the university this means "operating within the constraints of the university and opening it up to its own other, to something that its infinite Hegelian appetite cannot digest" (1988:63). Caputo refers to this politics as one of "responsible anarchy." And, indeed, poststructuralism *is* generally anarchic. It is not, however, interested in destroying reason, as its critics claim, but in redescribing a reason that is unencumbered by metaphysical prejudices and given over to free play, to openness to its other. Heidegger turned to the renegade mystical poet who subverts Reason by exposing it to its other in the sphere of play to break its deadly hold. But, Caputo (1987:226) warns, deconstruction should not be interpreted as wanting to escape the sphere of reason into that of play, but rather as wanting to "let play infiltrate reason itself" in order to subvert, not to overthrow it. Remaining active within the borders of reason, the object of deconstructive play is to "infiltrate its corporation, plant secret agents in its system," engage in guerrilla warfare. To its critics who contend that it throws us to the wolves, he replies, "reason is not undone by the foundering of metaphysics but liberated, emancipated from metaphysical prejudices which tended to make of it something less than it is and which in fact turned it into something more dangerous than wolves" (1987:209). Western Reason, he reminds us, does not have an unblemished past, it has "a fortune not unlike 'God' and 'country': some of the worst violence is committed in its name," so we have no valid motive to hold on to it at all costs (1987:210). To the contrary, we are well rid of it. A conclusion shared by poststructuralists generally, so that the virus they inject into Western civilization is not that of irrationalism but of skepticism over the hegemony of its Reason. And skepticism denotes not irresponsibility but, to the contrary, as Caputo says, a higher level of responsibility. What Foucault (1984a) in "What Is Enlightenment?" calls *maturity*. The maturity to do without the "comfort" of any supervising presence; to respond to and *take* responsibility for and on oneself.

Finally, poststructuralists share Heidegger's contempt for the idea of method, understood, as Caputo says, as something that rules rather than serves, something that constrains into a totality rather than frees into diffuseness. But neither Foucault nor Derrida regards this "contempt" for, this surrender of method, as surrender to irrationality. Method is abandoned in the struggle against the straitjacket of totality that suffocates freedom and creativity in the service of Reason. To put it differently, method is, like "reason," put within quotation marks as "method"—not abandoned. In this "'retrieved' Heideggerian sense," as Caputo (1987:213) says of deconstruction, it "is the suppleness by which thinking is able to pursue the matter at hand; it is an activity that knows its way about, even and especially when the way cannot be laid out beforehand; when it cannot be formulated in explicit rules." As Foucault (Rabinow 1984:47–48) says of genealogy, where "we are always in the position of beginning again," that "does not mean that no work can be done except in disorder and contingency." To the contrary, genealogy "has its generality, its systematicity, its homogeneity, and its stakes." Its stakes are the stakes of power, its homogeneity is obtained by focusing analysis onto the existing "forms of rationality," the "games of truth," and the "practical systems" that incorporate the technologies of power; "the realm of practices with their technological and their strategic side." A realm that can be systematically arranged within three broad areas of everyday relations: "relations of control over things, relations of action upon others, relations with oneself" (Rabinow 1984:48) and domains "of acts, practices, and thoughts that seem to me to pose problems for politics" (Rabinow 1984:384). Correspondingly, genealogy asks: "How are we constituted as subjects of our own knowledge? How are we constituted as subjects who exercise or submit to power relations? How are we constituted as moral subjects of our own actions?" (Rabinow 1984:49). All "how" questions, *practical* questions (unlike the theoretical "what" questions rationalists like Chomsky would have us ask: What is justice? democracy? reason? etc.) that lead to the ultimate question, the question of freedom, which asks, "How can the growth of capabilities be disconnected from the intensification of power relations" embodied in "technologies (whether we speak of productions with economic aims, or institutions whose goal is social regulation, or of technologies of communication): disciplines, both collective and individual, procedures of normalization exercised in the name of the power of the state, demands of society or population zones?" (Rabinow 1984:48). It is a question whose generality, Foucault says, arises from the fact that it has recurred insistently through human history.

Philosophy and Strong Poetry

Criticism that poststructuralist discourse is not, properly speaking, philosophical is often reflected by hostility toward it in philosophy departments, where—as Rorty put it in *PMN* (1980)—it is often regarded as "abnormal." In *PMN* and *Consequences of Pragmatism* (1982, henceforth *CP*), Rorty charged normal philosophy, the tradition originating with Plato and continued in modern times by Descartes and Kant that represents philosophy as an academic discipline or *fach*, with hegemonic designs justified through claims it makes about its epistemological status; namely, its authority to lay down the conditions of knowledge, and thereby to underwrite science and culture. His own writing project in *PMN* was to show that claim to be fraudulent and, therefore, to be abandoned—not to be replaced by some other foundational discipline but to abjure disciplines, or "games of truth" as Foucault calls them, altogether. At the time of writing *PMN* and *CP* Rorty (1980:315) thought hermeneutics could fill the resulting "cultural vacancy," not, however, intended as epistemology's "'successor subject,'" but to signal the end of the need for any such subject. Instead of searching for true foundations, an "antecedently existing common ground" for truth, hermeneutics contents itself with achieving temporary agreement in conversation (1980:318).

In *PMN*, inspired by Kuhn (but also on lines resembling Lyotard's distinction between normal and paralogical science and discourse), Rorty (1980:320) distinguished "normal" from "abnormal" discourse. The first is "rational" or rule-directed, "conducted within an agreed-upon set of conventions about what counts as a relevant contribution, what counts as answering a question, what counts as having a good argument for that answer or a good criticism of it," the second has the contrary characteristics and occurs "when someone joins in the discourse who is ignorant of these conventions or who sets them aside." Normal discourse is "disciplined" and conventional. For abnormal discourse, to the contrary, there is no discipline, "any more than there is a discipline devoted to the study of the unpredictable, or of 'creativity,'" and it may produce anything from nonsense to intellectual revolution. But creativity should not, Rorty goes on, be understood as "a view from nowhere."[84] To the contrary, it is always reactive, "parasitic upon normal discourse" (1980:365). Obviously, corresponding with these two kinds of discourse and ways of doing philosophy are two ways of being a philosopher; "systematic" and engaged in theory, working critically within predefined parameters, or "reactive" and skeptical, "primarily about systematic philosophy, and the whole project of universal commensuration" that has inspired the Western academic philosophical tradition since Plato. Systematic philosophers are *constructive*; they have a view about things, theories to offer and justify. Reactive philosophers "decry the very notion of having a view, while avoiding having a view about having views" (1980:371). The hermeneutic variety offers narratives that interpret and reinterpret the world within our familiar vocabularies. Dewey, Heidegger, and Wittgenstein are outstanding examples of reactive philosophers, their writing "therapeutic" instead of constructive. According to Rorty, reactive philosophers should not be confused with revolutionary, many of whom have been systematic (1980:368).

Hermeneutic writers show us "how the other side looks from our own point of view ... how the odd or paradoxical or offensive things they say hang together with the rest of what they want to say, and how what they say looks when put in our own alternative idiom" (1980:364–365). In *PMN*, however, Rorty (1980:360) hints toward a third kind of intellectual activity besides the constructive and therapeutic, namely the poetic, the Heideggerian "inverse of hermeneutics" involving "the attempt to reinterpret our familiar surroundings in the unfamiliar terms of our new inventions," through the writing of aphorisms, parodies, utopias, and ... dystopias; like Lyotard's paralogical fables and Foucault's genealogical fictions, for instance. Shortly after publishing *PMN* Rorty himself decided that hermeneutics continues to be metaphysical, equally hegemonic with the philosophy he intended to replace it with, and abandoned it. The move is announced in *CP* where he describes "textualism" as the philosophical replacement of idealism in more recent times, reversing the priority of thought over language characterized by Derrida as logocentrism. Textualism's intellectual "center of gravity" is in literary criticism rather than in academic philosophy (1982:139). Rorty (1982:143) defines it as "a specifically post-philosophical form" of romanticism rooted in "the thesis that what is most important for human life is not what propositions we believe but what vocabulary we use" (1982:142). And he describes it as an "attempt to think through a thorough-going pragmatism, a thorough-going abandonment of the notion of discovering the truth which is common to theology and science" (1982:150–151). Textualists "write as if there were nothing but texts," in the same way as idealists write as if there were nothing but "ideas" (1982:139). The *weak* textualist thinks her task is to break the code of a text, to get to its hidden meaning, while the *strong* simply "beats the text into a shape which will serve his own purpose" (1982:151). The weak textualist is "just one more victim of realism, of the 'metaphysics of presence,'" who wants to imitate science, who "wants a *method* of criticism," and "all the comforts of consensus," of being part of a community of like-minded people "who understand his jargon and care about his problem" (1982:152, italics in original). Gadamer is a weak textualist, Derrida a strong. By the time Rorty published his next book, *Contingency, Irony, and Solidarity* (1989, henceforth *CIS*), nearly a decade later, Derrida had replaced Gadamer in Rorty's favor and, as we shall see in the next chapter, the strong textualist becomes the *ironist*, and the intellectual hero of his liberal utopia.

My present point is to endorse Rorty's distinction between constructive and reactive writers and to locate the poststructuralists within the latter strain (which Rorty describes as the other of philosophy). The reflection relevant to the subject of this book is that poststructuralism is at odds with the approach to philosophy of education that works with the paradigm of the education research project described in Chapter 1, which is theoretical and constructive, contemplates a normative core or master narrative, operates with the modernist ideal of progress, and with a politics of community and consensus-seeking both between and within projects, where philosophers are fellow conversationalists with the other stake-holders.

The obvious point of reference for the politics of the research project was Gadamer, who influenced both the Rorty of *PMN* and Habermas. For Gadamer (1988:330), "to conduct a conversation means to allow oneself to be conducted by the object to which the partners in the conversation are directed." Personalities, as such, are bracketed out. The dialogue is addressed to the subject, not to one's fellow speakers, and is structured by the conversation itself. Thus, "it is generally more correct to say," Gadamer (1988:345) remarks, "that we fall into conversation, or even that we become involved in it," since it already has its own impetus and dynamic. What is required from the partners in a conversation is "that each opens himself to the other person, truly accepts his point of view as worthy of conversation and gets inside the other to such an extent that he understands not a particular individual, but what he says" (1988:347). A conversation of this kind sets all agonistic intent aside. It is not about "trying to discover the weakness of what is said," but about "bringing out its real strength" in the interest of eventual agreement. It is not, therefore, about winning victories, partial or total, but about "strengthening" its object by continually transforming it "into the uttermost possibilities of its rightness and truth and overcom[ing] all opposing argument which seeks to limit its validity" (1988:331).

Richard Bernstein (1991:337) contrasts this kind of conversation with the confrontational style of adversarial argumentation, where the other is regarded not as a partner in conversation but as an adversary to be exposed and defeated. Adversarial argumentation "requires attention to details, working through specific claims and arguments in order to show up their falsity and sometimes to expose their triviality. Therefore, Bernstein (1991:337) concedes, it has its merit, since "it is never satisfied with vague claims, it helps to pinpoint issues in dispute, and it can expose difficulties that need to be confronted." But, he maintains, it can also render us "blind to what the other is saying and to the truth that the other is contributing to the discussion." "Unfortunately, during the past few decades," he remarks, "'we' philosophers have not only perfected our adversarial skills but have carried them to excess" (1991:338). Dialogue, where civility between the partners and loyalty to the subject and its purposes is at a premium, has been replaced by polemic. Poststructuralists are interested in neither dialogue nor polemic. They are critical of attempts like Gadamer's and Habermas's to bracket out conflict from practical discourse, and argue that the search for universal agreement does violence to the heterogeneity of language games and modes of discourse that characterize the real world, and can, therefore, be achieved only *through* violence. Lyotard (1999:10) has also argued that the pragmatics of language of the project of universal agreement is fundamentally flawed. He reduces Wittgenstein's language games theory to three governing principles: (1) that the rules of the games do not carry within themselves their own legitimation but are rather the object of a contract between players; (2) that if there are no rules there is no game; and (3) that every "utterance" we make is best thought of as a "move" in a game. He charges Habermas and Wittgenstein—but he could have included Gadamer also—with ignoring the agonistic dimension of the language game; the fact that the language game is first and foremost a game of power.[85] That "to speak is to fight, in the sense of playing, and speech acts fall within the domain of a general agonistics," not of consensus (1999:10). The only truck that Foucault would have with hermeneutics, as

Dreyfus and Rabinow (1982:xix) point out, is with the hermeneutics of suspicion, which says that "man's" everyday self-interpretation is "surely deluded about what is really going on."

Deconstructive Politics

The same is not true, however, of Derrida, whose ethics, influenced by Levinas rather than Nietzsche, is one of openness to the other, not of combat and suspicion, and this renders it sympathetic to the politics of community and conversation. Caputo (1987:67) contrasts Gadamer's deep "philosophical" hermeneutics with a "radical" hermeneutics of Derridean inspiration that is playful and rejects the emphasis of the former on the "fusion of horizons," which is "preoccupied with digestion" of the other. Radical hermeneutics is permissively tolerant and lacks any assimilative ambitions. Gadamer represents the other as "a dialogue partner who appears 'across' the space of a conversation, on the same level, in a more or less homogeneous space." The space of a Derridean exchange, however, "is neither bi-polar nor level ... two neatly divided partners exchanging view, keeping the logos in the air" but "a tangled maze of messages ... not a dialogue but a colloquy" (Caputo 1987:68). Like Lyotard, Derrida "thinks perfectly level surfaces are artificial and can be found only in an unreal transcendental space... Real space is curved, unequal, unfair, where the voice of the different one is excluded, distorted, silenced" (Caputo 1987:68). Deconstruction curves it in the other's favor, so that the other comes to me with the power of a claim, "with the force of a disruption whose otherness I am not out to assimilate." It remains hermeneutic insofar as it remains concerned "to keep the conversation moving, mobile, to trust the dynamics of the *agora*," while doing everything to ensure fairness; that no voice is excluded or demeaned, and that the vested interests of the powerful are restrained as far as possible (Caputo 1987:261). Civility, in the sense of "knowing how to like and live with the dissemination of *ethos*," is its virtue. Caputo (1987:69) points out that difference is usually represented as "a fall from unity, a decline, a loss," but argues that the idea of community is compatible with an ethics of dissemination distinguished by "its high threshold for tolerating dissent and respect for differences" (1987:255). This is an ethics "bent on dispersing power clusters, constellations of power that grind us all under," including the binary schemes of Western metaphysics that create dichotomous relations between higher/lower, ruler/ruled, cause/effect, science/opinion, master/ slave, same/different, male/female, rich/poor, privileged/underprivileged, and so on (1987:260). What brings us together with others as a community is the sense of humility, the chastening that comes with the failure of metaphysics when, *owning up* to the embarrassment of one's limitations, and realizing that the best one can do is to "wade into the flux and try not to drown" (1987:258), one seeks the reassurance of others and, at the same time, experiences a certain compassion toward them as fellow "siblings of the same flux, brothers and sisters in the same dark night" sharing "our midnight fears, a common mortality." One sees oneself as a member of a "community of mortals" bound together by common fears and sharing "a common fate at the hands of the flux, sent by a *Geschick* which will not disclose its name, which does not have a name" (1987:259).

Caputo (1987:263) insists that a Derridean approach to ethics that is not opposed to the notion of community is not opposed to institutional organization either. In both cases it resists the tendency "to resist alteration, to suppress and normalize, to persist in place, in keeping with the metaphysics of presence." In this sense it does require "a genealogy of suspicion" like Foucault's, but also something more positive. An ethics of dissemination, Caputo (1987:264) says, works to "disrupt hardened shells ... but always in the *polis*," since there is no life outside the *polis,* no solitary, radically free subject. Though it operates "only in a community and in the ongoing conversation of mankind," however, this ethics offers no strategies or master plans for the whole of "mankind," but only tactics for local action "to keep the system in play wherever it has become inflexible, wherever anyone is overcome with the spirit of seriousness, wherever it finds the grim countenance of someone bent on saving us." And it operates on behalf of those who lack power or are "situated on the short end of any binary oppositional scheme." And Caputo's proposal of a Derridean politics of community that reassures without assimilating difference is shared by Richard Corlett (1989:4), who similarly suggests that a politics of community can be based on extravagance rather than unity, because, he says, the notions of "extravagance and community both turn on the notion of free gift-giving," which is also Derridean. Corlett (1989:xvii) argues that though a politics locked in binary opposition cannot "take seriously the remainder, the difference that cannot be reduced to opposition," it cannot contain it totally either. There is always excess to what binaries can contain that is unaccounted for, that lurks in the spaces and margins of a text, making unity impossible (1989:161). Foucault and

Lyotard make the same point that freedom is always possible. Corlett reminds us that the political problem Foucault set us was how to come to terms with the double bind of subjugation, namely the simultaneous individualization and totalization of the subject described in his work on disciplinary power structures.

A Derridean politics of community, in his view, provides a solution to it where Foucault doesn't: a compromise answer that accommodates people's demand for reassurance against the dissolution and anarchy of flux even as they seek their freedom from totality in extravagance or free play (1989:67). The notion of gift giving, Corlett argues, is important in this respect as a practice both extravagant and reassuring. Its economy, introduced as a language of hospitality, circumvents the oppositional relationship that lies at the heart of the politics of welfare, between the "caring" and the "needy," and which, he says, like Yeatman, reflects the language of domination. Derridean ethics, Corlett (1989:208) says, tell us that living life to the fullest is not living it on our own terms but in "the joy of being determined by the practice of community. This is because difference can be celebrated more effectively while being given over to the infinite play of substitutions." In the politics of a Derridean community, "to live extravagantly is to give gifts freely, to cultivate one's gifts in all directions"; to lose oneself in the practices of everyday life (1989:212). Such a politics projects a sense of community that is accidental and non-assimilative, that celebrates difference, regarding it as a gift, but provides a reassuring context at the same time. But while reassurance follows the logic of gift giving, "it makes little sense to expect people to cultivate gift-giving while denying their basic needs." In short, the logic of gift giving demands a politics of need satisfaction that disposes it politically to the left (1989:216). Derrida himself, making up for his earlier political reticence with a series of political books and interviews that reflect, as with Foucault, an ingrained suspicion of liberalism, has remained, nominally at least, loyal to Marx and the left, where Foucault has not.

Derrida's long-awaited engagement with Marx's texts came with *Specters of Marx* (1994). Other political works followed, among them a book on the subject of friendship and politics, *Politics of Friendship* (1997) (which followed on a seminar he gave in Paris in 1988–89). He has also, over recent years, become more forthcoming on the subject of politics in the interviews and seminars he has given. Justice, in particular, together with democracy, both defined within a politics of gift giving and hospitality, became a central concern for him, as it did not for Foucault.

In a roundtable at Villanova, he described his more recent approach to politics; the purpose of the "gestures I have made in recent years to deconstruct the political tradition, not in order to depoliticize but in order to interpret differently the concept of the political, the concept of democracy, and to try to articulate these concepts of the political and of democracy with what I said about the gift and about singularity" (Caputo 1997:18). Put differently, what he has tried to "think or suggest" over recent years "is a concept of the political and of democracy that would be compatible with that could be articulated with these impossible notions of the gift and justice" (Caputo 1997:19). "Impossible" in the sense that each implies a relation to the other that is not calculable, that goes beyond calculation. Politics, in general, he defines as "the place for hospitality, the place for the gift" (Caputo 1997:18), in contrast with Foucault, for whom it is the place of power, of resistance. It is not about choosing between unity and multiplicity, or attacking unity. Though unity is "a danger for responsibility, for decision, for ethics, for politics," he says, the politics of deconstruction is not about destroying it. Indeed, "some gathering, some configuration," is always needed. Deconstruction aims not to do away with the discourse of unity or consensus but to prevent it "from closing upon itself, from being closed up." It counters "the limit of every attempt to totalize, to gather, *versammeln*,' not with a limitless multiplicity but with "the heterogeneity, the difference, the disassociation, which is absolutely necessary for the relation to the Other" (Caputo 1997:13). "I can address the Other," Derrida says, "only to the extent that there is a separation, a dissociation, so that I cannot replace the other and vice-versa" (Caputo 1997:14). "A state in which there would be only *unum*, would be a terrible catastrophe"; it would be totalitarian and it wouldn't work. It wouldn't even be a state, properly speaking, he concludes (Caputo 1997:15).

In *Specters of Marx* he denounces the emergent liberal consensus of the postmodern world, the "new internationalism" or "new order" formed by global capitalism and media conglomerates, for creating an international hegemony on an unprecedented scale. With Marx he is considerably kinder, to the point of declaring deconstruction a radicalization of Marxism. Or, at least, a practice carried out within the tradition or spirit of Marxism. It turns out, however, that what attracts Derrida in Marx is not so much his politics, his economics, or his philosophy of history, all of which he more or less rubbishes, but the mystical part of Marx, his messianism. Indeed, he casts his own view of justice within the tradition of Marxian messianism, distinguishing it sharply from the law and defining it as what stands outside and beyond the law as a possibility or promise. And he does the same with democracy. "Justice is what gives us the impulse, the drive, or the movement to improve the law, that is, to deconstruct the law. Without a call for justice we would not have any interest in deconstructing the law. That is why I said that the possibility of deconstruction is a call to justice" (Caputo 1997:16). In *Force de Loi* (*Force of Law*, 1993), Derrida similarly refers to an "idea of justice" whose meaning cannot be read into either nature or reason, and is, therefore, "an experience of the impossible"; an idea that is infinitely irreducible and, therefore, cannot be articulated. It can only be experienced in a mystical way as a promise of what is still to come, as the Other. And if it cannot be articulated it cannot be deconstructed either. In brief, deconstruction *is* justice for Derrida, just as philosophy was justice for Socrates. He believes it can "serve to repoliticize the left with regards to positions which are not simply academic" (Lilla 1998:40, footnote 9, quoted from Chantal Mouffe).[86] As Mark Lilla (1998), on whose critique I am drawing, remarks, if justice cannot be articulated it cannot ground any substantial political program either; deconstruction leaves us with "decision pure and simple: a decision for justice or democracy, and for a particular understanding of both," nothing more (Lilla 1998:40). To put it into yet another nutshell, as Caputo would say, deconstruction comes across as an *ethos*, not as a program; a commitment to justice and democracy as care for the other that is indefinable and conceived of within the politics of hospitality and the logic of the gift.

Finally, this "care for the other" that marks Derrida's ethical approach appears to contrast sharply with Foucault's ethics of "care for self" that will be discussed in the next chapter. It is important to specify, however, that Derrida's is not intended to be an ethics of self-effacement any more than Foucault's ethics of care for self signifies an effacement of the other. Derrida even goes some way in agreeing with Foucault that ethics demands an element of narcissism. "There is not," he says, "narcissism and non-narcissism; there are narcissisms that are more or less comprehensive, generous, open, extended. What is called non-narcissism," he continues, "is in general but the economy of a much more welcoming, hospitable narcissism, one that is much more open to the experience of the other as other" (Caputo 1997:149). As we shall see, of the poststructuralists, Derrida, in fact, scores lowest on the scale of narcissism, while Baudrillard scores highest and Foucault is in between. Derrida (Caputo 1997:149) agrees with Foucault that without "a movement of narcissistic re-appropriation" there can be no relation to the other, since "love is narcissistic" by its very nature. But where Derrida's is an ethic of openness and hospitality to the other, and hints toward a utopian deconstructive politics of hope in what is to come in the name of justice and democracy, Foucault's is an ethic of suspicion and governance of oneself and of the other, his politics one of resistance and struggle articulated against the background of a dystopian narrative of modern institutions. A Foucaultian criticism of the Derridean ethos of justice and democracy as gift giving and hospitality is that it wishes to bracket out power from the relationships they involve and tends too heavily toward reassurance.[87] Foucault would insist that the economies of care as gift giving are also, ultimately, economies of power, and that we ignore this fact to our peril. So he is not impelled by the nostalgia for a power-free society that guides traditional anarchism and is detectable in a Marxian Derrida.

Derrida and the Learning Society

This observation that people need reassurance and not just freedom refers us back to the tension in the engagement we call education between enculturation, which is what gives reassurance, and individuation, which is what gives freedom and which poststructuralists identify with excess, extravagance, or transgression. Corlett and Caputo take the view—like MacIntyre, Habermas, and the left in general—that resolving the tension requires some account of community, but a sense of community that is very different from MacIntyre's in that its politics privileges dissemination over unity, voice over consensus, democracy over tradition. As with MacIntyre's, it is located at the local level; associates justice with generosity, solidarity, and the satisfaction of needs; is addressed toward the disabled in society of all kinds; and is critical of liberalism. None of the poststructuralists offers us the resources for a theory of a just and democratic learning society. At the same time, justice and democracy, Derrida tells us, are important notions that beckon us with their permanent possibility in the name of the other. His messianism invites us to be open to their possibility, to keep our hope in them alive and active through deconstruction. Like Dewey, he is interested in them more as forms of life than institutional arrangements—ways of living together marked by hospitality, by an openness to the other that is generous and that, though it coincides with the left's politics of needs satisfaction and reassurance, is at the same time suspicious of the focus the left puts on social cohesion, emphasizing the value of difference and free play instead, the dissemination of power, as its own political values. So that justice, apart from generosity, is also defined in these terms, as a radical tolerance, while injustice—and this is true of all the poststructuralists—is defined as the intolerance of difference and the totalitarian concentration of power in the *unum*, the one, whether of the community, of a culture or discipline, or of the state. The Derridean, just like the Foucaultian, will resist power whenever it appears in this form and will do so in the name of justice also— a justice that, like democracy, invites us with its promise, but has no name. That will remain unnamed and unnamable, undefined and indefinable, resists the lure of any controlling master narrative, that views all master narratives, including those of the learning society, with deep suspicion.

Both Corlett and Caputo, in fact, suggest that a Derridean approach to politics requires a Foucaultian genealogy of suspicion as its starting point. This is to keep the threat of unity in check, to prevent it from becoming total. The politics of resistance to this kind of threat that Caputo describes and that operates at the local level is addressed toward concrete issues with definable outcomes, and is intended to keep the system in play, not to overturn it. This is, again, typical of all the poststructuralists, as against the strategic resistance of social movements that is addressed to universal issues and that operates in the name of more abstract collective entities like humanity, society, women, a class, an ethnic group, and so on. Derrida, as Caputo points out, is as suspicious as is Foucault of the political space of modern social configurations, the space of power, describing it as inevitably unequal and unfair—a space within which the voices of difference, of the weak, the abnormal, tend to be marginalized, distorted, normalized, or just silenced. He, therefore, wants to see the space curved to favor these voices. And this means that for Derrida also, as for all the poststructuralists, there is a justice in conversation that is a justice of dissemination concerned with the exclusion of difference, but equally concerned with its assimilation. Thus, for the deconstructionist, as for any poststructuralist, an emergent unified discourse of a learning society controlled by an assimilative agenda for lifelong learning policies formulated by the EU or any other central agency, including the state, must be a major preoccupation.[88] From the deconstructionist's point of view, to avoid assimilation, the discursive model that defines the relationship between the central agency and its other (the transnational and the nation-states, the state and non-formal agencies), in defining the learning society (or the learning continent), must be colloquial rather than dialectical, open to a radical plurality as against the bipolar assimilation of the dialogue, which is facilitated, for instance, by conceiving the non-formal agencies collectively as a single movement or obliterating national identities.

A Derridean politics—and even more so a Foucaultian—demands of the individual, as Lengrand suggested, the courage of the Nietzschean hero, tempered with humility; the courage to stand in the flux without props and standpoints, to brave the world with its risk and laugh in its face, and the humility, from a Derridean viewpoint, to acknowledge one's inevitable limitations, one's weakness as a human being, and one's dependence on others with whom one shares one's fate—sentiments that drive one toward the need for reassurance, to belong to a community. For Caputo (as for MacIntyre), this humility before the realization of one's mortality, of one's dependence or weakness before an uncertain fate, is the basis of mutuality that ultimately presses one to respond generously to the needs of others. There is clearly a pedagogy that needs to be worked out here for learning communities that, contrary to MacIntyre's, are suspicious of projects to express a single mind and hospitable to difference instead. Corlett describes such a pedagogy as one based on the "performance" of the educator, where what is taught comes across as a gift given generously to the other to the extent of losing oneself in the performance, so that one's subjectivity is subordinated to the performance itself rather than, as in MacIntyre's case, a practice. MacIntyre argues that the logic of the gift doesn't stop with the giver, it also requires an ethic of receiving (and this is surely right) so that there is always the crucial part of the recipient, the pole of the receiver, the addressee to be considered and described in any account of a pedagogical relationship, just as the pole of the reader is crucial to the relationship of reading and writing, as all the poststructuralists insist.

In short, a Derridean political response to our postmodern liberal democratic learning society would be one that favors loose communities that resist assimilation by the state or its agencies, that are both hospitable and reassuring but avoid assimilating their members into sameness. One that encourages us to view justice and democracy as permanently unfulfilled promises, holding out hope for us and engaging our full commitment to their cause. A response that encourages us to think of lifelong learning in terms of such a commitment and of the learning community as a concrete endeavor to articulate it. That encourages us to think of learning as a gift given and received in generous gestures of mutual reciprocity by those who have the power to give (everybody, that is, who is in any sort of teaching-learning relationship with others) to those who have need for them. So we will think of learning communities in which the learning needs of others, especially of the weak, come to us with the power of a claim demanding our generous response to them. It seems reasonable that in cases where the resources available are limited, the giving should be tempered, as MacIntyre argues, with a principle of prudence, to prevent their being dissipated or lost and to ensure their fair distribution; i.e., their distribution according to the most pressing need. This is a very different conception of social justice from that of the quasi-meritocratic social investment state described by Giddens, where resources need to be earned and where there are no gifts.

Rorty's Liberal Utopia

Rorty is another poststructuralist who harbors a politics of hope, though one very different from Derrida's; one that is explicitly proliberal and pro-West, and that defines solidarity very differently. Rorty tells us that he gets his leftist politics not from Marx but from Dewey.[89] Sheldon Wolin (1990:7) describes his writings as constituting "one of the few, perhaps the only, major attempt to ally postmodernism with liberal democracy rather than with Marxism or social democracy." Rorty himself does not see it entirely this way. He has described himself as *both* a liberal and a social democrat and does not now believe that postmodernism can be allied politically with liberal democracy at all, though he may once have thought so. His view of the French poststructuralists—that they are "philosophically right though politically silly"—is possible because he thinks that philosophy has nothing to say to politics, that the two fall in different realms, different discourses, the private and the public, and should be kept separate, with philosophical discourse occupying us as private individuals, and pragmatic, practical discourse as public citizens. The attempt to weave the two—philosophy and politics, private and the public—together into a single discourse is, he holds, misconceived and mischievous. This being the case, he could pronounce his own political convictions without worrying that they could be out of phase with his philosophical thinking. The utility of philosophy, he tells us, only "lies in helping us to decide 'what to do with our aloneness'" (1987:572). Equally misconceived, in his view, would be the idea of abandoning the one or the other. We need to recognize them both, the ironic discourse of philosophy and the pragmatic of politics, as important in their respective spheres and put to their proper purposes.

Rorty, thus, radically reopens Rousseau's distinction between the spheres of interest of "the man" and the citizen, just as he radicalizes discourse into normal and abnormal. In his postphilosophical liberal utopia one can be a loyal and cooperative (and by no means uncritical) citizen at the same time as one is an ironist in private. While he dismisses philosophy from the public sphere, Rorty (1989:xiv) acknowledges the value of "historicist," "public" writers like Marx, Mill, Dewey, Habermas, and Rawls, not as political theorists or philosophers but as writers "engaged in a shared, social effort" with their "fellow citizens" through their narrative to "make our institutions and practices more just and less cruel." This is how, following Judith Shklar, he defines the institutions of a liberal society characterized by its deep aversion to cruelty. Writers who write as poets, on the other hand, help us cope with our aloneness. They are "private exemplars" rather than fellow citizens, in whom "the desire for self-creation, for private autonomy, dominates"; ironists like Kierkegaard, Nietzsche, Baudelaire, Proust, Heidegger, and Nabokov (1989:xiii). The French poststructuralists, Foucault especially, who have lost hope in the future of liberal democracy and express themselves in "terms infected by what seems to me a repellent Parisian world-weariness and hopelessness, as well as with leftover Marxist cynicism about gradual, non-revolutionary reform," are politically useless, though not, he thought early on, dangerous (1990a:44). He disagreed particularly with Habermas's (1990b) view that they are dangerous for the left. It is not really that, he argued, but that "they cannot be used for the purposes for which the left would like to use them."[90] Like Kierkegaard, Nietzsche, and the others, their proper use is for "roughly, private rather than public purposes—for giving us intellectuals a more coherent self-image, and a more coherent cultural utopia, rather than for giving us new political weapons or freeing us from old political illusions" (1987:572). Rorty blames Foucault in particular for fueling the error that philosophy could be relevant to politics. From Nietzsche, Rorty says, Foucault learned "to look twice at liberalism" (1989:62) and to distrust liberal institutions. Rorty's quarrel with Foucault is, therefore, a straightforward political one, since he regards liberal institutions positively himself. While with Habermas it is "'merely philosophical'", it concerns "*only* the self-image which a democratic society should have, the rhetoric which it should use to express its hopes," not its politics.[91] Unlike him, Habermas, he says, wants to ground liberal institutions in philosophical reflection (1989:67).

In short, where Foucault is an ironist without being liberal, Habermas is a liberal without being an ironist, but both encourage the view that philosophy is relevant to politics. Rorty wants to be both a liberal and an ironist and disclaims the relevance of philosophy to politics. His more recent writing has found him ever less favorably disposed toward Foucault. In *Achieving Our Country* (1998, henceforth *AC*), he blames Foucault's influence on the "cultural left" for its greater interest in abstract subversion than concrete political reform, and contends that the left should put a moratorium on theory, "kick its philosophy habit," and abandon its "futile attempt to philosophize" its way "into political relevance."[92] It should, especially, abandon the skeptical, anti-patriotic course it has taken over recent years—which, he argues, has stifled national progress—and embrace the politics of hope. "National pride is to countries," he contends in the book, "what self-respect is to individuals: a necessary condition for self-improvement" (1998:3). Besides, the left is, "by definition, the party of hope. It insists that our nation remains unachieved" (1998:14). Hope, however, cannot go together with the self-mockery and self-disgust that have become the key sentiments of its intellectuals and that produce not social progress but disinterest and immobility. Nor can it go with a spectatorial and retrospective attitude to politics. It looks to a future envisioned by Dewey and Whitman, who held up the ideal of a secular, democratic America as the first cooperative commonwealth and classless society in history.

Rorty (1998:18) encourages the American left to return to the early reformist days when it represented "the struggle for social justice to be the country's animating principle, the nation's soul," and blames Foucault's "Satanic" account of power for having taken it into "a gothic world in which democratic politics has become a farce" (1998:95), where "'liberalism' and 'humanism' are synonyms for naïveté," and where the nation-state is described as obsolete (1998:96). Foucault has thus turned from being harmless to being the enemy, a Platonist who contributes to "the endless attempt to make the intellect sovereign over the imagination"(1998:138), while Derrida remains "one of us," a "romantic utopian," even if his utopia is different. "The Foucauldian academic left in contemporary America," Rorty (1998:139) says, "is exactly the sort of left that the oligarchy dreams of: a left whose members are so busy unmasking the present that they have no time to discuss what laws need to be passed in order to create a better future." Though there is no doubting his subversive influence, these are not fair judgments of Foucault, as will be apparent in the next chapter. Contrary to Foucault, Rorty's view is "that contemporary society already contains the institutions for its own improvement," so that its basic structures, as Rawls calls them, need only reform (1989:63). We need a reformist left today, Rorty asserts, that recovers the old pragmatic spirit of Dewey and Whitman, and "smudges the line that Marxists tried to draw between leftists and liberals," not a subversive one (1998:44).[93] The value of liberalism is that it alone provides the practical political assurances required by the subjectivity of the cultural ironist whose activity is crucial to the cultural advancement of liberal democracies; for a postmetaphysical maturing of Dewey, Whitman, and Jefferson's vision of a secular, egalitarian society that guarantees individual liberty and endless diversity. A vision that recognizes that "our socialization goes all the way down," that there are no "truly human" wellsprings inside us from which it gushes, and that precludes the kind of solidarity envisioned by the revolutionary left (1989:xiii), which harbors the illusion "that the springs of private fulfillment and human solidarity are the same," and can be reconciled together within some legitimate moral or political conception of what it is to be "truly human" (1989:xiii).[94]

Dispensing with this illusion, Rorty argues, is as necessary for the progress of liberal societies today as it was for liberal societies in the past to dispense with religion. Demanding recognition of the inescapable contingency of our beliefs and values, it leads us to drop the rationalist notion of a "moral principle" in our dealings with one another. Rorty immediately recognizes the implications of this; it makes it difficult for us to justify our solidarity with others to ourselves. In response he suggests something like Wilfred Sellars's ethnocentric notion of morality as a matter of "we-intentions"—practices that we, whoever we are, recognize as *our* practices, reflecting *our* intentions, rather than as responding to universal principles of some kind (1989:59–60).[95] Within this dispensation, solidarity with others is rooted not in moral principles but in our ability to see them as "one of us," to feel a compassion for them that, as Freud showed us, has a "narcissistic origin." Freud, Rorty says, shows us how the ironist's narcissistic self-creation can be harmonized with compassion, which is an other-referring sentiment related to feelings of fraternity. In this sense, solidarity with others is "achieved not by inquiry but by imagination, the imaginative ability to see strange people as fellow sufferers ... by increasing our sensitivity to the particular details of the pain and humiliation of other, unfamiliar sorts of people," coming to see them as "'one of us' rather than as 'them.'" It is about expanding the range of our "we-intentions," "a matter of detailed description of what unfamiliar people are like and of re-description of what we ourselves are like" (1989:xvi).[96] It is not, however, in solidarity that Rorty (1989:xiv) recognizes the core political commitment of his liberal utopia but its individualism, the undertaking to let "its citizens be privatistic, 'irrationalist,' and aestheticist as they please so long as they do it in their own time—causing no harm to others and using no resources needed by those less advantaged." And he justifies liberal democracies as societies that give the ironist "the freedom to articulate her alienation," not as societies that are socially just (1989:89). Societies that share a "consensus that the point of social organization is to let everybody have a chance at self-creation to the best of his or her abilities, and that the goal requires, besides peace and wealth, the standard 'bourgeois freedoms'" (1989:84). Hardly a leftist statement!

His Rawlsian-sounding concern for the "less advantaged" quoted a few lines up is, in fact, the only concession he makes to the idea of social justice, but unlike Rawls, he does not twin any egalitarian principle with freedom in his discussion of justice. The key political issues he identifies for public debate in his liberal utopia are about balancing the needs for peace, wealth, and freedom when conditions require that one of these goals be sacrificed to one of the others, and how to equalize opportunities for self-creation without imposing it as a universal goal, letting people use or neglect these opportunities as they please. Social justice does not feature as an issue. Nor does he tell us how the "resources" they need will get to the less advantaged. Still less does he lay any responsibility for it on the state. Indeed, defining solidarity in terms of we-intentions and compassion rather than justice locates him not with Rawls, with whom he has frequently identified himself, but with minimalists like Nozick (1984) who argue that social redistribution should be left to charity, not state enforcement. The value he attributes to Rawls in "The Priority of Democracy to Philosophy" is as the philosopher who "following up on Dewey, shows us how liberal democracy can get along without philosophical presuppositions," just as it gets along without theological ones (1990b:179). Rawls shows us how persons holding different views of the self may be loyal citizens for pragmatic rather than moral reasons, Rorty says. He shows us that the liberal democracy requires no philosophical conception of the self. Such a conception, Rorty (1990b:292) believes, like those of justice and democracy, is useless for political purposes, or worse, and suitable only for private purposes, if, like his own, "one's vocation, one's private pursuit of perfection, entails constructing models of such entities as 'the self'"—in short, "if one has a taste for philosophy." The later Rawls, he points out, does not do political theory, he simply tries to systematize the principles and intuitions typical of American liberals, and this is how Rorty regards his own writing. Rawls "puts the democratic politics first, and philosophy second" (1990b:291). He shows us that at the concrete level of social policy no more authority is needed "than successful accommodation among individuals, individuals who find themselves heir to the same historical traditions and faced with the same problems" (1990b:286). In other words, social policy needs not philosophical foundations but the politics of reflective equilibrium (1990b:286). "The idea that liberal societies are bound together by philosophical beliefs seems to me ludicrous," he says. What binds them together "are common vocabularies and common hopes" (1989:86). Liberal societies are societies where ideals "can be fulfilled by persuasion rather than force, by reform rather than revolution, by the free and open encounters of present linguistic and other practices with the suggestions of new practices" (1989:60).

There is none of Foucault's suspicion of these procedures in Rorty's thinking, of the "free and open" encounters of liberal democratic societies. The hero of his utopia, a utopia with a "poeticized" rather than "rationalized" or "scientized" culture, is the liberal ironist (1989:53). The ironist, Rorty (1989:24) says, is the poet, the one who pursues the path of self-perfection rather than truth, who follows the Nietzschean path toward originality, who will "'have *demonstrated* that one is not a copy or a replica," of others. Her intellectual enemies are common sense and metaphysics, both of which, like Foucault's intellectual, she will regard as "immature." While the metaphysician deludes us into believing it possible to find a final vocabulary that will overcome the "problem" of contingency and accuses the ironist of "relativism"; and common sense has no worries that its final vocabulary, which it takes for granted, must always be uncertain, the ironist, having abandoned the idea that they "refer back to something beyond the reach of time and chance," faces up "to the contingency of his or her most central beliefs and desires" (1989:xv). Both cultures, metaphysical and common sense, feel uncomfortable with the ironist, who tells them a cruel truth about themselves: "that the language they speak is up for grabs by her and her kind." This is a truth they find humiliating in the sense that it makes "the things that seem important to them look futile, obsolete, and powerless." It is, Rorty (1989:89–90) says, like telling a child that her precious possessions are "trash" to be thrown away, or making them look ridiculous. To fail as a poet, he says, is to fail as a human being, but being a citizen is another matter, a matter of pragmatic adjustment, not creative poetry.

Philosophy and Achieving the Left

In *AC* Rorty (1998:52) militates politically for a broad left alliance among the old Marxist revolutionary left, erstwhile socialists and anti-communists, and Deweyan reformists, which would make it its business to struggle for the sake of leftist legislation and reform, and to reverse the story of despair told by the cultural left. He acknowledges that it would not be an easy alliance to achieve or maintain, but insists that it is possible nonetheless. He excludes the possibility of drawing the "cultural left" into it, accusing it of making "sadism," the humiliation of black Americans and other minority groups, the focus of its dissent rather than selfishness, thus deflecting the debate away from the left's traditional concern with economic injustice. The cultural left's "politics of difference," he argues, has few ties with those of the reformist left, which thinks "more about laws that need to be passed than about a culture that needs to be changed," and he accuses it of insensitivity to economic selfishness at a time when, in his view, "socially accepted sadism has steadily diminished," and problems of "economic inequality and economic insecurity have steadily increased," largely because of the globalization of the economy, which hinders national efforts "to prevent the immiseration of its workers" and has created an elite cultural and economic cosmopolitan upper class, or "overclass" (1998:78). He also accuses the cultural left of being selective of the "otherness" it exhorts Americans to recognize; namely that of women, blacks, gays, and so on, depicting them as the particular victims of sadism, when there are others (1998:83). In short, at the same time that he distances himself from what he describes as a Foucaultian-inspired left (the cultural left), he seeks to establish his own credentials as a Deweyan leftist reformist and politically orthodox social democrat.

His critics, however, have argued that he is neither. The outlook of the ironist, they say, conflicts with the description of liberals as people concerned to diminish suffering, who hope "that the humiliation of human beings by other human beings may cease," for this, as we saw, is just what the ironist does to those whose beliefs are metaphysical or backed by common sense—humiliate them (1989:xv).[97] Bernstein accuses Rorty of being "insensitive to the real pain, suffering and humiliation of human beings, that the other side of his ironical light-minded joshing is a cruel streak" (1990:35). Rorty argues back, however, that redescription is typical of intellectuals, not least the metaphysical, and must be expected in any society that grants them discursive space as a liberal society does. Besides, what people find objectionable in the ironist, he says, is not their humiliation but the fact that she doesn't claim to "educate" them; to uncover their true self and interests, real freedom, justice, and authenticity. In short, that the ironist has no spiritual or mental reassurance to offer. "What the ironist is being blamed for," he argues, "is not an inclination to humiliate but an inability to empower" (1989:91). Undermining people's beliefs she offers no alternative, casting them adrift and insecure in a hostile and alien ocean, demanding that they create themselves anew with their own efforts. The best the ironist can offer is the vocabularies of a Kierkegaard or a Nietzsche for their self-education, to help them deal with the sense of aloneness that irony brings. Matters are different in the public realm, where reassurance comes from the common language of citizenship and where irony, he argues against Foucault, has no place.

But even so, critics have attacked his leftist credentials and located him politically on the right. Bhaskar (1991:134) argues that his notion of a centerless self, like his anti-realism and his celebration of privatism, simply provides an ideological home for intellectual yuppies bent on justifying their political irresponsibility. Other critics of the left have quarreled with his self-declared ethnocentrism. Even his loyalty to Dewey, reaffirmed over the years as other influences and heroes have fallen by the wayside, has been put in question. Bernstein (1987:541) contends that he "distorts and betrays Dewey's legacy" and is really far removed from Dewey's vision of social democracy. Wolin (1990:26) has also questioned his democratic credentials, charging him with taking the *demos*, "the people," out of democracy with his brand of individualism. And feminists have also expressed strong opposition to his radicalization of the division of the public and private spheres. Fern Haber (1994:66) argues that the public/ private split cannot be sustained anyway since, "in the wedding of liberalism and ironism, one of the partners is dominated by the other," the former by the latter, and accuses him of encouraging a form of cultural imperialism.[98] She shares Wolin's complaint that "the masses" are conspicuously missing in his utopia, forgotten between the two social extremes; those silenced by pain and humiliation and its intellectual heroes, the strong poets (1994:55). Wolin (1990:27–29) also charges Rorty with encouraging the kind of "managed" democracy typical of the rich Western societies.[99] One that gestures rhetorically toward egalitarianism, widespread participation in power sharing, and respect for the sensibilities of ordinary people but does nothing to achieve them. Managed democracies "need intellectuals who are adept with words and images, who realize that words are more important than beliefs, that contingency is at fault, and who are sufficiently infatuated with their own self-importance as to believe that the 'founders' of the liberal utopia will be 'poets' rather than 'the people' who had discovered or clearly envisioned the truth about the world or about humanity" (1990:28). They have no use for the public sphere, for a society "in which privatization is publicly encouraged and proclaimed to be the highest value, and government treats its members benevolently, is a society where public space is, as a matter of policy, shrunken" (1990:24).

Fern Haber also questions Rorty's concern for the weak, charging him with articulating not the voice of the weak but of the dominant emerging bourgeois *ethos* of postmodern Western societies. She questions his "suggestion that there is no voice of the oppressed," and is less than sanguine "about the consequence that the leisured elite will speak for them." In any case, she contends that "the ironist is particularly ill-suited to serve as the social messiah" (1994:56), complains that Rorty's intellectuals are not so much the defenders of the weak but "the vanguard of the species" (1994:52), and charges him, as Wolin does, with anti-democratic elitism. "Rorty," she says, like Wolin, "believes that it makes sense to order our society to benefit the strong poets because it benefits all of us to protect that class of people not silenced by pain and suffering; only the poets can free the rest of us to be genuinely human" (1994:54). He is therefore, she contends, in bad faith. "It is not the voice of the marginalized Other, the oppressed, that occupies him, but that of the intellectual. In the end," she concludes, "the voice he wants to promote is not that of the Other, but that of the colonizer" (1994:74). By representing intellectuals as the "vanguard of the species," she argues, he contradicts his criticism elsewhere of "romantic" attempts of "leftist intellectuals to pretend that the avant-garde is serving the wretched of the earth," which he described as "a hopeless attempt to make the special needs of intellectuals and the social needs of the community coincide" (1994:57). In sum, Rorty's politics, she contends, are glaringly ill suited to serve the goal of demarginalizing the marginalized and giving a voice to the oppressed. A goal that is achieved, she argues like Foucault, by politicizing the voices of those who have been constrained institutionally within the sphere of their privacy, not by speaking on their behalf.

In short, notwithstanding his efforts to placate them, Rorty's political writings, continue to anger his critics on the left, who charge him with right-wing sentiments, as much as any of the French poststructuralists.[100] He responds by arguing that they misread him, and by insisting that he belongs to the reformist left. Early on, responding to their most general concern that his views are "likely to give aid and comfort to the wrong people" (1987:564), he described his "political credo" in eight "theses" about social democracy that broadly represented the political outlook of the West (1987:565). These theses, he contended, were shared with critics who, like himself, "might not mind describing themselves as 'social democrats'"(1987:567). Identity of viewpoints on them, he argued, was not necessary; "overlapping consensus" is enough to establish a common political identity and to make cooperation on political projects possible, even while disagreement on some aspects or issues continue to persist. Social democrats, he held, could live with these disagreements just as they could live with differences in their private philosophical tastes (1987:573). As he saw it, his key difference with his social democrat critics, as with Habermas, was not over politics but "over the utility of theory." His view being, of course, that "theory" serves no use in practical politics. That the best it can do is help us in "thinking through our utopian visions" (1987:569). In the same article he was already disassociating himself from those of the left "who find Marxist terminology more useful than we do" (1987:568), who subscribe to the "dreadful, pompous, mish-mash of Marx, Adorno, Derrida, Foucault and Lacan" (1987:570), and those who do *ideologiekritik* or critical theory, on the grounds of their partiality; that they criticize only the bourgeois ideology of late capitalism. "Unmasking," he declared, with Foucault also in mind, "has long been overworked, and has by now turned into self-parody" (1987:569).

However, notwithstanding what he says, one cannot put the criticism he receives from the left down simply to incomprehension on their part. His description of the liberal utopia in *CIS* certainly does convey the view that it belongs to the strong poets, not to ordinary people, much less the weak. It is also true that he intends his ironist intellectuals to be a cultural vanguard, even if their task is not, he says, to educate. More fundamentally, it is doubtful that dichotomizing the private and the public spheres will work politically. To create a cultural vanguard, in effect, is to create a political vanguard with crucial consequences for the practice of politics and the distribution of power in the society. It is naive to believe that those with cultural power will not use it in the public sphere. His defense of strong private individualism for his liberal utopia, his definition of justice as what permits an individualism of this kind to prosper, his lack of interest in any egalitarian principle to offset it, his ethnocentricity, his radical dichotomization of private and public realms, his weak account of solidarity and of sociality in general, his denial of any need for an emancipatory agenda, are foreign to the left's thinking. They are, on the other hand, familiar landmarks of a political landscape hostile to the left: the libertarian. It is a moot point whether his libertarian individualism is, whatever he says about the political irrelevance of philosophy, a product of his philosophical thinking (many, like Habermas, believe that the poststructuralist viewpoint inevitably leads either to it or to anarchism), or whether he is attracted to poststructuralism because of his libertarian outlook. Whichever may be the case, it is difficult to believe, as he suggests, that people can live in the schizophrenic way of keeping their irony private and containing it in the cultural sphere, excluding it, once it has been cultivated, from their thinking as public citizens. Once one starts thinking like a philosopher, that way of thinking infects all one's thinking, including one's thinking as a citizen. Once one is led by philosophical thinking to dismiss metaphysical outlooks as culturally immature, one is inclined to dismiss them as immature everywhere, including in the political realm, as Rorty effectively does in seeking to articulate a utopia without master narratives. In this respect, however, he may be more in touch with the new trends in social democrat party politics than his critics. In short, to what extent does Rorty's thinking, particularly his recent thinking in *AC*, resemble that of Giddens?

Certainly, like Rorty, the Third Way projects a strong individualism, though his is stronger. Like him it wants to redefine social justice and solidarity within a political text that is non-metaphysical, and like him it sees no alternative to capitalism and the free market. Like him it wants to bury Marx and socialism. Like him also it extols traditionally conservative values like patriotism, tradition, and a rugged self-dependence. In short, Rorty's politics, so heavily castigated by the old left, synchronizes very well with the new. Unlike Giddens, however, his concern with the politics of the left is not a concern with government but with reform and struggle. As we saw, the business of the broad left alliance he militates for would be to struggle for the sake of leftist legislation and reform, and to reverse the story of despair told by the cultural left (1998:52).

Unlike the traditional left, however, and like the Third Way social democrats, he refrains from blaming capitalism for this economic inequality and insecurity, and rejects the idea that it can be redressed by going back to, or restating, the protectionist policies of old. Instead, like Giddens and Habermas, he suggests that the left should think hard and look harder. This is something, he complains, the cultural left refuses to do, to engage in concrete national politics, nor does it offer alternatives to the market economy it attacks so relentlessly. The new left alliance, he insists, should stop attacking capitalism and "the system," and abandon inflammatory slogans like "power to the people" and the old revolutionary left's ambitions for a radical democracy. It should shed its "semi-conscious anti-Americanism," turn patriotic, and agree on a concrete political platform for reform together with the labor unions. In sum, it should, like all good social democrats of the Third Way, "get back into the business of piecemeal reform within the framework of the market economy" (1998:105). Nor should the alliance set itself up as a social movement of some kind. All movements, Rorty declares (quoting Kierkegaard), are inspired by "'the passion of the infinite'" (1998:114). The intellectuals of the new left, he contends, should harbor no such passion, rather they should "throw themselves into a lot of campaigns," a "campaign" being "something finite, something that can be recognized to have succeeded or to have, so far, failed" (1998:114). Like engineers and lawyers they should "find out what their clients need" and respond to it, rather than set the agendas themselves like the priests and sages of old (1995:198). Their work should have "inspirational value," and this "is typically not produced by the operations of a method, a science, a discipline, or a profession," but "by the individual brush strokes of unprofessional prophets and demiurges" (1998:133). Nor should they aspire for the eternal, like the creators of the great literary works of the past. They must hope for no more than "to say once again what has often been said, but to say it in a different way, to suit a different audience" (1998:136), and regard intellectual fashions to be "as changeable as the historical and personal situations of readers" (1998:137).

Rorty and Education

The political task that Rorty set himself in *CIS* as a philosopher who gave up on theory was to articulate the hopes and vocabularies of our liberal democracies within the changing vocabulary of the social democrat left.

The need for this type of articulation occurs, he says, when a "contest" develops "between an entrenched vocabulary which has become a nuisance, and a half-formed new vocabulary, which vaguely promises great things." This is how Giddens described the transition from the vocabulary of the old left to that of the Third Way. Then the "method" (the scare quotes are his) is not to theorize comprehensive new visions but to "try to make the vocabulary I favor look attractive by showing how it may be used to describe a variety of topics" (1989:9). This involves "redescrib[ing] lots and lots of things in new ways, until you have created a pattern of linguistic behavior which will tempt the rising generations to adopt it, thereby causing them to look for appropriate new forms of nonlinguistic behavior, for example the adoption of new scientific equipment or new social institutions," to match it (1989:9). In his "Reply to Arcilla and Nicholson" he describes this same task as that of helping societies, in his case liberal democracies, develop "a suitable rhetoric" to articulate their emerging hopes and aspirations, their "new, concrete alternatives" to the present, thus "making them a bit more palatable" for people, breaking the crust of convention in the process (1990a:41). This is how he describes his own writing in *CIS*, where he articulates what he takes to be the emerging hopes and aspirations of the liberal society (1989:9). In *PMN* and in *CP*, on the other hand, the task of the intellectual was that of intermediary between the liberal society's conventional language and alternative foreign, strange, or bizarre vocabularies and discourses that may appear threatening to it that she reinterprets reassuringly within the conventional language, showing how they hang within its "horizon of prejudices." He adopted the more poetic approach of articulating the emerging utopian vocabulary of the left, described in this paragraph, after retracting his support for a hermeneutic culture.

Meanwhile, he has continued to deny philosophy any relevance to politics, even arguing that its introduction into political dispute is harmful. In "Philosophy and the Future," before writing *AC*, he was insisting that intellectuals of the left "have to give up the priority of contemplation over action" (1995:198). In *AC*, as we saw, he complained about the cultural left's "futile attempts to philosophize one's way into political relevance" (1998:94), arguing that the left should put a moratorium on theory and kick "its philosophy habit" (1998:91). Like Marx, he says, "we" have to look to the future rather than the past. But puzzlingly, the "we" in "Philosophy and the Future," where he repeats from *CIS* that "our" task is "to replace a human self-image which has been made obsolete by social and cultural change with a new self-image, a self-image better adapted to the results of those changes," is "we philosophers" (1995:198)! He goes on to say, even more puzzlingly, that "philosophy cannot possibly end until social and cultural change end," and that "only a society run without politics—that is to say a society run by tyrants who prevent social and cultural change from occurring—would no longer require philosophers. In such societies," he continues, "philosophers can only be priests in the service of a state religion. In free societies, there will always be a need for their services, for such societies never stop changing, and hence never stop making old vocabularies obsolete" (1995:198). This at the same time as he warns against bringing philosophy into politics, and expresses his longing for a "postphilosophical" culture. It reveals an ambiguity on his part about the word "philosophy" and his uncertainty about whether he wants to describe himself as a "philosopher" and his work as "philosophical" or not, a problem shared by the other poststructuralists, who are sensitive to the fact that their writing is "abnormal"—outside the parameters of "normal" academic philosophy as these are defined by its practitioners, the other of philosophy.

It is clear that what Rorty rejects in *PMN* is a culture *founded* on philosophy. In *CP*, he rejects the representation of philosophy as a *fach* or discipline, in *AC* as "writing at a higher level of abstraction," introducing a "sweeping and novel ... conceptual apparatus," and "problematizing concepts" (1998:92–93). His work is certainly not philosophical in any of these ways, nor is it interested in arguing or justifying positions. So should it count as philosophy? The question is important only if one wants to define philosophy, to pin down its meaning. This, however, holds no interest to the poststructuralist, nor need it detain us here. Consistently with his view that philosophy has nothing to say to politics, Rorty (1990a:41) believes that it has nothing to say to education either. In "Education without Dogma" (1990c) he expressed himself strongly on the matter, describing its intrusion into education not just as irrelevant but harmful to the enterprise, clouding issues and rendering them intractable. He takes the issue dividing the political right and left over education about the proper relationship between "truth" and "freedom" (enculturation and individuation). He argues that philosophizing it has turned it into a protracted and unfruitful polemic about the "true nature" and interests of the learner, when a pragmatic compromise would be available were the opposing sides to realize that "truth" is already the agreed-upon province of "lower" education (schooling), and "freedom" of "higher" education (the non-vocational university). The simplicity with which he resolves the issue, MacIntyre's issue, is astounding! He does not contemplate—indeed he explicitly excludes—that "truth" (enculturation) and "freedom" (individuation) could be brought together in an educated public. Individuation, he says, is something to be achieved privately, and this is where philosophy *can* help. Apart from that, his solution clearly undermines the need for education theory, not to mention philosophy of education, as one of its subdisciplines. A Rortyian approach to the emerging vocabulary of lifelong learning and the learning society would be to articulate it as part of the language of an emerging liberal utopia in a postmodern world, and to point to its cruelties through different forms of narrative writings. The object of the former is to render the utopia, which he supports, "more palatable" or attractive to people, while that of the latter is to direct political activism toward specific reforms in favor of the weak and marginalized, and against institutions and practices of the emerging learning society insofar as they are cruel or humiliating. The liberal ironist is Rorty's model of what the educated person should be: one who seeks self-perfection in private, publicly promotes an ironist culture, and plays her role as a committed citizen in the liberal public sphere. Rorty does not provide any sociological account of our current liberal democratic societies as learning societies as Foucault does because, unlike Foucault, the narrative he wants to tell about them is one of hope and optimism, and because, again unlike Foucault, he thinks that fundamentally they have it right politically, socially, and institutionally, so there is no need for any close analysis, particularly of any "unmasking" of how they work, which is only of interest for those who want to resist them.

Rorty claims his beliefs on education, like his political beliefs, are close to Dewey, though both claims have been rejected by his critics and, in my view, are difficult to substantiate. His belief that the tension between the twin demands of enculturation and individuation experienced by modern education systems and teachers can be solved by making the latter a private matter correspond with current thinking in adult learning policy-making, but it is not Deweyan. Nor is his definition of the school's role in enculturation, or "conscious social reproduction," which, he says, should aim "primarily at communicating enough of what is held to be true by the society to which the children belong so that they can function as citizens of that society" (1990a:42). His very strategy of locating the two in separate spheres, which is consistent with his general strategy since *PMN* to resolve dichotomies (normal/abnormal, constructive/reactive, public/private, poetic/pragmatic, etc.) by separating their terms into different realms rather than synthesizing them into comprehensive resolutions, into an educated public for instance, as Dewey and other philosophers inspired by Hegel tend to do, or deconstructing them as Derrida does, is non-Deweyan. Teachers in schools and the present adult members of a society, Rorty argues, must recognize a "core commitment" to collectively recreate the society they share. "If a teacher thinks that the society is founded on a lie, then he had better find another profession" (1990a:42). This is the pragmatic Rorty (1990a:46), describing how things are in all societies. "It is not, and never will be," he says, "the function of lower-level education to challenge the prevailing consensus about what is true." And he is surely right here. Schooling in liberal democratic societies is protected from indoctrination, he says, by two things: A lot of students will go on to higher education, to non-vocational universities "where doubts about the society may become central rather than marginal to education," and "we have the good luck to live in a society which has managed to make social criticism part of the tradition which lower education is supposed to hand down" (1990a:42). Non-vocational, or liberal, universities he envisages and justifies on lines contrary to MacIntyre and Habermas (who wants to see universities politicized), as subversive places where the ironic reading of the canonical texts of the normal culture is cultivated and students take the path of private self-perfection.[101] The social criticism that is allowed in the schools, on the other hand, is not to be confused with subversion. Though teachers must tell children "that our society is the result of skeptical doubts about the past," their narrative must be one of hope and progress, a "story of increasing freedom," a patriotic narrative of a continuing if unfinished saga based on liberal achievements such as the emancipation of slaves, the enfranchisement of women, the rise of the trade unions, the development of the welfare state, and so on—in short, a narrative that will give the young "an image of themselves as heirs to a tradition of increasing liberty and rising hope" (1990a:42).

Rorty describes this account of education as "updating Dewey a bit," but it is really going against Dewey's (1934:12) most fundamental belief that the task of schools and teachers is to aid in social reconstruction, not social reproduction, and that they should ally themselves with "this or that movement of existing social forces" that is progressive, rather than undertake the conservative role Rorty prescribes for them. Dewey (1934:11) wanted teachers "to promote a new social order," not perpetuate the old one.[102] "The plea that teachers must passively accommodate themselves to the existing conditions" he denounced as "but one way and a cowardly one of making a choice in favor of the old and chaotic" (1934:12). Also, Dewey had a less optimistic story to tell of his country's growth than Rorty's. He was more than critical of the "rugged" individualism that emerged with capitalism, that vibrates through Rorty's own work, and that is fashionable today, and he was explicit in his discontent with the status quo: "I see little social unrest which is the straining of energy for outlet in action; I find rather the protest against a weakening of vigor and a sapping of energy that emanate from the absence of constructive opportunity; and I see a confusion that is an expression of the inability to find a secure and morally rewarding place in a troubled and tangled economic scene" (1930:14). In *The Public and Its Problems* he complained, like Habermas, that "the invasion of the community by the new and relatively impersonal and mechanical modes of combined human behavior is the outstanding fact of modern life" (1997:98). And the "new individualism" he advocated was pretty different from Rorty's. It was cast in terms of a recovered sense of community in the more intimate sphere of private life and of active citizenship in the public, and in both, as we saw, he promoted a politics of communicative action. More fundamentally, as I wrote a few lines up, Dewey would not have gone along with Rorty's radical separation of enculturation/individuation, and of private/public into dichotomous realms, just as he would not have accepted the radical separation of education/life into dichotomous realms that has characterized much liberal thinking inspired by Oakeshott.

Though he would have agreed with Rorty that no sense can be made of the idea of an "inner self," or private mind, or "human essence," and that we must think of the individual as socialized right through, Dewey would have strongly resisted Rorty's claim that the springs of self-fulfillment are different from those of solidarity with a community. For this reason he would also have rejected Rorty's radical individualism. Rorty was, indeed, close to Dewey in *PMN*, where his account of self-creation through conversation was influenced by Gadamer. There he defined education as *edification*, which serves to "take us out of our old selves by the power of strangeness, to aid us in becoming new beings" (1980:360), rather than *irony*. The outcome of edification could still be a "strong existentialist relativism," which it would be the task of enculturation to temper. But the difference between edification and irony is that while the former is achieved with others in conversation and is social, the latter is achieved alone or by interacting with a master skillful in exposing one to the limitations of one's thinking, to the contingency of one's beliefs, much as Socrates exposed his circle of friends and interlocutors and the citizens of Athens in general to the limitations of their vocabularies through aggressive questioning, insensitive to their humiliation, and it is essentially private. Rorty is right to refer to this pedagogical practice as cruel. The story of Socrates, the supreme ironist, also alerts us to the dangers if irony is transposed into the public sphere, if it is turned to the purposes of politics. But Rorty does not want to keep it out of the public sphere to protect the ironist but rather to protect public institutions that cannot, as he says, be founded on doubt. Socrates, like Foucault, as we shall see, used irony in subversive ways, to unmask the hypocrisy and failings of the political institutions of his time, and at great personal risk. In "The Masked Philosopher," Foucault (1997:322) cites Toni Negri, the Italian radical, as a contemporary example of the dangers of being an intellectual of this kind, but aspired to the same role himself. Like Rorty, on the other hand, he identifies education with self-creation that begins with the denial of one's self-identification with a "we." Like Rorty (1980:376) also, he insists that "we must first see ourselves as *en-soi*—as described by those statements which are objectively true in the judgment of our peers—before there is any point in seeing ourselves as *pour-soi*." "Even the education of the revolutionary or the prophet," as Rorty (1980:365) says toward the end of *PMN*, has to start from her culture. As Young (1995:13) puts it, "criticism always presupposes a schema, background, worldview, *vorhabe*, or tradition. It always works from within a historical/biographical horizon, to borrow Gadamer's terminology (Gadamer, 1975). Put crudely," he concludes, "in order to be critical you must first be indoctrinated." Given its usual association with the closing of the mind, however, "indoctrination" is too strong. It is not something a liberal society can tolerate, since it is intended to discourage education rather than lead to it. If enculturation is regarded as the necessary first step to education, as I agree it must be, it must be an enculturation that includes social criticism in its agenda.

Chapter Seven

The Politics of Suspicion

Dystopian Writing

Foucault's most direct contribution to the contemporary debate about the learning society is his critique of the workings of power within modern societies and his account of the growth of the institutional power structures of the modern state since it started to take shape in the classical period. Foucault, in fact, conceives of modern societies explicitly as learning societies, societies mobilized for learning in particular ways that accord with the motives of government and of the direct and indirect policing of populations. Like that of the Frankfurt theorists, which it resembles, his narrative is dystopian. The other dystopian narrative of the modern-postmodern learning society I shall take up in this chapter is Baudrillard's. Though Baudrillard set himself against Foucault, I shall treat their two narratives as complementary because he approaches the learning society from the angle of the media's role in an information society that Foucault does not consider or mention, notwithstanding the influence on him of Adorno and Horkheimer.[103] The two accounts, Foucault's and Baudrillard's, taken together with Lyotard's account of the workings of performativity, constitute a powerful description of the postmodern learning society seen through the eyes of these skeptical French poststructuralists. Together they raise the question of whether theirs is not, beneath the surface of the rhetoric of governments and employers, the *real* face of the postmodern learning society as it is emerging in our times, but with its roots already well entrenched in the modern world. None claims that it is. Foucault (Rabinow 1984:232) admits that his dystopia "isn't a very good description of 'real life,'" but he goes on to point out that "real life isn't the same thing as the theoreticians' schemes" either. So it isn't that he acknowledges theirs as "very good descriptions of 'real life,'" either.

The central concern that dominated Foucault's critical inquiry over the years, as he told us himself in one of his last interviews, was with how we are constituted as rational subjects today through different discourses and practices of power-knowledge, and at what cost to our freedom. A crucial part of his narrative concerns the contribution of the human and social sciences as "games of truth" to these discourses and practices. He classified his own genealogical narratives about the social world, as did Lyotard his paralogies, as "anti-sciences" or "fictions," abnormal discourses, in Rorty's language, that challenge the "normal," "truth-producing" narratives of the sciences. "I have never," he admits candidly in another interview, "written anything but fictions" (Gordon 1980:193).[104] The same can be said for utopian narratives, not just the purely fictitious ones drawn on the drawing board, like Plato's, but those grounded in the past or present like Rorty's. These are fictions too, with the difference that they are narratives of hope and optimism. Dystopian narratives, on the other hand, are narratives of fear or skepticism, depending on how strong they are and how one reads them. Neither, just because they are fictions, dispenses with the truth. "It seems to me," Foucault says in the same interview, "that the possibility exists for fiction to function in truth," and, "for a fictional discourse to induce effects of truth, and for bringing it about that true discourse engenders or 'manufactures' something that does not yet exist" (Gordon 1980:193). In short, the distinction truth/fiction is not clear-cut. It is *effects of truth* in particular, like Rorty's utopian narratives, that genealogical narratives seek to produce. And the fact that they make no claim to truth as accuracy of record or representation renders any criticism fetched against them—that they are historically inexact or inaccurate—off-beam. Accuracy is not the important issue, but this does not mean, Foucault insists, that there is no truth in his genealogical narratives, or that empirical elements are unimportant to them. His general point, as his remark about the "theoreticians' schemes" earlier shows, is that accurate representation can never be justifiably claimed for any narrative. But this does not mean that it cannot still "function in truth." In short, where Foucault's genealogical narratives are concerned it is their power of truth, not their accuracy of representation, that interests him; their ability "to induce effects of truth," to persuade. Hence, the criticism of Baudrillard's "sociological fictions" by Bryan Turner (Rojek & Turner 1993:84)—that they "are striking and challenging but they are not ultimately convincing"—though unimportant for Baudrillard, would be fatal for Foucault. This is because, as Couzens-Hoy (1986:14) suggests, Foucault's fictions have a political agenda where Baudrillard's do not; "because he hopes we will find the picture threatening," because he finds it so himself. And no one feels threatened by a narrative that does not carry with it some, perhaps a great deal, of "effects of truth."

"Effects of truth" or credibility is, in fact, a condition of all good dystopian, or utopian, writing with a political purpose, including such classics of the genre as those by Wells, Zamiatin, and Orwell. Were they incredible or beyond belief their political purpose would be blunted. Foucault represents his own dystopian narratives as "histories of the present," of realities already with us, not visions of the future, of the yet to come that is alarming to contemplate. Jon Simons (1995:5) remarks that if Foucault "is not obliged to tell the truth but free to invent a tale of oppression it would then be a question of choosing, arbitrarily or on aesthetic grounds, between his narrative and conventional accounts." The arbitrary and the aesthetic, however, are not the only grounds for choosing between narratives that are declared fictitious. It is not the case either that Foucault feels no obligation to tell the truth. Rather, "I believe too much in truth," he says, "not to suppose that there are different truths and different ways of speaking the truth" (Kritzman 1990:51). His declaration that his narratives are fictions stems not from disdain for the truth but from a respect that requires him to put it, like reason, in question. His dystopian writing is offered as one way of telling the truth that others may want to consider. But Usher and Edwards suggest another way of judging fiction besides the arbitrary and aesthetic: An account of how truth can lurk in fiction; how the texts of utopias and dystopias "function in truth" without claiming to be true, to tell things as they are or were. They describe the "truths" that lurk in Derrida's texts as a matter of *resonance* with experience rather than correspondence with facts or accuracy of representation. And this is what I think Foucault means when he refers to the "effects of truth" genealogical narratives induce, that they resonate with the experience of ordinary people.

Resonance, as Usher and Edwards (1994:123) say, is not easy to define or explain; "it refers to ways of seeing and thus of understanding where one is unsure of the exact meaning of what one has understood. Yet if something resonates," they continue, "one feels that something important is happening, and one can only feel this when what is happening has a certain purchase with one's concerns. In this sense resonance has to do with the familiar. But equally it has to do with the unfamiliar since that which resonates has a quality of strangeness about it which 'captures' and 'captivates.'" This is certainly an accurate description of Foucault's narratives. Resonance, they go on, is not about knowing more or going deeper into things but *seeing* them differently. What it arouses is "the recognition that there is more to be known and more to be said" than meets the eye. "When something resonates one is not at the end of a journey," Usher and Edwards (1994:123) continue, "one has not reached one's goal or *telos* but rather another starting point." This is, in fact, the kind of job dystopian (and utopian) narratives do when they impact the imagination; they resituate the reader at a new starting point (though they may, of course, leave one cold or angry instead, as some feel when they read Foucault). In Foucault's case the political purpose of his narratives is stated explicitly: "to show people that they are freer than they feel, that people accept as truth, as evidence, some themes which have been built up at a certain moment during history, and that this so-called evidence can be criticized and destroyed" (Martin, Gutman, & Hutton 1988:10). And to see this is to stand at the point of making a new beginning.

To repeat the point made earlier, the difference between writers of utopia and of dystopia is not one of truth or not truth but of outlook, of the political purpose to which they set their fictions. Utopian fictions are written in hope by those who are optimistic of the present and future, who think they know what a better (more just, more rational, more emancipated) society would be like, and believe it attainable, or, as with Rorty, perceive indistinct progressive trends in their society that they support and want to articulate as their society's hope. Dystopian narratives, on the other hand, are often told by those who, as with the Frankfurt theorists, think they know what a better society is like, see no signs of it in the present, and despair for its future. But they can be like those of Foucault, who does not claim to know what a better society would be like but is radically discontented with the present one. His lack of interest in saying what a better society would be like is, as we saw, what provokes his critics to charge him with irresponsibility and anarchism (though the two are not the same). One could react to them otherwise than by struggle; by resigning oneself to one's circumstances, conforming with or dropping out of the political universe, "looking elsewhere" as Baudrillard put it. Foucault assures us that his are not narratives of despair (otherwise there would be no point in struggling) though they are not narratives of hope either; and though it is true that he once described human history as a cycle of successive dominations with no exit into freedom, he is no cynic. His are narratives of suspicion rather than cynical hopelessness or even pessimism; narratives intended to open up the possibilities of freedom, not to close them down. This is different from Baudrillard (Gane 1993:152) whose cynicism is captured in his remark that hope today is a "rather unimportant value," and "not a very lucid idea." Baudrillard denies that lack of hope produces enervation. One does not have to hope or believe in things, he says, to do them. However, as we shall see, unlike Foucault, he sees no point in politics in the contemporary world. Foucault does not abandon hope but is suspicious of the hope of utopia, holding that the worst atrocities have been committed in its name. In this respect, he objects specifically to Habermas's view "that there could be a state of communication which would be such that the games of truth could circulate freely, without obstacles, without constraint and without coercive effect," in short, without power (Bernauer & Rasmussen 1994:18).

The Panopticon Society

Foucault's dystopian narratives are told in a series of books describing, as I said earlier, the emergence of modern institutions and practices, "economies" (in Greek *oikonomia*—*oikos*, a house, and *nomos*, a law) that have efficient policing and effective reform as their scope: "corrective" institutions like asylums, hospitals, clinics, prisons, military barracks, and, of course, schools. All of them are, in some way, pedagogical institutions incorporating regimes of learning, and all aspects of the learning society we tend to ignore. These institutions share a common agenda: to normalize, to render their inmates functional members of their society and productive in the economy. All have occasioned the need for a "science" (psychiatry, criminology, psychology, and so on) to tell them objective truths about normality and to find effective remedies for abnormality in their respective spheres. Their discourses (their technical jargon and vocabulary) thus function as "games of truth" within which the institution's life, including its pedagogical practices, is played. This is how, in Foucault's narratives, the modern state harnesses knowledge into an instrument of efficient and effective government, an instrument of power rendered silent but ubiquitous through its institutions. Arguably the most popular of these narratives, especially among those with an interest in education, is *Discipline and Punish: The Birth of the Prison* (1991a, henceforth *DP*), first published in 1975. Though, as its title indicates, the book is about the modern prison, it extends its scope to other modern corrective institutions, including schools, where discipline and punishment are at the core of everyday life. Indeed, Foucault's more general aim in writing the book was to describe how modern society became a carceral society through the evolution of these institutions, a *panopticon* society to be precise, a society obsessed with government. A panopticon is what, he tells us, today's learning society is.

The book begins famously with a harrowing account of the public torture and execution of the regicide Damiens in eighteenth-century France, emphasizing the publicness of the event and describing the elaborate and highly ritualized spectacle in detail. Foucault makes the point that the punishment was literally and explicitly inscribed on the *body* of the accused. The symbolic purpose of the spectacle, both juridical and political, he explains, was to combine the victim's punishment with the reassertion of the sovereign's absolute power. An intrinsic part of its rationale was the production of a confession from the victim, who thereby canceled out the offense caused by the crime and restored the *status ante quo* that was true and just. The spectacle was, however, as much about asserting the power of the sovereign as about reasserting truth and justice (which were, after all, encapsulated in the sovereign). It was hence deemed indispensable. Foucault goes on to describe the circumstances under which public execution was abandoned, replaced in modern times with a different regime of punishment, increasingly private and intended to reform its victims and reintroduce them into the mainstream of life and, especially, of the economy, requiring the invention of the modern prison. With this change of mentality came the redefinition of crime itself by the newly emerging science of criminology. Foucault points to the important part played by humanitarian activists in this transformation of punishment into more humane forms. But the cry for criminal reform was double-edged, since it was also, above all, the state's response to the call for a more efficient administration of the law in the face of alarming rises in petty and serious crime, before which the current judicial dispensations appeared powerless. And, for Foucault, the chief motive behind the reforms was not to punish less but to punish better, and "to insert the power to punish more deeply into the social body," in order to render it more governable (1991a:82). Something like the same story is told about the beginning of mass education during roughly the same period.

One very significant change the reforms brought to the politics of punishment was that, though its techniques and technologies continued to be practiced on the body, it increasingly addressed the "soul" of the punished. An equally important shift of focus was from punishment to discipline. And another still was the individualization of the crime, so that the juridical focus of the judgment became the criminal as "individual" rather than the crime in abstraction. In short, while "the coercive, corporal, solitary, secret model of the power to punish replaced the representative, scenic, signifying, public, collective model" of old, its object, shared by the host of other institutions of confinement that grew with the evolution of the modern state, was to reform the "individual soul" of the inmate (1991a:131). With the rise of capitalism and its industrial needs, another goal was to reinsert the inmate "morally and materially into the strict world of the economy" (1991a:124). Thus the coercive power of the state grew substantially, creating the framework for a punitive society. The understanding these institutions had in common was that "they should all, according to a strict economy, teach a lesson: that each punishment should be a fable," a moral "representation" built into the popular memory, around which "schoolchildren will gather with their masters and adults will learn what lessons to teach their offspring" (1991a:113). In short, the punitive society was inscribed into the social body as a learning instrument, its institutions forming a network, a grid, over which a learning society with a punitive and disciplinary *ethos* spread. And it had a model: Jeremy Bentham's nineteenth-century panopticon prison, whose qualities, according to Foucault's narrative, effectively infiltrated the whole institutional fabric of society through the modern bureaucracy.

The prison institution wanted to reform criminals into docile and obedient subjects and willing workers, but this was true of the other institutions of confinement also: the barracks, asylums, factories, schools, all with similar bureaucracies. Together they provided "a universal pedagogy of work for those who had proved to be resistant to it" (1991a:121). Their menus of forced labor were aimed principally at spiritual and moral transformation, but this was achieved by disciplining the body also. The practice of isolating prisoners, for instance, introduced into the English prison model had the explicit pedagogical purpose of encouraging the prisoner "to go into himself and rediscover in the depths of his conscience the voice of good" (1991a:122). The model required knowledge of the criminal's personality and the development of the behavioral sciences, for identifying effective corrective pedagogical techniques to address it with. It also required knowledge of physical space and its effective use, a scientific approach to the design and architecture of corrective buildings, in order to make the disciplining more effective. The panopticon prison structure was its outcome. Foucault vividly describes the infiltration of the modern partnership of behavioral sciences and panoptic techniques and designs into the social fabric, the partnership that made the modern state and the modern city, "follow[ing] the advance of power, discovering new objects of knowledge over all the surfaces on which power is exercised" (1991a:204).

Panopticon institutional spaces combine "surveillance and observation, security and knowledge, individualization and totalization, isolation and transparency" efficiently in their disciplinary regime (1991a:249). And this, Foucault tells us, is the regime of government and policing created more generally by the modern state.[105] The ambition of the panopticon institution is to maximize the utility of individuals as well as its control over them. It "functions as a kind of laboratory of power ... thanks to its mechanisms of observation," it "gains in efficiency and in the ability to penetrate into men's behavior." Its projects are "projects of docility," of behavioral regimentation and discipline practiced through "the meticulous control of the operations of the body, which assured the constant subjection of its forces and imposed upon them a relation of docility" (1991a:137). These mechanisms of disciplinary power, Foucault tells us, are at work in the schools and in the hospitals as well as in the prisons. Everywhere the same typical "political economy of detail" is followed through the distribution of individuals in space and time employing different techniques; for instance, through the invention of the "time-table," one of its most ingenious disciplinary inventions (1991a:139). He describes how this disciplining of space and time was pioneered in the schools and in other pedagogical establishments where "an analytical pedagogy meticulous in its details and also very precocious in its history" gradually emerged (1991a:159).

Power, Foucault (1991a:194) says, "produces"; it produces reality, it produces "domains of objects and rituals of truth." Discipline, he contends, "does not just control, it 'makes' individuals; it is the specific technique of a power that regards individuals both as objects and as instruments of its exercise" (1991a:170). Although its pedagogical techniques are aimed at reforming the soul, at the end of the day "it is always the body that is at issue" (1991a:25). The secret of its success lies in the fact that its instruments, mechanisms, and techniques are simple but effective: a hierarchical structure of observation, normalizing judgment, combined "in a procedure that is specific to it, the examination" (1991a:170). The examination, Foucault (1991a:172) tells us, lies at the heart of our modern pedagogical and corrective institutions, at the heart of modern policing and surveillance, at the heart of our learning societies; the rationale of the panopticon architecture is to enable an examination of the inmates to be as efficient and invisible as possible: "to permit internal, articulate and detailed control—to render visible those who are inside it," to place them under a "disciplinary gaze" that remains invisible and anonymous. The disciplinary gaze holds its subject firm "in a mechanism of objectification," rendering it a describable object, a "case," a statistic, a subject for a branch of knowledge, the behavioral sciences, and a handle for a branch of power (1991a:187). It is "a normalizing gaze, a surveillance that makes it possible to qualify, to classify, to punish." In short, it efficiently "combines the techniques of an observing hierarchy and those of a normalizing judgment" (1991a:184). On the panopticon model the examination renders modern power both "invisible" and pervasive through a range of institutions—from psychiatry to schooling to work, from the diagnosis of disease to the assessment of learners to the hiring of labor. It renders society an "infinitely minute web of panoptic techniques" where power/knowledge "regularly reinforce one another in a circular process," and from which there is no exit (1991a:224). Foucault refers to this panopticon learning society as "the dark side" of the Enlightenment.

Panopticon power is not, however, the only kind the modern state has developed to render its citizens more governable. In *The History of Sexuality Volume 1* (1984b), first published in 1976, in taking the case of the discourse of sexuality as his example, Foucault develops the startling thesis that efficient government is obtained as much, if not more, by encouraging a discourse to proliferate as by repressing it. Problematizing sexuality in the Victorian world led to the creation of a *scientia sexualis*, unique to Western societies, which defined normal sexuality, distinguished and explained the abnormal, and prescribed cures for the latter. In the same book Foucault introduces a different angle to the power of the modern state besides the disciplinary and repressive power described in *DP*—*pastoral* power—and subsumes both under the term *bio-power* (the power over life and death), as "two poles of development linked together by a whole intermediary cluster of relations" (1984b:139). Disciplinary power is "centered on the body as a machine ... an *anatomo-politics of the human body*." Pastoral power is "focused on the species body, the body imbued with the mechanics of life and serving as the basis of the biological processes: propagation, births and mortality, the level of health, life expectancy and longevity, with all the conditions that can cause these to vary." Pastoral power supervises these processes of life and death effectively "through an entire series of interventions and regulatory controls: a bio-politics of the population" (1984b:139), using the machinery of "demography, the evaluation of the relationship between resources and inhabitants, the constructing of tables analyzing wealth and its circulation," for the purpose (1984b:140). Putting the subject's existence as a living being in question, the modern state responded with "the proliferation of political technologies that ensued, investing the body, health, modes of subsistence and habitation, living conditions, the whole space of existence"—Habermas's colonization of the lifeworld by the system (1984b:143). Ideology "constituted the abstract discourse in which one sought to coordinate these two techniques of power," disciplinary and pastoral, "in order to construct a general theory of it" (1984b:140), and both together were "without question an indispensable element in the development of capitalism" (1984b:140–141). Pastoral, like disciplinary power finds its expression everywhere, not just in the modern state apparatus. It circulates through private ventures and initiatives like welfare societies, individual and corporate benefactors, and philanthropists, as well as families, modern medical practice, and so on. Like disciplinary power, it has "spread out into the whole social body, found support in a multiple of institutions," and is exercised in a multiplicity of sites (1984b:215). The language of modern rights, Foucault tells us, falls within its discourse. "The 'right' to life, to one's body, to health, to happiness, to the satisfaction of needs and, beyond all the oppressions of 'alienation,' the 'right' to rediscover what one is and all that one can be, this 'right,'" he says, "which the classical juridical system was utterly incapable of comprehending— was the political response to all these new procedures of power" (1984b:145). In short, it was ambivalent; a claim that could be made by the individual to "rediscover what one is," and by the state for its intrusion in the conditions of life.

Finally, the techniques of biopower and the challenges of modern government may be summarily described as those "methods of power capable of optimizing forces, aptitudes, and life in general without at the same time making them more difficult to govern" (1984b:141). They have to do with the twin aims of efficiently optimizing the potential of subjects for self-fulfillment and as human resources, and ensuring their docility.

Biopower "designate[s] what brought life and its mechanisms into the realm of explicit calculations and made knowledge-power an agent of transformation of human life" (1984b:143). In sum, it is the insidious way the modern state takes charge of life in general through the "continuous" deployment of "regulatory and corrective mechanisms," punitive and pastoral, in order to render individuals effective within the economy and happy with their lives (1984b:144). From Christianity, besides the technology of the examination, it has successfully appropriated those of pastoral care, secularizing and institutionalizing them for its purposes. Even here, as with its punitive reform, pastoral care resulted from a change of mentality in terms of which "the ancient right to take life, or let live was replaced by a power to foster life or disallow it to the point of death" (1984b:138). This change in mentality casts "life" as the central issue of government and the state in the role of the shepherd tending its flock and arbiter of individual well-being. To the extent that it projects the examination as the tool of government, the modern state continues to show the old classical concern with the production of truth, though the techniques of truth production today are typically the techniques of science. Besides these techniques that tell us the truth about us, Foucault also underlines the importance of those other techniques, ethical rather than scientific, by which the truth is told about the individual *by herself* and exercised through diverse practices of self-examination and self-confession. Their object being the promotion of *self*-regulation as the most efficient economy of control; more invisible than the gaze of the panopticon, though the subject renders herself no less visible. A self-regulation in conformity with norms that are set by others, their insidiousness lies in the illusion of personal freedom and control, of autonomy, they permit the subject.

The Obscene Society

Foucault (Gordon 1980:152) counterposes this reality of a modern-postmodern learning society dense with power relations to the Enlightenment dream of a transparent learning society "visible and legible in each of its parts, the dream of there no longer existing any zones of darkness, zones established by the privileges of royal power or the prerogatives of some corporation, zones of disorder," cherished by Rousseau and liberal reformists. Baudrillard startles us with a contrary thesis: The postmodern society, he says, is already an obscene society, a society that is transparent to a degree Rousseau and liberal reformists never contemplated. Bauman (MacLaren 1991:8–9), however, insists that the two are really complementary—not conflicting—accounts of postmodern society, and Douglas Kellner (1989) notes, behind Baudrillard's protestations against Foucault, a clear congruence between his account of the "society of simulations" and Foucault's "panopticon society."[106] "Michel Foucault's 'disciplinary society,'" Bauman (1987:81) says, "with its modes of surveillance and punishment, becomes for Baudrillard a society of simulated 'tests' and programmed differences." Both identify a complex of totalizing and individualizing techniques lying at the heart of the modern-postmodern society. Foucault's thesis about the self's "subjectification" to regimes of disciplinary, pastoral government and self-government is replicated by Baudrillard's claim that we do not have that kind of control over our destiny that we think we have, "we no longer exist as playwrights or actors but as terminals of multiple networks" (Rojek & Turner 1993:108). Foucault's disciplined subject is Baudrillard's mediatized terminal.[107] But their respective reactions to this state of affairs, their projects of freedom, are different.

Baudrillard's thinking about the obscene society began when, early on, in the 1970s, he turned away from the conventional way of representing advanced capitalist society as a "consumer society" as crude and out of touch with contemporary reality, because it fails to identify the manner in which the society has been transformed in the process of becoming an information society; a society that is, literally, a media society. At this stage, he was struck by Bataille's notion of a "general economy" that regards expenditure, waste, sacrifice, and destruction as more fundamental to life than the classical economies of production and utility, and argued that freedom from the imperatives of capitalism and utility comes from pursuing such an economy of "excess," gift giving, sacrifice, and destruction, instead of one of consumption and construction. Later, however, influenced by Marcel Mauss, he revised this idea and accepted that there are no such things as free gifts; that even the sun extracts "payment" or "compensation" and needs to be challenged constantly in order to expend itself. Drawing on Mauss's anthropology of the gift and countergift, he speculated a revolutionary return to a precapitalist society based on symbolic exchange; an almost primitive communism in which the non-productive or aesthetic is glorified in place of the productive and functional, and he regarded the "postmodern" turn in Western culture as the historical break, or rupture, that was likely to bring it about. Meanwhile, revolutionary action meant engaging in transgressive activities that are outside the logic of bourgeois semiotics or capital.

At this early stage, his attitude toward Marshall McLuhan, the obvious point of reference for anyone concerned with the media and communication, was entirely negative. He accused McLuhan of technological reductionism and determinism, showed real traces of technophobia, and expressed nostalgia for face-to-face modes of communication. A conversion later on, however, turned him more radical than McLuhan; "the medium is the message" became the key to his own thinking. Following McLuhan, he characterized modernity as an *explosion* of production and productive agencies, and an *implosion* of all boundaries, regions, all the distinctions between binary oppositions, particularly between subject and object, hitherto upheld by tradition and social theory, thus presaging the death of meaning. In *In the Shadow of the Silent Majorities* (1983a), first published in 1978, he described the format of the media as *fascinating*—it neutralizes meaning, leaving us with "a kind of 'neutered' passion, a stupefaction in front of the sequences, the events, the messages, etc." (Gane 1993:84). Fascination is "a way of blending in with the screen," of becoming "immanent with the screen," the screen being not a mirror that reflects but a surface that absorbs. To become fascinated in this way is to become "a gaze-simulacrum." Fascination "is a form of ecstasy ... an ecstatic state which is no longer reflexive... We have disappeared in a sort of ecstasy of the media, of information circulating with acceleration across everything. And one is no longer able to put a stop to the process. This is what I call fascination" (Gane 1993:85). In *Seduction* (1990b) Baudrillard adopted McLuhan's distinction of the media into "hot" and "cool" to show how the hot media literally devour information and exterminate meaning as they become more "cool" and abstract, the instruments of "cold seduction," fascinating us to the point where our subjectivity is no more than a reified consciousness.[108] We become the possessors of a privatized and serialized lifestyle resembling that of the television soap opera. More generally, for Baudrillard, the media today is "like a black hole" that fascinates us and into which disappears all meaning, political, social, and ethical, rendering these areas of life meaningless.

Baudrillard, in fact, describes the media as a hyperreality of simulations constituting an autonomous self-referential realm. Images, spectacles, and the play of signs have replaced the logic of production and class conflict, he says, to become the key constituents of our contemporary societies. Our inevitable interiorization of its fare signifies the obliteration in our consciousness of the distinction between public and private, between interior and exterior space. McLuhan's thesis that "the medium is the message" is pushed to the limit; to the situation where Baudrillard (1983a:102) hypothesizes not just the end of the message and of the social with it but the end of the medium itself. Rather than extensions of human power, as McLuhan had represented them to be, he represents the media as instruments that serve to turn societies into fascinated mass audiences, silent audiences, and presents us with an apocalyptic description (with a Heideggerian ring to it) of a world advancing toward a "universal semiotic of technological experience," a cyberniticization of society, which signifies the same sort of absolutist triumph as that of functionalism, administration, and control described by Adorno and Horkheimer. "Now the states, the institutions, the technical and technological systems, etc.," he says, "are so perfected and control everything in such a way that there is no longer any means of reversing these systems, no longer any subversive or revolutionary strategies which can bring about the overthrow of these systems" (Gane 1993:89). Dystopia, in the society of the spectacle, is not the subtle saturation of reality by dense power networks, as with Foucault, under the secret and subtle gaze of authority, but its complete transparency; a place where the media show us everything instantaneously and without any scruple or hesitation, rendering it for this reason "obscene." Not only do they occupy public space, exteriorizing it and rendering it transparent, they do the same to private space also. "In the media society," Baudrillard (1983b:72) claims, "the era or interiority, subjectivity, meaning, privacy and the inner life is over; a new era of obscenity, fascination, vertigo, instantaneity, transparency and overexposure begins: Welcome," he concludes ironically, "to the postmodern world," where the state's political project, as in Foucault's narrative, is "the control of a pacified society, ground up into a synthetic deathless substance: an indestructible artifact that will guarantee an eternity of power." A "project of political and cultural hegemony" (1983b:91).

We are historically, by Baudrillard's (1983b:111) account, at the stage of "third-order simulacra," where society has moved from "a capitalist-productivist society to a neo-capitalist cybernetic order that aims now at total control." With the destruction of meaning, no contradictions, crises, or real opposition are possible, no revolution or revolt, only complete inertia, "a kind of circularity between silence and the excess of information," creating "a kind of hysteria of information ... a rapture, an escalation." The information society, in short, is a death trap with no point of exit because it incorporates a paradox: "The more silent the masses, the more one talks of them, bombards them with messages, etc. But the more one produces information, the more one increases the masses" (Gane 1993:88). Mass society "is moving less and less; it is increasingly in a state of silence." The impression we have "of extensive mobilization, participation, circulation," is false, just an illusion of social interaction, not the real thing, because social interaction is also dead (Gane 1993:89). What exists is a simulation of the social, which kills off genuine sociality and renders the masses mere passive, apathetic, inert spectators of the media. But here he springs his surprise. This inertia is not, as with Adorno and Horkheimer, alienation but a strategic response of the masses themselves, who understand it as the only way they can resist (Baudrillard 1983a; Gane 1993:89). It is an instinctive strategy they adopt. Disappearing within it is the way they neutralize the media's power on them and exercise their own. "One wants to impose a political field, one wants to impose a social field, a cultural field," he says, "all of that comes from above; it comes through the media, and the masses reply to it all with silence; they block the process" (Gane 1993:88). They absorb the content of the media silently like insatiable sponges, demanding more and more spectacle and becoming more and more passive in the process.

In light of this analysis, Baudrillard unsurprisingly questions the relevance of contemporary political and social theories, declaring them all obsolete, their vocabularies dead. Ours, he declares, is simply an era of "hyperconformity." The masses are concerned with the spectacle and cynical about all else, so that the era of the social is over. "Society," interaction, communication, civility, and the rest, have imploded into mass indifference and silence. Interpersonal relations are "electrified" in media and computer networks that relate with and organize individuals through electronic circuits rather than face-to-face encounters and relations. And with the end of the social we are also at "the end of the body and of its history; the individual is henceforth only a *cancerous metastasis of its basic formula*" (1990b:233). The dystopia is complete, and it does not enclose us like Illich's box, or Weber's iron cage, or Adorno and Horkheimer's administered society, or Marcuse's one-dimensional society, or even Foucault's panopticon society. It is more frightening; a world where "all structures [are] turned inside out and exhibited, all operations rendered visible," transparent to the point of obscenity (1990a:29). The third is the last stage, the stage of counterfinality where the project of modernity, having completed itself according to its own internal utopian logic and superceded its limits, has turned inwards, imploded onto itself, producing "hypertelia"; "a kind of reversal" that projects produce when they "surpass" themselves, their own objective or finality, when "things go too far" and they destroy "their own objective." Baudrillard compares it with a cancerous state where "the cells are too lively; they reproduce too quickly. For the organism itself, it is a catastrophic process" (Gane 1993:90–91) that produces "esoteric" reaction as "the body rebels against its own internal organization, undoes its own structural equilibrium. It's as if the species has had enough of its own definition and thrown itself into an organic delirium" (1990a:33). "Hypertelia" is Baudrillard's metaphor for a postmodern society that has advanced the modernist project to the stage *beyond* the completion of its own internal logic of a technologized universe into a transpolitical, destructured, and dehistoricized universe emptied of event and rendered transparent and obscene by a glut of information.

The "transparency and obscenity of space in the promiscuity of networks, ... of the social in the masses, of the political in terror, of the body in obesity and genetic cloning .... The end of the sense of the historical, the end of the scene of the political, the end of the scene of fantasy, the end of the scene of the body—the irruption of the obscene. The end of the secret— the irruption of transparency" (1990a:25). This is how Baudrillard (1990a:61) envisions the postmodern world. There is, he says, no "good substance to the social, some ideality of social relationship that can and should be liberated, we are doomed to this diaphanous obscenity of change." And "we mustn't believe we are living the realization of some evil utopia, we are living the realization of utopia, period. That is to say, its collapse into the real."[109] That utopia is the liberal utopia of "a transparent universe," no more and no less (1990a:65). Exhausted through its own self-fulfillment it "breaks out of its social scientific box and becomes phantasmagorical, violent, paranoid, extreme" (Gane 1993:95), producing not an enlightened critical public but the stark anonymity of "the mass," not *anomic* but *anomalous,* like obesity, a "kind of monstrous conformity to empty space, of deformity by excess of conformity that translates the hyperdimension of a sociality at once saturated and empty, where the scene of the social as well as the body are left behind" (1990a:27).[110] A kind of terror; "a sort of convex and deforming mirror of order" where the political disappears also (1990a:34). Terrorism, like the mass, is blind, senseless, and unrepresentational. Both are extreme. "Not a step of violence," it is, he says, "everywhere in the normality of the social, such that from one moment to the next it can be transfigured into an inverse, absurd, uncontrollable reality" (1983a:57). It is misleading to describe it as the *product* of the mass, the two are simply simultaneous with each other in their brutality. In sum, Baudrillard (1983a:58) perceives a "triangular affinity" between mass, media, and terrorism. Together they create "the presently prevailing process of implosion." We are all of us hostages to this terror, submitting to its "proposition of universal responsibility"; we are its necessary accomplices because, unlike violence, terror needs spectators (1990a:36). The mass is the absolute prototype of the hostage and the spectator; "annulled in its sovereignty, abolished and non-existent as subject" but also "radically inexchangeable as object" (1990a:44). Terror, blackmail, the hostage, Baudrillard tells us, all have the quality of the obscenely transparent about them, they create the "political" vocabulary of our postmodern world.

Finally, the mass can in no way become "a protagonist of history," because what it generates is a profound cynicism about political action (1983a:2). It has no history to write, no virtual energies to release, nor any desire to fulfill; it is just a formless sponge whose power lies in its capacity to absorb and neutralize, not to initiate. It is an inertial power—"an opaque nebula whose growing density absorbs all the surrounding energy and light rays, to collapse finally under its own weight. A black hole which engulfs the social" (1983a:4). Bombarding it with information will not free its "energy" or fabricate the social anew. Quite the contrary, "information produces even more mass." Indeed, "the mass is only mass because its social energy has already frozen" in its fascination with information (1983a:26). Transparent and unreal, it is the media that makes it. Thus, the term "mass" itself causes Baudrillard some discomfort, as it does Adorno and Horkheimer. It does not, he specifies, stand for a sociological notion, nor for a concept explained through a survey or statistic. It is merely "a leitmotif of political demagogy, a soft, sticky, lumpen analytical notion" that he uses (1983a:4). To want to specify further, he contends, is a mistake—it is to provide meaning and identity for what has none. "The mass is without attribute, predicate, quality, reference... It has no sociological 'reality.' It has nothing to do with any *real* population, body or specific social aggregate" (1983a:5). It is "what remains when the social has been completely removed," a black hole (1983a:6–7). Its sociality is kept alive as a public fiction because it is required by the greater fiction of the political sphere, which survives only through the "credibility hypothesis, namely that the masses are permeable to action and discourse, that they hold an opinion, that they are present behind the surveys and statistics" (1983a:37). People "are encouraged to speak," in the name of this fiction. "They are urged to live socially, electorally, organizationally, sexually, in participation, in festival, in free speech etc." as a camouflage for reality (1983a:23).

The fiction is sustained through a "pedagogical plan," the utopia of a learning society, whose declared object is "to better inform, better socialize to raise the cultural level of the masses" (1983a:10) while exorcising the specter of the mass as a rabble and keeping it within reason. But the plan is nonsense, Baudrillard (1983a:14) says (obviously thinking of Foucault), for "power manipulates nothing, the masses are neither misled nor mystified." To the contrary, they "scandalously resist this imperative of rational communication" (1983a:10) and "retain a fascination for the medium which they prefer to the critical exigencies of the message" (1983a:35). What they demand is not more meaning or better understanding, or learning, never mind education, but more spectacle. Scenting "the simplifying terror which is behind the ideal hegemony of meaning" (1983a:10) they react to it "by absorbing and annihilating culture, knowledge, power, the social" (1983a:11), distrusting the supposed transparency of the political will like they do death. Hence the silence with which they defend themselves is not "a silence which does not speak, it is a silence which *refuses to be spoken for in its name*" (1983a:22). A silence that engulfs the political as will and representation (1983a:23), retreats into personal privacy, into the banality of everyday life, abjuring collective action. In its resistance to and impatience with the didactics of emancipation, the silent mass, Baudrillard (1983a:46) says, has understood that "there is no liberation, and that a system is abolished only by pushing it into hyperlogic, by forcing it into an excessive practice which is equivalent to a brutal amortization."

Not everyone agrees with this description of the postmodern information learning society. Baudrillard's account of the "mass" created by the media conflicts with that of Adorno and, more recently, Gianni Vattimo, who, on his part, rejects both accounts. Vattimo (1992:6) agrees that the postmodern "society of the mass media" is inhospitable to the idea of "a more enlightened, more 'educated' society (in the sense intended by Lessing, or Hegel, or even Comte or Marx)," and rejects the idea anyway "that a free society is one in which humanity can reach its self-awareness in a 'public sphere,' namely that of public opinion, open discussion, etc." (1992:17–18), a "community of unlimited communication," such as Apel and Habermas propose, and which he identifies with the "utopia of [the] absolute *self-transparency*," of reason (1992:17). But he also rejects the idea that the media society creates a mass. Referring to the "giddy proliferation of communication," he describes it as complex and opaque instead, even chaotic. Its "irresistible pluralization" (1992:6) and our experience of "continual oscillation between belonging and disorientation" in it, the tension between reassurance and excess, renders it hospitable rather to the ideal of emancipation (1992:10). Not, however, identified with humanity *tout court*, as Kant represented it, but with aesthetic communities, a "giddy proliferation" of communities. A vision of utopia that, as in Nozick, "comes about only through its articulation as heterotopia" (1992:69).[111] Vattimo (1992:25) agrees with Baudrillard that today "the images of the world we receive from the media and the human sciences, albeit on different levels, are not simply different interpretations of a 'reality' that is 'given' regardless, but rather constitute the very objectivity of the world." We need, he says, to regard the media society as "the 'context' for a multiplicity of fabling, and to consider the human sciences themselves as 'fables' aware of their own 'fabulous' character," rather than as purveyors of truth. Vattimo, like the early Rorty, thinks hermeneutics to be the proper philosophical response to our fabled world.

But Baudrillard, of course, disagrees, pronouncing meaning and, therefore, interpretation, dead. For Baudrillard there is no self-conscious critical distancing from the hyperreality of the fabulous. Levin (1996:174) refers to the digital "utopia" of a "fungible text (the body without organs, the void, the blank sheet, value, matter ... a kind of digital Solaris [that] has been growing into existence on the information networks linking the world's communications systems," for years: the Internet, Baudrillard's mass. Set up as a "parallel universe," a "realm of pure information," it functions like any other abstract system—capital, markets, writing, the genetic code—drawing randomly on "living" particularities in a generalizing, systematizing, metaphorical transaction with the "dead." Like the market, it is operated by an "invisible hand," resistant to administrative regulation, and difficult to control. A parasite, it feeds on everything it connects with, "converting all it encounters into self-substance," and its expansion is limited only "by the absolute parameters of its ecological niche: the continuing supply of labor, fresh blood, electronic interfaces." Like any parasite, "it depends for its survival on the evolutionary resilience of its host," namely, the human nervous system, and provides a "viral" scenario that "confirms Heidegger's vision of the historical emplacement of a biotechnical symbiosis (*Gestell*). This convergence exerts increasing pressure on both the human form and the technological forms to evolve—or destroy each other." This "would be Baudrillard's hypothesis," Levin (1996:174) says, that the Internet constitutes the ultimate technological realization of Heidegger's vision of Plato's metaphysics unfolding through the history of technology. A computerized intertextual utopia permitting "an illusion of identity, an ego experience of effortless thought expansion in an infinite field of spatial coordinates free of obstacles," a virtual reality to enter that we "translate ourselves into pure information, where there are no body doubles, no 'defiant enemies,' just infinitely malleable, endlessly reproducible, indefinitely branching 'clones'" (1996:176).

This state of affairs, Levin (1996:179) argues, signals not the end of logocentrism but its apotheosis, reproducing the imaginary structures of classical rationalism (the classical Platonic epistemology, according to which cognition and perception are rigorously counterposed) and the delusions of traditional moral reason, its genderless anonymity making toward an egalitarianism that will finally overcome all differences. Lyotard (1999), however, supports Vattimo's belief that the postmodern world can still be shocked by paralogical, nihilistic incursions, though he agrees with Adorno that the power and indispensability of its technologies make their control urgent for state and Establishment. Like Vattimo, he condemns the illusion of a "transparent society" that lives on because the notion of state and economic control is challenged by the illusion that knowledge and information circulate freely along the same lines as the economy, and work like the "invisible hand" ideal of social integration and justice propagated by capitalist economics, as an ideal resolution of the tension between the freedom and control of information. But he does not agree that the possibility of freedom lies in pluralism itself, because it can be a controlled pluralism. And Foucault argues the contrary thesis to Vattimo's, that the uncontrolled proliferation and circulation of discourses, which is itself what feeds the illusion of a transparent society, can make for more rather than less control. His example in the *History of Sexuality Volume I* is the circulation of the discourse on sexuality in the Victorian age, conventionally regarded as an age of censorship and repression. For Foucault, somewhat like Baudrillard, the more subtle form of control is to encourage the proliferation or excess of discourse and to make it the subject of a science, in this case, as we saw, a *scientia sexualis*, medicalizing it rather than overtly suppressing it. Lyotard, like Foucault, is particularly concerned that Habermas harbors and propagates the ideal of transparent communication so actively. Like Baudrillard, Lyotard believes that open communication based on the ideal of transparency produces not truth or enlightenment but intimidation and "terror." And Foucault attacks the ideal with even more absorbing thoroughness than Lyotard, even if he does not address his attack toward the media specifically, describing it as illusory. Far from being "transparent," Foucault insists, social reality is saturated with power through and through and this, obviously, applies to the way that it is infiltrated by information and its technologies, including the Internet, of course, which, as Levin points out, provides the ultimate illusion of open and transparent communication.

Radical Individualism

Charles Levin (1996:88) has remarked about Baudrillard that since *Symbolic Exchange and Death*, written in 1976, his social world has grown steadily darker—more and more explicitly understood as that core of death, disorganization, or undecidability that he now reads into every human construction. The contrary happened with Foucault, whose last works before his death grew lighter, concerned more with the ethics of freedom than with describing the technologies of oppression. So one expects different ethical and political responses to their respective diagnoses of the learning society from each. For Foucault, the object of genealogy is to uncover the contingency that has made us what we are, to "point out the drawbacks of this society, the ways in which it does *not* allow room for self-creation, for private projects," as Rorty (1989:63) put it, so that we can create ourselves anew and be what we want ourselves to be. A tool designed to give new impetus, as far and wide as possible, to the work of freedom, by revealing to us the contemporary limits under which we labor, the mechanisms of power that subjectify us, and pointing toward projects of freedom that enable us to constitute ourselves meaningfully as autonomous self-creating subjects. Baudrillard's writing shares nothing of this ethical and pedagogical concern, still less any political orientation. Its object is self-destruction, not self-creation. Shifting radically away from its early critical sociological posture, it became assiduously and uncompromisingly grounded *in himself*, in his own personal ambivalence; a "'transcendental immersion,' the hurling of his own discursive self into the abyss" of his future texts (Levin 1996:94).

He responds to the postmodern world by warding off its pieties, "dishing out ironic nonsense," letting his ideas "spin off in a tightening spiral, 'imploding' even their own internal logic" (Levin 1996:26). His general strategy is to "identify with the object, or even become one," with it (Levin 1996:26). To turn his writing, "as in Arthur Danto's definition of art," into "the 'self-consuming artifact'—the 'object'" that "is too useless to be 'recuperated' as a proper commodity." "Actually turning *himself* into a 'bizarre object'" in caricatures that, in his more intimate writings like *America* and *Cool Memories*, "have verged on self-disgust." He describes them as "a kind of 'theory-fiction' where things in the end simply fall apart by themselves," in "a kind of auto-destruction ... not, in any case, a centralization of the arguments" (Levin 1996:27). Influenced by Bataille and Marx's notion of commodity fetishism, he early deduced that social criticism is a form of fetishism that just plays the game of capitalism, and discounted the liberation of desire as a way out, because this is precisely what capitalist consumerism has already obtained in the shape of the mass. It can only lie in the nihilism of self-destruction; in pushing one's self to the limit-scale of meaninglessness and uselessness, becoming one with the object. Passing from fetishism to a strategy of pure seduction, to a fatal strategy, "the game of games," where "the object is considered more cunning, cynical, talented than the subject," as distinct from banal strategy where "the subject still believes himself more cunning than the object" (1990a:181). Fatal strategy is to duplicate the "profound duplicity" of the object; a "voluntary servitude," to "bend willingly" to its purposes (1990a:182). "There is," Baudrillard (1990a:184) insists, "no liberation but this one: in the deepening of negative conditions." This "worsening" (1990a:183), this "difficult and obscure" route of "siding with the object" and taking up its cause, which "threatens absurdity, and runs the risk of what it describes—but the risk is to be taken. The hypothesis of a fatal strategy must itself be fatal, too." Now that "all critical radicality has become useless, now that all negativity seems resolved in a world which pretends to realize itself, and now that the critical spirit has found its home in socialism, and the effects of desire are largely depleted—what remains," he asks, "but to bring things back to their enigmatic ground zero?" (1990a:190). To create a radical challenge internal to theory by sending theoretical approaches "spinning away like tops ... wholly embrac[ing] the movement that animates them ... amplify[ing] their concepts to the maximum, pulling them into the vortex of [their?] own dizziness ... draw[ing] them into an endless spiral" (1990a:125).

Writing as a fatal strategy is a game of illusion and challenge with no point of reference outside itself. Baudrillard is a master illusionist, the card trickster who gambles every time, not knowing how things will turn out. Producing the cards and showing them, then making them disappear and leaving his readers with a sensation of dizziness, playing a game that offers only "perverse" pleasure since there is nothing to be "done" with it; purely narcissistic in that it turns onto itself, and perverse in emphasizing its own self-destruction. Its "liberating logic" is that the struggle for self-affirmation is illusory, and it "is basically understood only by a few" who perceive the nature of our postmodern predicament; namely the total victory of the object (1990a:185). That trying to subvert it is a banal and fruitless exercise. That becoming free is becoming one with the object, turning oneself into pure spectacle, a self-consuming artifact, ecstatically transparent and bizarre and engaged in a permanent cycle of self-destruction; "ecstasy" being "the quality proper to any body that spins until all sense is lost, and then shines forth in its pure empty form" as simulation, as "anti-pedagogy"—the pure and empty form of pedagogy. Just as "anti-theatre is the ecstatic form of theatre: no more stages or scenes, no more content, but theatre in the street, actor-less, theatre of all for all, which even becomes confused with the regular unfolding of our lives without illusion" (1990a:9–10). Anti-politics, the ecstatic form of politics, is a disdain for politics, a nihilistic call to the death of politics just as anti-pedagogy is a disdain for education, a call to its death.

Baudrillard (Gane 1993:64–65) aims his political disdain at the left's yen for self-affirmation: the "leftist, moralizing, revolutionary positions of the seventies," which, he declares, "are finished." Like Derrida and Foucault, he sees no new political position emerging, one that is original and credible. Declaring this to be "the true problem," he denies that his response to it is one of prudence, denegation, passivity, or a retreat into disappointment. It is just not knowing for the moment what type of distance to take "in relation to this new society which has absorbed these margins." He concedes that political ideology, right or left, "will continue all the same to be in the foreground," but it is "a false foreground," operating only "as a system of simulation" (Gane 1993:66). Outworn, it serves only to divide people between good and bad. He describes himself as an example of how one can become its victim: "Nowadays I am taken to be a man of the Right, if not a fascist. Perhaps in objective terms I am on the Right, but I don't give a damn," he goes on defiantly, "I would be finished if I began to take this kind of judgment seriously" (Gane 1993:78). In fact, he really wants no part of politics; "it is no longer worth doing a critique of politics. Let's go somewhere else, to see what is going on elsewhere" (Gane 1993:66). Levin (1996:11) links this view, like Foucault's, with radical libertarian individualism, which is prepared to deal with the possibility that violence is in the human soul. It is deeply suspicious of the attempt to neutralize human aggression by bringing it out into the open, putting it into concrete words or images, processing it in semiotic or symbolic form, revealing the rules by which it plays, and proscribing it except with willing partners. For the radical, liberalism is just a "form of polite bad faith," its institutions and conventions "just an excuse, a rationalization, a cover" to protect individuality at the same time as it renders conviviality possible. What attracts the radical individualist about liberalism, Levin (1996:10–11) contends like Rorty, is what its critics complain about most: namely its inability to produce a collective culture rich enough to encourage solidarity. In a radical liberal utopia, "the myth of a connecting social substance will gradually fade, along with the theology of incorporation, the fantasy that we can escape from ourselves, that we are 'not alone,' because society is 'there for us, waiting.'"

Levin (1996:235) reads poststructuralism politically as a radical liberalism, not as an indictment of the West but as "a salutary rediscovery of its essential values of freedom, of openness for openness' sake: of play." And no one, he claims, has contributed more toward it than Baudrillard, though Rorty sympathizers, for instance, would undoubtedly disagree. But, politically, reading Rorty is not reading Baudrillard. Rorty unequivocally and unambiguously supports Western liberal democracy and declares himself of the left; Baudrillard expresses nothing but contempt for it and locates himself on the right. Besides, Baudrillard's belief that the state has "the power to reverse everything into indifferentiation, including that which denies it" (Levin 1996:39) and that political activism is, therefore, meaningless, echoes not Rorty's optimistic call for an activism that favors reform but Adorno and Horkheimer's stark pessimism. Indeed, as Levin (1996:13) says, Baudrillard is not himself tempted by the radical liberalism he promotes, he "simply drops out of the contemporary political universe," embracing the nihilism of ecstatic denial of the very will to live and writing self-destructively. Predictably, Baudrillard thinks that intellectuals, like constructive writers, are finished because they realize that they can make no social impact, never mind "influence in depth." Their utopian energies came to an end during the seventies, when they were all but used up. Most have since given up, not because their ideas are denied publicity, but because of "an over-circulation of ideas, of the most contradictory ideas, all in the same flux of ideas. What happens is that their specific impact is wiped out" by the media that mediates them. They have become a sort of "media-tape winding forward" (Gane 1993:76–77). Today the intellectual who "sacrifices himself in order to become the mere spokesman of a group or class, [he] is finished" (Gane 1993:80). And this doesn't worry him. "I wouldn't," he reflects, "be against envisaging a world without intellectuals as such. It's a possibility, and perhaps it's pessimistic. It would mean that the social order had eliminated every kind of discourse. On the other hand, it could mean a radiant and transparent world where there is no longer any need for thought, analyses, etc." (Gane 1993:79).

Self-Care and Self-Creation

Such a world, transparent and devoid of power, is, of course, impossible in principle for Foucault, and so is, therefore, the idea of a world devoid of politics. This being the case, the intellectual, in his view, will always be needed to "shake up habitual ways of working and thinking, to dissipate conventional habitualities, to re-evaluate rules and institutions, and starting from their re-problematization, to participate in the formation of a political will" (Fern Haber 1994:79). We have here Foucault's job description for the *specific intellectual*, as he represented himself to be. Otherwise, he says, people should be allowed "the possibility of self-determination and the choice of their own existence" (Fern Haber 1994:79). Contrary to what some critics say, Foucault does not believe that we are ever "trapped" by power (Gordon 1980:141–142).[112] All relations of power, he argues, imply the possibility of resistance, for if there were no possibility of resistance— of violent resistance, of escape, of ruse, of strategies that reverse the situation—then, he says, there would be no relations of power. His central task, over the years he worked on power, was "to create a history of the different modes by which, in our culture, human beings are made subjects" (Dreyfus & Rabinow 1983:7), which, we recall, included "ethical" practices, or "techniques of the self" by which the individual turns himself or herself into a subject of analysis through the operation of "something like a well-formed conscience." Practices of relations to self, that is, in which one is called upon to take oneself as an object of knowledge and a field of action, so as to transform, correct, and purify oneself, and find salvation. The job of education, Foucault says, is not, as Kant (and

MacIntyre, as we saw earlier) had suggested, "to discover what we are," but, as Nietzsche had countersuggested, "to refuse what we are," in order to promote "new forms of subjectivity" (Dreyfus & Rabinow 1983:216) that are authentically *ours* through the work of ethics (Dreyfus & Rabinow 1983:210) or "care for self."[113]

This is an ethics that he finds at work not in the modern world but in antiquity. But we can learn from it nevertheless, because the ethical questions of today are posed in the same terms as they were posed in antiquity, when the Greeks first, then the Romans, responded to them by seeking new kinds of subjectivity *from* and *within* experience, with the difference that for the ancients, there was no problematization of the constitution of the self as subject then as there is today, thanks to our modern experience. Moral experience, for them, was the experience of self-mastery. And this is how, pronouncing himself dissatisfied with today's account of moral experience as essentially centered on the subject, Foucault thinks we should experience it today, though he denies that he is presenting antiquity as a model for imitation in this respect. "You can't," he says, "find the solution of a problem in the solution of another problem raised at another moment by other people" (Dreyfus & Rabinow 1983:231). And anyway, the care for self on which the Greek notion of self-mastery was based was constructed within a "virile society with slaves, in which women were underdogs," and where the "dissymmetry, exclusion of the other, and obsession with penetration" was, as he put it, "quite disgusting" (Dreyfus & Rabinow 1983:233). Still, the Greek model does suggest valuable things to us. Foucault describes how it was subverted by the time of early Christian asceticism, when the precept to "take care of yourself" was supplanted by the equally ancient, related precept to "know yourself," and how Western moral thought and modern theoretical philosophy from Descartes to Husserl came subsequently to prioritize the notion of the self as a thinking subject.

Alcibiades I provides an early philosophical elaboration of the practice of "care for self." Plato sets out four problems that it raises and that were to recur through antiquity: (1) the proper relation between being occupied with oneself and political activity; (2) the proper relation between being occupied with oneself and pedagogy; (3) the proper relation between concern for oneself and knowledge of oneself; and (4) the proper relation between care of self and philosophical love, or the relation to a master. Foucault describes how writing became an important part of the culture of self-care; how the self became a theme to write about and how this involved taking notes on oneself, writing treatises and letters, keeping notebooks and eventually keeping a diary, thus creating a relationship also with self-vigilance. And how, once these practices lost their original link with politics and lifelong education in Hellenistic and early Roman times, they came to be related to a "medical" instead of a "pedagogical" model, associated with a culture of silence, of listening and reflecting on truth from outside, and of listening to the self within, instead of with dialogue and speaking as had previously been the case. Foucault tells how they lost their lifelong character by adopting Stoic techniques of examination of conscience, self-disclosure through letters, and the interpretation of dreams that related to old age and to the process of completion of life. How self-examination became concerned with thought rather than with action, with scrutiny rather than review, with sorting out the good from the bad, and with the present.

Foucault describes how Christianity—as a confessional religion of self-disclosure and exposure through penitence with strongly ritualistic and symbolic, theatrical elements—brought further important changes to this practice of self-examination. Monasticism, in particular, added two important principles of spirituality to it borrowed from the Stoics but understood very differently; those of obedience and contemplation, so that self-examination and care for self came to be subordinated to obedience and required the permanent verbalization of thought through the instrument of confession. Monasticism marked the beginning of the Christian hermeneutics of the self, with its deciphering of inner thoughts, implying that there is something hidden within us and that we are always in a state of self-illusion. It created, Foucault contends, the basis for the modern "hermeneutics of suspicion" as Paul Ricour refers to it, a "deep hermeneutics" Foucault himself shares, that "holds that actors do not have direct access to the meaning of their discourse and practices, that our everyday understanding of things is superficial and distorted" (Dreyfus & Rabinow 1983:123). It is not difficult to see how these Christian practices prepare the way for the modern practices of self-examination and self-confession that Foucault describes in his other genealogical works, with their related economies. The notion of self-examination as the deciphering of one's inner thoughts encourages the notion of a self that is there as text awaiting an authentic reading rather than one that has to be made in practice, as Foucault himself views it. Like Nietzsche, Foucault, in fact, speaks of a self that is constantly *made*, not discovered. This is why he connects the ethics of self-care "with the practice of creativity—and not of authenticity." We have, he says, "to create ourselves as works of art" in different ways including, if this is the case, through the activity of writing. Derrida (Derrida & Ewald 1995:290) similarly describes his writing as *experience*, "a word which means all at once crossing, journey and ordeal," and contrasts it with authoring a philosophy. And he describes experience as preference; "not a preference which I prefer, but the preference within which I find myself inscribed, and which gives body to the decision or the singular responsibility without which there would be no morals, no rights, no politics." Foucault echoes these views, denying his own authorial status and referring to his own writing as experience in similar terms, as something whose outcome is uncertain from the beginning and remains so until the end, something that "you come out of changed" (1991b:27). This *making* of the self through writing is to be contrasted with writing as a mode of self-disclosure or confession. He identifies Nietzsche, Bataille, Blanchot, and Klossowski, writers who "didn't have the problem of constructing systems, but of having direct, personal experiences," as those who influenced his thinking in this respect (1991b:30). In an interview with Catherine Porter he also contended that "the key to the personal poetic attitude of a philosopher is not to be sought in his ideas, as if it could be deduced from them, but rather in his philosophy-as-life, in his philosophical life, his *ethos*"(Rabinow 1984:374), his "manner of being" a philosopher (Rabinow 1984:377). This is what, as we shall see, he also thought about being a citizen.

Critics like Blake, Smeyers, Smith, and Standish (1998:64) remark that with this orientation toward an ethic of self-care and self-creation, "the intersubjective relationship as a focus of ethics seems to have evaporated, or at least lost its importance" for Foucault, making him a complete narcissist. This is not correct. In Vol. 3 of *The History of Sexuality* (*The Care of the Self*) he describes how the ethics of self-care that followed the Hellenistic and Roman world did indeed become related "to the 'private' aspects of existence, to the values of personal conduct, and to the interest that people focused on themselves" (1990:41) and how its demand for rigorous discipline over oneself coincided with a weakening of the political and social framework of people's lives. He questions the orthodox thesis that this individualism grew out of the increasing necessity for self-reliance in a world that had suddenly become distant and anonymous, describing ancient societies broadly as "societies of promiscuity, where existence was led 'in public,'" and individuals "situated within strong systems of local relationships, family ties, economic dependence, and relations of patronage and friendship." And points out that even the doctrines that were most attached to austerity of conduct—the Stoic, for instance—insisted on the respect of one's obligations to others, whether humankind in general, one's fellow citizens, or one's family, and "were quickest to denounce an attitude of laxity and self-satisfaction in practices of social withdrawal" (1990:42). He refers to a Socratic strand of "individualism" in the modern world that promotes an active cultivation of the self, subsidiary to the care for the self, that is social, and that is the proper object of philosophy because it is meant to be reflected upon, developed, and taught. It requires different kinds of exchanges and communications between people, and at times even institutions and communities (1990:45), where the task of tutoring others or acting as their counselor, or even spiritual guide, is regarded as a duty (1990:51). This conception of self-care, Foucault tells us, was originally conditioned to a great extent by the changing sociocultural and political climate, by changes in the political game, which, with the advance into the modern world, concerned a far more extensive and complex field of power relations than the past, and made the problematizing of political activity essential. Such that it could not be responded to with a simple decision between participation or withdrawal, although it may often have been presented in this form.

In distinguishing the "conversion to self" that care for self signified in this context from the self-devotion of the narcissist, and describing it as an objective one sets oneself, a path to oneself in which one escapes all dependencies and enslavements but not one's social and political responsibilities, Foucault describes the path he chose for himself. A shift in the ethics of self-mastery, "a change of orientation, a difference in emphasis," (1990:67) that was marked, yes, by a certain narcissism, by a sense of one's delight in oneself "as a thing one both possesses and has before one's eyes" (1990:65), but not that of the aesthete, the recluse, or the political dropout, even if one recognizes that politics is a "game of violence, excess, rebellion, and combat," which encourages such reactions (1990:67). To the contrary, it requires "an intensification of social relations" (1990:53), the weakening of the self that Nietzsche suggested in his later work, where the accent of combat is placed more on self-protection than assertion, and is never guided by the will to dominate (1990:67). And this is how Foucault himself understands self-care, as a practice of creative freedom but also as an intensification of social relations in which care is extended to others who are helped to care for themselves. He states this explicitly: "The care of the self is ethical in itself; but it implies complex relationships with others insofar as this ethos of freedom is also a way of caring for others ... the problem of relationships with others is present throughout the development of the care of the self." His interlocutor in this interview I am quoting from suggested that maybe he meant that "The care of self always aims for the well-being of others; it aims to manage the space of power that exists in all relationships, but to manage it in a non-authoritarian manner." Foucault concurs and goes on to describe "the particular position of the philosopher" as "the man who cares about the care of others." Not one, however, he adds quickly, who puts such care before care for self. To the contrary, "the care of the self is ethically prior in that the relationship with oneself is ontologically prior." Or to put it more simply, one must first care for oneself before one can properly care for others. "A city in which everybody took proper care of himself," Foucault (1997:287) concluded in "The Ethics of the Concern for Self as a Practice of Freedom," "would be a city that functioned well and found in this the ethical principle of its permanence."

Foucaultian Politics and the Specific Intellectual

This is not a conclusion that either today's neoliberals or new social democrats would quarrel with. But, of course, Foucault, as we have seen, understands care of self very differently from mere self-dependence and the individualization of responsibility, and even more from the care of self that produces the self-fulfillment of consumerism, of having. He understands it in the sense of the ethics of strong self-mastery just described, its self-creative narcissism very different from Baudrillard's self-destructive narcissism, and from Rorty's self-creative privatism. In the political sphere Foucault, as Rorty points out, would have us suspicious of the discourse of justice and democracy in our liberal democracies, and of their institutions. On the other hand, as he tells Chomsky, he is not interested in theorizing justice or democracy in some other way. Justice, he tells us, is a good political invention for those interested in conserving political and economic power, but not for those who are more interested in seeing it dispersed. Though he rarely, if ever, spoke or wrote about it again after his exchange on the subject with Chomsky, one can read into his ethics, if one wishes, a notion of justice as a non-oppressive and non-manipulative governance of the self and others, and a notion of injustice in discourse as blocked. But he nowhere calls this management of power just himself. He was also concerned that no voice is demeaned or excluded, and that the vested interests of the powerful are restrained as much as possible (Caputo 1987:261), but he did not call this justice either.

Dewey and Habermas regard democracy as a game of truth, openness, and transparency, a "conduit of consent—and thus, ideally, of consensus—and a guarantee of a rational politics, a politics that represents rather than dominates" (Seitz 1995:115), its power "borrowed" from the sovereign people by representatives. Foucault, however, as Brian Seitz (1995:115) argues, renders this account of representation and the "communication" of consensus problematic in different ways.[114] His thesis is that "practices of communication are forms of production," they are never neutral; "what the political subject is, is not independent of the various networks of 'information' and 'communication,' but is to a large extent produced by it." There is, then, no public opinion formulated independently of "the multi-faceted machinery of representation, which, again, is not just instrumental; it is itself connected to history, economy, and technology, particularly the 'technology of speed' that lies at the heart of the postmodern society" (1995:125). "The people," as such, do not express any will or consent, and the notion of the people's sovereignty is vacuous. From a Foucaultian perspective, democratic government should be understood independently of any fiction of a will of the people. As Seitz says, it requires us to approach the procedural rules of democracy themselves with suspicion, and to keep them under careful scrutiny and in contention. Seitz (1995:5), from his Foucaultian standpoint, contests the way the problem of representation is posed: "how to translate the originary political subject into a consolidating, effective, *true* representative, or, more simply, how to get government 'to stand in the place of' the people in order to accurately reflect or express society." We should, he says, rid ourselves of the idea of a political subject (who or what a political discourse is about) with an "originary consciousness that simply uses representation as an instrument—uses it well or poorly—in order to achieve certain fundamentally rational ends." As Foucault teaches us, "there is no subject independent of the different discourses to which it belongs" (Seitz 1995:8). Once we accept this, the way is open to explore "the possibility that the discursive and practical mechanisms of political representation produce this political subject at the same time that they produce a representative of it" (Seitz 1995:5).

The political subject of democracy, from a Foucaultian perspective, is numbers, not a mythical "will of the people" or a "general will," and since in a modern democracy the numbers are multiple and divided, it is "conflictual in nature rather than, ultimately, consensually constituted." So that the proper way of describing how its political will is produced is as "a form of warfare, and if its conflicts ever cease, democracy will be dead" (Seitz 1995:13). Put more plainly, it is conflict, not consent, that produces the democratic subject, from a Foucaultian viewpoint. The dynamics of the representative democracy are the expression of ongoing conflict rather than those of a developing reason. Understood in this way, democratic representation is seen not as a kind of relation but as an ongoing self-reflexive process incorporating various kinds of power emanating from many different sources and, rather than speak of a political polity, it makes sense to speak of different polities. In this sense, power in a democracy, from a Foucaultian viewpoint, "is better characterized as dispersed rather than as fundamentally hierarchical (this includes the inverted hierarchy of democratic power, the pyramid turned upside down)," one that "incorporates and constitutes itself through a multiplicity of processes of dissemination" (Seitz 1995:134). And the democratic will is better thought of not as a pluralism actively pursuing consensus but as "a more conflictually conceived diversity of voices at war with one another, voices marked and legitimated as number" (Seitz 1995:148), its dynamics a "dynamics of power, of multiple, clashing powers," a "dynamics of war" (Seitz 1995:153) than as a progressive effect of developing reason. "Public opinion" does not exist outside "the technological *topos* in which it gets aired (a *topos* that is never entirely controlled, despite the maintenance forces continually at work there)." Seitz (1995:160) argues that "it is in the production of 'information' that the political subject gets produced, at least the one we associate with public opinion, with 'the people.'" And this confirms and adds strength to the maximalist view that such production is "a significant dimension of the process of education," of the learning society (1995:161).

Within this approach to politics as essentially dispersed and combative, Foucault describes the role of *specific intellectuals* active "within specific sectors, at the precise points where their own conditions of life and work situate them (housing, the hospital, the asylum, the laboratory, the university, family and sexual relations)," (Gordon 1980:126) as against *universal intellectuals* acting as "the consciousness/conscience of us all," and raising the consciousness of the masses (Language Counter-Memory). Unlike Baudrillard, Foucault does not feel happy working with concept of the mass, since his concern is to do justice to the complex localized, particular, and concrete struggles that ordinary people engage in in the course of their everyday lives, and that are located in the capillaries of the lifeworld, where, he believes, politics can be effective. Like Kundera, Baudrillard, and others he believes that the time of the universal intellectual is up anyway. In an interview with Fontana and Pasquino (Gordon 1980), he describes the growth of a new breed of intellectuals after World War II: technicians, magistrates, teachers, functionaries of the state or capital, technologists, scientists, and professionals within it whose roles became politicized through their growing participation (beginning with the nuclear scientists after World War II) in political debate and public affairs. How the category of intellectual, traditionally derived from the figure of the jurist or notable, was broadened in the process to include the savant or expert, and how the latter's power grew with the extension of technoscientific structures in the economic and strategic domain. How the former, the "writer of genius" and "rhapsodist of the eternal" who opposed injustice in state and administration, was replaced by the latter, the "absolute savant" at the service of state and administration, a "strategist of life and death," in the game of biopower (Gordon 1980:129).[115] It is against this expert that Foucault counterposes his specific intellectual, who is at the service of ordinary people, not of the state or administration, whereas Habermas continues to dream of reinstating the universal intellectual.

The dangers that would neutralize the specific intellectual's contribution to politics, Foucault says, are those of being entirely theoretical and abstract, or being manipulated by the political parties or trade unions that already control much of public life. Or, being completely isolated from public life and ignored. Thus, apart from her engagement in specific issues, she should not fight shy of the general issue of "that regime of truth which is so essential to the structure and functioning of our society" (Gordon 1980:132). Here she struggles not "on behalf" of or against some ideological rendering of the truth in science or politics, against "error or illusion, alienated conscience or ideology," or to change people's views, "what's in their heads," or, even less, to emancipate truth from every system of power, which is impossible, but "truth itself" in its circular "relationship" with power (Gordon 1980:133). It is "about the status of truth and the economic and political role it plays" in our everyday lives that the intellectual speaks (Gordon 1980:132), her object "detaching the power of truth from the forms of hegemony ... within which it operates at the present time" (Gordon 1980:133). The intellectual challenges the political, economic, and institutional regime of the production of truth, and ascertains the possibility of constituting a new politics of truth that is not hegemonic. Her task is "to sap the power, to take the power, it is an activity conducted alongside those who struggle for power, and not their illumination from a safe distance" (1980:207). *Alongside* is important. It denies the ownership of the struggle to the intellectual and calls up the image of comradeship and solidarity, which, his critics think, Foucault's politics precludes. Specific intellectuals speak for or on behalf of no one in general; the proletariat, the poor, women, the human race, the abused other. They speak for no one but themselves. Foucault, Deleuze says, is one who teaches us about "the indignity of speaking for others" (1980:209).

"I have a dream," Foucault himself says, "of an intellectual who destroys self-evidence and universalities, who locates and points out in the inertias and constraints of the present the weak points, the openings, the lines of stress; who constantly displaces himself, not knowing exactly where he'll be nor what he'll think tomorrow, because he is too attentive to the present" (Peters 1996:57). This is his idea of the specific intellectual. Not one who is the purveyor of truth or the articulator of utopian aspirations (the intellectual's or someone else's), or part of an avant-garde of freedom or humanity, nor the supreme strategist of an emancipatory movement, but one who plays a freewheeling role in the tactics of resistance, making temporary alliances with others when required but constantly moving her site of action to wherever a worthy cause emerges. This was an ideal he tried to embody in his own life and that explains his resistance to political labels, left or right. Foucault regarded this ideal as the height of responsibility and modeled it on the figure of the *parrhesiastes*, who speaks frankly on all occasions—especially those that are dangerous and involve risk to oneself. *Parrhesia* is primarily a specific relationship to oneself; choosing to live as "a truth-teller rather than as a living being who is false to himself" (2001:17). The object of the *parrhesiastes* is not to demonstrate the truth to someone else but to be critical, to tell someone where one has gone wrong. One obviously speaks as a *parrhesiastes* from a position of inferior power, otherwise there is no risk in what one says or danger to oneself. At the same time, the *parrhesiastes* is usually one who is educated, since she needs to know her own status within the discourse. Finally, the last characteristic of *parrhesia* is that truth-telling is regarded as a duty; the *parrhesiast* is always free to be silent but chooses to speak instead.

In the Greek democracy, where one had to be a citizen in order to speak, what one risked in speaking the truth was the displeasure of the majority. In the Greek context, this often meant exile.

> To summarize the foregoing, *parrhesia* is a kind of verbal activity where the speaker has a specific relation to truth through frankness, a certain relationship to his own life through danger, a certain type of relationship to himself or to other people through criticism (self-criticism or criticism of other people), and a specific relation to moral law through freedom and duty. More precisely, *parrhesia* is a verbal activity in which a speaker expresses his personal relationship to truth, and risks his life because he recognizes truth telling as a duty to improve or help other people (as well as himself). (Foucault 2001:19)

The obvious technique typical of this verbal activity is the dialogue, and the most evident model of the *parrhesiastes* is, of course, Socrates. Foucault goes on to say "that *parrhesia* was a guideline for democracy as well as an ethical and personal attitude characteristic of the good citizen" (2001:22). The Athenian constitution guaranteed *isegoria* (the equal right of speech), *isonomia* (the equal participation of all citizens in the exercise of power), and *parrhesia*, which occurred between citizens as individuals and between citizens in an assembly, so that it also appeared in the *agora* (2001:22). With Socrates, of course, the link is made between *parrhesia*, philosophy (regarded, as Foucault also regarded it, as the art of life), and care for self which, again, as Socrates warned Alcibiades, is the necessary prerequisite for one willing to take the responsibility of caring for others.

Foucault's attitude toward the modern liberal state resembled MacIntyre's in that, though he did not approve of it, he was prepared to acknowledge the social improvements it has achieved over the years. May (1994:7) describes him as a weak anarchist, distinguishing weak anarchism from political philosophical approaches that are *formal* (dealing with "ought" questions and exploring the tension between what is and what ought to be, and regarding any recourse to history as irrelevant), and *strategic* (which asks the eminently practical question raised by "that classical political strategist Vladimir Ilyich Lenin: 'What is to be done?'"), take history seriously, and reject any demarcation between doing political philosophy and devising political programs. The strategic approach holds that "all problems can be reduced to the basic one; justice is a matter of solving the basic problem" (1994:10) and pictures the world "as a set of concentric circles, with the core or basic problematic lying at the center, and the derivative problematics surrounding it at various distances" (1994:11). Tactical anarchism resists this reducibility and the model of structured concentric circles. For a tactical anarchist like Foucault there is no one center of power; power is disseminated everywhere, "consequently politics are irreducible" to a focused strategy by a vanguard group, party, or movement (1994:11). This is not to say that there are no concentrations of power, places, sites where it intersects, but these are sites where it conglomerates rather than originates, dangerous sites that attract suspicion, where the tactics of resistance and dispersion may be demanded. Foucault, May says, shares this political outlook with Deleuze and Lyotard. Derrida, in his view (and mine also), "remains without a clearly articulated political philosophy" (1994:12). Baudrillard, on the other hand, is a strategic thinker, whose "thought tends toward the reductionist and comprehensive rather than the multiple and the local" (1994:12). May does not mention Rorty, but his politics, as we also saw in the previous chapter, are tactical like Foucault's, though aimed not at resistance but at reform.

As a tactical anarchist, Foucault (May 1994:51) rejects the "top"-"bottom" imagery with which strategic thinking approaches power, especially the idea of the state as top-down government by a minority over the masses. He sees "intersecting networks of power rather than a hierarchy." Moreover, the repressive relations tactical anarchists address are not only at the economic and state level but the epistemological, psychological, linguistic, sexual, religious, and ethical, as well (May 1994:94). Finally, they do not presume connections of power but discover them by political analysis. May (1994:55) goes on to identify tactical anarchism with "federalism"; the view that "in any area of social life, there has to be a balance between, on the one hand, the power of individuals and small groups to decide their lives and, on the other, the fact that these decisions affect and are affected by the social context in which they are made." The question the tactical anarchist asks "is how to keep power from being delegated to representatives while still accomplishing the larger tasks that social life requires." Acting on a fundamental distinction between political and administrative powers, federalism holds that political decisions should be made directly by those affected by them, not by representatives or surrogates, while administrative decisions, where no one speaks in anybody's name or acts on anybody's behalf, can be left to boards, committees, and so on. The distinction between political and administrative power, as May points out, is not really so hard and fast (anarchists, in fact, are typically suspicious of both), but the point federalism wants to make is that, as much as possible, power is to stay with those who must bear its effects.

May distinguishes different articulations of federalist thought in anarchist literature; as blueprints, however vague, for a new society; as suggestions for alternative arrangements; or for the tactical interventions in specific sectors of the social network favored by tactical anarchism, which is genealogical and recognizes the productivity of power. While it engages in micropolitics, tactical anarchism has two views about political conduct at the macrolevel: that the practices of institutions often emerge from local practices, and that when they do, the local practices that generated them do not become a mere corollary or auxiliary aspect of them, but enter into a complex relationship with them (1994:98). Thus, while tactical anarchists like Foucault and Deleuze regard macropolitics as founded on micropolitics and recognize that understanding the former requires understanding the latter, they also recognize that this does not mean that the former is simply the latter writ large. The two they regard as irreducible both upward and downward: "Everything is political, but every politics is simultaneously a macro-politics and a micro-politics" (1994:100). Their point is that, though the two necessarily interact and must be understood together, it would be a mistake to view them as sharing identical structures. Finally, May (1994:112) summarizes the general guidelines to political action offered by Foucault, Lyotard, and Deleuze to "include the call for social, personal, and political experimentation, the expansion of situated freedom, the release of subjected discourses and genres, and the limitation and reorientation of the role of the intellectual." They are the same guidelines offered by Rorty, naturally in a different political spirit.

Foucault, the Learning Society, and Education

Marshall (Ball 1990:7) believes that "the methodological imperative" that emerges from Foucault's work is "to examine processes of modern power in modern schools." Not so. If a "methodological imperative" does come across to us in Foucault's work, it is to examine processes of power *in postmodern learning societies in general* in order to determine what work of freedom and education is possible within them both in the private and the public sphere.[116] The former through the work of self-mastery as we interact with others in our informal relationships with them, and, in the more intimate sphere, through our ethical and aesthetic care for ourselves as transgressive self-creating poets, the latter through the equally transgressive outlook of *parrhesia*. Foucault tells us, like all the poststructuralists, to forget about theorizing a utopian learning society of the future and to wake up to the nature of present societies as *de facto* learning societies, societies that mobilize learning in different ways. He tells us, in particular, to forget the ideal of a truly rational learning society or public transparent and free from power where information circulates openly, aspired for by liberal modernists, as a dangerous pipe dream with totalitarian implications. At the end of the day the postmodern learning society he describes is not so different from that described by the Frankfurt theorists. Like Adorno and Horkheimer he was much impressed by the battery of technologies of containment at the disposal of the liberal-capitalist state, by its efficiency in absorbing conflicts or crises, or significant challenges to its power and security. Only, though he was not optimistic like Rorty he was not pessimistic about its future like the Frankfurt theorists either.

A Foucaultian concern with the learning society would be one with its micropolitics, with the circulation of learning and its relation with power/knowledge lifewide in all its sites; in all its veins, arteries and capillaries, its pressure points in particular, in how it happens in the streets, the shop, the neighborhood, the home, the marketplace, the workplace, apart from the school and the university, but also the prison, the barrack, the asylum, the clinic, the hospital, and so on. In short, wherever there are relations between people that are always, in all cases, relations of learning, pedagogical relations, just as they are always relations of power. This concern with the lifewide manifestations of power and learning coincides with that of the lifelong education writers, with their maximalist model of the learning society. Enjoining us to look at lifewide learning relationships from the angle of power, Foucault cautions us against blanket optimistic messages like Dewey's, that living together educates. While insisting that living together is living relationships of power, he reminds us that not all agendas of power are agendas of education; many are agendas of domination, suppression, or manipulation, and that we should approach them all, all learning agendas, with care and suspicion. Apart from the fact that he introduces the dimension of power into lifewide learning, or "living together," Foucault's particular interest in its "negative" institutional sites associated with the correction of abnormality in different behavioral forms—criminal, immature, ignorant, mad, and so on—draws our attention to a side of the learning society that is rarely, if ever, considered by those who write about it: its corrective institutions. He also suggests that experiments in systems, technologies, and practices of learning tried out at these sites find their way into other sectors of society and that we should be alert and sensitive to this fact. In fact, he makes the even more startling claim that their learning regimes are not really that much different in essence from those at work in other institutionalized settings that we tend to regard positively, like schools and universities. What a Foucaultian approach to the learning society suggests also is that one should be concerned not simply with its social spaces but with the *physical* also, with the positioning of bodies within physical spaces and with their architecture as well. That these, and not just the practices that go on within it, are also crucial to the character of the learning society.

What Dewey meant by "living together educates," of course, was that living with others helps us grow personally and socially, and he shared Foucault's view that where it stunts growth, where the power to learn is blocked and does not circulate freely, living together does not educate. Growth, as we saw, was Dewey's operational definition of education. For his normative definition he turned to the typically human potential of creativity; to change the world, one's circumstances, to be active in reconstructing one's life and one's society as a participative citizen in a democracy. Foucault's operational definition is different—education for him requires the genealogical deconstruction of experience that permits us to constantly *recreate* ourselves anew, rather than *reconstruct* ourselves in an ongoing way. Foucault wants us to be suspicious, not optimistic, of our enculturation, even if it appears to offer us the power of agency, freedom, and control of our lives. He wants us to aim for self-mastery and to value the knowledge of ourselves that comes from the genealogical practice of telling the truth about oneself, about what one is, how one is made by the different regimes of power/knowledge to which one is subjected, as indispensable to one's unfolding project of freedom. Self-mastery is shown by the way we care for ourselves, govern our lives privately and our relations with others, and, therefore, also, by the way we govern others and the way we acknowledge our governance by others. Ethically, a society "in which everyone took proper care of himself" is how Foucault would see a learning society. To repeat a point made earlier, care for self as he intended it is not, however, to be confused with the philosophy of self-dependence encouraged by the neoliberal and the new social democrat and reproduced in the lifelong learning literature: the economic self-dependence of an indulged consumer in a learning society conceived as a learning market. Foucault instigates us to regard this kind of discourse of self-dependence as a trap and to see it for what it is, a "technique of the self" with a hidden agenda, a subtle aspect of a self-discipline that is imposed on us and that we need to challenge with the ethical project of self-mastery that is the true project of freedom.

The Foucaultian citizen who practices self-mastery feels responsible for and is responsive to the other, not in a generic sense as a universal other (some group, category, social class, gender, or the whole of humanity), but an identifiable other, an individual or individuals, with a face and name, especially when the other is subjected to specific forms of violence. Then the citizen speaks against the violence, lending not just her voice but her physical action to the protest also. As a citizen she speaks the truth against violence; as a specific intellectual she speaks for the truth, particularly in situations that are dangerous to herself. This is how she "absorbs the power." "It seems to me," Foucault said, "that 'what is to be done' ought not to be determined from above by reformers be they prophetic or legislative, but by a long work of comings and goings, of exchanges, reflections, trials, different analyses" (Fern Haber 1994:95). In short, pragmatically in the course of doing things by those involved in doing them. "And it is because of the need not to tie down ... or immobilize," with a theory, he concluded, "that there can be no question for me of trying to [say] 'what is to be done'" (Fern Haber 1994:95). There is a sense of indignity that anyone who is not already dehumanized beyond any conception of self-dignity experiences at the suggestion, "I shall speak for you," even if it is meant to reassure one, to set one's mind at rest that one is being spoken for. There is a kind of arrogance in assuming that one can speak, indeed that one has the right to speak, on behalf of others. One can never properly speak for anyone but oneself. Care for the other ought to mean empowering the other to speak, where empowerment is, as Habermas suggests, connected with "the idea of the undisabled subject" rather than with emancipation. And the way this is done is not, or not principally, pedagogically, by *teaching* the other to speak, though this will be appropriate where the relation with the other is that of master or teacher, but socially, by attacking the causes, the systems and practices, that prevent the other from speaking, that block the circulation of discourse and constitute themselves as disabling to the other. This does not mean, of course, that there are not (as MacIntyre points out, and as we well know) those in society for whom, because of their particular condition, their disability, speaking for themselves is temporarily or maybe permanently impossible. But even with them one does not do them the indignity of speaking *for* them, one speaks the truth of their condition; the pain, the humiliation, they suffer.

The Foucaultian citizen regards the game of democracy, as I wrote earlier, as a game of combat and struggle, and her political education is, therefore, an initiation into the arts, skills, and norms of fair combat; i.e., a Nietzschean kind of combat that, while it does not disguise the will to power, is uninterested in the conclusive defeat and assimilation of the other and interested rather in keeping power dispersed and differences alive. Similarly, for Foucault the self is a site of combat and resistance rather than growth and reconstruction. Foucault emphasizes that when we stop thinking of the self in a Cartesian way we can start to acknowledge that that site is a body also and not a mere mind or intellect. That the disciplinary practices of modern-postmodern institutions are inscribed quite as much on the body as they are on the mind. And that, therefore, the body must be as much at issue as the mind when the self is called in question and self-creation cited as an ideal. We need to see how we are situated physically in our world, in the learning society, by the different configurations of power with which we intersect. The world we inhabit is, after all, just as much a physical world, a world of physical sites and spaces (as I remarked earlier) as it is a social world. The other way in which we are situated in our world is through discourse. Parlo Singh (1995) cites Davies's and Harre's argument that people's understanding and experience of social identity is constructed through discourse, so that using the metaphor of an unfolding narrative, the self is best seen as fluidly located within different discourses, rather than as a stable *telos*. This is, of course, the poststructuralist view also. In this sense, the Foucaultian self lives and grows in a tension between self-governance, or mastery, and the transgressiveness that goes both with the politics of resistance and the ethics of self-creation. There is no question in Foucault's conception of things, any more than in Rorty's, that the tension can be resolved with one's membership in some public. The technologies of communication and dialogue in which the self is produced, whether of institutional practices or informal publics, are, for Foucault, always technologies of power/knowledge. From a Foucaultian perspective, the parameters of one's association with others are set not by an accommodating mutuality but by rules of governance, which are rules of struggle and accommodation. Thus, the Foucaultian self, like the Nietzschean self, must learn to live dangerously without the reassurance of a public if it is to be truly free.

The link Foucault makes between autonomy and self-government or mastery is evidently Kantian, but given a Nietzschean twist so that it begins with self-refusal; with rejecting what we are in order to actively consider what we are not as a possibility. In this sense it starts narcissistically, with an active problematizing of one's own existence as a product of social forces, in relationship with others. But the self its produces, as Nietzsche also taught us, is a self weakened ethically by its relationships with others. Relationships governed not just by the negative principle of non-domination and non-assimilation, but by the positive principle of undisabling others. This, in turn, permits a solidarity with them that arises wherever we perceive them to be subjected to relations of governance that dominate, oppress, or exploit. The sentiment arises not from selflessness, nor, as Rorty described it, from one's imaginative ability to see others as "one of us," of some collective entity, or from identification with their suffering, but from seeing them as "part of me," part of my project of self-care and affirmation, and, therefore, also as an obligation or duty for me. Thus, while in Rorty's sense we experience a sense of solidarity with other only to the extent that we experience their pain, for Foucault we recognize it as part of the essential sociality of our own being. Finally, while by affirming the difference between enculturation (the disciplining of the subject, the process involved in its subjectification) and individuation (as a project of freedom founded in care of self and self-creation), Foucault reclaims education and agency (rather than destroys their meaning as his critics have charged). He does not believe, any more than does Rorty, that we can become individuals without enculturation, without a point of reference. Our education begins when we become sensitive to the historicity and contingency of that point of reference, and are ready to resist its hegemony on us who it has rendered its subjects.

The fact that Foucault regards education in this way, as the work of freedom won in revolt against how one has been produced by others, evidently renders it "dangerous" in the eyes of those who enjoy hegemonic power over us, since it threatens them with the subversion of their power. But this is what the game of education is about in Foucault's eyes. Rorty—who shares this view that education is subversive and also links it with self-creation, an emphasis on individuality rather than its assimilation into a public—blunts the danger by insisting that, like philosophy, it has to do only with our aloneness and not with any political purposes. Politically I have distinguished Foucault and Baudrillard from the other post-structuralists—Derrida, Lyotard, Vattimo, and Rorty—who see their politics in some way as being of the left. Foucault, as we saw, denies himself a specific political location. Though his early militancy was radically leftist, he held no lingering nostalgia for the left later moving entirely out of the political game of left and right, though not, like Baudrillard, out of the game of politics as such. He renounced only established affiliations and positionings and pledged himself to *parrhesia* and to tactical resistance in alliance with others of repressive or manipulative relations of power where they appear in the polis, in the learning society, as his political work. Though interested in government, to the extent that he defines all political and ethical relations as forms, styles, practices, of government, of self and of others, his tactical anarchism and his philosophical disposition precludes him from coming up with any positive *theory* of government of the learning society. As a political activist concerned with repressive and manipulative concentrations of power, he was particularly attentive to the silent and intimidated, the discursively disabled for whom he struggled to create spaces within which they could speak. Otherwise, his attitude toward the state and its institutions, and toward official power in general, was, as we saw, like MacIntyre's, one of suspicion and selective collaboration. This seems to me to be a far more coherent and concrete approach to politics in our times than Derrida's romantic utopianism or any project to reconstitute Habermas's democratic public sphere or MacIntyre's educated publics.

Our experience of contemporary Western society today echoes the panopticon image Foucault conveys to us as the state, armed with advanced digital and camera technologies and sophisticated data banks, brings us under ever closer scrutiny and intrudes ever more into our lives. In short, the panopticon society is a reality that is not hard to detect as we look around us in today's world. Political events following the September 11 attack on New York, justifying the so-called "war against terror" and the heightened state of tension caused by the anticipation of further terrorist attacks, have given the postmodern state the perfect excuse to strengthen its surveillance technologies and assume intrusive powers into the lives of its citizens to a degree unprecedented in modern democratic societies. As the cry goes up for more efficient and effective surveillance against terrorism and subversion, to add to that for the more efficient and effective management of information and human resources for our knowledge-based societies and economies, the panopticon features of our societies grow ever stronger. Foucault's "imperative" is not just to examine those features, but to *unmask* the workings of power/ knowledge that they hide. The way they work also as learning societies; the hidden way in which the politics of learning in our contemporary societies reproduce and consolidate these features in institutions of formal learning, in the media and through the sociocultural and political environment as informal learning, and in non-formal learning environments and initiatives, those that are spontaneous also. Foucault would want us to challenge the discourse of lifelong learning and the knowledge-based society that is normal today; to regard it with suspicion, problematizing it and exposing it to its other, which are the discourse of education and the learning individual.

His writings, however, must always be understood as being about individual resistance and spontaneous collective action, not as a substantive political program. Those who, like many of his critics on the left, want a program for action, for reform or government, who want a manifesto like Giddens's, or a revolutionary project, must look elsewhere. For these his thinking is irrelevant just as it is irrelevant for anybody who wants to theorize a learning society that is just, democratic, and educated. In this respect, however, one needs to recall the two approaches to politics he distinguished in his exchange with Chomsky, that of the governors and of the governed. The governors are interested in making the rules of the game of justice and democracy they want the governed to play with; the governed, on their part, try to influence the game in different ways by playing within them, subverting, or transgressing them. Foucault's point against Chomsky was that resistance needs no theory or program of justice or democracy, nor need one's resistance be blind or irrational if one doesn't have such a program. Government, however, at the state and institutional level, does. At this level Foucault, as a poststructuralist interested in the pole of the reader, is interested politically in the pole of the governed but not in canceling out the pole of the governor. Rorty's point in distinguishing normal from abnormal discourse (that of government and that of resistance or subversion, respectively, in this case) was that these are alternative but complementary, the abnormal discourse being parasitic on the normal. And this applies to the political discourses of government and resistance; they do different jobs related to their different ways of engaging with politics. The discourse of government is constructive and reconstructive of policies, programs, projects, and so on, and requires a theoretical and institutional framework. That of resistance is deconstructive, tactical, creative, and need be concerned with nothing other than resisting the abuse of power wherever it occurs. Which returns me, finally, to the education research project discussed in Chapter 1 and subsequently. Though, as I have said, it is certainly useless and uninteresting for the poststructuralist way of engaging with politics, it could still be an important strategic tool for those strategically interested in the government of the learning society, the policy-makers and advisors for whom it could profitably serve as a model.

Notes

Chapter 1: The Lifelong Education Movement

1   Ettore Gelpi, who directed the UNESCO Lifelong Education Centre in Paris at the time, told me that it was the only course he knew of anywhere.

2   According to Parkyn (1973), in December 1965 the UNESCO International Committee for the Advancement of Adult Education, having discussed a commissioned paper on the subject by Paul Lengrand, recommended that UNESCO should endorse the principle of lifelong education. It was apparently Lengrand (1975:57) also who first recommended the adoption of the principle of integration and proposed its distinction into vertical and horizontal.

3   H.W.R. Hawes (1974) points out that the antecedents of lifelong education are also to be found in other parts of Asia and Africa inherent in the structure of their societies, where the extended family is a major force. In Kenya, for instance, the older members provide instruction while the closeness and support of the family enables individuals to learn from each other. Age groups, possibly originally sharers in a common initiation or coming-of-age ceremony, remain linked together throughout life. The same is true, he says, of the pomdok system in Malaysia.

4   Pierre Furter (1977:13) credits Yeaxlee with giving the term "lifelong education" its definite form in English.

5   Beck identifies the origin of the risk society with the beginning of the industrialization process in the early nineteenth century. Its shape, he says, was determined by ongoing contributions to its knowledge base by the scientific and technological revolution. The risks and hazards experienced by contemporary societies are the long-term fruits of this revolution.

6   Besides ensuring the all-round harmonious development of the personality, Lengrand (1975:57) continues, lifelong education also needs to achieve its own unity as a process over time; it needs "to reconcile and harmonise these different stages of training in such a manner that the individual is no longer in conflict with himself. By laying stress on the unity, the all-roundedness and the continuity of development of the personality," he says, lifelong education "leads to the formulation of curricula and instruments of education that create permanent communications between the needs and lessons of professional life, of cultural expression, of general development and of the various situations for and through which every individual completes and fulfils himself."

7   It should be viewed not, in Lengrand's (1975:61) words, as "an addendum to life imposed from outside," or as "an asset to be gained ... to use the language of philosophers, it lies not in the field of 'having' but in that of 'being'" (1975:61). The Faure report (1972:143) makes basically the same point both in its title, *Learning to Be*, and in its pages. It declares like Lengrand that education ought not to be defined in relation to a fixed content that needs to be assimilated, but as a process in individual

human beings who learn to express themselves, communicate and question the world through their various experiences, attaining their own increasing self-fulfillment in the process.

[8] The literature on the subject was already quite voluminous in the United States in the 1960s where, as Oddi (1987) points out, there were some ten different understandings of the term floating about at the time and research was of an empirical nature addressed to adults. In the UNESCO Institute of Education's work in the 1970s, however, it took the form of "a comparative evaluation of school curricula (Skager & Dave, 1977; Ingram, 1979)" and concerned itself with "more general analyses, often in the form of speculations and of a normative character (see e.g. Cropley, 1980)" (Rubenson & Borgstrom 1981:116). Outside UNESCO, much of the research still related to Tough's (1979) studies of learning projects that tried to operationalize self-directed learning with adults, and "many surveys" were directed to the question of adults' deliberate learning in different settings and with various populations. Rubenson and Borgstrom (1981:118) made an important distinction between the approach to self-directed learning in Tough and in other approaches where society and the educational system is taken to be supportive, and that of lifelong education writers like Ettore Gelpi where "quite the opposite premise applies, the existing educational system being taken, in common with social mechanisms generally, to counteract and suppress the emergence of self-directed learners."

[9] The idea of a "scientific humanistic" culture, in fact, came to the writers of the movement from Julian Huxley rather than Dewey, unsurprisingly given his close association with UNESCO as its first director general. I have come across little direct reference to both in the lifelong education literature, though Dewey's indirect influence is, as Cross-Durant (1984) rightly says, evident everywhere.

[10] See *PLE* pp. 61–63.

[11] F.W. Jessup (1969) rejects the term "continuing education" because it tends, he says, to obscure the fact that lifelong learning is compatible with discontinuous education.

[12] Denis Kallen (1979) gives a detailed account of the development of the concept of recurrent education since its launching in 1968 by Olaf Palme, the then Swedish minister of education. He quotes an OECD document of 1971, saying that "Recurrent education is formal, and preferably full time education for adults who want to resume their education interrupted earlier for a variety of reasons." Another document in 1973 describes it as "the distribution of education over the life span of the individual in a *recurring* way." Kallen made important distinctions between recurrent education and education permanente while Charles Boyle (1982) did the same for recurrent and continuing education.

[13] Cropley's book gives an excellent account of the diverging accounts of lifelong education and the different purposes to which it has been put.

[14] Martin Yarnit (1997) has suggested another reason for dropping education for the normatively neutral learning: education, he says, is too *passive*. I'm not sure exactly what this means but what I take him to mean is that education conjures up the idea of something received from others, something one submits to rather than something one does for oneself. This certainly does not square with how it has been understood either by liberal philosophers, who emphasize autonomous learning, or by Dewey with his emphasis on personal growth.

[15] See Rozycki, E.G. (1987), and my reply (1989).

16 Asked why he seemed more concerned with developing new adult education structures than with school reform, and why he considered adult education rather than schooling as the "locomotion" of lifelong education, Lengrand (1975:150) answered that history shows that what has brought about "desirable progress in the status of workers, women and young people is not reason but the impatience and revolt of those concerned." Children who feel unhappy and ill at ease at school can make nuisances of themselves, but the child "is not equipped to rebel because he has not had the adult's experience of independence."

17 The other "gap" Lengrand (1975:152) wanted lifelong education, as a philosophy of education, to bridge was the generation gap. More than that, he wanted it to be conceived as a joint undertaking and experience not only between generations but "all categories of human beings whose relationship is that of dominant-dominated, e.g. men and women, men of different races, or developed and developing countries."

18 Peters (1996:96) adds Yoneji Masuda, who, like Illich, "talks of 'knowledge networks' that avoid the restrictions of formal schooling and concentrate on a 'personal type' of education and 'self-learning'" to the group and argues that these networks are becoming ever more possible with the passing of time, thanks to the increasing development of computer technology.

19 Parkyn (1973:9) referred to Dewey as the one who has made the most relevant conceptual analysis of the relationship between living and education, and who explicitly stated the characteristics of education as a lifelong process.

20 van der Zee (1996:166–167) uses different names for formal, non-formal, and informal learning: *guided learning* (all sorts of learning activities that involve a measure of instruction or tuition), *do-it-yourself learning* (all activities people undertake on their own initiative, without the mediation of teachers or course-makers, with the intention of broadening their horizons or improving their capacity to accomplish some task), and *spontaneous learning* (all learning one "bumps into"—like a serious accident, a conflict at work, a failed relationship—and as a by-product of an activity guided primarily by other motives). He usefully suggests key areas we need to address in order to extend our interest in education lifewide, namely: *informal contacts* (friends, neighbors, members of the family); the *mass media* (books, radio, television, newspapers, magazines, audio- and videocassettes); *labor organizations* (the place of work); *cultural institutions* (museums, libraries, theatres, cinemas, creative centers); and *utilitarian facilities* (trade fairs, labor exchanges, banks, do-it-yourself shops). As he points out, uncovering the educational potential of this spectrum of learning experiences is a daunting task, though some work has already been done through recent studies of learning in the workplace, the public library, television, and museums.

21 Bagnall (1990:2) takes it to have the following implications: that "(1) all learned change is education (in the sense of outcome or product), (2) any event that contributes to any such outcome is educational or educative (in the sense of process), and (3) no distinction can be drawn in education between what should be the case, and what is the case—between its normative and descriptive aspects."

22 My response to Bagnall is found in "Lifelong Education: Illiberal and Repressive?" (1993).

23 My point of view, similar to Lakatos's with respect to scientific projects, is that philosophical projects or viewpoints are rarely if ever conclusively defeated; they can always make comebacks. This is what MacIntyre hoped would happen with respect to

Aristotelianism in *AV*. It has been true of pragmatism, a largely defeated project in the middle part of the twentieth century that has made a remarkable comeback over recent years. And it may be true also in the future for other currently defeated projects. Often it takes a philosopher of genius like MacIntyre, or Rorty in the case of pragmatism, for the star of an apparently moribund project to rise again.

Chapter 2: Death of the Movement

24   Whether one refers to the phenomenon as postmodern or "late" or "high" or whatever, is of no great consequence. What is important, as Crook, Pakulski, and Waters (1992:1) say, is that "the observation that radical social change is in process is shared widely" today, and because it "is now so widespread in its penetration of various social and cultural realms and because it reverses so many of the normal patterns of modernity," we cannot regard it as a mere extension of the modern world.

25   Field's (1997) paper contains a useful summary of the EU's foray into policy-making in education in these early years and later, starting with its early interest in vocational training—culminating in the launching of ERASMUS in the mid-1980s; and continuing with a wide-ranging general review of its policies between 1990 and 1992 and with the consequent launching of the SOCRATES and LEONARDO programs shortly afterwards. Field is skeptical about these programs, judging them inaccessible to adult learners, work-based learners, part-time learners, and distance learners, and he puts this down to a mixture of deceit on the EU's part and spending constraints, particularly after Maastricht.

26   Cropley (1979:11) had described learning as "a normal and natural process which does not need teachers or even awareness that the process is occurring," while education "focuses on the experiences which influence learning, and is naturally used to refer to those activities which have a conscious educative purpose." Put differently, "discussion of lifelong learning focuses attention on what the people who are engaged in learning do, lifelong education concentrates on the people, processes, methods and materials, institutions, organizations and sites, and administrative and organizational conditions which hopefully facilitate learning (Gestrelius 1979)." Cropley was writing about a shift at the time from lifelong learning to lifelong education, which he disagreed with, not the other way around. This was a time when the debate about the learning society as "the supportive infrastructure" needed to put lifelong education into effect, about "how to do it," was "a feature of recent writing in the area" (1979:10). In short, he proposed lifelong education as the operational definition of lifelong learning, which, of course, I disagree with.

27   A claim was made for similar and more spectacular developments across the Atlantic by Henry A. Spille, then vice president of the American Council on Education. "All over America," Spille (Longworth & Davies 1996:xi) declared, "educational, business, labour and governmental organizations are preparing to meet the challenge of the 21st century by focusing on lifelong learning. Companies are becoming 'Learning Organizations.' Cities are proclaiming themselves to be 'Cities of Learning.' Labour unions are negotiating contracts that include continuing education benefits. Professional associations are setting up task forces and work groups to study lifelong learning implications." This alliance of education, business, labor, and government is

the alliance of forces defining the learning society in the United States, according to Spille, and it was no different in Europe.

[28] The point that an information society is not necessarily a society in which people are informed evidently plays with the ambiguity of the word "informed," where "x is informed" can mean that x has information, knows the "facts," but that her information is inert, that she can do nothing with it. Or it can mean that "x's opinions or ideas are informed," which implies an intelligent attitude to the information that one has. One can have a learning society that is informed in either sense of the word, though it is the second sense of an informed society that is desirable.

[29] Admittedly, it is difficult to specify just what this obligation amounts to in a world where "survival" is a complex business. The lifelong education writers countered it with five major strategies: making self-direction a major goal for learning at the schooling age; ensuring accession to a wide range of formal adult learning initiatives both vocational and non-vocational at the postschooling age; encouraging the proliferation of non-formal and ad hoc learning initiatives originating from sources outside the formal sector and in the local communities; encouraging (in accordance with the principle of lifewide learning) all the institutions in society to recognize their responsibility to educate; and ensuring an informal learning environment harmonious with their humanistic outlook. This whole package of strategies constituted the maximalist approach to the learning society.

[30] They express what I take to be a considerable amount of sympathy with my notion of an education research project, but have clearly misread my proposal to adopt "touchstone theory" between competing research projects, which I did in the interest of interproject communication—not, as they say, extra-project comparison. I had no wish to propose the need for "some extra- or supra- paradigm criteria of intelligibility and corrigibility," which would certainly clash with my "relativism" (Aspin & Chapman 2000:11).

[31] Hughes and Tight (1995:297) do not suggest what could lie beyond the discourse of the learning society; they leave the matter open. They do, however, refer to the "division" in the literature between two ways of approaching the learning society; that of the *visionaries* and that of the *analysts*. Again they do not elaborate on this distinction either.

[32] Young (1998:150) has identified not one but three myths of the learning society going about today (though he refers to them not as "myths" but as "models"); the "schooling model," the "credentialist model," and the "access model." He proposes a fourth model himself, the "connective" or "educative," arguing that the three other models fail because they do not "focus directly on learning relationships nor on learning processes but on participation in institutions, gaining qualifications and on access to learning opportunities for individuals," and fail to problematize the central concept of learning itself, though this is not true of the literature of the lifelong education movement, at any rate (see Lengrand 1986). For Young a learning society is measured according to how much it pursues the policy of encouraging expanded learning or, to use Dewey's term, growth.

Chapter 3: MacIntyre's Educated Public

[33] As MacIntyre (1987:16) put it, their task is "to shape the young person so that he or she may fit into some role or function that requires recruits," while teaching her "how to acquire independence of mind, how to be enlightened, as Kant understood 'enlightenment.'"

34   As Abraham Edel and Elizabeth Flower (1983:427) point out, MacIntyre uses the term emotivism very loosely. Strictly speaking, it was the name of a specific metaethical theory of the second quarter of the twentieth century, in the positivist stage of the analytic revolution, and was tied to a specific theory of language and psychology, which was criticized by analytic philosophers themselves in the ordinary language stage.

35   This dissatisfaction with plurality reminds one of Plato, for whom it was a source of problems with democratic politics and culture, which he also regarded as intrinsically barbaric. Like MacIntyre, Plato responded by setting up an educated public of philosophers, who were to be the society's moral guardians. But the question of what to do with plurality, or fragmentation, whether to rationalize and contain it in some way or to give it its head and go along with it, goes even further back to pre-Socratic antiquity, though the postmodern world may finally have rendered it truly dramatic in existential terms. In politics it becomes an issue about freedom and containment, risk and reassurance.

36   MacIntyre (1981:25) himself classifies Weber as an emotivist in the book.

37   Though a committed Christian, Marxism held a very strong attraction for him in his earlier years because of the strong international movement that sustained it and because of its commonalities with the Christian social doctrines he admired. In his early, pre-*AV* writings, he described Marx as "having been able to give fuller expression to the forms of Christian thought which he inherited from Hegel" (McMylor 1994:12). Marxism's orientation toward science and scientific method also gave it greater historical success than Christianity in coming to terms with the modern age. In his very first book, *Marxism: An Interpretation,* written in 1952, he already identified liberalism, which effects a division between the secular and the sacred, as the natural enemy of Christianity. He said in a later interview with Cogito ("An Interview with Alasdair MacIntyre 1991:67) that the work that issued in *Secularization and Moral Change* in 1967, taught him that "all attempts to adapt Christianity to liberal modernity are bound to fail." In *AV* he attributes his loss of interest in Marxism to the fact that, like liberal individualism, it embodies the central defects and failures of the modern and modernizing world (1981:18). More recently he has pronounced it as being neither useful nor interesting, since it has also lost whatever political relevance it once had.

38   Caputo (1987:253–254) concedes that MacIntyre is very conscious of the injustices and violence of the medieval world. While MacIntyre thinks they can be remedied, Caputo argues, he himself thinks its exclusions and repressions "were not merely a minor flaw in the classical world, an unfortunate blind spot, which we can mend," but the logical outcome of any teleological scheme: "In a teleological scheme, woe unto them who are a means to the *telos,* who get grounded up by the teeth of the *telos.*"

39   Heidegger, Caputo (1987:250–251) says, "leaves the thinker mute in the face of the ethico-political," does not exploit the ethico-political cutting edge of his own deconstruction of metaphysics. Caputo (1987:252) also criticizes Heidegger's rhapsodic account of Greek *techne* for obscuring the real divisions within the polis, "the systematic exclusivity and repressiveness of the Greek democracy," describing it as a kind of blindness typical of escathological visions in general.

40   Feinberg (1991:93–94) accused MacIntyre with overstating his case against the modern world "in a number of ways." He had not shown that life today has become so

complex that it is beyond the grasp for a person with a reasonable amount of education, nor that it *must* remain complex so that we must put our fate in the hands of experts themselves limited by their disciplinary training. But this criticism was largely off beam, because MacIntyre did not put down the impossibility of a public in today's world to any difficulty people have in grasping its complexities, but to more basic problems with its modernist culture.

41 I attended the London lecture because I imagined that it would say be relevant to my work on the chapter on the learning society in *PLE* at the time. I did not expect him, of course, to make any specific link with or refer to the learning society. I also knew from reading *AV* that the intellectual tradition within which he worked was very different from that which inspired the lifelong education movement or the tradition of the social democrat left I embraced. The movement, on its part (to my knowledge at least), never used the expression "educated public" or theorized anything like one in its conception of a learning society. But that factor added to the interest. I also knew, of course, that the wish to reclaim the notion of a public was very strong in Dewey, whose work I was much influenced by at the time, and I wanted to know how MacIntyre's thinking on the subject related with Dewey's, if at all.

42 Graham Haydon (1987) is a case in point. Not only did he miss the note of polemic with Peters in the lecture but also the entire point MacIntyre was making that the current education system *cannot*, as it is, "work well," and that our current philosophical culture *cannot* produce any "genuine dialogue" at all. And this not because of any inefficient internal communication or lack of good will that may or may not exist within the ranks of educationalists and philosophers, but because of the deep-seated sociocultural causes and the kind of philosophical culture MacIntyre has identified in his books, particularly the brand of pluralism embraced by liberal modernity.

43 In *EP* he suggested Aquinas's *Summa Theologiae* as the suitable canonical text for his preferred public. In *TRV* it is the papal encyclicals (Pope Leo XIII's *Aeternae Patris*, also of Thomist inspiration, published in 1879), which have the advantage of addressing the modern age in an ongoing manner and updating Catholic doctrine, and are unequivocal pronouncements drawn from traditional sources (the Bible, Gospels, revelation, and Christian tradition). They, therefore, provide clear guidelines for the faithful to follow on moral issues. In short, in *TRV*, MacIntyre looks to the popes through their encyclicals to provide the spiritual and moral leadership the modern secularized state is incapable of. And he cannot have been disappointed, as the last years have witnessed a proliferation of these encyclicals addressing the secularist *ethos* of the late modern age.

44 The close coherence of the notion of "a craft" with "a practice" is not hard to see; crafts are similarly "virtue-guided" and they also denote internal standards of excellence (1981:69). Also, "to be adequately initiated into a craft," MacIntyre (1981:70) says, "is to be adequately initiated into a tradition."

45 MacIntyre identifies Nietzsche's *Genealogy of Morals* as the canonical text of the genealogist, and the genealogists he refers to fairly extensively in *TRV* are Foucault and Deleuze, probably because he regards them (with some justice) as being Nietzsche's most faithful followers.

46 MacIntyre (1990:3–4) himself does not underestimate the difficulty. In his introduction to *TRV* he describes it very well: "The extent and depth of these differences in approaching and reacting to my lectures was by itself enough to raise sharply such

questions as: Are the differences and divisions which exist within academic communities by now so great that any notion of addressing the academic community as such, and indeed the wider educated community as such ... has become vain and empty?"

47   Where Foucault was concerned, though he continued to hold his prestigious professorship at the College de France until the end of his life, it was not in philosophy but in history of ideas. Lyotard, Rorty, and Derrida have all had problems with mainstream philosophers. Rorty left the philosophy department at Princeton University to become professor of humanities at the University of Virginia and expresses more sympathy for literary critics and journalists than professional philosophers.

48   Yeatman (1994:45) remarks that their inclusion could be described neither as a spontaneous outgrowth of the liberal curriculum nor as the result of "the self-regulation of the collegial community of the autonomous university." It came only after intense struggle and as a result of the powerful demand by militant feminists that institutionalized knowledge be made accountable and responsive to contemporary politico-ethical challenges like their own (1994:42).

49   Nussbaum (1997:278), who defends the liberal university as a "community of reason" in her friendly evaluation of Notre Dame University, says that on the whole it had "succeeded well in constructing a distinctively religious campus that is also a place of genuine inquiry and debate." But it is a campus where "continued vigilance is needed to preserve a space for free argument on every topic, including those arguments that challenge orthodoxy and ask the tradition to change in order to be 'all that it could be.'"

50   The language MacIntyre and I use is different. He distinguishes the different voices in the pluralistic world in terms of competing rationalities instead of research projects (though he does refer to the Enlightenment as a "project" in *AV*), and to "rational traditions" instead of normative cores, but we are essentially on the same wavelength. MacIntyre, however, seems to believe that the mere fact that a project is at a later stage means that it has progressed over its past stages, which could imply a belief that progress is historically linear, which is not my view. I also think that unhealthy projects may be recuperated.

51   Dunne (MacIntyre & Dunne 2002:13) points to the dangers this will create: that entertaining other people's narrative "may enforce a more or less radical retelling of *our* narrative," which would raise questions about the truth of narratives, and risk the possibility of one's self-understanding being put at stake. To which MacIntyre replies that it is "important not to force on students questions that they may not yet be able to face."

Chapter 4: Habermas: The Rational Society

52   Held (1980:14) believes that Habermas's is a separate branch of critical theory rather than one that simply follows on the Frankfurt tradition. Habermas himself has described his differences with the Frankfurt theorists in various places. In "A Reply to My Critics," he describes his project as one of renewing a critical social theory that secures its normative foundations by taking in the experience of thought gained along the way from Kant through Hegel to Marx, thence through Peirce and Dilthy to Weber and Mead, which avoids falling prey to historicism, or sociology of knowledge, and does not stand over against history and the complex of social life (1982:232).

53 I don't wish to read any conscious intention on MacIntyre's part to exclude Habermas. MacIntyre has also been accused of being particularly selective in his narrative of the Enlightenment, leaving out its French influences.

54 While acknowledging its dark side, his attitude toward the Enlightenment is that whether we like it or not we continue to be its heirs: "[T]hese criticisms and self-criticisms still sustain themselves from the light of the enlightenment—we have no other criteria, save for its own." The lesson Adorno and Horkheimer teach us is that the Enlightenment project can make "humanity more independent but not automatically happier" (Habermas 1994b:107).

55 Connelly (1996:241) himself is intensely critical of both Mezirow's work and that of his followers, accusing them of failing to "demonstrate the necessary familiarity with Habermas's work," and of not recognizing "the critical assessments of Habermas's work taking place in the non-educational world."

56 Horkheimer believed that some phenomena of social life can be shown to be the natural properties of the species, although they can come to the fore only under certain conditions. Freud's libido theory, for instance, had shown that human beings share a striving for pleasure and self-preservation and that this stratum of human existence is an ever-flowing, permanent source of stimuli that are potentially revolutionary. Capitalism, he argued, enforces restrictions on these libidinal drives, thus putting in motion the repressions, feelings of guilt, and a general suffering that instigate revolt.

57 The later Horkheimer's interest turned toward reevaluating different metaphysical and theological traditions, which he researched through an interdisciplinary methodology employing the same method of immanent criticism. So that, while traces of his earlier concerns with the possibility of a "rational society" still covertly remained in his writing, particularly since he saw theology itself as an expression of humanity's unrepressible longing to go beyond its immediate reality and to establish a free and just community, these were very faint indeed.

58 Marcuse (1994:18) described the "one-dimensional society" as a society in which "domination—in the guise of affluence and liberty—extends to all spheres of private and public existence, integrates all authentic opposition, absorbs all alternatives," where "technological rationality reveals its political character as it becomes the great vehicle of better domination, creating a truly totalitarian universe in which society and nature, mind and body are kept in a state of permanent mobilization for the defence of this universe."

59 Marcuse (Fromm 1971:xxii) was the member of the Frankfurt School who quarreled with his former colleague, seeing in the publication of *Escape from Freedom* in 1941 signs of Fromm having compromised with American capitalism, shallow optimism, and "positive thinking," of having capitulated to the status quo, of being a "revisionist," of "pure conformist ideology."

60 Theology, jurisprudence, and medicine would be excluded from its range of discursive competence. These were, in his view, areas of concern best left to the state and its experts.

61 The use Hegel wanted to make of the public sphere as a "means of education" was "to integrate subjective opinions into the objectivity assumed by the spirit in the form of the state" (Habermas 1989a:120). Marx's countermodel failed historically also.

62 As early as "A Reply to My Critics," he insisted that now "I do not regard the fully transparent society as an ideal, nor do I wish to suggest *any* other ideal—Marx was not the only one frightened by the vestiges he saw of utopian socialism." He also acknowledged that the ideal speech situation encounters counterfactual instances in everyday life: "which deviates in many ways from everyday communicative practice" (1982:235–236).

63   Calhoun (1992:32) points out that he "seems to have been persuaded more by his account of the degeneration of the public sphere than by his suggestion of its revitalisation through intra-organizational reforms and the application of norms of publicity to inter-organizational relations."

64   The task of universal pragmatics, as Habermas (1979:1) described them, is "to identify and reconstruct universal conditions of public understanding," which are general presuppositions of communicative action including other forms of verbal social action like conflict, competition, and strategic action in general, all "derivatives of action oriented to reaching understanding." Its key thesis, vindicated by Habermas also in terms of a Kantian reconstructive transcendental analysis, is that linguistically competent subjects acting communicatively must raise universal normative validity claims and suppose that they can be vindicated or redeemed.

65   The same complaint is made by Parsons (Calhoun 1992:438), who criticizes him for not having taken any account of the role taken by the "educational revolution" in the nineteenth century in his narrative. Parsons remarks that Habermas underestimates "the positive influence of formal schooling, especially of its expanding secondary level, on cultural mobilization, and the promotion of critical attitudes."

66   Habermas (1990b:13) denies that utopianism has interested only intellectuals and points to its influence on the European labor and political movements in Europe during and after World War I, before the advent of the economic crisis. The only one to survive as national policy today, he says, is social-democratic reformism, whose "main success" lay precisely in "managing to establish a welfare state compromise, whose effects reach deeply into the structures of society."

67   "We still live in the modern epoch—not in some post-modern sequel to it," Habermas (Dews 1992:216) asserted in a later interview with Perry Andersen and Peter Dews. "Everyday politics remains mediated by a Zeitgeist in which utopian and historical modes of thinking constantly intermingle."

68   In *The Philosophical Discourse of Modernity*, making the same point about the decline of "the production paradigm," he says that "the emancipatory perspective" now proceeds not from a definition of the conditions of labor but "from the paradigm of action oriented towards mutual understanding" (1990a:82).

69   Habermas began his engagement with hermeneutics and his long polemic/debate with Gadamer in his essay "On the Logic of the Social Sciences," which appeared in 1967.

70   Habermas (1990b:18) wants these otherwise autonomous, or "wild," publics to "also enter into communication with one another," thus countering the danger of self-absorbed isolation and parochialism. Collaboration would strengthen their solidarity and their collective capacity for action and enable them "to focus on social processes and demand a redistribution of power."

Chapter 5: The Learning Society and the Third Way

71   Yeatman makes the point that it is a politics of difference rather than welfare that most directly challenges domination and that, responding to the problem of internal exclusion and the vulnerability of social groups, demands more than social investment in welfare or self-help. It involves the development of a politics of voice and representation that actively tackle the problems by making their systematic character

visible, and through needs-based social planning. In this sense she wants to redefine rights as primarily dialogical rather than fixed by some notion of citizenship or of a human essence.

72 Yeatman (1994:37) has no problem with the idea of expert authority or professional erudition. What matters is how that authority is practiced, namely that it is problematized and made accountable to different audiences, and that it is placed at the service of non-dominant groups or classes with whom the particular experts have a flexible, "service-delivery" relationship, which works with the other as a partner, so that each is recognized as "the appropriate 'expert' for their distinctive role" (1994:51). Since differences in judgment and policy, some irresolvable, are more than likely to arise from it, the parties need "to be dialogically accountable to each other for these differences, and to be responsible for negotiated pragmatic compromises which permit, if not consensus, a decision with which all can live for the time being" (1994:51).

73 Illich's edu-credit cards would presumably be issued by the state, so that it would be the state alone that would shoulder the financial burden of the learning society rather than the state in partnership with the other agencies cited by the Commission. The Commission's proposal varies with Illich also in that its learning initiatives would be structured along different lines, on a well-managed and programmed modular basis rather than through a system of *ad hoc* and temporary networking. Besides, the Commission evidently does not contemplate destroying the whole fabric of contemporary schooling and formal education.

74 New Labour's schooling policies respond to the employers' demand to raise the quality of schools, and it appears to share the same aversion to "progressivism" as neoliberals. Thus, like the Conservatives, it continues to look to business for its inspiration and to gauge school progress on performativist criteria. The policies announced in the Green Paper reflect this approach: raising the standards of teaching and learning effectiveness, setting clear measurable targets for both, and emphasizing the traditional value of literacy and numeracy as the basic skills for the new learning age. Not even promoting self-directed learning at least!

75 Blake et al. (1998:1) contend that the Green Paper's view of lifelong learning, of the continuous acquisition of knowledge and skills and of work-based learning, "could revolutionize post-compulsory education in the UK more than anything to be found in Dearing." They point to the agenda for the universities in the first paragraph of the Green Paper, namely to respond efficiently to the twin demands of coping with rapid technological change and with the economic impact of market globalization by producing flexible graduates capable of constant retraining, and the increasing tendency to prioritize the teaching of highly abstract "transferable skills" (1998:4). It is not, they say, that these skills are unimportant but that "the university's role in the transformation of individuals and of their understanding of their world," namely their education, "is marginalised" in the process (1998:4). More particularly they worry about the kind of citizens this approach will produce. The state (Blairite no less than Thatcherite), they say, "says to the citizen, 'As far as the economy goes, we don't really care just what kind of person you are. In fact, we would rather you were no one in particular, otherwise you will be less flexible'" (1998:4–5). The state views the citizen "either as a redeployable cipher or as an individualistic nuisance." In short, its ideal of citizenship "lacks appeal at best." At worst, it is "ethically bankrupt, and it leaves us with a conception of the individual which is worryingly thin" (1998:5). They respond

with renewed commitment and loyalty to the old tradition of liberal learning and inquiry that places its commitment to critique "at the heart of academic endeavor" (1998:5). This tradition, however, as MacIntyre, Lyotard, and others rightly say, is in crisis. But the point of Blake et al.'s critique is that, bar the rhetoric, there is really very little to choose from between the politics of the new social democrats and that of its neoliberal predecessor in government where educational policy is concerned.

76   Dewey (1938:16) did not elaborate. "The nature of a newly emerging individualism," he said, "cannot be described until progress has been made in its actual creation."

77   The Third Way title of Giddens's book, *Beyond Left and Right*, sounds Nietzschean, and though he specifies that it does not signify a trans-valuation of political values but a redefinition of the values of the left, the title says it all in this respect. Postmodern politics is the implosion of the politics of left and right into a center where the values of the left are redefined beyond recognition and performativism reigns supreme.

Chapter 6: The Politics of Hope

78   Jean François Lyotard (1999) designates as "modern" any discourse that legitimates itself with reference to a metadiscourse, that makes appeal to some metanarrative; to use his own examples, to the dialectics of Spirit, the hermeneutics of meaning, the emancipation of the rational or working subject, the creation of wealth, and so on.

79   Michael Peters (1996:19) comments that "the uses of the terms 'postmodernism' and 'poststructuralism' are now so commonly conflated that I have not bothered to consistently differentiate throughout the text," but I am not in agreement with this approach.

80   Lyotard (1999) identifies the beginning of the postmodern outlook with the end of the nineteenth century, with transformations that altered the "game rules" of science, literature, and the arts. Best and Kellner (1991) say that Rudolf Pannowitz first used the word "postmodern" in 1917 to describe a new fascist generation following the historical collapse of values in contemporary European culture. Ihab Hassan (Docherty 1993:147) contends that the real origin of the term remains uncertain, but credits Federico de Onis in 1934 as the first to use the term *postmodernismo*. Docherty, however, ascribes it to Arnold Toynbee, who first dated the end of the modern age at 1875, then shifted it to the end of the First World War. Best and Kellner point out that postmodernism first came into solid focus as a cultural phenomenon in the field of architecture in the 1950s, where it was theorized by such as Robert Venturi, Denise Scott Brown, and Charles Jencks in reaction to the self-referential modernist purism of the Bauhaus. Before long, in the United States in particular, it spread to other disciplines and areas of culture and life.

81   Foucault expressed puzzlement with the term "postmodernity." "What are we calling postmodernity? I'm not up to date," he asked (Kritzman 1990:33). In any case, he saw no signs of the "disappearance of reason" occurring in our times. "I can see multiple transformation," he observed, "but I cannot see why we should call all this transformation a collapse of reason" (Kritzman 1990:35).

82   The impression Foucault gives of being "neutral" about the power/knowledge regimes and the disciplinary technologies he describes in *Discipline and Punish* and elsewhere has led "to complaints that he is normatively confused or that he deprives himself of

any basis for criticism of the social phenomena he describes" (Patton 1989:260). While his "refusal to specify either a prescription or a prognosis for the social illnesses he diagnoses suggests to some readers that genealogy is as unserious and irresponsible as archeology" (Couzens-Hoy 1986:7), Michael Walzer (1986) has dismissed Foucault's politics as a form of "infantile leftism" and Rorty has referred to it as "self-indulgent radical chic."

83 Fraser was referring to his intervention at the Cerisy conference on his work, where he explained his silence over Marxism and the student revolution in 1968 as itself a political strategy, determined by his wish not to contribute to the "anti-Marxist concert" of the time, or to weaken or split the left. Later, Thomas McCarthy (1989–90:146) quoted him as saying that he had "never succeeded in directly relating deconstruction to existing political codes and programmes," because "the available codes for taking a political stance are not at all adequate to the practicality of deconstruction."

84 The expression is Thomas Nagel's (1986).

85 Lyotard, like Foucault, locates freedom within the agonistic dimension of discourse, ties it with creative experimentation, and identifies it with *paralogy* which, as Jameson (Lyotard 1999:xix) notes, he describes in the rhetoric of "struggle, conflict, the agonic in a quasi-heroic sense." A sense in which it is linked with his "related vision of non-hegemonic Greek philosophy (the Stoics, the Cynics, the Sophists), as the guerrilla war of the marginals, the foreigners, the non-Greeks, against the massive and repressive Order of Aristotle and his successors."

86 Lilla quotes Derrida from Chantal Mouffe (Ed.). (1996). *Deconstruction and Pragmatism*, London: Routledge.

87 Derrida (Caputo 1997:18–19) says about the logic of gift giving: "A gift is something that never appears as such and is never equal to gratitude, to commerce, to compensation, to reward... A gift is something you cannot be thankful for. As soon as I say 'thank you' for a gift, I start canceling the gift, I start destroying the gift, by proposing an equivalence, that is, a circle which encircles the gift in a movement of reappropriation. So, a gift is something that is beyond the circle of reappropriation, beyond the circle of gratitude." In short, it lies beyond the circle of power and is not, strictly speaking, political at all but "theological."

88 Usher and Edwards (1994:119) point out that because he appears to say nothing directly about education, there is the temptation to describe Derrida as "irrelevant." But they suggest that he enables us to do battle against the neglect and marginalization of other forms and levels of education that are not schooling or aspects of it: adult education, which has been "confined to the ghettos of 'training' and 'leisure-time activity,'" (1994:131) and is therefore an ally to the cause of regarding education from the perspective of the learning society.

89 Rorty (1987:568) is constantly dismissive of Marx, sustaining that "what was useful in Marxism has been absorbed into the social democratic, Deweyan tradition, and the residue can be safely neglected."

90 At one stage he actually thought the French poststructuralists politically useful, not because they "have given us some new weapons to use in unmasking the rottenness of the system," but because "among other things," they help us "envisage a social democratic utopia—a future for the human race in which Enlightenment liberalism is carried through to its limit, eradicating in the process the last traces of Enlightenment rationalism"

(1987:571). Even in *CIS* he describes Foucault as politically useful to show us "how the patterns of acculturation characteristic of liberal societies have imposed on their members kinds of constraints of which older, premodern societies had not dreamed" (1989:63).

[91] On the other hand, Rorty (1989:65–66) admits, the strong poeticized culture of his liberal utopia with its associations with "neo-Nietzschean figures such as Heidegger and Foucault," is one Habermas would, in fact, "deeply" dislike.

[92] Foucault's error, in Rorty's (1991:195) view, lay in "projecting his own search for autonomy out into public space"—that is where he becomes politically dangerous.

[93] Rorty had already written a few articles on the left and America before *AC*, notably: "Intellectuals in Politics," *Dissent* (Fall 1991, Vol. 38 , 483–490); "The Intellectuals at the End of Socialism," *Yale Review* (1992, Vol. 80, 1–16); and "Movements and Campaigns," *Dissent* (Spring 1995, Vol. 42, 55–60).

[94] As Rorty (1990a:45) put it, "there is only the shaping of an animal into a human being by a process of socialization, followed (with luck) by the self-individualization and self-creation of that human being through his or her own later revolt against that very process," to consider.

[95] From an ethnocentric viewpoint, the question is not "What is it to be a human being?" but, for an American, "What is it to inhabit a rich twentieth-century democratic society?" and "How can an inhabitant of such a society be more than the enactor of a role in a previously written script?" (1989:xiii). His ethnocentrism and his patriotic nationalism, though it "does not speak with narrow ferocity for the nation" (Billig 1993:82), are reasons why he is identified with the right.

[96] Rorty (1989:192) does not wish to diminish the power of the idea of "human solidarity," only to "disengage it from what has often been thought of as its 'philosophical presuppositions.'"

[97] To be fair to Rorty (1989:92), he requires the liberal ironist to have "as much imaginative acquaintance with alternative final vocabularies as possible ... in order to understand the actual and possible humiliation" of non-ironists.

[98] Rorty is ambiguous about an ironist public culture. "I cannot," he says in *CIS*, "go on to claim that there could or ought to be a culture whose public rhetoric is *ironist*. I cannot imagine a culture which socialized its youth in such a way as to make them continually dubious about their own process of socialization" (1989:87). In the same book, however, he also says that he wants irony to be the *culture* of his liberal utopia, even referring to a culture of "ironism" (1989:xvi).

[99] Managed democracies are not "managed" in the crude sense that their citizens are puppets manipulated by the centers of economic or political power. Rather, the managed democracy "is a created world of images, sounds, and scenarios that makes only occasional contact with the everyday reality of most people. The rest of the time that world floats in dissociation, a realm wherein reference has been suspended" (Wolin 1990:27–28). The spectacle is meant to show that "the system works." But nobody, Wolin (1990:28) contends like Baudrillard, is really taken in by it. Ordinary citizens "understand very well that it doesn't work for them: it only imposes surcharges on vital services."

[100] Rorty is not exactly popular among conventional philosophers either. Alven Neiman (1993:206) puts it colorfully: "[T]hese days the name Rorty is about as welcome in most philosophy departments as is the name Ted Kennedy in meetings of young Republicans for Pat Buchanan."

101   "The point of non-vocational higher education" is "to help students realize that they can re-shape themselves—that they can re-work the self-image foisted on them by their past, the self-image that makes them competent citizens, into a new self-image, one that they themselves have helped to create" (Rorty 1990c:45).

102   Indeed, Dewey was unhappy with a liberal politics of reform, which is "just messing around ... doing a little of this and a little of that in the hope that things might improve" (Festenstein 1997:75). He was disenchanted with piecemeal liberal reform, writing in 1935 that "liberalism must now become radical, meaning by 'radical' perception of the necessity of thorough-going changes in the set-up of institutions and corresponding activity to bring the changes to pass. For the gulf between what the actual situation makes possible and the actual state itself is so great that it cannot be bridged by piecemeal politics undertaken *ad hoc*" (Bernstein 1987:540).

Chapter 7: The Politics of Suspicion

103   According to Foucault's own account in his interview with Roulet (Kritzman 1990), he had long been thinking along lines that were parallel to the Frankfurt theorists without knowing it.

104   This connects with the way he describes his writing. "An experience," he says, "is neither true nor false: it is always a fiction, something constructed, which exists only after it has been made, not before; it isn't something that is 'true,' but it has been a reality" (1991b:36).

105   "The practice of placing individuals under 'observation,'" he says, "is a natural extension of a justice imbued with disciplinary methods and examination procedures. Is it surprising that the cellular prison, with its regular chronologies, forced labour, its authorities of surveillance and registration, its experts in normality, who continue and multiply the functions of the judge, should have become the modern instrument of penality? Is it surprising that prisons resemble factories, schools, barracks, hospitals, all resemble prisons?" (1991a:227–228).

106   Baudrillard (Gane 1993:89), distinguishing his own views on power and resistance from Foucault's, criticized Foucault for not seeing inertia as a strategy and for thinking in terms of *active* strategies that have a molecular, interstitial nature only. He argued that though Foucault's analysis is "perfect" within its own parameters, it is "traditional" in articulating itself in terms of power. Baudrillard's own view is that there is no more active power. That it is neutralized as it is perfected, in the process of becoming more and more anonymous and indeterminate. He also accused Foucault of being infatuated with the imaginary force of his own narratives and installing power in the same hegemonic relationship to discourse as those other notions he had tried to demolish, particularly truth (1980:20).

107   Foucault (1990:252) uses the word "subjectification" to describe "the procedure by which one obtains the constitution of a subject, or more precisely, of a subjectivity which is of course, only one of the given possibilities of organization of self-consciousness." His invention of the term is interesting. It gives more force to the aspect of discipline in the process, which he wants to emphasize, than words like socialization or enculturation, which he could have used instead.

108   Seduction, in Baudrillardian terms, is not to be confused with fascination, which is a different game. Seduction is always a dual relation; it involves defiance, provocation, and is reversible, while in fascination there is no defiance— "on the contrary there is a kind of respective neutralization of things." This makes it the "inverse" of seduction, which, in Foucault's language, is the game of freedom, rather than its corollary (Gane 1993:85).

109   "There is not even a utopian world any longer," he says. "There is no utopia. There is not even a 'scene' of utopia." Why, because we have lost hope in utopia? No. Because "utopia has gone into the real, we are in it" (Gane 1993:62).

110   The mass is "the irruption of the more social than social," a social that "has absorbed all the inverse energies of the antisocial, of inertia, resistance and silence." The stage where the logic of the social reaches its limit—the point where it inverts its finalities and reaches its point of inertia and extermination, but at the same time approaches ecstasy. Masses are "the ecstasy of the social, the ecstatic form of the social, the mirror where it is reflected in all its immanence" (Baudrillard 1983a:10–11).

111   Foucault (1989:xvii–xviii) also used the word heterotopia and wrote about heterotopia. Differently, however, from Vattimo. In *The Order of Things*, he distinguishes heterotopias as "disturbing, probably because they secretly undermine language," from utopias, which are tied to a politics of hope and "afford consolation." In "Different Spaces" he describes utopias as "emplacements having no real space," while heterotopias are "other places, a kind of contestation, both mythical and real, of the space in which we live" (1998:178–179). He distinguishes "crisis heterotopias" from "heterotopias of deviation" where "individuals are put whose behavior is deviant with respect to the mean or the required norm. These are the rest homes, the psychiatric hospitals," the prisons and old people's homes. The latter being particularly interesting since "old age is a crisis and also a deviation" (1998:180). Foucault goes on to describe the traits and principles of heterotopia, their extent and limits, their relationship to more ordinary spaces in life, and their relationship to freedom.

112   In *Discipline and Punish* (1975) he remarked, in fact, that we pass from one domination only to enter another. Charles Taylor (1985) subsequently criticized him for identifying power exclusively with power over, with domination; for not opposing it with some counternotion of freedom. In particular, he argued, Foucault does not consider the other dimension of power, which is its use as a positive, enabling force. Michael Walzer (1986) argues that his political epistemology is quite simply incoherent. But Foucault (Dreyfus & Rabinow 1983:237) himself described his life work as covering three possible domains of genealogy; the truth axis, the power axis, and the ethical axis, which concerns freedom. Simons (1995:3) distinguishes two sides to Foucault, the "heavy" and negative, where he comes across as a "prophet of entrapment" and the "light," aesthetic, affirmative of "untrammelled freedom and an escape from all limitations." Foucault works within the tension of these two moods.

113   Foucault (1990:55) refers specifically to the culture he describes as one where "educating oneself and taking care of oneself are interconnected activities."

114   On the matter of consensus, Foucault declared that though he cannot be "for consensuality," understood as a politics of intimacy advocated by Habermas, he is also "against nonconsensuality," against a politics of non-cooperation (Rabinow 1984:379).

115 In "The Tomb of the Intellectual," Lyotard (1993:3–4) similarly describes the growth of a new cadre of professionals, whose expertise is "essentially linked to the technosciences of language, along with the concentration of civil, economic, social, and military administration," who have "changed the nature of intermediary and higher occupational tasks, [and] have attracted numerous thinkers trained in the hard sciences, high technology and the human sciences," and whose interest and competence is not, as with the traditional intellectual, in the "fullest possible embodiment of the universal subject" but in performativity as such.

116 Keith Hoskin (1990:29) refers to Foucault as a "crypto-educationalist" "who really discovered something very simple (but highly unfamiliar nevertheless)—the centrality of education in the construction of modernity." Hoskin (1990:31) insists that what Foucault was doing all the time, "whether he thought he was talking about power or knowledge, was an educational analysis," in which the notion of "the examination" is central.

Bibliography

Adorno, Theodor. (1989). "The Culture Industry Reconsidered." In Stephen Eric Bronner & Douglas MacKay Kellner (Eds.), *Critical Theory and Society: A Reader*. Routledge (New York, London).

Adorno, Theodor, & Horkheimer, Max. (1992). *Dialectic of Enlightenment*. Verso (London, New York).

Anyon, Jean. (1994). "The Retreat of Marxism and Socialist Feminism: Postmodern and Poststructural Theories in Education." *Curriculum Inquiry*, Vol. 24, No. 2, 115–133.

Aronowitz, Stanley, & Giroux, Henri. (1991). *Postmodern Education*. University of Minnesota Press (Minneapolis; Oxford, UK).

Aspin, David, & Chapman, Judith. (2000). "Lifelong Learning: Concepts and Conceptions." *International Journal of Lifelong Education*, Vol. 19, No. 1, (January–February), 2–19.

Aspin, David, & Chapman, Judith. (Eds.). (2001). *International Handbook of Lifelong Learning* (2 vols.). Kluwer Academic Publishers (Dordrecht, Boston, London).

Bagnall, Richard G. (1990). "Lifelong Education: The Institutionalisation of an Illiberal and Repressive Ideology?" *Educational Philosophy and Theory*, Vol. 22, 1–7.

Bagnall, Richard G. (2000). "Lifelong Learning and the Limitations of Economic Determinism." *International Journal of Lifelong Education*, Vol. 19, No. 1 (January–February), 20–35.

Bailey, Charles. (1988). "Lifelong Education and Liberal Education." *Journal of Philosophy of Education*, Vol. 22, No. 1, 121–126.

Bain, William. (1995). "The Loss of Innocence: Lyotard, Foucault, and the Challenge of Postmodern Education." In Michael Peters (Ed.), *Education and the Postmodern Condition*. Bergin & Garvey (Westport, CT).

Ball, Christopher. (1995). "Learning Does Pay." In David Bradshaw (Ed.), *Bringing Learning to Life*. The Falmer Press (London; Washington, DC).

Ball, Stephen. (Ed.). (1990). *Foucault and Education, Disciplines and Knowledge*. Routledge (London, New York).

Bamburg, Jerry D. (1997). "Learning, Learning Organizations, and Leadership: Implications for the Year 2050." *New Horizons for Learning*, newhorizons.org/restr.

Baudrillard, Jean. (1980). "Oublier Foucault." Translated as "Forgetting Foucault." *Humanities in Society*, 3, No. 1 (Winter), 87–111.

Baudrillard, Jean. (1983a). *In the Shadow of the Silent Majorities*. Semiotext(e) (New York).

Baudrillard, Jean. (1983b). *Simulations*. Semiotext(e) (New York).

Baudrillard, Jean. (1990a). *Fatal Strategies*. Semiotext(e) (New York).

Baudrillard, Jean. (1990b). *Seduction*. Macmillan (London).

Bauman, Zygmunt. (1987). *Legislators and Interpreters: On Modernity, Post-Modernity and Intellectuals*. Cambridge University Press (Cambridge, UK).

Bauman, Zygmunt. (1996). *Postmodern Ethics*. Blackwell Press (Oxford, UK).

Bauman, Zygmunt. (1997). *Postmodernity and Its Discontents*. Polity Press (Oxford, UK).

Beck, Ulrich. (1994). *Risk Society: Towards a New Modernity*. Sage Publications (London; Thousand Oaks, CA; New Delhi).

Bell, Daniel. (1976). *The Coming of Post-Industrial Society*. Penguin Books (Harmondsworth, UK).

Benhabib, Seyla. (1992a). *Situating the Self*. Polity Press (Oxford, UK).

Benhabib, Seyla. (1992b). "Models of Public Space: Hannah Arendt, the Liberal Tradition, and Jurgen Habermas." In Craig Calhoun (Ed.), *Habermas and the Public Sphere*. The MIT Press (Cambridge, MA; London).

Bernauer, James, & Rasmussen, David. (Eds.). (1994). *The Final Foucault*. The MIT Press (Cambridge, MA; London).

Bernstein, Richard J. (1987). "One Step Forward, Two Steps Backward: Richard Rorty on Liberal Democracy and Philosophy." *Political Theory*, Vol. 15, No. 4 (November), 538–563.

Bernstein, Richard J. (1991). *The New Constellation*. The Polity Press (Oxford, UK).

Bertens, Hans. (1995). *The Idea of the Postmodern: A History*. Routledge (London, New York).

Best, Steven, & Kellner, Douglas. (1991). *Postmodern Theory*. Macmillan (London).

Beyer, Landon E, & Liston, Daniel P. (1992) "Discourse or Moral Action? A Critique of Post-modernism." *Educational Theory* 42, 371–393.

Bhaskar, Roy. (1991). *Philosophy and the Idea of Freedom*. Blackwell (Oxford, UK).

Billig, Michael. (1993). "Nationalism and Richard Rorty: The Text as a Flag for *Pax Americana*." *New Left Review*, No. 202 (Nov–Dec), 69–83.

Blake, Nigel. (1995). "Ideal Speech Conditions, Modern Discourse and Education." *Journal of Philosophy of Education*, Vol. 29, No. 3 (November), 355–367.

Blake, Nigel; Smeyers, Paul; Smith, Richard; & Standish, Paul. (1998). *Thinking Again: Education after Postmodernism*. Bergin & Garvey (Westport, CT).

Blake, Nigel; Smeyers, Paul; Smith, Richard; & Standish, Paul. (2000). *Education in an Age of Nihilism*. Routledge Falmer (London, New York).

Boshier, R. (1998). "Edgar Faure after 25 Years: down but not out." In J. Holdord et al. *International Perspectives on Lifelong Learning*. Kogan Page (London).

Boyle, Charles. (1982). "Reflections on Recurrent Education." *International Journal of Lifelong Education*, Vol. 1, No. 2, 5–18.

Bradshaw, David C.A. (Ed.). (1995). *Bringing Learning to Life: The Learning Revolution, the Economy and the Individual*. The Falmer Press (London; Washington, DC).

Calhoun, Craig. (Ed.). (1992). *Habermas and the Public Sphere*. The MIT Press (Cambridge, MA; London).

Caputo, John D. (1987). *Radical Hermeneutics*. Indiana University Press (Bloomington, IN).

Caputo, John D. (1988). "Beyond Aestheticism: Derrida's Responsible Anarchy." *Research in Phenomenology*, Vol. 18, 59–73.

Caputo, John D. (1997). *Deconstruction in a Nutshell*. Fordham University Press (New York).

Carr, Wilfred. (1995). "Education and Democracy: Confronting the Postmodern Challenge." *Journal of Philosophy of Education*, Vol. 29, No. 1, 75–91.

Coffield, Frank. (1996). "A Tale of Three Little Pigs: Building the Learning Society with Straw." Paper presented at EU conference at Newcastle University, November 1996, revised and published in Coffield, Frank (Ed.). (1997). *A National Strategy for LLL.* Department of Education, University of Newcastle (Newcastle, UK).

Commission on Social Justice. (1996). "Investment: Adding Value through Lifelong Learning." In Peter Raggatt, Richard Edwards, & Nick Small (Eds.), *The Learning Society: Challenges and Trends.* Routledge and the Open University (London, New York).

Connelly, Brian. (1996). "Interpretations of Jurgen Habermas in Adult Education." *Studies in the Education of Adults,* Vol. 28, No. 2 (October), 241–252.

Connolly, William E. (1982). "Book Review: *After Virtue.*" *Political Theory* (May), 315–319.

Corlett, William. (1989). *Community without Unity.* Duke University Press (Durham, NC).

Cornelis, François et al. (1994). *Education for Europeans: Towards the Learning Society.* European Round Table of Industrialists (Brussels).

Couzens-Hoy, David. (1986). *Foucault: A Critical Reader.* Basil Blackwell (Oxford, UK).

Crook, Stephen; Pakulski, Jan; & Waters, Malcolm. (1992). *Postmodernization: Change in Advanced Society.* Sage (London).

Cropley, Arthur J. (Ed.). (1979). *Lifelong Education: A Stocktaking.* UIE Monographs 8 (Hamburg, Germany).

Cross-Durant, Angela. (1984). "Lifelong Education in the Writings of John Dewey." *International Journal of Lifelong Education,* Vol. 3, No. 2, 115–125.

Cross-Durant, Angela. (1986). "Further Education and the Promotion of Lifelong Education." *International Journal of Further and Higher Education,* 10 (2), Summer, 45–53.

Dave, R.H. (1973). *Lifelong Education and School Curriculum.* UIE Monographs 1 (Hamburg, Germany).

Dave, R.H. (Ed.). (1976). *Foundations of Lifelong Education.* Pergamon Press (Oxford, UK).

Deflem, Mathieu (Ed.). (1996). *Habermas, Modernity and Law.* Sage Publications (London; Thousand Oaks, CA; New Delhi).

Deleon, Asher. (1984). "Some Thoughts Regarding Education Versus Communication." In Kenneth Wain (Ed.), *Lifelong Education and Participation.* The University of Malta Press (Malta).

Delors, Jacques. (1996). *Learning: The Treasure Within.* UNESCO (Paris).

Denzin, Norman K. (1991). *Images of Postmodern Society.* Sage Publications (London; Thousand Oaks, CA; New Delhi).

Department for Education and Employment. (1998). *The Learning Age: A Renaissance for a New Britain* (London, UK).

Derrida, Jacques. (1983). "The Principle of Reason: The University in the Eyes of Its Pupils." *Diacritics,* 3–20.

Derrida, Jacques. (1993). "Force of Law: The Mystical Foundation of Authority." In Drucilla Cornell & Michael Rosenfeld (Eds.), *Deconstruction and the Possibility of Justice.* Routledge (New York).

Derrida, Jacques. (1994). *Specters of Marx.* Routledge (New York, London).

Derrida, Jacques. (1997). *Politics of Friendship.* Verso (London, New York).

Derrida, Jacques, & Ewald, François. (1995). "A Certain Madness Must Watch Over Thinking." *Educational Theory* (Summer), Vol. 45, No. 3, 273–291.

Dewey, John. (1930). "Toward a New Individualism." *The New Republic* (February) 19, 13–16.

Dewey, John. (1934). "Can Education Share in Social Reconstruction?" *Social Frontier 1* (October), 10–13.

Dewey, John. (1938). *Experience and Education*. Macmillan (New York).

Dewey, John. (1966a). *Democracy and Education*. Macmillan (New York).

Dewey, John. (1966b). *The Child and the Curriculum*. In F.W. Garforth (Ed.), *John Dewey: Selected Educational Writing*. Heinemann (London).

Dewey, John. (1997). *The Public and Its Problems*. Swallow Press, Ohio University Press (Athens).

Dews, Peter. (1986). *Habermas, Autonomy, and Solidarity*. Verso Books (London).

Dews, Peter. (Ed.). (1992). *Autonomy and Solidarity: Interviews with Jurgen Habermas*. Verso Books (London, New York).

Docherty, Thomas. (Ed.). (1993). *Postmodernism: A Reader*. Harvester Wheatsheaf (New York, London).

Dohman, Gunther. (1996). *Lifelong Learning.* Federal Ministry of Education, Research and Technology (Bonn).

Dreyfus, Hubert L., & Rabinow, Paul. (1982). *Michel Foucault: Beyond Structuralism and Hermeneutics*. University of Chicago Press (Chicago).

Edel, Abraham & Flower, Elizabeth. (1983). Book review of *After Virtue*. *Journal of the History of Philosophy*, 21 (July), 426–429.

Edwards, Richard; Raggatt, Peter; Harrison, Roger; McCollum, Ann; & Calder, Judith. (1998). *Recent Thinking in Lifelong Learning*. Department for Education and Employment (DfEE) Research Report No. 80.

Elliott, Philip. (1986). "Intellectuals, the Information Society and the Disappearance of the Public Sphere." In R. Collins et al. (Eds.), *Media, Culture and Society: A Critical Reader*. Sage (London).

Etzioni, Amitai. (1968). *The Active Society*. Collier and Macmillan (London).

European Commission White Paper. (1995). *Teaching and Learning: Towards the Learning Society*. European Union (Brussels).

European Commission Staff Working Paper. (2000). *A Memorandum on Lifelong Learning*. European Union (Brussels).

Eurydice European Unit Survey. (2000). Lifelong Learning: The Contribution of Education Systems in the Member States of the European Union. (Brussels)

Ewert, Gerry D. (1991). "Habermas and Education: A Comprehensive Overview of the Influence of Habermas on Educational Literature." *Review of Educational Research* (Fall), Vol. 61, No. 3, 345–378.

Faure, Edgar et al. (1972) *Learning to Be*. UNESCO (Paris).

Feinberg, Walter. (1991). "The Public Responsibility for Public Education." *Journal of Philosophy of Education*, Vol. 25, No. 1, 17–26.

Fern Haber, Honi. (1994). *Beyond Postmodern Politics*. Routledge (New York, London).

Festenstein, Matthew. (1997). *Pragmatism and Political Theory*. Polity Press (Oxford, UK).

Field, John. (1996). "Open Learning and Consumer Culture." In Peter Raggatt, Richard Edwards, & Nick Small (Eds.), *The Learning Society: Challenges and Trends*. Routledge and the Open University (London, New York).

Field, John. (1997). "The European Union and the Learning Society: Contested Sovereignty in an Age of Globalisation," first draft of a document later revised and published in Frank Coffield (Ed.), *A National Strategy for Lifelong Learning*. Department of Education, University of Newcastle (Newcastle, UK).

Field, John. (2001). "Lifelong Education." *International Journal of Lifelong Education*, Vol. 20, No. 1/2 (January–April), 3–15.

Foucault, Michel. (1980). *Language, Counter-Memory, Practice*. Donald F. Bouchard (Ed.), Cornell University Press (Ithaca, NY).

Foucault, Michel. (1984a). "What Is Enlightenment?" In Paul Rabinow (Ed.), *The Foucault Reader*. Pantheon Books (New York).

Foucault, Michel. (1984b). *The History of Sexuality Volume 1*. Penguin Books (London).

Foucault, Michel. (1989). *The Order of Things*. Tavistock/Routledge (London New York).

Foucault, Michel. (1990). *The Care of the Self*. Penguin Books (London).

Foucault, Michel. (1991a). *Discipline and Punish: The Birth of the Prison*. Penguin Books (London).

Foucault, Michel. (1991b). *Remarks on Marx: Conversations with Duccio Trombadori*. Semiotext(e) (New York).

Foucault, Michel. (1997). *Essential Works 1: Ethics* (Paul Rabinow, Ed.). Allen Lane, Penguin (London).

Foucault, Michel. (1998). *Essential Works 2: Aesthetics* (Paul Rabinow, Ed.). Allen Lane, Penguin (London).

Foucault, Michel. (2001). *Fearless Speech* (Joseph Pearson, Ed.). Semiotext(e) (New York).

Frangiere, Gabriel. (1976). *Education without Frontiers*. Duckworth (London).

Fraser, Nancy. (1984). "The French Derrideans: Politicizing Deconstruction or Deconstructing the Political?" *New German Critique*, Vol. XXXIII (127–154).

Fraser, Nancy. (1992). "Rethinking the Public Sphere: A Contribution to the Critique of Actually Existing Democracy." In Craig Calhoun (Ed.), *Habermas and the Public Sphere*. The MIT Press (Cambridge, MA; London).

Fromm, Eric. (1971). *The Sane Society*. Routledge (London).

Furter, Pierre. (1977). *The Planner and Lifelong Education*. UNESCO International Institute for Educational Planning (Paris).

Gadamer, Hans-Georg. (1988). *Truth and Method*. Sheed and Ward (London).

Gane, Mike. (Ed.). (1993). *Baudrillard Live*. Routledge (New York, London).

Gelpi, Ettore. (1984a). "Lifelong Education and International Relations." In Kenneth Wain (Ed.), *Lifelong Education and Participation*. The University of Malta Press (Malta).

Gelpi, Ettore. (1984b). "Lifelong Education: Opportunities and Obstacles." *International Journal of Lifelong Education*, Vol. 3, No. 2, 79–87.

Gestrelius, Kurt. (1979). "Lifelong Education—A New Challenge." *European Journal of School Education*, Vol. 1, No. 3, 277–292.

Gibbins, John R., & Reimer, Bo. (1999). *The Politics of Postmodernity*. Sage Publications (London; Thousand Oaks, CA; New Delhi).

Giddens, Anthony. (1991). *Modernity and Self-Identity: Self and Society in the Late Modern Age*. Polity Press (Oxford, UK).

Giddens, Anthony. (1998a). *Beyond Left and Right*. Polity Press (Oxford, UK).

Giddens, Anthony. (1998b). *The Third Way: The Renewal of Social Democracy* Polity Press (Oxford, UK).

Gilbert, Rob. (1992). "Citizenship, Education and Postmodernity." *British Journal of Sociology of Education*, Vol. 13, No. 1, 51–68.

Giroux, Henri. (1992). *Border Crossings*. Routledge (New York, London).

Gordon, Colin. (1980). *Michel Foucault Power/Knowledge*. Harvester Wheatsheaf (New York).

Green, Andy. (1994). "Postmodernism and State Education." *Journal of Educational Policy*, Vol. 9, No. 1, 67–83.

Greene, Maxine. (1982). "Public Education and the Public Space." *Educational Researcher*, Vol. 11, No. 6 (June–July), 4–9.

Griffin, Colin. (1983). *Curriculum Theory in Adult and Lifelong Education*. Croom Helm (London).

Habermas, Jurgen. (1970). *Toward a Rational Society: Student Protest, Science and Politics*. Beacon Press (Boston).

Habermas, Jurgen. (1974). *Theory and Practice*. Heinemann (London).

Habermas, Jurgen. (1979). *Communication and the Evolution of Society*. Heinemann (London).

Habermas, Jurgen. (1981). "Modernity versus Postmodernity." *New German Critique 2*, 3–14.

Habermas, Jurgen. (1982). "A Reply to My Critics." In John B.Thompson & David Held (Eds.), *Habermas Critical Debates*. Macmillan Press (London).

Habermas, Jurgen. (1989a). *The Structural Transformation of the Public Sphere*. Polity Press (Oxford, UK).

Habermas, Jurgen. (1989b). *Legitimation Crisis*. Polity Press (Oxford, UK).

Habermas, Jurgen. (1989c). *The New Conservatism*. Polity Press (Oxford, UK).

Habermas, Jurgen. (1990a). *The Philosophical Discourse of Modernity*. Polity Press (Oxford, UK).

Habermas, Jurgen. (1990b). "What Does Socialism Mean Today? The Rectifying Revolution and the Need for New Thinking on the Left." *New Left Review*, No. 183 (Sept/Oct), 1–21.

Habermas, Jurgen. (1992). "Further Reflections on the Public Sphere." In Craig Calhoun (Ed.), *Habermas and the Public Sphere*. The MIT Press (Cambridge, MA; London).

Habermas, Jurgen. (1994a). *The New Conservatism*. Polity Press (Oxford, UK).

Habermas, Jurgen. (1994b). *The Past as Future (Interviews with Michael Haller)*. Polity Press (Oxford, UK).

Habermas, Jurgen. (1996). *Habermas, Modernity and Law* (Mathieu Deflem, Ed.). Sage Publications (London; Thousand Oaks, CA; New Delhi).

Habermas, Jurgen. (1998a). *The Theory of Communicative Action: Volume 2*. Polity Press (Oxford, UK).

Habermas, Jurgen. (1998b). *Between Facts and Norms*. The MIT Press (Cambridge, MA).

Habermas, Jurgen. (1998c). *The Inclusion of the Other*. Polity Press (Oxford, UK).

Hall, Stuart; Held, David; & McGrew, Tony. (Eds.). (1996). *Modernity and Its Futures*. Polity Press (Oxford, UK).

Harris, Kevin. (1979). *Education and Knowledge*. Routledge and Kegan Paul (London).

Hawes, H.W.R. (1974). *Lifelong Education, Schools and Curricula in Developing Countries*. UIE Monograph 4 (Hamburg).

Haydon, Graham. (Ed.). (1987). *Education and Values: the Richard Peters Lectures*, Institute of Education, University of London (UK).

Heidegger, Martin. (1993). *Basic Writings*. Routledge (London).

Held, David. (1980). *Introduction to Critical Theory, Horkheimer to Habermas*. University of California Press (Berkeley CA).

Hirst, Paul H. (1974). *Knowledge and the Curriculum*. Routledge and Kegan Paul (London).

Hoskin, Keith. (1990). "Foucault Under Examination: The Crypto-Educationalist Unmasked." In Stephen Ball (Ed.), *Foucault and Education, Disciplines and Knowledge*. Routledge (London, New York).

Hughes, Christina, & Tight, Malcolm. (1995). "The Myth of the Learning Society." *British Journal of Educational Studies*, Vol. XXXXIII (September), 290–304.

Hunter, Ian. (1994). *Rethinking the School*. Allen and Unwin (New South Wales, Australia).

Hutcheon, Linda. (1989). *The Politics of Postmodernism*. Routledge & Kegan Paul (London).

Illich, I. & Verne, G. (1976). *Imprisoned in the Global Classroom*. Writers and Readers Publishing Company (Montreal). "An Interview with Alasdair MacIntyre." (1991). *Cogito* (Summer), 67–73.

Illich, Ivan. (1978). *Deschooling Society*. Penguin Books (Harmondsworth, UK).

Ireland, Timothy. (1978). *Gelpi's View of Lifelong Education*. Manchester Monographs 14 (Manchester, UK).

Janne, Henri. (1976). "Theoretical Foundations of Lifelong Education: A Sociological Perspective." In R.H. Dave, *Foundations of Lifelong Education*. Pergamon Press (Oxford, UK).

Jansen, Theo, & van der Veen, Ruud. (1996). "Adult Education in the Light of the Risk Society." In Peter Raggatt, Richard Edwards, & Nick Small (Eds.), *The Learning Society: Challenges and Trends*. Routledge and the Open University (London, New York).

Jessup, F.W. (Ed.). (1969). *Lifelong Learning*. Pergamon Press (London).

Jones, Alan. (1995). "A Learning in Organizations Model." In David Bradshaw (Ed.), *Bringing Learning to Life*. The Falmer Press (London; Washington, DC).

Kallen, Denis. (1979). "Recurrent Education and Lifelong Learning: Definitions and Distinctions." In Tom Schuller & Jaquetta Megarry (Eds.), *World Yearbook of Education 1979: Recurrent Education and Lifelong Learning*. Kogan Page/Nichols Publishing Co. (London).

Kanpol, Barry. (1995). "Is Education at the End of a Sovereign Story or at the Beginning of Another? Cultural-Political Possibilities and Lyotard." In Michael Peters (Ed.), *Education and the Postmodern Condition*. Bergin & Garvey (Westport, CT; London).

Kateb, George. (1982). "Looking for Mr. Good Life." *The American Scholar*, 51 (Summer), 432–436.

Kellner, Douglas. (1989). *Jean Baudrillard: From Marxism to Postmodernism and Beyond*. Polity Press (Oxford, UK).

Kenway, Jane. (1995). "Having a Postmodernist Turn or Postmodernist *Angst*: A Disorder Experienced by an Author Who is Not Yet Dead or Even Close to It." In Richard Smith & Philip Wexler (Eds.), *After Postmodernism: Education, Politics and Identity*. The Falmer Press (London; Washington DC).

Kirpal, P.N. (1976). "Historical Studies and the Foundations of Lifelong Education." In R.H. Dave (Ed.), *Foundations of Lifelong Education*. Pergamon Press (Oxford, UK).

Kiziltian, Mustafa U; Bain, William J; & Canizares, Anita M. (1990). "Postmodern Conditions: Rethinking Public Education," *Educational Theory* 40, 3 (Summer), 351–369.

Knight, John. (1995). "Fading Poststructuralisms: Post-Ford, Posthuman, Posteducation?" In Richard Smith & Philip Wexler (Eds.), *After Postmodernism: Education, Politics and Identity*. The Falmer Press (London, Washington, DC).

Kritzman, Lawrence D. (1990). *Michel Foucault: Politics, Philosophy, Culture*. Routledge (New York, London).

Kundera, Milan. (1991). *Immortality*. Faber and Faber (London).

Ladwig, James G. (1995). "Educational Intellectuals and Corporate Politics." In Richard Smith & Philip Wexler (Eds.), *After Postmodernism: Education, Politics, and Identity.* The Falmer Press (London; Washington, DC).

Lakatos, Imre. (1980). *The Methodology of Scientific Research Programs.* Cambridge University Press (Cambridge, UK).

Lawson, Kenneth. (1982). "Lifelong Education: Concept or Policy?" *International Journal of Lifelong Education*, Vol. 1, No. 2, 97–108.

Lengrand, Paul. (1975). *An Introduction to Lifelong Education.* Croom Helm (London), and the UNESCO Press (Paris).

Lengrand, Paul. (1986). *Areas of Learning Basic to Lifelong Education.* Pergamon Press (Oxford, New York).

Levin, Charles. (1996). *Jean Baudrillard: A Study in Cultural Metaphysics.* Prentice Hall/ Harvester Wheatsheaf (New York, London).

Lilla, Mark. (1998). "The Politics of Jacques Derrida." *The New York Review*, (June) 25, 36–41.

Long, Huey B. (1974). "Lifelong Learning: Pressures for Acceptance." *Journal of Research and Development in Education*, No. 7, 2–12.

Longworth, Norman, & Davies, Keith W. (1996). *Lifelong Learning.* Kogan Page (London).

Lyotard, Jean-François. (1993). *Political Writings.* University College London Press (London, UK).

Lyotard, Jean-François. (1999). *The Postmodern Condition: A Report on Knowledge.* Manchester University Press (Manchester, UK).

Macey, David. (1994). *The Lives of Michel Foucault.* Vintage Press (London).

MacIntyre, Alasdair. (1981). *After Virtue.* Duckworth (London).

MacIntyre, Alasdair. (1987). "The Idea of an Educated Public." In Graham Haydon (Ed.), *Education and Values.* London Institute of Education, University of London.

MacIntyre, Alasdair. (1988). *Whose Justice? Which Rationality?* Duckworth (London).

MacIntyre, Alasdair. (1990). *Three Rival Versions of Moral Inquiry.* Duckworth (London).

MacIntyre, Alasdair. (1992). "Democracy Ancient, Modern and Postmodern" (book review). *The Review of Politics*, 54, 311–313.

MacIntyre, Alasdair. (1994). "A Partial Response to My Critics." In John Horton & Susan Mendus (Eds.), *After MacIntyre.* Polity Press (Oxford, UK).

MacIntyre, Alasdair. (1999). *Dependent Rational Animals.* Duckworth (London).

MacIntyre, Alasdair, & Dunne, Joseph. (2002). "Alasdair MacIntyre on Education: In Dialogue with Joseph Dunne." *Journal of Philosophy of Education*, Vol. 36, No. 1, 1–19.

MacLaren, Peter. (1991). "Postmodernism, Post-Colonialism, and Pedagogy." *Education and Society*, Vol. 9, No. 1, 3–22.

MacLaren, Peter. (1995). "Critical Pedagogy and the Pragmatics of Justice." In Michael Peters (Ed.), Education and the Postmodern Condition. Bergin & Garvey (Westport, CT, and London).

Makino, Atsushi. (1997). "Recent Developments in Japan's Lifelong Learning Society," Internet text, apec-hurdit.org.

Marchand, Marianne H., & Parpart, Jane L. (Eds.). (1995). *Feminism/Postmodernism/ Development.* Routledge (London, New York).

Marcuse, Herbert. (1969). *An Essay on Liberation*. Beacon Books (Boston).

Marcuse, Herbert. (1994). *One-Dimensional Man*. Routledge (London).

Margalit, Avishai. (1996). *The Decent Society*. Harvard University Press (Cambridge, MA; London).

Martin, Luther H.; Gutman, Huck; and Hutton, Patrick H. (1988). *Technologies of the Self: A Seminar with Michel Foucault*. Tavistock Publishers (London).

Masschelein, Joseph. (1991). "The Relevance of Habermas' Communicative Turn." *Studies in Philosophy and Education*, 11, 95–111.

May, Todd. (1994). *The Political Philosophy of Poststructuralist Anarchism*. Pennsylvania State University Press (University Park, PA).

McCarthy, Thomas. (1989–90). "The Politics of the Ineffable: Derrida's Deconstructionism." *The Philosophical Forum*, Vol. XXI, Nos. 1–2 (Fall–Winter), 146–168.

McMylor, Peter. (1994). *Alasdair MacIntyre: Critic of Modernity*. Routledge (London, New York).

Mendus, Susan. (1992). "All the King's Horses and All the King's Men: Justifying Higher Education." *Journal of Philosophy of Education*, Vol. 26, No. 2, 173–182.

Merquior, J.G. (1985). *Foucault*. Fontana Press/Collins (London).

Miller, David. (1994). "Virtues, Practices and Justice." In John Horton & Susan Mendus (Eds.), *After MacIntyre*. Polity Press (Oxford, UK).

Mouffe, Chantal. (Ed.). (1996). *Deconstruction and Pragmatism*. Routledge (London).

Nagel, Thomas. (1986). *The View from Nowhere*. Oxford University Press (Oxford, UK).

Neiman, Alven. (1993). "Rorty, Irony, Education." *Studies in Philosophy and Education*, Vol. 12, Nos. 2–4, 205–209.

Nicholson, Carol. (1995). "Postmodern Feminisms." In Michael Peters (Ed.), *Education and the Postmodern Condition*. Bergin & Garvey (Westport CT; London).

Nozick, Robert (1984). *Anarchy, State and Utopia*. Basil Blackwell (Oxford, UK).

Nussbaum, Martha. (1997). *Cultivating Humanity: A Classical Defense of Reform in Liberal Education*. Harvard University Press (Cambridge, MA).

Oakes, Edward T. (1996). "The Achievement of Alasdair MacIntyre." *First Things*, 65, 22–26.

O'Brien, Stephen. (1999). "New Labour, New Approach? A Critical Review of Educational Theory." Paper presented at the *BERA Annual Conference*, Queen's University of Belfast, August 27–30.

Oddi, L.F. (1987). "Perspectives on Self-Directed Learning." *Adult Education Quarterly*, 38 (1), 21–31.

Parkyn, George W. (1973). *Towards a Conceptual Model of Life-long Education*. UNESCO Monograph (Paris).

Paterson, R.W.K. (1979). *Values, Education and the Adult*. Routledge and Kegan Paul (London).

Patton, Paul. (1989). "Taylor and Foucault on Power and Freedom." *Political Studies*, 37, 260–276.

Peters, Michael. (1996). *Poststructuralism, Politics and Education*. Bergin & Garvey (Westport, CT; London).

Peukert, Helmut. (1992). "Basic Problems of a Critical Theory of Education." *Papers of the Philosophy of Education Society of Great Britain*, (April) 26–28, 116–123.

Popper, Karl. (1965). *The Open Society and Its Enemies, Vols. 1 & 2*. Routledge and Kegan Paul (London).

Quicke, John. (1997). "Reflexivity, Community and Education for the Learning Society." *Curriculum Studies*, Vol. 5, No. 2, 139–161.

Rabinow, Paul. (Ed.). (1984). *The Foucault Reader.* Penguin Books (London).

Raggatt, Peter; Edwards, Richard; & Small, Nick. (Eds.). (1996). *The Learning Society: Challenges and Trends.* Routledge and the Open University (London, New York).

Ranson, Stewart. (1994). *Towards the Learning Society.* Cassell (London).

Ranson, Stewart; Martin, Jane; & Dixon, John. (1997). "A Learning Democracy for Cooperative Action." *Oxford Review of Education*, Vol. 23, No. 1, 117–131.

Ranson, Stewart, & Stewart, John. (1994). *Management for the Public Domain: Enabling the Learning Society.* St Martin's Press (New York).

Rawls, John. (1980). *A Theory of Justice.* Oxford University Press (Oxford, UK).

Rinne, Risto. (1998). "From Labour to Learn: The Limits of Labor Society and the Possibilities of Learning Society." *International Journal of Lifelong Education*, Vol. 17, No. 2, 108–120.

Rojek, Chris, & Turner, Bryan S. (Eds.). (1993). *Forget Baudrillard.* Routledge (London, New York).

Rorty, Richard. (1980). *Philosophy and the Mirror of Nature.* Basil Blackwell (Oxford, UK).

Rorty, Richard. (1982). *Consequences of Pragmatism.* The Harvester Press.

Rorty, Richard. (1987). "Thugs and Theorists." *Political Theory*, Vol. 15, No. 4 (November), 564–580.

Rorty, Richard. (1989). *Contingency, Irony, and Solidarity.* University of Cambridge Press (Cambridge, UK).

Rorty, Richard. (1990a). "The Danger of Over-Philosophication: Reply to Arcilla and Nicholson." *Educational Theory*, Vol. 40, No. 1 (Winter), 41–44.

Rorty, Richard. (1990b). "The Priority of Democracy to Philosophy." In Alan Malachowski (Ed.), *Reading Rorty.* Basil Blackwell (Oxford, UK).

Rorty, Richard. (1990c). "Education without Dogma." *Dialogue*, No. 2, 44–47.

Rorty, Richard. (1992). "Trotsky and the Wild Orchids." *Common Knowledge*, Vol. 1, No. 3, 140–153.

Rorty, Richard. (1995). "Philosophy and the Future." In Herman J. Saatkamp Jr. (Ed.), *Rorty and Pragmatism.* Vanderbilt University Press (Nashville, TN; London).

Rorty, Richard. (1998). *Achieving Our Country.* Harvard University Press (Cambridge, MA; London).

Rorty, Richard. (1999). *Philosophy and Social Hope.* Penguin Books (London).

Rozycki, Edward G. (1987). "Policy and Social Contradiction: The Case of Lifelong Education." *Educational Theory* (Fall) 37, No. 4, 433–443.

Rubenson, Kjell, & Borgstrom, Laen. (1981). "Equality in the Context of Lifelong Education: Consequences for Policy and Research." In Brian Hervey, David Jones, John Dames, & John Wallis, *Policy and Research in Adult Education* (The First Nottingham International Colloquium 1981). Department of Adult Education, University of Nottingham (Nottingham, UK).

Schuller, Tom. (1998). "Three Steps Towards a Learning Society." *Studies in the Education of Adults*, Vol. 30, No. 1 (April), 11–20.

Seitz, Brian. (1995). *The Trace of Political Representation.* State University of New York Press (Albany).

Simons, Jon. (1995). *Foucault and the Political.* Routledge (London, New York).

Singh, Parlo. (1995). "Voicing the 'Other,' Speaking for the 'Self,' Disrupting the Metanarratives of Educational Theorizing with Poststructural Feminisms." In Richard Smith & Philip Wexler (Eds.), *After Postmodernism: Education, Politics and Identity.* The Falmer Press (London; Washington, DC).

Skager, Rodney. (1978). *Lifelong Education and Evaluation Practices.* Pergamon Press (Oxford, UK).

Smart, Barry. (1992). *Modern Conditions, Postmodern Controversies.* Routledge (London, New York).

Smith, Richard, & Wexler, Philip. (Eds.). (1995). *After Postmodernism: Education, Politics and Identity.* The Falmer Press (London; Washington, DC).

Standish, Paul. (1995). "Postmodernism and the Education of the Whole Person." *Journal of Philosophy of Education.* Vol. 29, No. 1, 121–135.

Stock, Arthur. (1996). "Lifelong Learning: Thirty Years of Educational Change." In Peter Raggatt, Richard Edwards, & Nick Small (Eds.), *The Learning Society: Challenges and Trends.* Routledge and the Open University (London, New York).

Stout, Jeffrey. (1988). *Ethics after Babel.* Beacon Press (Boston).

Strain, Michael, & Field, John. (1997). "On 'The Myth of the Learning Society.'" *British Journal of Educational Studies*, Vol. 45, No. 2 (June), 141–155.

Suchodolski, Bogdan. (1976). "Lifelong Education—Some Philosophical Aspects." In R.H. Dave, *Foundations of Lifelong Education.* Pergamon Press (Oxford, UK).

Suchodolski, Bogdan. (1979). "Lifelong Education at the Crossroads." In Arthur J. Cropley (Ed.), *Lifelong Education: A Stocktaking.* UIE Monographs 8 (Hamburg, Germany), 34–49.

Superintendent of Documents. (1983). *A Nation at Risk: The Imperative for Educational Reform.* U.S. Government Printing Office (Washington, DC).

Taylor, Charles. (1985). "Foucault on Freedom and Truth." In *Philosophy and the Human Sciences: Philosophical Papers 2.* Cambridge University Press (Cambridge, UK).

Taylor, Charles. (1994). "Justice After Virtue." In John Horton & Susan Mendus (Eds.), *After MacIntyre.* Polity Press (Oxford, UK).

Taylor, Richard. (1998). "Lifelong Learning in the Liberal Tradition." *Journal of Moral Education*, Vol. 27, No. 3, 301–312.

Tett, Lyn. (1996). "Education and the Marketplace." In Peter Raggatt, Richard Edwards, & Nick Small (Eds.), *The Learning Society: Challenges and Trends.* Routledge and the Open University (London, New York).

Thomas, Alan M. (1991). *Beyond Education: A New Perspective on Society's Management of Learning.* Jossey-Bass (London).

Tight, Malcolm. (1998). "Education, Education, Education! The Vision of Lifelong Learning in the Kennedy, Dearing, and Fryer Reports." *Oxford Review of Education*, Vol. 24, No. 4, 473–485.

Tuijnman, Albert C. (1996). "The Expansion of Adult Education and Training in Europe: Trends and Issues." In Peter Raggatt, Richard Edwards, & Nick Small (Eds.), *The Learning Society: Challenges and Trends.* Routledge and the Open University (London, New York).

Usher, Robin, & Edwards, Richard. (1994). *Postmodernism and Education: Different Voices, Different Worlds.* Routledge (London, New York).

van der Zee, Hendrik. (1996). "The Learning Society." In Peter Raggatt, Richard Edwards, & Nick Small (Eds.), *The Learning Society: Challenges and Trends*. Routledge and Open University Press (London, New York).

Wain, Kenneth (Ed.). (1984). *Lifelong Education and Participation*. The University of Malta Press (Malta).

Wain, Kenneth. (1987). *Philosophy of Lifelong Education*. Croom Helm (Kent, New South Wales).

Wain, Kenneth. (1989). "The Case of Lifelong Education—A Reply to Rozycki." *Educational Theory* (Spring), Vol. 39, No. 2, 151–162.

Wain, Kenneth. (1993). "Lifelong Education: Illiberal and Repressive?" *Educational Philosophy and Theory*, Vol. 25, No. 1, 58–70.

Wain, Kenneth. (1995). "MacIntyre and the Idea of an Educated Public." *Studies in Philosophy and Education*, 14, 105–123.

Walzer, Michael. (1986). "The Politics of Michel Foucault." In David Couzens-Hoy (Ed.), *Foucault: A Critical Reader*. Basil Blackwell (Oxford, UK).

Waterman, Ruth H.; Waterman, Judith A.; and Collard, Betsy A. (1996). "Toward a Career-Resilient Workforce." In Peter Raggatt, Richard Edwards, & Nick Small (Eds.), *The Learning Society: Challenges and Trends*. Routledge and the Open University (London, New York).

Wolin, Sheldon D. (1990). "Democracy in the Discourse of Postmodernism." *Social Research*, Vol. 57, No. 1 (Spring), 5–30.

Worpole, Ken. (1996). "The Age of Leisure." In Peter Raggatt, Richard Edwards, & Nick Small (Eds.), *The Learning Society: Challenges and Trends*. Routledge and the Open University (London, New York).

Yarnit, Martin. (1997). "Living Together, Working Together: Key Issues for Lifelong Learning in the UK and Europe." Adult Learners' Week, Australia, bace.nsw.gov.au.

Yeatman, Anna. (1994). *Postmodern Revisioning of the Political*. Routledge (London, New York).

Young, Michael F.D. (1998). *The Curriculum of the Future*. Falmer Press (London).

Young, R.E. (1990). "Habermas' Ontology of Learning: Reconstructing Dewey." *Educational Theory*, Vol. 4, No. 4, 471–482.

Young, Robert. (1995). "Liberalism, Postmodernism, Critical Theory and Politics." In Richard Smith & Philip Wexler (Eds.), *After Postmodernism: Education, Politics and Identity*. The Falmer Press (London; Washington, DC).

Zaret, David. (1992). "Religion, Science, and Printing in the Public Spheres in Seventeenth-Century England." In Craig Calhoun (Ed.), *Habermas and the Public Sphere*. The MIT Press (Cambridge, MA; London).

INDEX

A

Adorno, Theodor 140, 143, 267, 296; culture industry 145-146, 151, 178.

Adorno, Theodor & Horkheimer Max xi, xv, 45, 53, 55, 97, 135, 140, 159, 164, 239, 277, 290, 291, 293, 300, 314; culture industry 58, 144, 146, 152; Enlightenment 95, 96, 329

adult education/learning, *passim*; as commodity, 77, 79, 151, 178, 217; as human/ moral right, 81, 83-84; as leisure industry, 71, 77, 79-80, 178, 217; as welfare right, 81-82, 86; vocationalization of, 69, 77, 80

Alcoff, Linda 235

Andersen, Perry & Dews, Peter 164, 330

Anyon, Jean 237

Apel, Karl-Otto 101, 294

Apple, Michael 136

Aquinas, Thomas 103, 115, 122, 133, 327

Arcilla, Rene 270

Arendt, Hannah 51, 101

Aristotle 9, 97, 102, 105, 115, 133, 323, 333

Arnold, Matthew 2

Aronowitz, Stanley &Giroux, Henry 231, 233, 234, 238

Artaud, Antoine 238

Aspin, David & Chapman, Judith 22, 23, 36, 88, 89

B

Bachelard, Gaston 2

Bagnall, Richard 34-36, 37, 39, 88, 323

Bailey, Charles 6-9, 24, 44, 86, 214

Bain, William 55

Baker, Keith Michael 154

Ball, Christopher 68, 73, 74

Ball, Stephen 234

Bamburg, Jerry D. 74

Barthes, Roland 240

Bataille, George 122, 238, 240, 304

Baudelaire, Charles 238, 259

Baudrillard, Jean x, xii, xiv-xv, 59, 61, 146, 227, 229, 234, 238, 280, 295-296, 312, 318, 347; and learning society 277, 294, 297; and McLuhan 289-290; and politics 281, 299-300; and postmodern society/ world 290, 292-294, 298; and utopia 292, 294, 336; dystopian narrative/writing 277, 290-291; mass/mass society 290-294, 308, 349; media/information society 288-291, 293, 294; narcissism 299, 254, 306; obscene society xiii, 287-297; on fascination 289, 293-294, 336; on Foucault 277-279, 288, 290, 335; on intellectuals 300-301, 309; on modernity 289, 291, 292; on power 294, 335; on seduction 289, 298, 336; radical individualism xiv, 300; self-destruction xiv, 297-300, 306; silent masses 291, 294; strategy banal/fatal 298-299; terror/ ism 292-293, 297; the object 298-299; writing 297-300

Bauman, Zygmunt 190-193, 288

Beaufret, Jean 96

Beck, Ulrich 5, 8, 10, 51, 53, 167, 168-169; and the risk society 195, 219, 321

Bell, Daniel 57-58

Benhabib, Seyla 155, 165-166, 235

Bentham, Jeremy 283

Bernd, Magnus 240

Bernstein, Richard 249, 264-265

Bertens, Hans 240

Best, Steven 52, 332

Best, Steven & Kellner, Douglas 238

Beyer, Landon & Liston, Daniel P. 230

Bhaskar, Roy, 265

Blake, Nigel; Smeyers, Paul; Smith, Richard; & Standish, Paul 213, 304, 331, 332
Blanchot, Maurice 304
Bloch, Ernst 164
Bofill, Joan 216
Boyle, Charles 322
Bradshaw, David 67, 71
British Labor Party/Government xii, 75, 89, 194, 198, 204, 210, 218, 331; Green paper 84, 210, 212-214, 331; lifelong learning policies 202, 210-213, 223; learning society 89-90, 202, 210-211, 213, 219
Buchanan, Pat 334

C

Calhoun, Craig 156-157, 160, 330
Caputo, John 97-99, 112, 243-244, 245, 250-251, 254, 255-257, 326
Carr, Wilfred 231-232
Chomsky, Noam 242, 245, 306, 320
Cohen, Joshua 173
Comenius, John Amos 2
Commission for Social Justice 75, 83-84, 194, 212, 331
Connelly, Brian 136-137, 329
consensual discourse/politics 99, 125-126, 193, 231, 248
continuing education *see* education
conversation (politics of) 99, 125-126, 248-251 *see* Bernstein, Gadamer, Habermas, MacIntyre, poststructuralism, Rorty
Corlett, William 251-252, 255-257
Council of Europe 10, 20, 48
Couzens-Hoy, David 279
critical pedagogy 136, 230, 235
critical theory 230, 234, 267 *see* Frankfurt School, Habermas, Horkheimer
Crook, Stephen; Pakulski, Jan; & Waters, Malcolm 54, 55, 324
Cropley, A.J. 15, 38, 322, 324
Cross, Patricia 81
Cross-Durant, Angela 20, 33, 322
culture industry 145, 150-151, 160 *see* Adorno & Horkheimer, Habermas
Cynics 346

D

d'Arcy, Jean 58
Dahrendorf, Ralf 169
Danto, Arthur 298
Dave, R.H. 9, 15, 21, 49
Davies, B. 317
de Onis, Federico 332
deconstruction 226, 234, 240-241, 243-245, 273, 320 *see* Caputo, Derrida
deconstructionism 240, 256 *see* post-structuralism
Deleon, Asher 58
Deleuze, Gilles 229, 240, 310, 312-313, 327
Delors Commission 63
democracy 58, 100, 115, 116-118, 149, 153, 158, 173, 186, 204, 223, 227, 231, 232, 234, 241, 245, 255-257, 259, 307-308, 320 *see* Derrida, Dewey, Giddens, Habermas, MacIntyre, Popper; Greek 149, 310, 326; learning *see* Ranson; 'managed' 266, 334 *see* Wolin; participatory ix, 185-186, 188
democratic learning society *see* learning society, learning democracy
democratic public sphere 116, 208, 232 *see* Dewey, Habermas
Dennett, Daniel 229
Denzin, Norman 59, 61
Derrida, Jacques x, xii, xiiv, 122, 229, 240, 245, 247, 248, 250, 258, 267, 273, 279, 299, 304, 312, 328; and education 333 *see* Usher & Edwards; and Marx/Marxism 243, 252-255, 333; deconstruction 243, 253-255, 333; ethics (care for the other/gift giving/hospitality) 198, 250-255, 333; on narcissism 254-255; politics xiii, 243-244, 251, 252-257, 319, 333 *see* Caputo
Descartes, Rene 96, 100, 239, 240, 246, 302, 317
deschooling movement 20, 25-26, 28, 29, 38, 86
Dewey, John 2, 10, 16, 24, 26, 81, 83, 115, 135, 138, 173, 179, 185, 216, 232, 247, 255, 258, 259, 261, 273, 335 *see* lifelong education, Rorty; and democracy 7, 21, 34, 36, 115, 171, 307, 315; and the

learning society 33, 215, 314-315; and the public 101, 102, 154, 163, 327; democratic learning communities 103, 124, 215; education as growth 6-8, 21-22, 33, 35-36, 82, 104, 152, 214-215, 315, 322, 325; individualism (new/rugged) 136, 215, 274, 333; informal learning 34-36, 40; learning environments 8, 34-36

Dews, Peter 330

difference (politics of) 193, 236, 237, 253, 256-257

Dilthey, Wilhelm 328

Di Stefano, Christine 236

distance/open learning 78-80, 111, 113

Dixon, John 184, 186

Docherty, Thomas 332

Dohman, Gunther 199-202, 215

Dreyfus, Hubert & Rabinow, Paul 250

Dunne, Joe 129, 130, 328

dystopia/dystopian narratives/writing xiii, 91, 141, 247, 279, 280 *see* Adorno and Horkheimer, Baudrillard, Foucault, Marcuse

E

Edel, Abraham 325

educated person (man) 43-44, 66, 100, 121, 196, 272

educated public xiii-xiv, 101-102, 111, 113, 158, 160, 184, 187-188, 217, 273, 318 *see* Dewey, learning society, MacIntyre, university

education ix-x, 8-9, 13, 35, 41, 75, 85, 89, 97, 150, 160, 179, 184, 186, 200, 203, 209-210, 230, 282, 232-233, 321-322, 325 *see* adult education, Dewey, Habermas, MacIntyre; and life 16, 35, 323 *see* Dewey; and performativity x, 74, 89, 111, 129, 138, 225; as subversive *see* Foucault, Marcuse, Rorty; continuing 10, 19-20, 24, 37, 40, 42, 71, 322; crisis/death of ix-x, 91, 214-225, 227, 233; democratic *see* democratic education; liberal 23, 43, 82, 335; lifewide 21, 24, 42, 81, 200, 323; normative definition/

concept 6, 10, 21-22, 35, 40, 41, 89, 214, 215 *see* Dewey; operational (technical) definition 6, 10, 21-22, 35, 41 *see* Dewey; permanent 10, 19-20; postmodern agenda/politics of xiv, 161, 225-226, 230, 233; recurrent 10, 19-20, 24, 37, 40, 42, 49-50, 322; self- *see* self-education

education research project xii-xiii, xv-xvi, 41-44, 88, 89, 100, 125, 128, 174, 183, 248, 320, 323, 325 *see* MacIntyre

educational theory ix, xii, 41, 226, 231, 233, 236, 272 *see* postmodernism

educative society 9, 47-48

Edwards, Richard 74

Edwards, Richard; Raggatt, Peter; Harrison Roger; McCollum Anne; & Calder, Judith 66, 70, 203, 222

Eley, Geoff 153-154

Elliott, Philip 58-59, 61, 178

emancipation/empowerment 82, 96, 112, 146, 166, 172, 217, 223, 226, 229, 232, 235, 236, 237, 244, 268, 316, 332 *see* Habermas

emancipatory pedagogy *see* critical pedagogy

emancipatory politics 206, 230 *see* feminism, Habermas, Vattimo

enculturation/individuation xiv, 138, 255 *see* Foucault, MacIntyre, Rorty

Enlightenment x, 55, 58, 91, 96, 100, 101, 108, 136, 150, 158, 166, 205, 231, 232, 235, 237, 244, 328, 329, 333 *see* Adorno and Horkheimer, Foucault, Habermas

European Commission x, 62, 63, 68, 87; and lifelong learning 68, 221, 223; white paper (1995) 63, 69-70, 204, 211, 219, 221, 224

European Round Table of Industrialists 68-69, 72

European Union (EU) x, xiv, 38, 54, 55, 62, 90, 177, 198, 207, 221; and learning society 90, 189, 223, 256; and lifelong learning 39, 63, 74, 189, 205, 213, 220-221, 223, 256 *see* Field, Yarnit; education policy 63-64, 90, 224, 337

Ewert, Gerry D. 136

F

Faure Report ix, 10-11, 16-18, 25-26, 29, 38-39, 45-48, 62, 64, 68, 87, 89, 223, 224, 321

Feinberg, Walter 98, 101, 158, 326

feminism 56, 114, 229, 230, 235, 265, 341; criticism of postmodernism 235-238

Fern Haber, Honi 242, 265, 266

Field, John 49-50, 62, 63, 78, 79, 80, 324

Flower, Elizabeth 325

Fontana, Alessandro & Pasquino, Pasquale 309

Foucault, Michel x, xii, 14, 27, 95, 112, 114, 142, 167, 172-173, 175, 183, 196, 229, 234, 235, 237, 245, 251, 267, 275, 286, 290, 297, 299, 327, 328 *see* Baudrillard, Rorty; anarchism xiii, 280, 241-242, 252, 255, 310-313, 319; and democracy 306-307, 311, 316 *see* Seitz; and Frankfurt theorists 97, 277, 335; and Habermas 166, 177, 241, 281, 296-297, 336; as poststructuralist 97, 318, 320; carceral/ disciplinary/ punitive society 281-285, 288, 317; dystopian narratives/writing, 255, 277, 279-281; enculturation/ individuation xiv, 318; ethics xiv, 254-255, 281, 297, 301-306, 311, 313, 315-316, 318, 336; genealogy xiv, 240, 245, 247, 256, 278-281, 297, 303, 315, 333, 336; hermeneutics 249-250, 303; individualism xiv, 304-305; learning society 277, 281, 283-285, 287, 297, 313-315, 317, 319-320; narcissism 254, 304-306, 317; on education 301, 313-316, 318, 336, 337; on examination 285, 287, 303, 335, 350; on government/ governance 286, 287, 317, 318, 319, 320; on intellectuals xv 263, 275, 301, 308-310, 316; on justice 242-243, 256, 306-307; on liberalism/liberal democracy 259, 306; on modern state 277, 281, 283-287, 311; on power (bio/ disciplinary/ power/knowledge) xiv, 241-243, 245-246, 252-253, 255, 277, 278, 281, 282-288, 297, 301, 305-307, 309-310, 312, 314, 315-317, 318, 319, 332, 335-336; on schooling 283-284, 335; on self-creation, xiv-xv, 275, 297, 304, 306, 317, 318; on self-examination/confession 287, 303; on self-government/-mastery 287, 288, 302, 303, 305, 306, 313, 315-317, 319; on subjectification xiv, 245, 288, 301, 315, 318335; on truth 246, 278-279, 281, 287, 307, 309-311, 315; panopticon society 282, 288, 291, 319; *parrhesia* 310-311, 313, 318; politics xiii-xiv, 241-242, 252, 255, 257, 280-281, 307-310, 312, 316-317, 319, 320, 333; writing as fiction 247, 278-279, 304, 335

Frangiere, Gabriel 39

Frankel, Boris 85

Frankfurt School/theorists xi, 59, 95, 97, 101, 102, 135, 141, 143, 144, 147, 148, 166, 280, 314, 329; rational society xi, 97, 135, 139, 314 *see* Habermas, Horkheimer; totally administered society 95, 112, 177

Fraser, Nancy 153, 155, 241, 243, 333

Frazer, Elizabeth 119

Freud, Sigmund 157, 234, 261, 329

Fromm, Eric xiv, 143-144, 216, 329

Furter, Pierre 48, 50, 165, 321

G

Gadamer, Hans-Georg xiv, 101, 172, 185, 205, 250, 330; on conversation 206, 248-250

Garnham, Nicholas 154

Gelpi, Ettore 17, 24-25, 32, 46-47, 49, 89, 216, 321, 322

Gestrelius, Kurt 40

Gibbins, John & Reimar, Bo 57

Giddens, Anthony 10, 52, 189, 204-206, 209, 218-219, 226, 268-269, 320, 332; on democracy/social democracy 204-208, 208, 210, 216-217; philosophic conservatism 205-206, 208, 226; risk society 3-5, 53, 219; social investment/ welfare state 205, 206, 208-209, 219

Gilbert, Rob 57, 231

Giroux, Henry 136, 234

globalization 51, 53, 54, 58, 204, 206, 207, 219, 331

Godot 94

Goffman, Irving 93
Gramsci, Antonio 169
Green, Andy 71, 230, 233, 234
Greene, Maxine 101-102
Griffin, Colin 40
Guattari, Felix 229, 240

H

Habermas, Jurgen xi-xii, xiv, 59, 90, 91, 141, 143, 183, 186, 216, 229, 240, 255, 259, 268-269, 274, 297 *see* democratic education, Foucault, Rorty; and critical theory/ Frankfurt School 97, 138, 156-157, 177, 328; and education 136-138, 152, 160, 170, 179; and Enlightenment 155, 168, 180; and Marxism 135, 153, 157; and social democracy 135-136, 157, 159, 168-169, 177, 330; and social movements 142, 153, 162, 164, 168; anti-postmodernism 137, 142, 166, 168, 170, 172, 176, 180-181, 229, 238-239; communicative action/practice xi, 115, 136-138, 156-158, 161-163, 165, 167, 171-174, 176, 181, 188, 215, 230, 329, 330; communicative community xi, 139, 176, 179, 181, 185, 295; consensual/ conversational politics 99, 161, 163, 170, 181, 249; critical public sphere xi, 58, 136, 138, 139, 147-148, 150, 153, 158, 160, 163-164, 170, 179; culture industry 146-147, 151-152, 160, 178, 188; democracy xi, 115, 136, 147, 149, 153, 156-157, 159, 162-164, 170-180, 188, 307; emancipation/ emancipatory politics xi, 115, 137-139, 149, 157-158, 163-164, 167, 170-173, 178-181, 316; ideal speech 137-138, 157, 162, 164, 167, 170-171, 176, 179, 329; learning society 137-139, 144, 161, 163, 177, 179, 180, 187; liberal bourgeois public xi, 148-149, 152, 155-156, 159-160, 163, 179; media 146, 151-153, 160, 177, 178, 188; on adult education 136-138, 151, 178; on enlightenment 137, 171, 178, 180; on intellectuals xv, 163, 168, 177-180, 309; on justice 115, 175, 180-181; on

modernity x, 164, 227; on publicity/ public relations 138, 147, 150-153, 155-156, 164, 170, 174, 178-179; on theory 170-172; on welfare state 164, 167-170, 176-177, 179, 184, 189, 330; politicization of university 147-148, 273; public sphere 137-138, 148-149, 150, 152-153, 155-159, 162-163, 174, 177-179, 187, 215, 319; publics (wild/ autonomous/bourgeois) xi, 101, 154, 158-163, 174, 179, 184, 188, 215, 330; rational society xi, 135, 137, 139, 142, 146-147, 156-159, 172; systems/ lifeworld xi, 137-138, 147-149, 155, 158, 161-163, 169, 174-179, 187, 188, 286; utopianism xi, 157, 163-169, 171, 179, 180, 330
Haddab, Mustapha 216
Hall, Stuart 231
Hall, Stuart; Held, David; & McGrew, Tony 52
Haller, Michael 171
Harre, Rom 317
Harris, Kevin 41
Hassan, Ihab 332
Hawes, H.W.R. 321
Haydon, Graham 126, 327
Hegel, G. 150, 166, 244, 273, 294, 326, 328, 329
Heidegger, Martin 45, 97, 98, 238, 240, 243, 244, 245, 247, 259, 295, 326, 334; anti-humanism 96-97, 239-240; on technology 95-96, 112, 296
Held, David 328.
hermeneutics 295, 303, 332 *see* Caputo, Foucault, Gadamer, Rorty
Hirst, Paul 43
Hitler, Adolf 61
Hobbes, Thomas 118, 166
Hobsbawm, Eric 5
Hohendahl, Peter 170-171
Horkheimer, Max 135, 139-140, 143, 145, 329
Hoskin, Keith 337
Hughes, Christina & Tight, Malcolm 70, 72, 78, 87, 88, 89, 184, 197, 325
Hume, David 106
Hunter, Ian 27
Husserl, Edmund 302

Hutcheon, Linda 235
Huxley, Julian 18, 322

I

Illich, Ivan 33, 37, 38, 39, 50, 85, 86, 194, 200, 291, 323, 331 *see* deschooling; edu-credit card 29, 85, 331
individual learning accounts *see* Learning Bank
individualism 74, 76, 118, 159, 189, 198, 268, 294 *see* Baudrillard, Derrida, Dewey, Foucault, MacIntyre, Rorty, self-responsibility
informal learning *see* learning
information society x, 9, 57-62, 324 *see* Baudrillard, Elliott, Foucault, postmodern information society, learning society
intellectuals xv-xvi, 53, 59, 146, 160, 233, 313 *see* Baudrillard, Foucault, Habermas, Kundera, Rorty
Internet 32, 295-297

J

Jameson, Frederic 112, 333
Janne, Henri 21, 40
Jansen, Theo & van der Veen, Ruud 195
Jefferson, Thomas 261
Jenks, Charles 332
Jessup, F.W. 2, 322.
Jones, Alan 72, 73
justice 118, 118-123, 167, 176, 184-187, 192, 198, 218, 223, 227, 229, 241, 245, 255, 258, 320 *see* Derrida, Foucault, Giddens, Habermas, MacIntyre, social justice; conversational 121, 122, 179, 256 *see* Derrida, Habermas, MacIntyre

K

Kallen, Denis 322
Kanpol, Barry 230, 235, 241
Kant, Immanuel 86, 100, 118, 150, 156, 158, 174, 176, 179, 240, 246, 295, 301, 317, 325, 328, 329.

Kateb, George 97, 116
Kellner, Douglas 52, 288, 332
Kennedy, Ted 334
Kenway, Jane 112
Kierkegaard, Soren 259, 265, 269
Kiziltian, Mustafa; Bain, William; & Canizares, Anita 232-233
Klossowski, Pierre 304
Knight, John 27
knowledge-based society/economy 90, 211, 319 *see* EU, lifelong learning
Kuhn, Thomas 246
Kundera, Milan 309; imagology/intellectuals xv, 61-62, 153, 179

L

Lacan, Jacques 240, 267
Lacey, Nicola 119
Ladwig, James G. 28
Lakatos, Imre 41-42, 323
Landers, Joan 153
Lash, Scott 5
Lawson, Kenneth 34-35
learning *passim*; formal 9, 33, 37, 40, 130, 201 319, 323; informal 9, 33, 36-37, 40, 42, 70, 130, 143, 201, 222, 319, 323, 325 *see* Dewey, lifelong education; lifewide 21, 24, 42, 43, 132, 137, 210, 222, 314, 325; non-formal 9, 28, 33, 37, 40, 70, 76, 130, 143, 199, 201, 222, 319, 323, 325; nonvocational *see* adult education/learning; self-directed *see* lifelong education, self-directed learning; to learn 11, 15, 25, 81
Learning Bank 83-84, 194, 212
learning community 97, 199, 200, 220, 257-258 *see* Derrida, MacIntyre; democratic *see* Dewey
learning democracy *see* Dewey, Giddens, Ranson
learning industry 80, 145, 178, 200
learning market 6, 77, 85
learning organization 51, 68, 69, 72-75, 145, 217, 224, 324
learning society *passim*; and social justice 70, 188-189, 195; and the welfare state 81,

187, 189, 194; as information society 49, 59, 80-81, 202, 324-325; as liberal utopia *see* Rorty; as myth 72, 87-89, 197, 325 *see* Hughes and Tight; as panopticon *see* Foucault; deschooled 28-32, 39, 331; democratic, 69, 71, 72, 255, 320 *see* Habermas, learning democracy; dystopian *see* Baudrillard, Foucault, Habermas; Employers' 67-72, 73, 87, 189, 331; Japanese model of 199-202, 215, 216, 220 *see* Dohman; market/consumerist model of 78-79, 85, 184, 201, 315; maximalist model of 37-40, 199, 211, 308, 314, 325; modern/postmodern xiii-xv, 95, 144, 201, 277, 313-314; neoliberal 70, 74, 80, 125, 189; non-participation in 84, 85, 86, 204, 213; obscene *see* Baudrillard; social democratic xii-xiii, 69, 74, 88, 183, 189, 194, 217-219 *see* British Labor Party, Habermas; state's responsibility for 40, 75, 85, 194; utopian 88, 89, 313-314 *see* Faure Report

Learning to be (see Faure Report)
learning webs 29, 30, 38 *see* deschooling
left *see* political left
Lengrand, Paul 3, 10, 12-14, 16, 18-19, 24, 75-76, 82, 145, 214, 216, 257, 321-323
Lenin, Vladimir Illyich 116, 311
Levin, Charles 295-297, 300
Levinas, Emmanuel 250
liberal (nonvocational) university xiv, 108-115, 272-273, 332 *see* Lyotard, MacIntyre, Nussbaum, Rorty
liberal utopia *see* Rorty
liberalism xii, 118, 121, 174, 226, 229, 237, 252, 253 *see* Habermas, MacIntyre, poststructuralists, Rorty
lifelong education xiv, 86-87, 132, 189, 194, 210, 216, 233, 234, 303, 321, 323. Chapter 1 *passim*; and informal learning 20, 33-36, 40, 42; and lifelong learning x, 22-23, 49, 224, 322, 324; and self-directed learning 15-16, 24, 30-31, 40, 70, 214, 325; institutionalization of 37-39; normative definition of 10, 23-25, 42; pragmatic argument for 1-3, 6-9 *see* Aspin & Chapman, Bailey; technical

(operational) definition of 10, 15, 20, 20, 23-25, 37, 40, 324
lifelong education movement/writers ix-xi, 72, 75, 82, 83, 86, 132, 142, 188, 194, 215, 216, 217, 221, 232, 314, 325, 327 Chapter 1 *passim*; and deschooling 20, 25-26, 33; and learning society 9, 81, 125, 184; educational philosophy 1-2, 9, 24, 37, 66, 125; maximalist project xii, 37-40, 42, 44, 70, 88; politics ix 9, 16-18, 70, 233, 321; pragmatist strand ix, 19, 24, 46-47, 49, 58, 89 *see* Gelpi; scientific humanism ix, 18-19, 42, 43, 45, 233, 322; utopian strand/utopianism ix, 19, 22, 45-47, 49, 140, 200 *see* Faure report
lifelong learning *passim*; and self-fulfillment 69, 78, 79, 202; as welfare right/service 76, 81-82, 189, 194; consumerist view 5, 66, 78-79; economic agenda/project 2, 5, 70, 213; Eurydice report 74, 203-204; informal, 20, 33-36, 40 *see* lifelong education; self-responsible/self-dependent 73, 74, 75, 76, 82, 225
lifeworld 117, 151, 162, 309 *see* Habermas
Lilla, Mark 254, 313
Long, Huey B. 10
Luhmann, Nicolas 161
Lyotard, Jean-Francois x, xii, 52, 53, 95, 234, 229, 237, 238, 249, 250, 251, 312-313, 318, 328, 337; on paralogy 246, 247, 278, 296, 333; on performativity 61, 111; on postmodern university 31, 111-113, 147, 332

M

Maastricht Treaty 63, 64, 221, 334
MacIntyre, Alasdair xii, 26, 32, 61, Chapter 3 *passim*, 138, 156, 158, 163, 169, 183, 257, 273, 302, 325 *see* Caputo, Feinberg, Mendus, Stout; and democracy 115-117, 124, 326; and Marxism 135, 326; antiliberalism 94-95, 115, 121, 136, 137, 159, 255, 326; antimodernism x, 91-95, 98, 101, 107, 126, 136, 159, 227, 238; antipluralism 92, 93, 94, 107-108, 114, 116-117, 124-125, 127, 326, 327;

Aristotelianism 94, 105, 107, 118, 119, 120, 128; communitarianism 118-119, 124; conversational politics 125-126, 162, 134; criticism of modern state 94, 117, 119, 123-124, 129, 311, 319; educated public (university) xi, 38, 91, 100-103, 105-108, 115, 121, 124, 125, 128, 130, 133, 150, 159-161, 187, 188, 272, 319, 326, 327; education project/ research project 102, 124-127, 129-130, 323, 328; emotivism 92-94, 107, 108, 326; enculturation/individuation xi, 91, 102, 272; ethics of gift-giving 121-124, 198 *see* justice; independent practical reasoner 120-123, 130, 131-133, 161, 179; learning community/society xi, 128-134, 161; on education x, 91-92, 105, 120, 126, 129, 160; on intellectuals xv, 127-128; on justice (as generosity, desert, needs, conversational) 107, 115, 118-123, 125, 179, 197, 257, 258; on modern public sphere 91, 93, 94, 102; on modern self 93-94, 105; on practices 102-104, 119, 120, 128, 131-132, 134, 327; on rights 118, 195-198; on schools 129-131; on virtues 104, 115, 119, 120, 128, 131, 132; politics of community 104-105, 115, 117-124, 133; Scottish public xi, 101-103, 105-107, 115, 148-149, 159-160, 188; self-discovery/ interrogation 105, 132, 186; universities xi, 106, 108-110, 112-118, 125, 129, 130, 133, 165, 332; utopianism 97-98, 165 *see* Caputo, Kateb

MacLaren, Peter 55-56, 136, 234-235

Makino, Atsushi 202

Mannheim, Karl 164

Marchand, Marianne & Parpart, Jane 237-238

Marcuse, Herbert 140-144, 147, 159, 164; one-dimensional man/society 12, 291, 329; politicization of the university 142, 147

Margalit, Avishai 192-193, 198

Marshall, James 313

Martin, Jane 184, 186

Marx, Karl xiii, 8, 96, 97, 123, 139, 143, 150, 151, 157, 234, 243, 252, 253, 258, 259, 267, 268, 294, 298, 326, 328, 329 *see* Derrida, Rorty

Marxism xii, 135, 139, 153, 229, 234, 237, 243, 253, 326, 333

mass media xv, 9, 46, 48, 57, 59, 61, 80, 144, 234 *see* Baudrillard, culture industry, Habermas, Kundera, McLuhan, postmodern information societies, postmodern learning societies, Vattimo

mass schooling (schooling) ix, 24-28, 50, 69, 82, 85-86, 91, 160-161, 188, 233 *see* Habermas

mass society/culture 144, 147 *see* Adorno and Horkheimer, Baudrillard

Masschelein, Joseph 137

Masuda, Yoneji 323

Mauss, Marcel 288

May, Todd xiii, 311-313

McCarthy, Thomas 239, 243, 333

McLuhan, Marshall *see* Baudrillard

Mead, George Herbert 341

media society *see* Baudrillard, Vattimo

Melo, Alberto 216

Mendus, Susan 99-100

Merquior, J.G. 241

Mezirow, Jack 136, 329

Mill, John Stuart 108, 151, 259

modern world ix, xiii, 52-53, 82, 101, 105, 107, 108, 119, 136-140, 143, 158-160, 179, 198, 230, 233, 326

modernism 57, 196, 229, 231, 233, 234, 235, 248, 327, 332; anti- 236, 238 *see* Heidegger, MacIntyre

modernity x-xi, 4-5, 9, 52-53, 95-96, 99, 111, 135, 158, 166, 229, 230, 235, 236, 324, 337 *see* Habermas, MacIntyre; crisis of x, 5, 16, 91, 97, 233, 241

Mouffe, Chantal 254, 333

N

Nabokov, Vladimir 259

Nagel, Thomas 333

Negri, Toni 275

Neiman, Alvin 334

neoliberal state/government (responsibility for education) 74, 76, 80

neoliberalism 56, 183, 185, 204, 205, 212, 216-218, 226-227, 230, 306, 332

Nicholson, Carol 237, 270
Nietzsche, Freidrich xiv, 8, 12, 14, 93, 97, 98, 114, 142, 192, 238, 239-240, 244, 250, 257, 259, 263, 265, 301, 303, 304, 305, 317, 327, 332, 334
Nozick, Robert 118, 171, 189, 192, 262, 295
Nussbaum, Martha 114

O

Oakes, Edward 91
Oakeshott, Michael 205-206
Oddi, L.F. 334
OECD 10, 20, 48-50, 322
Orwell, George 279

P

Palme, Olaf 322
Pannowitz, Rudolf 332
Papandreu, George 216
Parkyn, George 33, 323
Parsons, Talcott 330
Paterson, R.W.K. 82-83
Peirce, Charles Sanders 341
performativity x, 60-61, 74, 82, 89, 96, 111, 113, 125, 214, 223, 227, 332 *see* Lyotard
Peters, Michael 58, 85, 323, 332
Peters, Richard 23, 100, 129, 340
Peukert, Helmut 27, 139
philosophically educated public *see* MacIntyre educated public
philosophy: and education, and politics, as hermeneutics, constructive and reactive, hegemonic status of, normal/abnormal, public/private use, utility of *see* Rorty; as conversation *see* Bernstein, Gadamer, Rorty; of the subject/consciousness, 97, 159 *see* Habermas
philosophy of education ix, xv, 41, 44, 82, 100, 128, 226, 248; liberal 36, 43, 100
Plato 9, 91, 95, 96, 102-103, 105, 175, 240, 246, 260, 278, 296, 302, 326
politica! activism *see* Baudrillard, Derrida, Foucault, Rorty

political left xii-xiii, 56, 84, 168, 177, 183-184, 204, 205, 217-218, 226-227, 230, 233, 235, 252, 255, 268-269, 310, 320 *see* Derrida, Giddens, Habermas, postmodernism, poststructuralism, Rorty, Third Way; social democrat 327, 332
political right 56, 207-208, 226-227, 310 *see* neoliberalism
politics of resistance *see* Baudrillard, Caputo, Foucault, Lyotard, May
Popper, Karl 7
Porter, Catherine 304
positivism 60, 95, 148, 159, 166, 325
postindustrial society/world/workplace 28, 50-52, 58, 71-72, 85, 238
postindustrialism 234, 238
postmodern condition ix-x, 52, 54, 91, 95, 112, 195, 229, 232-233, 324 *see* Lyotard
postmodern societies/information societies x, 4, 52, 57, 102, 195, 232, 266, 288, 307
postmodern university 111-112 *see* Lyotard
postmodern world ix-xi, xiii, xv, 28, 44, 52, 53-56, 57, 59, 61, 82, 102, 108, 111, 129, 136-138, 198, 214, 219, 224, 226, 230, 232-233, 240, 253, 272, 296, 326
postmodernism ix-x, xii, 52, 57, 94, 183, 226, 227, Chapter 6 *passim*; and poststructuralism 238, 332; criticism of 229-238 *see* critical pedagogy, feminism, Habermas, Rorty
postmodernist politics 229-238
postmodernists x, xii, 166, 195, 205, 229, 234, 236, 238
postmodernity 52-53, 59, 60, 91, 112, 235
poststructuralism x, 97, 239, 241-245, 248, 268 *see* postmodernism; anti-humanism, 97, 239-240
poststructuralist politics 31, 244, 249-250, 255, 320 *see* Derrida, Foucault
poststructuralists xiii, xv, 196-197, 236, 238-246, 248, 249, 254-257, 258, 268, 271; French 258, 259, 267, 277, 313, 333

Q

Quicke, John 5, 71

R

Raggatt, Peter; Edwards, Richard; & Small, Nick 67, 69, 70, 71, 76, 77, 83, 84, 87, 195

Ranson, Stewart xii, 5, 183-188, 189, 198, 207, 215-217

rational society 143, 144 *see* Frankfurt School, Habermas, Horkheimer

Rawls, John 99, 118, 166, 171, 174, 186, 259, 261, 262, 263

reassurance (politics of) xi, 252, 255, 257, 265 *see* Corlett, Derrida, Foucault

recurrent education *see* education

Reid, Thomas 106

Ricour, Paul 303

Riesman, David 144

right *see* political right

rights human/moral/welfare 55, 173, 175, 177, 184, 186, 191, 193-197, 206, 208-209, 219 *see* MacIntyre

Rimbaud, Arthur 238

Rinne, Risto 51, 72

risk society x, 51, 72, 84, 89, 191-192, 195 *see* Bauman, Beck, Giddens, Rinne

Rorty Richard x-xi, xiii, xv, 180, 183, 196, 229, 232, 246, 278, 280, 295, 312, 313, 314, 317, 328; and Dewey xiii, 258-260, 264, 272-274, 333; and justice 262, 265, 268; and Marx/Marxism 258, 259, 261, 264, 267, 270, 333; and social democracy 258, 264, 265, 267-269, 333; conversationalist politics 41, 99, 206, 274; democracy (liberal) 258, 260, 262-263, 265-266, 269-270, 272; enculturation/ individuation, xi, xiv, 272, 274-275, 318, 334; ethnocentricity 261, 265, 268, 334; hermeneutics, xii, xv, 246-247, 270; individualism xiv, 262, 265-266, 268, 274; intellectuals xv, 259-260, 263, 265-267, 269-270, 334; irony/ironism xv, 259-261, 263, 264-268, 272, 274-275; leftist politics 258-262, 264-270, 334; learning society 269-275; liberal ironist 248, 260, 263, 272, 334; liberal utopia 248, 259, 262, 265-268, 272, 300, 334; liberalism 258-261, 263, 265, 270, 275; normal/abnormal discourse 246-247, 259, 271, 272, 320;

on education 269-275; on Foucault xiii, 259-261, 263-265, 267, 272, 333-334; on Habermas 259-260, 267334; on philosophy xv, 240, 246-248, 258-260, 262-263, 268, 270-272, 318; on public sphere 259, 266, 268, 272, 275; on solidarity 258, 261-262, 268, 300, 318, 334; politics of hope xiii, 258, 260, 280, 334; privatism 259, 262-263, 267-268, 272, 275, 306; public/private distinction xv, 258-259, 265, 267-268, 272; self-creation/perfection xiv-xv, 259, 261-262, 265, 272, 273-275, 297, 306, 318, 334; utopianism, xiii, 247, 259, 263, 265, 267-268, 270, 272

Roulet, Gerard 259, 335

Rousseau, Jean-Jacques 175, 287, 288

Rozycki, E.G. 322

Rubensen, Kjell & Borgstrom, Laen 322.

Ryan, Mary 153

S

Sade, Marquis de 238

sane society *see* Fromm

Sartre, Jean Paul xiv, 93, 96

St Augustine 115

St Benedict 94, 98

Schaller, K. 137

Schuller, Tom 78

Scott Brown, Denise 332

Scottish public *see* MacIntyre

Scruton, Roger 205, 206

Seitz, Brian 307-308

self-care/governance/legislation 175, 179 *see* Foucault

self-creation 13, 185 *see* Foucault, Rorty

self-dependence/responsibility/reliance xiv, 188, 189, 194, 195, 204-206, 208, 213, 214, 217-219, 224, 226, 268, 306, 315 *see* individualism, lifelong learning

self-directed learning 24, 73, 74, 81, 194, 322, 331 *see* lifelong education

self-education 81, 265 *see* Baudrillard, Derrida, Faure Report, Foucault, Habermas, lifelong education, MacIntyre, performativity, postmodernism, Rorty self-examination/confession *see* Foucault, MacIntyre

self-fulfillment 72, 179, 194, 214-215, 217, 226, 274, 306 *see* education as, Foucault, lifelong learning, Rorty

self-interrogation *see* Foucault, MacIntyre

self-perfection 177 *see* Rorty

self-refusal 317 *see* Foucault, Nietzsche

Sellars, Wilfred 261

Shklar, Judith 259

Simons, John 279, 336

Singh, Parlo 236, 317

Skager, Rodney 15

Smart, Barry 3

social democracy, xii, 136, 183, 188, 189, 204-207, 215, 217, 226-227, 332 *see* Dewey, Giddens, Habermas, learning society, left, Rorty, Third Way

social investment state 213, 218, 258, 330 *see* Giddens

social justice 82, 84, 167, 188, 189, 192, 206, 217, 219, 226, 234, 258, 260, 262, 268 *see* learning society, lifelong learning, Rorty, Third Way

social movements 230, 256, 269 *see* Habermas, Rorty, Yeatman

Socrates 105, 254, 305, 311

solidarity 141, 174, 190, 192, 197-198, 205, 207, 216, 218, 230, 235-236, 255, 268, 274, 318 see MacIntyre, Rorty

Sophists 333

Spille, Henry A. 324.

Standish, Paul 231

Stewart, John 106, 185

Stock, Arthur 76, 77

Stoics 303, 305, 333

Stout, Jeffrey 98-99, 161

Strain, Michael & Field, John 77, 78, 89

Suchodolski, Bogdan 2, 6, 11, 12, 14, 16, 17-18, 47, 77, 140

Swartz, Bertrand 48

T

Taylor, Charles 118, 119, 336

Taylor, Richard 203, 241

Tett, Lynn 86

Third Way social democracy xii-xiv, 168-169, 184, 188, 202, 204-210, 214, 216, 218-219, 226, 268-270, 332 *see* Giddens

Thomas, Alan A. 49

Thomism 108, 340

Thompson, John & Held, David 157

Tight, Malcolm 211, 213

Tocqueville, Alexis de 151

Tough, A.M. 322.

Toynbee, Arnold 332

Tuijnman, Albert 76, 77

Turner, Bryan 278

UNESCO ix, 2, 10, 48-50, 62, 87, 221, 321, 322

university xi, 106, 111-112, 113-114, 160, 212, 243-244, 331 *see* Caputo, Habermas, Lyotard, MacIntyre, Marcuse, Nussbaum, Yeatman

U

Usher, Robin & Edwards, Richard 82, 233, 279-280, 235, 333

utopianism 139-141, 279-280 *see* Benhabib, Derrida, Foucault, Furter, Habermas, Horkheimer, MacIntyre, Marcuse; escathological 97-98, 326 *see* Caputo, Kateb

V

van der Zee, Hendrick 80, 85, 323

Vattimo, Gianni xv, 59, 296, 318, 336; media society 294-295

Venturi, Robert 332

Verne, E. 37

W

Walzer, Michael 241, 333, 336

Waterman Ruth H.; Waterman Judith A.; & Collard Betsy A. 73

Weber, Max xi, 32, 45, 95, 148, 291, 326, 328

welfare politics/society 192, 252, 286

welfare state 56, 82, 85, 86, 187, 188-190, 195,
    198, 218 *see* Bauman, feminism,
    Giddens, Habermas, Illich, Margalit,
    Nozick, Ranson, Suchodolski, Yeatman
Wells, H.G. 279
Whitehead, A.N. 2
Whitman, Walt 260, 261
Williams, Bernard 99
Wittgenstein, Ludwig 197, 247, 249
Wolin, Sheldon 258, 265-266, 334.
Wynne, Brian 5

Y

Yarnit, Martin 63, 64, 67, 203, 322
Yeatman, Anna 114, 189-190, 193, 194, 218,
    236, 237, 252, 328, 330, 331.
Yeaxlee, A.B. 2, 334
Young, Michael. F.D. 89, 325.
Young, Robert 136, 138, 275

Z

Zamiatin, E. 279

Studies in the Postmodern Theory of Education

General Editors
Joe L. Kincheloe & Shirley R. Steinberg

Counterpoints publishes the most compelling and imaginative books being written in education today. Grounded on the theoretical advances in criticalism, feminism, and postmodernism in the last two decades of the twentieth century, Counterpoints engages the meaning of these innovations in various forms of educational expression. Committed to the proposition that theoretical literature should be accessible to a variety of audiences, the series insists that its authors avoid esoteric and jargonistic languages that transform educational scholarship into an elite discourse for the initiated. Scholarly work matters only to the degree it affects consciousness and practice at multiple sites. Counterpoints' editorial policy is based on these principles and the ability of scholars to break new ground, to open new conversations, to go where educators have never gone before.

For additional information about this series or for the submission of manuscripts, please contact:

> Joe L. Kincheloe & Shirley R. Steinberg
> c/o Peter Lang Publishing, Inc.
> 275 Seventh Avenue, 28th floor
> New York, New York 10001

To order other books in this series, please contact our Customer Service Department:

> (800) 770-LANG (within the U.S.)
> (212) 647-7706 (outside the U.S.)
> (212) 647-7707 FAX

Or browse online by series:

> www.peterlangusa.com